/. 00

Approaches to the Bible

VOLUME 1
COMPOSITION, TRANSMISSION
AND LANGUAGE

Approaches to the Bible
The Best of Bible Review

VOLUME 1
COMPOSITION, TRANSMISSION
AND LANGUAGE

EDITED BY
HARVEY MINKOFF

BIBLICAL ARCHAEOLOGY SOCIETY
Washington, DC

To my parents, wife and children–
links in the chain of tradition.
H.M.

Hershel Shanks/general editor
Suzanne F. Singer/managing editor
Judy Wohlberg/production manager
Carol R. Arenberg/special projects editor
Laurie Andrews/copy editor
Sean O'Brien/special projects assistant
Designed by Sharri Harris Wolfgang, AURAS Design, Washington, DC

Library of Congress Cataloging-in-Publication Data
Approaches to the Bible: the best of Bible review / edited by Harvey Minkoff.
p.   cm.
Includes bibliographical references and indexes.
Contents: v. 1. Composition, transmission, and language.
ISBN 1-880317-16-8 (v. 1)
1. Bible–Introductions. 2. Bible–Study and teaching.
I. Minkoff, Harvey. II. Bible review.
BS475.2.A66 1994
220.6–dc20   94-21126
CIP

©1994 Biblical Archaeology Society
4710 41st Street, NW
Washington, DC 20016

Contents

PART II

Transmission of Biblical Texts

EVOLUTION OF THE TEXT

MANUSCRIPTS

Foreword

I f we have learned anything from publishing *Biblical Archaeology Review* and *Bible Review*, it is that there is a tremendous need, one might say thirst, for up-to-date, first-class biblical scholarship for a lay audience. And that audience is much larger than even we suspected.

Articles from these two magazines are now so widely used in study groups, in college, university and seminary classes and in church and synagogue religious schools that it is no longer remarked upon. But when articles are used in this way, they tend to lose some of the sweep and depth that characterize them when they are carefully arranged and understood as a developing whole.

We first sensed this in the case of *Biblical Archaeology Review*, which prompted us to put together the two-volume set entitled *Archaeology and the Bible: The Best of BAR* (1990). Volume 1 covered "Early Israel," and volume 2 covered "Archaeology in the World of Herod, Jesus and Paul." These volumes have been so successful and so widely adopted for classroom use that we decided to compile another collection of articles, this time from *Bible Review* (or *BR*, as it is known to its friends).

Approaches to the Bible: The Best of Bible Review is the result. Edited with flair and erudition by Harvey Minkoff (see his introductions to the various sections), this series also consists of two volumes, the first subtitled "Composition, Transmission and Language" and the second subtitled "A Multitude of Perspectives."

Even we were surprised at how neatly these articles could be grouped into a comprehensive whole, an overview of various approaches to the biblical text. Just glancing at the intriguing titles, the articles beckoning to be read, impresses us with the importance and excitement of approaching the Bible from a variety of perspectives.

I venture to suggest there is no more readable or comprehensive introduction to the greatest, most inspiring, most influential collection of books ever written—what we call the Bible—than you will find in these pages. The reader will be introduced not only to the latest scholarship, but also to an even-handed presentation of different and sometimes conflicting points of view—

all designed to deepen an appreciation of the many levels on which the Bible can be read and studied.

This is an exciting venture, and I envy those who are coming to it for the first time. We hope you will find it a never-ending source of enrichment.

Hershel Shanks
President
Biblical Archaeology Society

Composition, Transmission and Language
A General Introduction

T he word Bible comes from the Greek word *biblia*, a plural form meaning "books," rather than "book." And the Bible is best understood as a multiplicity. But understanding the Bible is not a straightforward proposition because readers come to the text with a variety of conflicting religious, cultural and academic preconceptions.

People read the Bible for many reasons. To some, it is the defining text of a faith community. To others, it is a source of personal comfort, inspiration and guidance. To still others, it is a monument of English literature or Western culture. Some students of the Bible are scholars; others are guileless believers. Some contributors to *Congregation*,[1] a collection of essays on the Bible by writers of secular fiction and poetry, offended scholars, who objected that their essays were self-centered, overly personal or poorly informed. But these failings on a scholarly plane contributed to the influence of *Congregation* on another level. Unlike bloodless scholars, who, as Wordsworth charged, sometimes "murder to dissect," these nonspecialists, these laypersons, described their personal engagement with the text.

To complicate matters further, in both content and order, the Bible of Jews differs from the Bible of Protestants, which in turn differs from the Bible of Catholics. As Frank Kermode notes in *The Genesis of Secrecy*,[2] the meaning of Jewish Scripture changed when it was renamed the "Old Testament" from a story with an open-ended promise of redemption to part one of an entirely different story of salvation.

How, then, can we get at the meaning of a book—or books—written two to three thousand years ago, in Hebrew, Aramaic and Greek, in a milieu very different from ours? Despite the implied unity of a bound volume, the Bible is a collection of histories, laws, prophecies, rituals, narratives, poems and short stories written by many authors at different times and under varying conditions. In light of the composite nature of the Bible, can it still be considered a unified work with a single, consistent theme? Can it—should it—be read sequentially from Genesis to Revelation, the way one reads a book from first chapter to last?

The scholarly answer is that we cannot interpret the Bible until we learn more about life, languages and ideas in the biblical world; only then can we hope to comprehend what "son of man" or Sheol—or God—meant to a distant people long ago. Another answer is that, if we engage the text in an empathetic way, we can derive a personal sense of the Bible's longing, hope and promise, as well as its literary merit.

The two approaches need not be mutually exclusive, or even sequential, although a dichotomy has, unfortunately, developed. Scholars who subscribe to the historical-critical school sometimes become so immersed in mining the text for details that they lose sight of the reasons people care about the Bible. And readers who seek a personal relationship with the word of God or an appreciation of the Bible as literature often ignore or dismiss questions about the accuracy or historicity of the text or the significance of textual allusions.

From its inception in 1985, BR has tried to walk the narrow line between these two positions and, at the same time, bring first-rate scholarship to lay readers as well as scholars. As a nonconfessional publication, BR provides a forum for discussing the background, context, structure, language and meaning of the Bible, rather than a pulpit for espousing any particular interpretation. All the authors, however, share the belief that the Bible is important. The essays in this collection deal with issues circumscribed by the editorial policy of BR, but they also—or consequently—contribute to greater personal engagement as well.

The articles reprinted in volume 1 focus on the composition, transmission and language of the Bible in ways that illustrate the searching and theorizing, defining and redefining, give and take, thrust and parry that, although lacking in neatness, can enhance knowledge and appreciation of the greatest book of all—the Bible.

Harvey Minkoff

PART I

Composition of the Biblical Text

Overview

The traditional understanding of the Bible is that it was written by a series of inspired authors—judges, kings, priests, prophets, apostles and favored associates. Moses composed the Pentateuch, David the Psalms, Solomon Ecclesiastes; Samuel, Isaiah, Ezra, Paul and others are credited with writing the books that bear their names. According to one theory, these individuals filtered God's word through their human understanding; according to another, they transcribed what God dictated. But in either case, (1) an author conceived and composed the unified work we have before us, and (2) the Bible provides a record of the time, place, circumstances and personalities of most of the authors.

From the start, historical critics have challenged both conceptions of biblical composition. The biblical books, they contend, are composites—sometimes careless pastiches—of earlier documents. Eponymous authors are nothing but shadows with names. Historical critics argue that the Bible is not a unified record of God's plan, but a haphazard, accidental accretion that should be studied as a record of the past, an archaeological site where ancient ideas, primitive literature and eastern Mediterranean culture can be unearthed.

Stated in such harsh terms, critical scholars may seem hostile to the object of their study. As much as 200 years ago, Friedrich Schleiermacher, a pioneer of "empirical theology" and modern hermeneutics, argued that any investigation of the New Testament not informed by a personal interest in Christianity would undermine the canon. Indeed, this possibility is recognized by some modern practitioners as well. In *Exploring Exodus*, Nahum Sarna supports "a lurking suspicion that authentic scholarly concerns are occasionally beset with an ingrained prejudice that finds it all but impossible to credit the people of Israel with any originality."[1] And Joseph Blenkinsopp, in "The Documentary Hypothesis in Trouble,"[2] acknowledges that Julius Wellhausen, whose name has become a catchword for 19th-century biblical criticism, was hostile to both Judaism and institutional Christianity.

Wellhausen produced the classic synthesis of the documentary hypothesis, an idea first put forward in the 17th century and the cornerstone of biblical scholarship for at least the last 100 years. According to this theory, the Bible as a whole, as well as many individual biblical books, is a composite of orig-inally independent sources written by different authors at different times for different purposes. According to an early version of the hypothesis, when Moses wrote the Pentateuch, he drew on ancient sources distinguishable from each other by the use of either Elohim or Yahweh as the divine name. Later, a Priestly document was hypothesized, and Deuteronomy was recognized as a separate work. Wellhausen argued that these four documents might also illustrate the evolution of religious ideas in Israel and early Judaism.

Now, however, scholars recognize the limits—if not necessarily the errors—of this approach. Philosophers like Paul Ricoeur and Hans-Georg Gadamer ques-tion the existence of scientific objectivity. Knowledge is not value free, they con-tend, and any interpretation of data starts with presuppositions, either acknowl-edged or subconscious. Historical critics may dismiss older attitudes toward the Bible as being based on culture-specific assumptions—and therefore false—but they overlook the fact that they also make culture-specific assump-tions. They are, after all, situated in the post-Enlightenment milieu of Western humanism and are subject to the limitations and underlying assumptions of that world view.

In *Truth and Method*, Gadamer observes that these critics are always look-ing for something behind the text, a "reality" of which the text is "the involuntary expression."[3] And, according to Blenkinsopp, this has led to increasing frus-tration as attempts to characterize the Elohistic, Yahwistic, Priestly and Deuteronomistic strands of the text have revealed that they, too, are compos-ites. Although Blenkinsopp does not believe the historical-critical approach should be jettisoned, he believes we must pay closer attention to the question, which is seldom asked by documentary critics, of how the narrative reached its final form.

Implicit in this question is a new respect for the work of the final editors, or redactors, a change from the attitude at the beginning of the 20th century, when, in *General Introduction to the Study of Holy Scripture*, the influential scholar Charles A. Briggs defined historical criticism as "digging through this mass of rubbish....in order to recover the real Bible."[4] Redaction critics exam-ine how each editor put his own stamp on the material by choosing among various sources to create a finely crafted work.

The editing is no longer caricatured as mindless cutting and pasting. As Richard Elliott Friedman notes in *The Creation of Sacred Literature*, juxtapos-ing the Yahwistic and Priestly Creation stories in the first chapters of Genesis created "exegetical possibilities which neither of the original documents pos-sessed independently."[5] Adding a hopeful ending to the story of the Exile (in Chronicles) completely changed the theological import of the events, just as the New Testament altered the meaning of the Hebrew Bible by turning it into the Old Testament.

Binding particular books in a single volume in a particular order is also meaningful, a point John Barton highlights in *Reading the Old Testament* when he asks what Ecclesiastes would mean to us today if, instead of having been included in the Bible, it had been discovered among the sectarian documents at Qumran.[6] And Frank Kermode argues, in *The Literary Guide to the Bible*, that the Jewish response of closing the biblical canon at the end of the first century after the loss of political independence and the destruction of the Temple in Jerusalem "is sufficient evidence not only of the significance of the individual books, but of the belief that their power was enhanced by membership in a whole greater than the sum of the parts."[7]

In the field of biblical theology, the "canonical approach," which is espoused by Brevard Childs in such books as *Introduction to the Old Testament as Scripture*[8] and *The New Testament as Canon*,[9] is based on studying the received text as a meaningful unity rather than a source to be mined for buried nuggets of truth. In *The Art of Biblical Narrative* and elsewhere,[10] Robert Alter uses techniques of literary criticism to demonstrate the verbal cohesion in supposedly unrelated original strands of text. And in David Noel Freedman's recent book, significantly titled *The Unity of the Hebrew Bible*, he maintains that a firm editorial hand can be detected in the final shape of the Hebrew Scriptures.[11] He notes, for instance, the almost perfect word-count symmetry in the bipartite division of the Hebrew Scriptures into Torah/Former Prophets (150,000 words) and Latter Prophets/Writings (156,000 words), and in the quadripartite division into Torah (80,000), Former Prophets (70,000), Latter Prophets (72,000) and Writings (84,000). He also contends that the Torah and Former Prophets develop the theme that breaking the Ten Commandments—"one by one, book by book"—led to Israel's destruction. According to Freedman, this proves that, without violating the integrity of his sources, the final redactor was able to infuse the Bible with his own point of view.

A thoroughgoing attack on the standard documentary hypothesis was mounted by Isaac M. Kikawada and Arthur Quinn in *Before Abraham Was: The Unity of Genesis 1-11*.[12] They argue that modern scholars see a lack of unity and multiple authors because they are not attuned to the characteristic subtleties of ancient Near Eastern literature. In particular, they maintain that the Genesis story as a whole exhibits a classic structural unity that is lacking in the individual sources that have been proposed. However, P. Kyle McCarter, Jr., counters that the unity of Genesis does not mitigate against multiple authors because the structure in the text before us could have been imposed by the final editor.

How this might have been done is illustrated by a well known problematic passage in the Book of Samuel. Students of the Bible noticed long ago that the David and Goliath story is 80 percent longer in the Hebrew of the traditional Masoretic text than in the Greek Septuagint. The usual explanation for this is that the Septuagint version is an abridged version of the Masoretic version. But Emanuel Tov points out that this explanation does not account for the 17 "pluses" in Greek that are missing from the Hebrew. He argues that the Septuagint is, in fact, a literal translation of a different Hebrew original and that this source has been combined with another in the Masoretic version.

The composition of the Gospels, too, exemplifies how creative editing melds into authorship as individuals stamp their purposes and personalities on the material. Mark created a chronological framework for earlier collections of stories and sayings. Luke tried to improve on Mark with a more sophisticated and well wrought narrative. Obvious and subtle echoes of the patriarchs and prophets resound throughout the story of Jesus, but the Jewish scriptural background has been assimilated into the literary conventions expected by a Greco-Roman audience. In fact, Helen Elsom suggests that the Hellenistic biographies of the Gospels, along with the epistles that Paul styled after the epistles of Greek philosophers and Roman rulers, made possible "the transformation of the Messiah of Scripture into a Greco-Roman cultural hero."[13]

If we abandon the idea that God dictated the words of the Bible to various authors and accept the idea that human authors shaped source material to suit their purposes, we must confront the question of accuracy. Participants in the Jesus Seminar, for example, worked for five years rating the sayings attributed to Jesus as "almost certainly" to "almost certainly not" authentic. Once mainstream biblical scholars accepted the idea that the Gospels were part of a developing tradition among early Christians, they had little trouble accepting the notion that memories of Jesus may have been adapted to meet the needs of particular Christian communities and that sayings or anecdotes may have been included for reasons other than authenticity. On the other hand, Helmut Koester and Stephen J. Patterson suggest that the "lost" Gospel of Thomas, discovered in Nag Hammadi in 1945, may have been excluded from the canon because it did not conform to the accepted view that Jesus' death and resurrection, rather than his teachings, were the vehicles of salvation.

If Thomas and other books were omitted from the Bible because they did not conform to accepted dogma, then it would seem that doctrine antedated the Bible. In other words, rather than starting with "the Bible" and deriving doctrine from the text, someone used preexisting doctrine to decide what to include in the Bible. The word *canon*, after all, derives from a Greek word meaning measuring rod. The books in the biblical canon somehow measured up. But to what standard did they measure up and by whom were they chosen?

These questions are just as germane to Hebrew Scriptures. According to an ancient Jewish tradition preserved in the Talmud (Sukkah 20a): "Long ago the Torah was forgotten in Israel, until Ezra came from Babylonia and reestablished it; when it was forgotten again, Hillel the Babylonian came and reestablished it." Some scholars interpret this to mean that canonical literature—probably the Pentateuch, Psalms and Prophets—existed at the time of the Babylonian Exile in 586 B.C.E. and was reconstituted by Ezra in the fifth century, after it had been destroyed during a period of persecution; an expanded canon was established 500 years later in the days of Hillel.

The Gospels, in many references to sacred Jewish Scripture, also suggest the existence of a canon. One widely held theory is that a rabbinic council at Jabneh (Jamnia) established the Jewish canon toward the end of the first century C.E. Marc Brettler argues, however, that the Jewish canon was the result of a democratic process that extended over a long period of time rather than a one-time fiat by a religious elite. In light of the suggestion that the Gospel of Thomas was rejected because it did not conform to Pauline doctrine, Brettler's argument that canonization of the Hebrew Bible was an "inclusive" process is especially interesting; he believes contradictions among the texts reflect a desire to enfranchise various philosophies within Judaism.

The canonization of the New Testament is somewhat easier to trace because manuscript collections and conflicting lists by early theologians have survived. Manuscript evidence indicates that Paul's letters, written about 50-60 C.E. and collected some 35 years later, were often circulated in one volume with Hebrews. A number of gospels were in circulation before the four canonical Gospels were assembled in the mid-second century, an arrangement that, ironically, destroyed the unity of the two-volume work Luke-Acts. In 160-170 C.E., Tatian produced the *Diatessaron* (Through Four), which combined the four Gospels into a single running narrative, but this work was later declared heretical.

At first, the issue of official canonization was not considered important because Christians already had holy scriptures—the Jewish Bible. In the middle of the second century, however, as part of his attempt to remove all traces of Judaism from Christianity, Marcion proposed a canon that included only Luke and ten of Paul's letters. In reaction, his opponents defended the importance of other documents and proposed alternative canons. Although the exact criteria for determining canonization have yet to be established, it seems clear that books written by apostles or close associates of apostles were included, as were writings that conformed to "orthodox" Christian theology and works that had already been adopted for use by the church—such as Hebrews and Revelation, which had been quoted as "Scripture" from earliest times.

By definition, if some books were judged fit for inclusion in a canon, others must have been judged unfit. But not everyone agrees which was which. The Jewish Bible consists of the 24 books of the Hebrew Scriptures, called Tanakh, an acronym for Torah (Law), Nevi'im (Prophets) and Kethubim (Writings). These books and several others—among them Judith, Maccabees and the Wisdom of Ben Sirach—were collected in the Septuagint. The texts, names and order of the books in the Septuagint sometimes differ from the Hebrew text. For example, the Hebrew text of Samuel is longer than the Greek version, and two Hebrew books, Samuel and Kings, correspond to four books, 1-4 Kings, in the Septuagint.

Christian Bibles are derived from the Jewish Greek Bible—renamed the Old

Testament—plus the New Testament. But Greek manuscripts varied, and the status of certain books was equivocal. For example, 3 and 4 Maccabees are included in some manuscripts of the Septuagint but not as part of the canon. The Protestant Old Testament is limited to the 24 books of the Hebrew Scriptures, arranged, however, as they are in the Septuagint; the additional books of the Greek canon formed the basis of the Apocrypha. In Catholic tradition, these books are included in the Old Testament.

Then there are Pseudepigrapha, books attributed to ancient figures that are not in anyone's Bible. Nonetheless, James H. Charlesworth, editor of a new edition of Old Testament Pseudepigrapha, is one of many scholars who believe that these documents are essential to a proper understanding of Christian origins. Because of conceptual similarities between these works and early Christian works, he rejects the notion that "primitive Christianity" was radically different from its Jewish roots. Charlesworth maintains that the long tradition of denying the Jewish origins of Christianity has falsified the histories of both Judaism and Christianity.

The Documentary Hypothesis

Discussions of the composition of the Bible call attention to at least three meanings of the word composition: the make-up of the sources; the act of authorship; and the creation, from separate texts, of a unity called the Bible. In the two articles in this section, Joseph Blenkinsopp, in "The Documentary Hypothesis in Trouble," and P. Kyle McCarter, Jr., in "A New Challenge to the Documentary Hypothesis," introduce and analyze the documentary hypothesis, which is the reigning scholarly explanation of the biblical sources.

CHAPTER 1

The Documentary Hypothesis in Trouble

Joseph Blenkinsopp

What is the documentary hypothesis and why have Bible scholars been arguing about it for more than a century? Joseph Blenkinsopp surveys the development of the theory (which was formulated by Julius Wellhausen in the 19th century)–from the tentative questions of medieval commentators through the identification of separate textual strands distinguishable from each other by different divine names. Blenkinsopp then explains why the theory has recently been overshadowed by new theories like structuralism, canonical criticism and redaction history. Finally, he analyzes the Flood story in Genesis to demonstrate that there is still much to be learned from a historical-critical approach to the Bible.–Ed.

How was the Pentateuch, the five books of Moses–Genesis, Exodus, Leviticus, Numbers and Deuteronomy–formed? What is the history of its composition? The traditional view of both Judaism and Christianity has been that it was written by Moses under divine inspiration.

As early as the 12th century, however, the Jewish commentator Ibn Ezra raised questions about certain unmistakable references to events that occurred or circumstances that existed much later than Moses' time. Some of the difficulties besetting the traditional dogma–for example, the circumstantial account of Moses' death and burial at the end of Deuteronomy–are obvious to us today. This was not the case in the early modern period, however. Richard Simon, a French Oratorian priest now regarded as one of the pioneers in the critical study of the Pentateuch, discovered this the hard way when he published his *Histoire critique du Vieux Testament* (Critical History of the Old Testament) in 1678.[1] Simon tentatively attributed the final form of the Pentateuch to scribes, from the time of Moses to the time of Ezra. Simon's work was placed on the Roman Catholic Index, most of the 1,300 printed copies were destroyed, and Simon was exiled to a remote parish in Normandy.

One way modern source critics distinguish among different sources or strands in the biblical text is by the use of different divine names. This technique was first employed more than 250 years ago. Some biblical passages consistently refer to God by the name Yahweh; others by Elohim. The first person to distinguish between different sources on the basis of divine names was an obscure German pastor named Witter, whose work, published in 1711, went unnoticed to such an extent that it was rediscovered only in 1924, when a French scholar, Adolphe Lods, came across the book, written in Latin, while researching early Pentateuch criticism. Interestingly enough, Witter had not abandoned the dogma of Mosaic authorship but suggested that Moses used sources recognizable by the generic divine name Elohim, as distinct from Yahweh. Yahweh was the name revealed to Moses in the wilderness (Exodus 3:13-15, 6:2-3).

This idea was developed further, apparently independently of Witter, by a French physician, Jean Astruc. In 1753 Astruc, on the basis of his study of Genesis, identified three sources in the text—the Elohistic source (using the name Elohim), the Jehovistic source (using the name Yahweh—or Jehovah in its Germanic form) and a third source that could not be attributed to either. These *mémoires*, as Astruc called the sources, were combined by Moses to produce the Pentateuch as we have it.

Astruc's formulation was further refined by Johann Gottfried Eichhorn, author of the first scientific *Introduction to the Old Testament* (1780).[2] Eichhorn also maintained that Moses was the author of the Pentateuch, but, as a child of the Enlightenment, he did so not for dogmatic reasons but because he believed that Moses began life as an Egyptian intellectual and then became the founder of the Israelite nation.

By the beginning of the 19th century, most Bible critics outside the conservative ecclesiastical mainstream agreed that the Pentateuch had undergone a long process of formation and was made up principally of two types of material identified in general by use of the divine names Elohim and Yahweh. Later, the Elohist source was subdivided into the Elohist (E) and another source designated as the Priestly source (P). As it was first formulated, the P source was regarded as the product of priestly authors writing sometime after the Babylonian Exile (586 B.C.E.), when the priests assumed a dominant role in the religious life of the community. Generally, the E source was thought to be earlier than the J source, largely because, according to one biblical tradition (Exodus 6:2-3), the personal divine name Yahweh was first revealed to Moses; prior to Moses' time, God was referred to as Elohim.

One problem—and it is still a problem today—is apparent. These conclusions were based primarily on Genesis. Today we recognize that an explanation that works well for one section of the Bible—for example, the primeval history recounted in Genesis 1-11—might not work as well for another section—for example, the Exodus story in Exodus 1-15.

A closer study of key passages, beginning with the work of German the-ologian Wilhelm de Wette in 1807, led to a reversal of the chronological order in which the sources were arranged, so that J was dated earlier than E. De Wette also made a significant contribution by recognizing Deuteronomy as a sepa-rate source and identifying it with the book discovered, according to the Bible, during repair of the Temple fabric in the twenty-second year of the reign of King Josiah (622 B.C.E.), the last great king of Judah. King Josiah's religious reforms, as described in 2 Kings 22-23, included disestablishing the "high places" and insisting on the exclusivity of a single central sanctuary in Jerusalem. Because these reforms correspond closely with the legal viewpoint expressed in Deuteronomy (especially 12:1-14), de Wette was able to identify the fifth book of the Pentateuch as the book the Bible tells us was discovered in the cleansed Jerusalem Temple or, as de Wette maintained, as the book that was "planted" in the Temple by the priests. De Wette's hypothesis, which was widely ac-cepted, became a pivotal point in the study of the Pentateuch because it made possible a distinction between earlier legislation, which was not in accord with Deuteronomy, and later legislation, which presupposed it.

The groundwork was thus prepared for the classic statement of the documentary hypothesis, developed by Strasbourg professor Eduard Reuss (1804-1891) together with his student and friend Karl Heinrich Graf (1815-1869). The hypothesis was formulated with unsurpassed brilliance and clarity by Julius Wellhausen in *Prolegomena to the History of Israel* in 1883.[3] This so-called higher criticism was carried on mostly in Germany, which has been the heartland of biblical and theological study in the modern period. In the English-speaking world, where conservative ecclesiastical influences were more in evidence, the documentary hypothesis took root much later. As late as 1880, the vast majority of biblical scholars in Britain and America still espoused the Mosaic authorship of the Pentateuch.

The literary analysis embodied in the higher criticism not only attempted to explain the compositional history of the Pentateuch, it was also the basis for reconstructing the evolution of religious ideas in Israel and early Judaism. The earliest sources, J and E (which Wellhausen wisely did not try to distin-guish too systematically), were thought to reflect a more primitive stage of nature religion based on the kinship group. Deuteronomy (D), on the other hand, recapitulated prophetic religion; at the same time, Deuteronomy brought the age of prophecy to an end with the written law. Most scholars in the 19th century agreed that the prophets, who elevated ethics over cultic practices and whose approach to God was unmediated, represented the apex of religious development. Accordingly, after the age of prophecy came to an end, there was nowhere to go but down. The last stage in Israel's religious development, which reflected a theocratic world view, found expression in the Priestly source (P) during the Exilic or early post-Exilic period (sixth-fifth centuries B.C.E.).

This kind of evolutionism, which drew heavily on German Romanticism

Julius Wellhausen

Julius Wellhausen (1844-1918), a seminal but stormy figure in the history of biblical studies, brought together the work of earlier documentary critics in a brilliant synthesis that dominated the study of the Pentateuch for the next hundred years. In his *Prolegomena to the History of Israel* (1883), Wellhausen reconstructed the history of Israel based on a revised sequence of Pentateuchal sources. He regarded the earliest sources, the Yahwist (J) and Elohist (E), as reflections of a primitive, spontaneous stage of nature religion. The latest source, the Priestly source (P), which included a great many cultic regulations, corresponded to the rigid ecclesiastical institution established in the post-Exilic period (after 586 B.C.E.). In this scheme of things, Deuteronomy (D) marked the passage from the old order to the new.

According to Wellhausen, publication of the Deuteronomic law (Deuteronomy 12-26) toward the end of the Israelite monarchy in the late seventh century B.C.E. put an end to the old freedom of worship and sealed the fate of classical prophecy. The Deuteronomic reformers insisted that there be one central sanctuary—the Temple in Jerusalem—and that religious authority be based exclusively on written law. Deuteronomy thus prepared the way for the legalism and ritualism of Judaism in the post-Exilic period. According to Wellhausen, Judaism as we know it originated in this period. The legalistic and ritualistic character has been maintained to the present.

Although Wellhausen was sharply critical of the outcome of this historical process—he referred to it, for example, as a "petty scheme of salvation"—it would be wrong to call him anti-Semitic. His animus was directed as much against religious institutions in general, including institutional Christianity, as it was against Judaism. Unfortunately, his enormously influential book appeared at a time when anti-Semitism was endemic in German universities and public life in general. In 1879, for example, Heinrich von Treitschke, a renowned professor of history at the University of Berlin, coined the phrase *Die Juden sind unser Unglück* (the Jews are our misfortune), which became a widely used Nazi slogan.

Although critical study of the Bible is rightly part of the intellectual history of the modern world, it was traditionally conducted in an atmosphere prejudicial to Judaism—which may explain why relatively few Jewish scholars participated until recently. Now, a century after Wellhausen formulated his hypothesis, Old Testament scholars are searching for alternatives to his theories. Most scholars today recognize that critical study of the Old Testament bears directly on Christianity as well as Judaism and relations between the two faiths.

and the philosophy of Hegel, is fortunately no longer in favor. What remains as a task for scholars today is a more careful evaluation of the arguments on which the documentary hypothesis is based.

Since the publication of Wellhausen's *Prolegomena*, it has become apparent that all four strands of the Pentateuch—J, E, P and D—are also composites. But attempts to break them down into their components (J[1], J[2], for example) have been frustrated and have contributed to widespread disillusionment with the documentary hypothesis.

There have always been those who questioned one or another aspect of the documentary hypothesis or, like the Jewish scholars Yehezkel Kaufmann and Umberto Cassuto, rejected it outright. In the last decade, however, doubts have begun to be raised by biblical scholars in the critical mainstream. A more detached investigation of key passages, especially in Genesis, has suggested that the criteria for distinguishing between the "classical" sources (J, E, P, D and their subdivisions) can no longer be taken for granted. The distinction between J and E (J's ghostly *Doppelgänger*) has always been problematic, and there has never been consensus on the existence of E as a separate coherent narrative. In the years just after World War II, the Yahwist (J) was endowed with a high degree of individuality as the great theologian of the early monarchy (tenth or ninth century B.C.E.), largely as a result of the influential work of the Heidelberg Old Testament scholar Gerhard von Rad. In the last decade, however, doubts have emerged about the date, extent and even the existence of J as a separate and cohesive source spanning the first five or six books of the Bible. Similar, if less insistent, doubts have been voiced about the date of the Priestly source (P) and its relation to earlier traditions in the Pentateuch.

The net result is that the earlier consensus, which was never absolute, has suffered some erosion, but no paradigm capable of replacing the classical documentary hypothesis of J, E, P and D has yet emerged. Some continue to pay the hypothesis lip service but do not use it. A few—for example, the prominent German Old Testament scholar Rolf Rendtorff—have abandoned it altogether.

In short, the critical study of the sources of the Pentateuch, which has been the focus of Old Testament studies since the late 18th century, seems to have lost its sense of direction in recent years. Many Old Testament scholars, especially in the English-speaking world, excited by the discovery of the New Criticism (no longer new after about half a century), have lost interest in investigating the sources and original settings of biblical texts. The same goes for those who now apply structuralist theory to biblical narrative; the essence of structuralist literary theory is that a text must be read as a closed system. A more traditional approach to the biblical text, which goes by the name of canonical criticism (represented preeminently by Professor Brevard S. Childs of Yale Divinity School), insists on the final canonical form of the Pentateuch, rather than hypothetical sources, as the proper subject of theological exposition.

These influences have resulted in a great diminution of interest in the kind of literary archaeology that produced the documentary hypothesis in the 19th century.

Those who are still concerned with the problem are desperately seeking new answers. For example, many now question the idea that J (or the Yahwist, as he is often called) was an author with a distinctive theology. In reaction to this view, many scholars are now questioning the unitary and cohesive nature of this source and no longer consider it the foundation of the story line in the Pentateuch. As suggested earlier, doubts continue to be entertained about the existence of the Elohist (E) as a distinct strand, once thought to be a source parallel to J that originated in the northern kingdom of Israel some time after the death of Solomon. P has survived recent attacks on the documentary hypothesis best of all, because P is characterized by distinctive language, a fondness for genealogies and exact chronological indicators. But scholars now recognize that P too is a composite document that has gone through a number of compositional stages involving editing (redaction) and expansion of the text. There is even debate about whether P should be considered an independent narrative source or a reworking of earlier traditional material.

Moreover, other lines of inquiry have proved to be more promising than efforts at refined source criticism—for example, studying the literary character and structure of the text and the social origin of small textual units (form criticism), identifying and tracing the growth of traditions embodied in the texts (tradition history), and identifying editorial procedures in the development of the text and their ideological or theological presuppositions (redaction history).

To obviate any possible misunderstanding, let me emphasize that there is no question of returning to a precritical reading of the biblical text. If the documentary hypothesis is in crisis, the question for those still interested in the formation of the Pentateuch is whether the hypothesis is salvageable and, if not, what might take its place. But it is clear that we cannot simply jettison a historical-critical approach to the biblical text.

Perhaps we can best illustrate the problems and possibilities by examining one section of the Pentateuch, the Flood story (Genesis 6-9). Any conclusions we reach will have to be tentative and will not necessarily apply to other biblical texts. We might expect, however, to pick up some ideas worth pursuing throughout the Pentateuch.

With few exceptions, documentary hypothesis scholars agree that the Flood story, like the rest of the primeval history in Genesis 1-11, is a combination of two strands—the Yahwist, or J, source from the early Israelite monarchy (tenth or even ninth century B.C.E.) and the Priestly, or P, source from the Exilic or early post-Exilic period some four centuries later. With few exceptions, scholars also agree that the earlier strand, J, is a source for the later strand, P. That is, P incorporated J and, at the same time, gave the narrative its final form.

In the box at right, we show how the primeval history (Genesis 1-11) is generally divided by documentary hypothesis scholars. Although the Flood story is listed as a composite of the two sources, there are enough repetitions in the story to warrant drawing up two roughly parallel versions with distinctive and recurring linguistic and stylistic differences. We shall focus here on one short passage in the Flood story, the account of Noah's entry into the ark, to illustrate how the two strands can be separated. The lines in the following chart have been divided so that parallel aspects of each version are opposite one another. Italics are used to identify language that is identical or almost identical in both sources.

J (Yahwist) Source (Genesis 7:7-10)	**P (Priestly) Source** (Genesis 7:13-16)
Noah, his sons, his wife and *his daughters-in-law* with him *went into the ark* to escape the waters of the Flood.	On that very day *Noah, the sons of Noah,* Shem, Ham, and Japhet, *the wife of Noah,* and *his* three *daughters-in-law went into the ark,*
Of clean animals and of animals that are not clean, of fowl and *everything which creeps on the ground,*	together with every living thing according to its kind, and every animal according to its kind, and *every* crawling *thing which creeps on the earth* according to its kind, and every fowl according to its kind;*
two by two they went to Noah into the ark, male and female, as God had commanded Noah.	*they went to Noah into the ark, two by two,* from all flesh which has in it the breath of life; those who entered, *male and female* from all flesh, went in *as God had commanded him.*
After seven days the waters of *the Flood came upon the earth.*	(Noah was 600 years old when *the Flood* of waters *came upon the earth,* verse 6)

*The Hebrew text adds "every bird, every winged thing," but this phrase is not in the Old Greek (Septuagint) and is probably a later gloss.

Note that the P text is about a third longer than J, and yet about half of P is *verbally* identical with J. Repetition per se does not, of course, prove plurality of authorship. But because the repetitions amount to parallel versions with different recurrent linguistic, stylistic and thematic features, and because this phenomenon is found throughout the Pentateuch, the likelihood of plurality of authorship is no longer a mere possibility but a strong probability. Note that the only significant thematic difference between the versions quoted above is that J distinguishes between clean and unclean animals, and P does not. Similarly, after the Flood, J records Noah's sacrifice on the purified earth (Genesis 8:20-21), but P does not. Assuming the existence of a Priestly source,

The Sources of Genesis 1-11 according to the Documentary Hypothesis

J (Yahwist) Source		P (Priestly) Source
	The Creation of the World	Genesis 1:1-2:4a
Genesis 2:4b-3:24	The Creation of the World and the Garden of Eden	
Genesis 4:1-16	Cain and Abel	
Genesis 4:17-26	The Descendants of Cain (including Lamech) and Seth	
	The Descendants of Adam (10 members including Lamech and Noah)	Genesis 5
Genesis 6:1-4	The Divine Beings and the Daughters of Men; the Heroes of Old—the Nephilim.	
	The Flood; Genesis 6:5-9:19 (see chart on p. 18)	
Genesis 9:20-27	The Drunkenness of Noah	
	The Table of Nations	Genesis 10
Genesis 11:1-9	The Tower of Babel	
	The Descendants of Noah (10 members)	Genesis 11:10-26

Modern source critics usually divide the primeval history in Genesis 1-11 (from the Creation through the Tower of Babel) into two major strands or sources—J (the Yahwist—Jehovah in its Germanic form) and P (the Priestly source). According to the traditional formulation of the documentary hypothesis, J, itself a composite source, is the oldest. P later took J material, edited it and incorporated parts of it into the narrative, which gave P its final form. This chart shows how the material is traditionally divided between J and P. Note that there are two Creation stories, one by J and one by P, but only one Flood story, which is a composite, or conflation, of the two strands.

The division of sources is not quite as neat as this outline may suggest; it is generally assumed, for example, that the Table of Nations (Genesis 10), although designated P, includes earlier material, perhaps from J. But by and large, this is how the narrative is divided according to the documentary hypothesis.

In the primeval history, two distinct but overlapping story lines were juxtaposed, with one exception—the Flood story, which is a conflation of the two sources. P's seven-day Creation account (Genesis 1:1-2:4) is followed by J's (Genesis 2:4-25), which is written from a different perspective. The Cain and Seth genealogies in 4:17-26 are paralleled by the descendants of Adam in Genesis 5:1-31 (with, however, some significant differences—five names are identical; four are variants).

Recent scholars have found serious flaws in details of the documentary hypothesis, and P is no longer regarded as the editor of the final version of the biblical text. Moreover, both J and P may be composites of earlier and later material.

this is what we would expect because in Leviticus 1-7 and 11 (attributed to P) P is careful to note that the laws governing sacrifices and ritual purity were transmitted much later to Moses at Sinai. Therefore, they were not incorporated into P's Flood story in Genesis.

On the basis of this kind of testing—and by demonstrating internal consistency—carried out over the entire Pentateuch, the existence of parallel versions has been established with a fair degree of probability.

At this point, however, problems arise with the classic formulation of the documentary hypothesis, especially with the explanation of the relationship between different sources and the process by which they were combined in the final text. I will illustrate some of these problems in connection with the Flood story. (The chart at left shows the traditional divisions between J and P for the entire Flood story.)

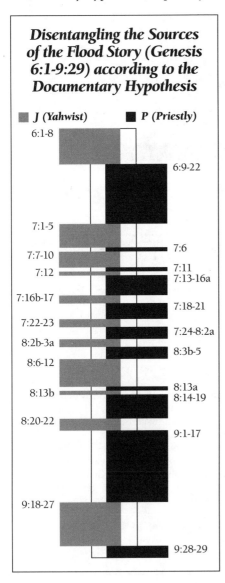

Disentangling the Sources of the Flood Story (Genesis 6:1-9:29) according to the Documentary Hypothesis

■ J (Yahwist)   ■ P (Priestly)

6:1-8
6:9-22
7:1-5
7:6
7:7-10
7:11
7:12
7:13-16a
7:16b-17
7:18-21
7:22-23
7:24-8:2a
8:2b-3a
8:3b-5
8:6-12
8:13a
8:13b
8:14-19
8:20-22
9:1-17
9:18-27
9:28-29

1. P's Flood story is a complete and logically coherent narrative, beginning with the chapter heading "These are the generations of Noah" (6:9) and ending with Noah's death (9:29). This is not true of the J version, where the ark is introduced suddenly and without explanation (7:1), and the story goes directly from Noah looking out of the ark to the sacrifice on dry land (8:13b, 20).

Consider the interesting detail that after Noah entered the ark, "Yahweh shut him in [the ark]" (7:16b). Documentary critics have attributed this statement to J, but it does not fit in J's version, where it comes too late because the Flood is already underway (7:7-10,12). Noah must have been shut in earlier in the P version. The statement that Yahweh shut Noah in the ark follows his entry into the ark, and the statement is intelligible only as a footnote explaining how the ark could have remained watertight (6:14) *after* Noah and his family had gone aboard. In its generally accepted form, similar difficulties are encountered throughout Genesis 1-11.

2. A much stronger case can be made for P as an internally consistent and well organized narrative source than for the balance of the narrative in the Flood story. The same is true throughout the primeval history. The non-P material in Genesis 1-11 is not nearly as consistent.

3. Arguments for a very early date for the non-P material are far from conclusive. In his standard book *The Old Testament: An Introduction*, German Bible scholar Otto Eissfeldt,[4] who expounds the documentary hypothesis with his own variations, offers only one argument for dating J to the period of the early monarchy—the "enthusiastic acceptance of agricultural life and of national-political power and status." Whatever validity this criterion might have for other parts of the Pentateuch, however, surely does not apply to Genesis 1-11. The passages of the primeval history generally attributed to J, rather then emphasizing the acceptance of agricultural life, stress the curse on the soil (Genesis 3:17), banishment from the Garden of Eden and the divine repudiation of human pretensions (for example, the Tower of Babel story). "National-political power and status" are hardly endorsed.

4. Recent scholars have noticed that some key passages attributed to J— the Garden of Eden story (Genesis 2:4-3:24) and the preface to the Flood story (Genesis 6:5-8)—have a strong sapiential flavor, that is, a flavor characteristic of the late post-Exilic wisdom literature that flowered in biblical books like Job and certain sections of Proverbs. Moreover, the supposedly J portion of Genesis 1-11 even includes terminology found in late wisdom writings. For example, the "tree of life" (Genesis 3:22,24) is mentioned in Proverbs (3:18 et al.) and nowhere else, and the word for the mist or spring that watered the ground (Genesis 2:6, *'ed* in Hebrew) occurs in Job 37:27 and nowhere else.

5. This brings us to our final question, one not often asked by documentary critics. How did the narrative reach its final form? The general assumption has been that the Priestly author or authors took over, edited and expanded the early material and thus produced the Pentateuch as we know it. But other evidence, including the late reworking of what is supposedly J, seems to point in a different direction. If P had been responsible for the final version of the text, it is inconceivable, for example, that P would have left in the distinction between clean and unclean animals in the Flood story because the distinction was not introduced until Moses' time (see Leviticus 11). For the same reason, P uses the divine name Yahweh only *after* it had been revealed to Moses (Exodus 6:2-3). In the final Bible text, in non-P materials, which are presumably from an earlier tradition, Yahweh is venerated under that name from the very beginning (Genesis 4:26). Why would P leave these references in the text if he was the final editor?

Similar problems can be found throughout the Pentateuch. For example, it is hard to believe that the Priestly source, which understandably venerates

Aaron as the ancestor of the priesthood, would have left in the Golden Calf incident (Exodus 32) in which Aaron plays, at best, a dubious role. We are, therefore, led to think that there must have been an even later editorial stage in the development of the text that built up the history of early humanity around a basically Priestly work supplemented by other available narrative material. The precise details of the process are obviously obscure. But the point is that the traditional formulation of the documentary hypothesis does not fully explain the development of the biblical text.

On the other hand, you may ask what difference it makes. Why does it matter? It is obviously possible to read and appreciate the Flood story without all this critical reconstruction of literary history, as people have done for centuries. What is the point of a historical-critical reading of biblical texts? What are the advantages of this approach over other methods, e.g., literary, allegorical, midrashic, formalist, structuralist, etc.? More and more people are asking this question, not only because the academic study of the Bible has had relatively little impact outside the academy (biblical scholars generally write for each other), but also because critical scholars have tended to assume that this is the *only* way to read a biblical text.

One answer is that the realization that the Flood story has a literary history at least eliminates a simplistic approach to the historicity of the text—the kind of simplicity that has recently led to another expedition to scale Mount Ararat in search of the ark. To put it differently, we will have to face the literary problem before we can even raise the issue of historical accuracy. Moreover, the literary history of the Flood story is not confined to the Bible. The biblical Flood story is a rather late version of a narrative theme that developed in the Near East over a very long period of time and was often copied. We know it, for example, in prebiblical form from the 11th tablet of the Gilgamesh epic. In 1914, a substantial fragment of a much earlier Sumerian version of the Flood story was published. Essentially the same version appears in a shorter form in a history of Babylon written by Berosus, a Babylonian priest in the third century B.C.E. All of this material must be taken into account in interpreting and reconstructing the literary history of the biblical text. As philosopher R. G. Collingwood pointed out a long time ago, the first question to ask is not if something really happened but what it means.

The object of historical-critical analysis has never been the esthetics of the text but the historical, social and religious realities that generated the text. In this sense, the text is a point of access to the religious experience of Israel at the time of writing. If, for example, the Priestly core narrative of the Flood comes from the time of the Exile or shortly after, it can be expected to reflect aspects of religious thought in Israel at that time. Only in the P source of the Flood story, for example, does God make a covenant with humankind in the person of Noah (Genesis 9:8-17). This is a remarkable breakthrough in religious thinking, prompted by the entirely new situation created by the loss of Israel's national independence in 586 B.C.E. and the Babylonian Exile. We would not understand this breakthrough in the same way if the passage were not attributed to an Exilic or post-Exilic source.

The point, then, is that there are aspects of religious experience and levels of meaning in biblical texts that cannot be easily understood without a historical-critical approach of some kind. This is not the only way to read the Bible, but it has an important role to play. Although the documentary hypothesis has been shown to have serious flaws, it is perhaps too soon to jettison it entirely. Our task is to find better ways of understanding how the biblical narrative was generated without writing off the advances of our predecessors.

AFTERWORD

Claiming that the documentary hypothesis "continues to look fairly healthy," Rev. Kit Wilke of Cranston, Rhode Island, faults Blenkinsopp for not taking into account the nature of preliterate society:

Very large portions of the tradition of that society are memorized and could be repeated by rote by fairly large numbers of people. Any major alteration in existing texts would cause a great deal more trouble than the women's movement is having rewriting some of our favorite hymns. Insertions and deletions are always far easier than alterations. The Priestly editors could not easily have expurgated Yahweh from the ancient texts without appearing to be rebels against the tradition. One thing the Priestly writers were clearly not is rebellious. With this in mind, the documentary hypothesis continues to look fairly healthy. **BR** *2:2 (1986), p. 10*

Pastor Floyd Hale of Caseyville, Illinois, argues that Blenkinsopp tries too hard to make the hypothesis appear shaky:

He [Blenkinsopp] admits—in vague terms—that such an hypothesis is not in trouble; the problem is just fitting the many details into the original system. What I sense in Blenkinsopp is typical of a lot of today's scholars. I don't doubt his scholarship, but he chooses to make it support the present trend (landslide) back to conservatism in all things religious. Most of the conservatives (who protect themselves by not exposing themselves to scholarship in Bible) would find this article proof that the documentary hypothesis does not need to be taken seriously, when they do not even know what it is. This article means nothing to the person who knows very much about the documentary hypothesis— he is already aware of such problems.

The only thing I found in support of the hypothesis was "it is perhaps too early to jettison it entirely," and that is a left-handed compliment (and in the last paragraph). His own treatment of the Flood story is proof that more than one source was used. **BR** *2:2 (1986), p. 10*

CHAPTER 2

A New Challenge to the Documentary Hypothesis

P. Kyle McCarter, Jr.

McCarter also defends the historical-critical approach as he answers "A New Challenge to the Documentary Hypothesis." He concedes that some aspects of the traditional formulation need revision, but he rejects the argument of Isaac M. Kikawada and Arthur Quinn in Before Abraham Was *that the creation myths of many cultures share a layered and sequenced organization that is evident in the Genesis story as a whole but not in any of its supposed underlying sources. McCarter counters that the structure Kikawada and Quinn posit is so loosely defined that "it is difficult to think of a story to which such a scheme...could not be applied." Even if Genesis does exhibit such a structure, this does not prove single authorship because "one could argue that the scheme was imposed on the story by its last editor." McCarter concludes that "the fundamental theory that the Pentateuch contains within it diverse sources joined together by editors seems as sound today as it did a century ago."–Ed.*

According to the documentary hypothesis, the Pentateuch, the first five books of the Bible, is a compilation of several originally independent documents. Ancient editors or redactors collected these documents, which were composed at various times in the history of the ancient community, and combined them in a single extended narrative. In this way, the Pentateuch as we know it came into being. This hypothesis is one of the fundamental assumptions of modern biblical scholarship. In one form or another, it has been accepted by most scholars since the 18th century, when the traditional view that Moses wrote the first five books of the Bible was widely questioned for the first time.

A recent book by Isaac M. Kikawada and Arthur Quinn, *Before Abraham Was: The Unity of Genesis 1-11,*[1] offers a thoroughgoing challenge to the documentary hypothesis. Kikawada is a Japanese biblical scholar who holds the position of visiting lecturer in the Department of Near Eastern Studies at the University of California, Berkeley, where Quinn is a professor of rhetoric. They believe that the documentary hypothesis has outlived its usefulness and, indeed, that a case can be made for the Pentateuch as the work of a single author. In their book, they introduce their argument by presenting a new analysis of the biblical primeval history, Genesis 1-11, a section chosen because of the central role it played in the development of the documentary hypothesis.

Attempting to demonstrate the unity of the primeval history is a formidable undertaking, not only because so many generations of scholars have labored to demonstrate its disunity, but also because it impresses the reader as anything but a unified composition. In Genesis 2:4 there is a marked change in style in the Creation story, and the story that follows seems to repeat or contradict some of the things that happened in the preceding story. In Genesis 1:27, for example, human beings are created, both male and female, after the creation of the animals in earlier verses. In Genesis 2:7, however, there is another creation of man, this time before the animals (cf. verse 19) and without woman, who is not created until verse 22. Such disjunctions led scholars who formulated the documentary hypothesis to conclude that two distinct accounts of creation are preserved in Genesis 1-2, the second beginning at Genesis 2:4. The same pattern, moreover, persists throughout Genesis 1-11, which seems to break down into two groups of passages with contrasting styles and several thematic inconsistencies between them. The two groups also display differences in theology. In one, the deity is referred to as *'elohim*, God, and presented as a transcendent lawgiver; in the other he is called *yahweh* (usually rendered "the Lord") and depicted as an anthropomorphic god who actively consorts with human beings. According to proponents of the documentary hypothesis, therefore, the biblical primeval history is a composite narrative embracing two originally distinct accounts of primordial history.

Kikawada and Quinn admit that Genesis 1-11 appears heterogeneous rather than homogeneous to the modern reader. As they put it, "It seems to be a number of loosely collected tales, with genealogies intruding here and there. We can find certain overlapping themes and styles. But the primeval history as a whole appears to be more a collection of narratives than a single narrative."

But is this impression valid? Kikawada and Quinn argue that it is not. They attribute this impression to the modern reader's inability to perceive the subtleties of ancient composition. Indeed, the central assumption of their book is that an ancient Near Eastern reader or listener would have seen unity where we see disunity. They test this assumption by comparing Genesis 1-11 to several other ancient compositions, and the comparisons lead to two assertions. First, many of the peculiarities of Genesis 1-11, which modern scholars have interpreted as evidence of multiple authors, are, in fact, present in other works of ancient literature. Second, ancient primeval histories share a comprehensive pattern or structure, which is also recognizable in Genesis 1-11.

The first assertion is not presented systematically, but examples are scattered throughout the book. On pages 39-40, for instance, Kikawada and Quinn compare the fact that man seems to be created twice in Genesis 1-2 to a Sumerian myth in which a general creation of man is followed by a contest in which the god Enki and the goddess Ninmah fashion some new human creatures with special characteristics. This comparison suggests to Kikawada and Quinn that there may have been a double-creation motif in the tradition with which a single author of Genesis 1-2 was working.

At this point, however, it is not clear how Kikawada and Quinn want us to understand the story. Are we to suppose that other men and women already existed when the man in Genesis 2:7 was created? The comparison with the Sumerian myth, in which Enki and Ninmah form new creatures after the world is already populated with human beings, seems to imply such an interpretation. It is difficult to believe, however, that any biblical writer thought of Adam as anything other than the first man, the progenitor of all mankind (*'adam*), and the genealogy at the beginning of Genesis 5 seems to identify him as such unambiguously. But if the man created in Genesis 2:7 is the first man, then the contradictions between Genesis 1 and 2 remain regardless of the influence of a double-creation tradition. If, as Kikawada and Quinn suggest, a single Israelite author composed both of these chapters in conformity with an ancient pattern, why did he introduce these problems? No such contradictions exist in the myth of Enki and Ninmah.

Elsewhere, Kikawada and Quinn consider the two divine names. They pay particular attention to this phenomenon in the Noah story, where the names alternate frequently. For comparison, they adduce several examples of the "doubling of divine names within a single passage" from Akkadian and Ugaritic literature. The implication is that the alternation of divine names in the Noah story is a Hebrew example of a widespread literary phenomenon and not, as proponents of the documentary hypothesis suppose, a consequence of combining two different accounts. It is troubling, however, that the nonbiblical parallels are all poetic. Name alternation is a familiar characteristic of ancient Semitic poetry, and the alternation of divine names in Hebrew poetry is not taken by scholars as evidence of multiple authors. The Noah story, however, is prose, not poetry, and the divine name alternation there corresponds generally to a number of other variations (duration of the Flood—40 days and 40 nights in one account [Genesis 7:17], more than a year in the other [Genesis 7:24]; the number of animals taken aboard—two of each animal in one account [Genesis 6:19], seven pairs of clean animals and one pair of unclean in the other [Genesis 7:2], etc.).

On the basis of their discussion of the double creation of man, the alternation of divine names in the Noah story and other peculiarities of Genesis 1-11, therefore, Kikawada and Quinn cannot be said to have made a compelling case for the first assertion, that the heterogeneous appearance of the biblical primeval history can be explained by appealing to ancient Near Eastern literary conventions. The second assertion, however, that Genesis 1-11 shares a common structure with other ancient primeval histories, turns out to be more important for their case. Much of the book is devoted to supporting this assertion.

The argument begins in chapter 2, where Kikawada and Quinn call attention to the Atrahasis epic, a Mesopotamian account of primordial events. Drawing upon the work of previous scholars, they suggest that the structure of this epic can be described according to a five-point outline—Creation, First Threat, Second Threat, Final Threat and Resolution. They then proceed quickly to identify the same five-part structure in the biblical primeval history. They outline the two stories as follows:

ATRAHASIS

A. Creation (I. 1-351)
   Summary of work of gods; creation of man
B. First Threat (I. 352-415)
   Man's numerical increase; plague; Enki's help
C. Second Threat (II. i. 1-II. v. 21)
   Man's numerical increase
       1. Drought; numerical increase
       2. Intensified drought; Enki's help
D. Final Threat (II. v. 22-III. vi. 4)
   Numerical increase; Atrahasis' flood; salvation in boat
E. Resolution (III. vi. 5-viii. 18)
   Numerical increase; compromise between Enlil and Enki; "birth control"

GENESIS

A. Creation (1:1-2:3)
   Summary of work of God; creation of man
B. First Threat (2:4-3:24)
   Genealogy of heaven and earth; Adam and Eve
C. Second Threat (4:1-4:26)
   Cain and Abel
       1. Cain and Abel; genealogy
       2. Lamech's taunt (in genealogy)
D. Final Threat (5:1-9:29)
   Genealogy; Noah's Flood; salvation in ark
E. Resolution (10:1-11:32)
   Genealogy; Tower of Babel and dispersion genealogy; Abram leaves Ur

Further examination reveals the presence of the same structure in a Greek primeval history, which includes the story of the Trojan War, and an Iranian primeval history, the Zoroastrian tale of Yima and the vessel of salvation.

In other words, Kikawada and Quinn contend that in ancient times there was a conventional pattern according to which primordial events were described. This pattern was widespread and exerted influence as far west as the Aegean Sea and as far east as the Iranian Plateau. The pattern is reflected, therefore, in several ancient primeval histories, including the one in the Bible. Moreover (and here we come to the main point), the conventional five-part structure occurs in Genesis 1-11 *as a whole* but not in either of the alleged documentary sources. Because such a sophisticated structure could hardly have arisen accidentally from a loose combination of independent documents, the biblical primeval history must be the work of a single author.

In the next two chapters, Kikawada and Quinn reinforce this conclusion with detailed internal analyses of Genesis 1-11 as a whole (chapter 3) and the Flood story in particular (chapter 4). In chapter 3 they attempt to demonstrate the unity of the larger story in terms of the five-part scheme. In part A, the story of Creation, mankind is blessed with the words "Be fruitful and multiply and fill the earth" (Genesis 1:28). This looks ahead to the resolution of the story in part E, in which human beings are dispersed into various lands, thus "realizing this blessing/command concretely." And between these two events are the three central stories—Adam and Eve, Cain and Abel, and Noah—which exhibit symmetry and progressive repetition, according to a subtle structure discerned by Kikawada and Quinn. The whole is held together by a series of genealogies, which, far from being extraneous interruptions of the narrative, are the links that hold the stories together and serve, at the same time, as reminders of the effectiveness of the blessing.

In chapter 4, the Noah story receives special attention because of its peculiar place in the documentary analysis of Genesis 1-11. Whereas other major episodes seem to be drawn almost entirely from one source or another, the Flood story is apparently an intricate interweaving of two documents, or so proponents of the documentary hypothesis believe. Kikawada and Quinn disagree. They offer a detailed unitary reading of Genesis 6-9 in which they refute many of the standard arguments of source analysis. They note, for example, that in Genesis 6:19 Noah is told to bring two of every living thing on board the ark, while in Genesis 7:2 he is told to bring "seven pairs of all clean animals...and a pair of animals that are not clean." According to the authors, this is not an internal contradiction arising from the combination of divergent accounts. In Genesis 7:2 Noah is told to bring *more* animals on board. Why? Kikawada and Quinn explain: "As soon as Noah's voyage is over, he sacrifices in thanksgiving clean animals and birds. Without the extras, Noah's sacrifice would have rendered these species extinct." The purpose of the several repetitions in the story—such as recounting that Noah, his family and the animals are twice said to have entered the ark (7:7-9 and 7:13-16)—is emphasis, a rhetorical device for clarity and reinforcement. The overall unity of the Flood story is most clearly demonstrated, furthermore, by the internal structure, an intricate pattern carefully worked out by Kikawada and Quinn.

How are we to evaluate this structural argument for the unity of Genesis 1-11? In the first place, we agree that the biblical primeval history and the Mesopotamian Atrahasis story have many structural and thematic features in common. This, however, is not conceding much because the relationship of the stories in Genesis 1-11 to Mesopotamian parallels has been generally recognized for more than a century. In fairness to Kikawada and Quinn, we must grant that they have succeeded in bringing this relationship into better focus. Their approach forces us to concentrate on the structural features the two traditions share, and their extension of the comparison to Greek and Iranian parallels helps distinguish the essential components of the shared pattern from the structural peculiarities of one tradition or another. In short, they have accomplished one of their objectives—to demonstrate the existence of a common pattern or structure that is shared by various ancient accounts of primordial events, including the biblical primeval history.

The pattern common to these ancient stories seems to be approximately the following. After the creation of human beings, the population steadily increases until it causes a problem. Then the gods send some kind of calamity to reduce the population to tolerable limits.[2]

The problem caused by the growth of the human population is manifested in various ways in different traditions. In the Old Iranian tradition, it is apparently a simple lack of room, while in Mesopotamia it is noise, a constant din that keeps the old gods from sleeping. In the Greek tradition, the problem is partly the sheer number of people, which overburdens Mother Earth, and partly impiety, which is offensive to the gods. In Israel, the problem is human wickedness, in consequence of which the earth is corrupted. The divine solutions to the problem also takes various forms. In ancient Iran, a bitter winter is sent by Ahura Mazda; in Greece war is sent by Zeus; and in Mesopotamia and Israel a deluge is sent by Enlil and Yahweh, respectively.

Note that the biblical story differs from the others in that population growth is not a part of the problem. On the contrary, human reproduction is presented in a wholly positive light, as expressed in the blessing of creation, "Be fruitful and multiply, and fill the earth..." (Genesis 1:28). In the early chapters of Genesis, human *behavior*, not human *increase*, provokes the imposition of divine checks and limits.

This difference suggests to Kikawada and Quinn that the Hebrew author made ironic use of the tradition. In fact, the purpose of the biblical account was to oppose consciously the Atrahasis tradition. In that tradition, which was the literary achievement of the urbanized culture of Mesopotamia, a population increase was perceived as a serious threat to society. In contrast, the author of Genesis 1-11 offers "the nomadic or pastoral life as a means to unlimited human reproduction." In Genesis, population increase is a blessing, and agriculture, city-building and other forms of "the old sedentary sin" are doomed to failure.

To inherit the blessing of creation, human society must remain nomadic: "To have progeny as numerous as the sands we must be willing to move over those sands." The story of Adam and Eve demonstrates the failure of agriculture. The story of Cain, the first city-builder (Genesis 4:17), demonstrates the failure of urban civilization. Things go well for Noah until he plants a vineyard (Genesis 9:20), but at that point the curse enters his family. A final statement on city-building is made in the story of the Tower of Babel, and the solution to the problems that arise there—and, in fact, the continuing problems that arise throughout the primeval history—is to scatter human beings over the surface of the earth. Kikawada and Quinn explain that dispersion represents a return to the nomadic way of life.

One wonders if many readers will be persuaded by this interpretation of Genesis 1-11. Certainly there seem to be easier and better ways to understand these same episodes. It is difficult to see how Adam's agricultural lifestyle is responsible for his trouble. The story of the garden is not intended to show the failure of agriculture but to explain (among other things) why farming is so difficult (cf. Genesis 3:17-19). Perhaps Cain was the first city-builder (although most modern scholars have thought it was his son Enoch), but he was also "a wanderer upon the earth" (4:14), a nomad—indeed the quintessential biblical nomad—whom the Israelites probably thought of as the ancestor of the Kenites—the Cain-ites!—the quintessential biblical nomadic tribe. To equate the indictment of Cain with an indictment of urban civilization is extraordinarily bold, to say the least. Even the family history in Genesis 4:17ff. depicts Cain as the ancestor of nomads. His descendant Jabal was "the father of those who live in tents and have cattle" (Genesis 4:20). To be sure, Kikawada and Quinn argue that *cattle* means "property" here, including slaves, so that Jabal becomes the father of "the flesh trade." But even if this is correct (which seems unlikely), Cain's descendants bought and sold their slaves while living "in tents."

Nor can we agree that Noah's vineyard is mentioned to show that the righteous man had finally fallen into "the old sedentary sin." On the contrary, it shows that agriculture is possible again after the cleansing of the earth by the Flood. There is no suggestion in the biblical narrative of any wrongdoing on Noah's part in planting a vineyard (or in becoming drunk, for that matter, as we are told he became in Genesis 9:21). The curse on Canaan in Genesis 9:25 was provoked by Ham, whose crime, whatever it was, had nothing to do with agriculture or urban civilization. Finally, there seems to be little basis for associating the dispersion of human families at the end of the story of the Tower of Babel with the nomadic way of life. As the so-called Table of Nations in

Genesis 10 shows, the people are scattered into different lands where they will speak different languages and adopt different lifestyles, a few nomadic but many more urban and agricultural.

Returning to the structural argument, we must ask ourselves if the five-part scheme is a useful way of displaying and comparing the structures of various primeval histories. The scheme does seem to fit the stories fairly well, at least as Kikawada and Quinn analyze them. Some readers may wonder, however, whether the five-part scheme is so flexible and generalized that it can be applied to almost any story. The first part of the scheme is called Creation, but creation takes place only in the Israelite and Mesopotamian examples, and only the creation of human beings in the latter case. Introduction or Initialization might be better designations than Creation. In the case of the Threats, it may be too precise to speak of three as a conventional number. In the Atrahasis story, the flood is Enlil's fourth attempt to reduce the human population, although Kikawada and Quinn, following the analysis of other scholars, describe the third attempt as an intensification of the second. There are only two threats in the Greek story, but Zeus does contemplate a third at one point. As it then turns out, the "unifying five-part structure" discovered by Kikawada and Quinn is a scheme in which a situation is introduced (Creation), a series of approximately three complications is described (First, Second and Final Threats), and the outcome of the situation is reported (Resolution).

It is difficult to think of a story to which such a scheme, given sufficient ingenuity, does not apply. Kikawada and Quinn themselves apply it not only to primeval histories, but also (in chapter 5) to numerous other narratives as well. They find it to be ubiquitous in the Bible, underlying not only Genesis 1-11, but also the so-called Court History of David in Samuel and Kings, the story of the Exodus, Genesis as a whole and the Pentateuch as a whole!

Let us suppose, however, that Kikawada and Quinn are correct about the five-part scheme. Let us suppose that the biblical primeval history does share this structure with other ancient compositions. Would this constitute evidence for the unity of Genesis 1-11? Unfortunately, it would not. The scheme could have been introduced at the earliest or the latest stage of the development of the narrative as described by the documentary hypothesis. All five elements are already present in the oldest sources according to the analyses of most contemporary critics. Alternatively, one could argue that the scheme was imposed on the story by the last editor or redactor. In any case, it is not necessary to conclude that Genesis 1-11 was the work of a single author.

In short, Kikawada and Quinn have not succeeded, at least in the opinion of this reviewer, in casting doubt on the validity of the documentary hypothesis as it applies to Genesis 1-11. This is not to say, however, that the book is not valuable. It is. It is interesting, provocative and filled with acute and insightful observations. Biblical scholars will find many things to interest them and at least a few things that are new—quite enough to expect from any book.

Before Abraham Was is not only for scholars. It is written in clear, non-technical, informal English against the backdrop of a sympathetic presentation of the documentary hypothesis. As a result, their case is accessible to almost any reader, and it is reasonable to expect that their views will be evaluated not only by biblical scholars, who will be predisposed to be skeptical, but many others as well.

Perhaps it is fitting to conclude this review with a few words on behalf of the documentary hypothesis. Many people today, including a few able scholars like Kikawada and Quinn, seem to believe that this old theory about the origin of the pentateuchal narrative is no longer tenable. These people are mistaken. It is true that many of the traditional components of the hypothesis are under close examination at present, and it is reasonable to expect that the hypothesis will undergo substantial revisions in the future, as it has in the past. But the fundamental theory that the Pentateuch contains within it diverse sources joined together by a number of editors seems as sound today as it did a century ago.

In fact, the hypothesis seems more sound today because we can now cite both biblical and extrabiblical evidence showing that it was precisely in this manner—by combining and editing documentary sources—that sacred literature was composed in biblical times. A careful reading of 1 and 2 Chronicles, for example, shows that the composer of those books drew heavily upon the narrative of Samuel and Kings, selecting long passages to be included in his own work within a distinctive editorial framework. In this case, where both the source document (Samuel-Kings) and the final product (Chronicles) have been preserved, the validity of a documentary hypothesis is established beyond dispute.

Another type of documentary composition can be demonstrated by comparing the Greek and Hebrew texts of the story of David and Goliath.[3] The Hebrew Bible contains two different accounts of the story, which have been carefully woven together, much the same way the two flood stories were combined in Genesis 6-9. The Greek version is a translation of a much shorter Hebrew text that contained only one of these stories. In the case of the Flood story we have only the composite account, but in the case of the story of David and Goliath we have both the composite account (in the Hebrew text) and one of the two source accounts (underlying the Greek text).

Consider finally the Samaritan Pentateuch, the form of the Five Books of Moses handed down within the Samaritan community. Here we often find part of the text expanded by the addition of materials drawn from other passages. Where Exodus and Deuteronomy contain information on the same subject, for example, we often find the text of Exodus expanded by materials drawn from Deuteronomy. By studying the Samaritan Pentateuch and other texts from Qumran and elsewhere, we can observe firsthand the editorial combination of documentary sources.

Biblical Authors and Editors

The second aspect of biblical composition is the creative work of authors and editors. As we have already noted, earlier critics often caricatured the received biblical text as a cut-and-paste pastiche. Many current scholars, however, have come to admire the contributions of the final redactors. In particular, they argue that combining material from various sources and earlier versions does not necessarily result in texts filled with contradictions. A skilled editor, they believe, can craft a coherent and cohesive whole with a clear point of view.

CHAPTER 3

The Nine Commandments
The Secret Progress of Israel's Sins

David Noel Freedman

David Noel Freedman, the general editor of the Anchor Bible series, illustrates how a skilled redactor can "organize and arrange the material...to shape a unity that is inherent but not fully realized in the component parts." In Freedman's opinion, the final editor, without violating the integrity of separately authored texts, was able "to construct a history of his people on the framework or scaffolding of the Decalogue...by the strategic highlighting of particular themes and devices to bring out the central story." Freedman maintains that the structure of the Torah and Former Prophets–what he calls the Primary History of Israel–reinforces the theme that "[t]he violation of God's law, step by step, commandment by commandment, results in Israel's destruction."

The moral terms of God's promise to Israel are summed up in the Ten Commandments at the beginning of the Primary History. But these laws are violated "one by one, book by book," until the community of Israel goes into exile in the last book. As Freedman explains, the editor "was responsible for assembling the constituent elements of this great narrative....Furthermore, while scrupulously preserving the materials...he nevertheless was able to contribute to the final assemblage and to produce a unified work."–Ed.

Embedded in the sequence of books from Genesis through Kings is a hitherto unnoticed sequence of violations of the Ten Commandments, one by one, book by book, by the community of Israel, which leads, in the end, to exile.

I would suggest that this sequence of violations reveals the hand of the final editor of the Primary History–Genesis through Kings–and reinforces an overarching theme–the violation of God's law, step by step, commandment by commandment, results in Israel's destruction. Explaining this is a tall order. I hope you will find it as gripping to read as I found it exciting to explore.[1]

The Primary History in the Hebrew Bible consists of nine books:

A. TORAH (PENTATEUCH)	**B. FORMER PROPHETS**
1. Genesis	6. Joshua
2. Exodus	7. Judges
3. Leviticus	8. Samuel
4. Numbers	9. Kings
5. Deuteronomy	

In the Bible today, Samuel and Kings are divided into two parts. In the official Hebrew canon, however, Samuel and Kings were a single long book, which was subsequently divided into two parts, presumably for ease in handling and for reference purposes. The same is true, incidentally, of Chronicles, which, however, is a later composition and not part of the Primary History and which appears at the very end of the Hebrew Bible.[2] In English and Greek Bibles, the Book of Ruth is attached to Judges, but that insertion reflects secondary and derivative arrangements; in the Hebrew Bible, the Book of Ruth appears near the end.

The nine books from Genesis through Kings form the Primary History of Israel as recounted in the Hebrew Bible. They constitute a single narrative sequence, tracing the story of Israel from its origins—and the origins of everything—to the end of the nation, the downfall of the southern kingdom of Judah in 587/586 B.C.E. and the exile of the survivors in Babylon.

This central block of material, almost half of the entire Hebrew Bible, was compiled and promulgated, in my opinion, sometime in the latter part of the Exile not long after the story ends, about 550 B.C.E. The last dated entry in the story is 561 B.C.E., when the king of Babylon released King Jehoiachin of Judah from prison (2 Kings 25:27). The exiles began to return under the Persian monarch Cyrus in 539 B.C.E.

Clearly, the Primary History is comprised of compositions by several authors and includes materials derived from a wide spectrum of sources, some cited, some alluded to, some implied. The Primary History is generally regarded by scholars as an assemblage or aggregation of at least four major written sources—J (the Yahwist), E (the Elohist), P (the Priestly code) and D (the Deuteronomist). J and E, the earliest sources, were soon combined as JE. Then JE was incorporated into the Priestly code to form what I call the P-work, which consists of Genesis, Exodus, Leviticus and Numbers. The next five books—Deuteronomy, Joshua, Judges, Samuel and Kings—are also generally regarded as a unitary sequence known as the Deuteronomic history. We may call this the D-work. So together our nine books are composed principally of the P-work and the D-work, which were combined by a final editor.

Although the finished product obviously underwent a great deal of editorial activity, the Primary History nevertheless exhibits certain, I would say unmistakable, marks of unity. Over the years, I have devoted considerable research to this unity, and what I have to say here results from this research.

Briefly, my argument is that a single person (or a small editorial committee dominated by one person) was responsible for assembling the constituent elements of this great narrative and arranging them in the order in which we now have them. Furthermore, while scrupulously preserving the available materials entrusted to his care and observing the rules of the editorial task, he nevertheless contributed to the final assemblage and produced a unified work.

The work of the editor, or redactor, has always interested me—for obvious reasons[3]—and although my experience is doubtless different from an ancient editor's, there must also be some common elements. The first obligation of an editor is to recognize his (or her) constraints or limitations. But without encroaching on the province of the author, the editor, especially when assembling or compiling a composite work with contributions from several authors, has the right to organize and arrange the material to bring out continuity and coherence, in other words, to shape a unity that is inherent but not fully realized in the component parts. In fact, he has an obligation to do so. In essence, I believe this was done with the Primary History by the compiler, who was probably a Jerusalem priest during the Babylonian Exile.

Evidence of unifying editorial activity can be found in the links between the sections that derive from different authors. The further apart the links in the story, the more likely they are to reflect the work of the editor. Thus, editorial touches that connect Genesis with Kings are especially indicative of the work of the redactor or compiler. Consider, for example, the apparent, if superficial, link between the first stories in Genesis (Adam and Eve, Cain and Abel), both of which deal with punishment for sin or crime, and the fate of the nation at the end of Kings. In the Adam and Eve and Cain and Abel stories (Genesis 1-4), the punishment for disobedience is banishment or exile, precisely the fate of the exiles in Babylon, the presumed readers of those stories and the subject of the final chapters of Kings.

Moreover, Babylon itself is the subject of the story of the Tower of Babel (Genesis 11), the first narrative after the renewal of life on earth following the Flood. The Tower of Babel story supplies the transition to the beginning of the patriarchal narrative, the account of Abraham's family. So the story that began in Babylon more than a millennium before ends in the same place for Abraham's remote descendants. From Babylon to Babylon provides a neat framework, or envelope, for the Primary History. Only a compiler-editor would have made explicit what was implicit in the separately authored blocks of material.

Let us turn now to a more elaborate structural feature that pervades the Primary History, cutting across source and authorship lines and giving us an entirely new perspective on how the compiler managed this vast enterprise.

It is generally agreed that a principal theme of the Primary History—and of the major components, certainly the D-work and perhaps the P-work as well—is how the Israelites, the chosen people of God who were rescued from bondage in Egypt and established in a new homeland, lost their independence and their land and ended up in exile. Although the details of this tragedy, the decline and fall of the two nations, Israel and Judah, are given in political/ military terms, if not socioeconomic ones, the overriding theme is that just as Israel was created by God, so it could be, and was, destroyed by him. The reason for the destruction was that, from the beginning, the relationship between God and his people was understood to be morally conditioned and was explicated in a binding agreement, or covenant, between them. Thus, the deliverance of Israel from bondage and the establishment of the nation were the deeds of a gracious God acting on the basis of a commitment to the patriarchs beginning with Abraham. But the continued existence of the nation, not to mention its success, security and prosperity, depended upon behavior, adherence to a code of conduct pleasing to God. This code was spelled out in the hundreds of rules and regulations—moral and cultic, civic and religious, social, political and economic—that permeate the pages of the Torah.

The code of conduct is summed up in the Decalogue, or the Ten Commandments, which was known to every Israelite. Here, in a word (or Ten Words, as they are called in the Hebrew Bible), is the epitome of the covenant, a summary of the rules by which all Israel must live under the sovereign rule of God. The covenant is both a promise and a threat, as both Moses (in the speeches in Deuteronomy) and Joshua (in his speeches in Joshua 23-24) make clear. If Israel obeys the laws of the covenant, then all will be well and Israel will prosper under the aegis of its God; if, however, people disobey the commandments and rebel against the authority of God, then everything will be lost— prosperity, security, nationhood and homeland.

The Primary History is the story of how Israel failed to keep its side of the bargain. Because Israel did not adhere to the requirements of the compact with God, the nation was ultimately punished for dereliction of duty.

Most readers—scholars and laypeople—will probably agree about this. There are, of course, other themes and important features of the Primary History, but the interpretation of Israel's history and destiny properly emphasizes the covenant obligation and Israel's repeated failure to live up to God's central demands.

Now I want to try to put myself in the shoes of the redactor-compiler, or to sit at his desk, and ask how I can sharpen the focus or highlight the drama of this decline and fall and bring home to the survivors the necessary, if onerous, lesson of the past so as to strengthen their resolve in their present affliction and prepare them for a future that holds a similar combination of threat and promise.

The first thing I would do as redactor-compiler would be to highlight the Decalogue as the core and center of the covenant. The simplest way to do this, of course, would be by repetition. The Decalogue is found in both the P-work (in Exodus 20:2-17) and the D-work (in Deuteronomy 5:6-12), which contains an older source of the Decalogue. Instead of combining the two or conflating them, the compiler keeps them separate. So the Decalogue appears twice in the story, near the beginning of Israel's 40-year march from Egypt to Canaan and just before the end of the journey, when Israel is about to enter Canaan.

Moreover, the repetition of the Decalogue occurs at strategic points in the literary structure. The Book of Deuteronomy is at the center, the fifth book of the nine books in the sequence, and thus is the pivot or apex of the entire work. The contents of Deuteronomy suggest that this is not an accident or coincidence. Moses, the central figure of the Primary History, dominates the Book of Deuteronomy, which consists of a series of addresses by Israel's greatest leader toward the end of his life, in essence, his valedictory. In these sermons, Moses not only reviews the history of his people (thereby providing a legitimate reason for repeating the Ten Commandments), but also, as a true prophet, he forecasts what will happen in the future, depending upon their behavior. So the Decalogue stands at the beginning of the national history and at the center of the narrative.

Further, the Decalogue symbolizes and summarizes the covenant, the obligations of which fall on all Israelites, as individuals personally responsible for obeying the commandments and as members of a community answerable to God for the behavior of individual members.

We can outline the sequence of events as follows. Israel is delivered from bondage in Egypt and brought to Sinai, the sacred mountain. There the Decalogue is given as a *précis* of the covenant. The people agree to its terms, and the covenant is solemnly ratified by sacrifices and a common meal at the mountain (Exodus 24). In the succeeding books, repeated violations of the covenant, interrupted by occasional reversals and reforms, culminate in the repudiation of Israel by its maker and founder and the destruction of the nation, the northern kingdom of Israel in 722 B.C.E. and the southern kingdom of Judah in 587/586 B.C.E. The end is captivity in Babylon.

How did the final editor of this mighty history make the case dramatic and suspenseful and, at the same time, guide the reader through the complex details of this 600-year history? Using the Decalogue as his point of departure, the editor portrays Israel as violating each of the commandments directly and explicitly. The commandments are violated in order, one by one. Given the fact that the editor has a group of books (i.e., scrolls) to deal with, he assigns, in general, one commandment and one violation to each book.

Wherever possible, the seriousness of the episode is stressed to show how the violation (usually by an individual) involves or implicates the whole nation, putting the very survival of the nation in jeopardy. Only the extraordinary intervention of a leader or a precipitous change of direction on the part of the people is reason to spare them. In each instance, God relents and the relationship is patched up. But after each episode, the threat and warning are strengthened, so that succeeding violations bring Israel (and Judah) ever closer to destruction. In the end, all of the commandments will have been violated and God's patience will have run out. Let us now see if, and how, this happens.

The Ten Commandments,[4] in abbreviated form, are listed below:

1. Apostasy
2. Idolatry
3. Blasphemy
4. Sabbath observance
5. Parental respect

6. Murder
7. Adultery
8. Stealing
9. False testimony
10. Coveting

Because the editor is working with existing literary texts and not just a collection of bits and pieces, he is naturally limited as to how much he can arrange or rearrange, organize or reorganize, or otherwise manipulate his material. Hence we can expect certain deviations and adjustments as we go along. For example, the story of covenant-making and covenant-breaking properly begins with the Book of Exodus, which presents something of a problem. Genesis has covenants and covenant ceremonies (for example, with Noah in Genesis 9 and with Abraham in Genesis 15 and 17), but these are not like the covenant made at Sinai/Horeb and mediated by Moses; nor are they related to the Decalogue. The editor deals with this problem by beginning with Exodus and doubling up the commandments violated in that book.

Apostasy and Idolatry

Immediately after the Ten Commandments are given on Mount Sinai and the Israelites agree to them, Moses goes up the mountain to receive instructions for building the Tabernacle. During his absence, the incident of the golden calf occurs (Exodus 32). The episode is described in such a way as to make it clear that the Israelites have violated the first and second commandments: "You shall have no other gods beside me" (Exodus 20:3) and "You shall not make for yourself a graven image" (Exodus 20:4).

The Israelites not only make the golden calf (a graven image), but they also speak of it as symbolizing one or more gods (apostasy): "And they said, 'These are thy gods, O Israel, who brought thee up from the land of Egypt'" (Exodus 32:4). Thus, we have accounted not only for the first two commandments, but also for the first two books of the Primary History.

If we probe a bit deeper into this episode, we find another feature that will be repeated in book after book for commandment after commandment. Although some Israelites are guilty of violating the covenant in connection with the golden calf and others are not (the Levites), the existence of the whole community is threatened. God tells Moses that he will wipe out Israel and create a new people from Moses' progeny (Exodus 32:10). Only after Moses intercedes and some of the apostates are slaughtered does God relent and spare the community (Exodus 32:11-14, cf. verses 31-35).

This episode is the paradigm for the whole subsequent history of Israel. A violation of any of the commandments is a violation of all of them, indeed of the whole covenant, but the primary category is always expressed in terms of apostasy and idolatry, which are at the heart of the Decalogue, just as the Decalogue is at the heart of the rules and regulations of the covenant.

Blasphemy

The third book is Leviticus, and the third commandment prohibits misuse of the name of God, that is, blasphemy: "You shall not invoke the name of Yahweh your God for falsehood" (Exodus 20:7).

There is just such a story in Leviticus. An unnamed man, the son of an Israelite woman and an Egyptian man, "went out among the people of Israel...and quarreled" (Leviticus 24:10). Then he "cursed the name and committed blasphemy" (Leviticus 24:11). He is brought before Moses and placed in custody to await Yahweh's decision. Yahweh then instructs Moses to take the blasphemer outside the camp where everyone who heard the blasphemy lays hands upon his head, and the whole assembly stones him (Leviticus 24:12-14). Yahweh tells Moses to tell the people: "Any man, if he curses his God, then he shall bear [the consequences of] his sin. The one who curses the name of Yahweh shall surely be put to death, and the whole congregation will stone him—the alien resident as well as the native born—when he curses the name he shall be put to death" (Leviticus 24:15-16).

Of the hundreds of laws and regulations imposed on Israel by the covenant, the Ten Commandments stand out because no specific penalty is attached to them. These are not casuistic laws stated in terms of cause and effect or crime and punishment; they are apodictic laws, flat regulations that demand unqualified obedience. In the case of the blasphemy in Leviticus, the guilty party is detained until the matter of punishment has been resolved. The Israelites recognize that there has been a serious breach of the covenant, but no one, not even Moses, knows how to deal with the matter.

When word is received from Yahweh, the whole community, including those who witnessed the crime, must participate in the act of judgment. In that way, the community is cleared of complicity with the guilty person and escapes the consequences of this breach of the covenant. This particular occurrence may seem trivial compared to the golden calf, but the special treatment accorded this passing event shows that the writer (or editor) had in mind the highest level of covenant obligation—the Decalogue.

Sabbath Observance

The fourth book in the Primary History is the Book of Numbers, and the fourth commandment is Sabbath observance:

> Remember[5] the Sabbath Day to keep it holy. For six days you shall labor and do all your work, but the seventh day is a sabbath of Yahweh your

God. You shall do no work at all, neither you nor your son nor your daughter, your male or female servant, nor your cattle, nor the alien who is within your gates.

Exodus 20:8-10

In Numbers we find a story about a man who gathered sticks on the Sabbath, thus violating the prohibition against doing work on that day:

While the Israelites were in the wilderness, they found him gathering wood on the Sabbath Day. So those who found him gathering wood brought him to Moses and to Aaron and to the whole assembly. They detained him in the guardhouse, because it had not been explained what should be done to him. Then Yahweh said to Moses: "The man shall surely be put to death. The whole assembly shall stone him with stones, outside the camp." So the whole assembly brought him outside the camp and they stoned him with stones and he died, as Yahweh had commanded Moses.

Numbers 15:32-36

This story is much like the one in Leviticus concerning blasphemy. In each case, a violation of one of the Ten Commandments is recorded and the man responsible is arrested pending sentencing and appropriate punishment. In each case, the determination of the penalty (death by stoning by the whole assembly) is made by Yahweh and communicated directly to Moses. Action by God supplements the Decalogue, which lists injunctions but does not specify punishments. And the severity of the penalty emphasizes the centrality and essential nature of the terms of the covenant. Anything less than removal of the offender would implicate the whole community in the offense and ultimately lead to abrogation of the compact and dissolution of the nation.

Parental Respect

The fifth book is Deuteronomy, and the fifth commandment reads as follows: "Honor your father and mother, so that your days may be prolonged on the land that Yahweh your God is going to give you" (Exodus 20:12).

Once again, there is an account of a violation of a particular commandment. This time, however, the incident is couched in the hypothetical terminology of case law, prescribing the punishment for a specific crime. In other words, the formulation in Deuteronomy goes a stage beyond Leviticus and Numbers. In the earlier books, we are given the incident or episode that is the basis or precedent on which the punishment was fixed. Here we have a general formulation, derived presumably from a particular incident, which has been lost or is no longer included in the biblical tradition.

If a man has a son, who is contumacious and rebellious [i.e., stubbornly rebellious] and will not obey the orders of his father or his mother; and if they chastise [discipline] him and he persists in his disobedience, then his father and his mother shall lay hold of him and bring him forth to the elders of his city and to the gate of his place. And they [the parents]

shall say to the elders of his city: "This son of ours is contumacious and
rebellious, and he will not obey our orders; he is [also] an idler and a sot."
Then all the men of his city shall stone him with stones until he is dead.
So shall you destroy the evil from your midst. And as for all Israel, let them
pay heed and show reverence.

Deuteronomy 21:18-21

We turn now to the last four books in the Primary History—Joshua, Judges,
Samuel and Kings—and the next four commandments, numbers six, seven, eight
and nine. An adjustment is necessary here because the order in which these
books take up three of the four commandments is not the same order in which
they appear in Exodus and Deuteronomy. This may be because the editor or
redactor of the Primary History was not entirely free to choose his material and
therefore had to make some adjustments; or it may be that he was working from
a different order of the commandments; or perhaps he was familiar with other
traditions concerning the order of the commandments and justified his
rearrangement by this diversity.

In this connection, we note that the order of commandments six, seven and
eight varies among the sources, as the chart at right reflects. These three commandments are short (only two words each in Hebrew, one of which is
equivalent to the English *do not*), so it would be easy to transpose them.

In an abbreviated version of the Decalogue in Jeremiah's Sermon in the
Temple Courtyard (Jeremiah 7:9), these three commandments are listed in
the order they are dealt with in the next three books of the Bible (stealing, murder, adultery) rather than the order in which they are listed in Exodus and
Deuteronomy (murder, adultery, stealing). There may even be a connection here,
in view of well documented literary affinities between the Book of Jeremiah and
the Deuteronomic history (Deuteronomy through Kings). As far as the prose
sections of Jeremiah are concerned, the similarity of style, as well as the similarity of themes and motifs, strongly supports the connection. Baruch
ben-Neriah, the scribe who was responsible for at least two versions of the Book
of Jeremiah (Jeremiah 36:1-32, especially verses 4 and 32), may also have
played an important role in compiling and producing the great Deuteronomic
history, and this may account for the fact that the order in which the commandments are violated in the next three books of the Primary History is the
same as in Jeremiah's sermon.

Stealing

Let us turn once again to the books of the Primary History as they continue
the story of Israel's journey to destruction and exile. The sixth book is the Book
of Joshua. Here the major crime or transgression of the covenant is theft, a violation of the eighth commandment in the conventional ordering of the Hebrew
Bible but the sixth in the order in Jeremiah.

The episode in Joshua is described in great detail. The Israelites destroy
Jericho but are defeated at the next site on their march, Ai. Yahweh announces

Order of Commandments Six, Seven and Eight

Hebrew Bible (Exodus, Deuteronomy)	6. Murder	7. Adultery	8. Theft
Septuagint*	7. Adultery	8. Theft	6. Murder
Nash Papyrus;** Luke 18:20; Romans 13:9; Philo†**	7. Adultery	6. Murder	8. Theft
Jeremiah 7:9; the order of violations in Joshua, Judges and Samuel	8. Theft	6. Murder	7. Adultery

*The Septuagint (LXX) is an early Greek translation of the Hebrew Bible.

**The Nash Papyrus, dated to the second century B.C.E., is a 24-line Hebrew text containing the Ten Commandments and part of the *Shema* prayer (Deuteronomy 6:4-5). Of unknown provenance, the papyrus was purchased from an Egyptian antiquities dealer in 1903 by W. L. Nash, for whom it is named.

† Philo was a Jewish philosopher who lived in Alexandria from the first century B.C.E. to the first century C.E., roughly contemporaneous with Jesus, Paul and the Jewish sages Hillel and Gamaliel.

that the reason for the defeat is that someone "stole" some of the booty from Jericho that was dedicated to Yahweh. The man is identified by lot as Achan ben-Carmi of the tribe of Judah. From the outset, the focus of the story is on the crime:

> The Israelites committed a grave offense regarding the dedicated booty. Achan, the son of Carmi, the son of Zabdi, the son of Zerach of the tribe of Judah took some of the sacred booty, and the wrath of Yahweh was kindled against the Israelites.
>
> Joshua 7:1

As a result, the Israelites are defeated at Ai, and this setback jeopardizes their foothold in the land of promise and threatens their whole settlement. The punishment is even more severe than in the previous cases. Achan and his family are executed by stoning at the hands of the whole community.

The story shows that the crime of theft was construed as a capital offense on a par with the other commandments and was punishable in the same manner (by community stoning). In most cases, theft would not be considered a capital offense, and the wrongdoer would be punished by a fine, the imposition of damages (requiring payment of double or more the amount stolen) or restitution of some other kind. Such cases would hardly serve the purpose here, but the extraordinary case of Achan fits admirably into the scheme we have outlined. As he did in the previous cases, God again takes a direct hand in exposing the crime and the criminal and again dictates the punishment.

The editor-compiler adapted the commandment and structured the story to fit the overall pattern, thereby emphasizing the importance of obeying the commandments to the survival of the community, as well as the divine provision for dealing with violations. In each case, the nation narrowly escapes the consequences of divine wrath.

Murder

The seventh book, Judges, involves murder, following the order in Jeremiah 7:9. Judges includes many instances in which someone is killed—Eglon by Ehud (Judges 3:15-26, especially verses 21-22), Sisera by Jael (Judges 4-5, especially 4:17-21, 5:24-27) and numerous Philistines by Samson (Judges 14-16, especially 14:19, 15:15, 16:30)—but none of these qualifies for our purposes because they are not considered violations of the commandment against murder but are regarded as righteous deeds for the sake of the community.

The story we have in mind is at the very end of the book (Judges 19-21). It is the story of an unnamed woman, identified only as the Levite's concubine. The men of Gibeah in Benjamin took her by force in the night and mass raped her (Judges 19). She crawled back to the house where her master was staying and died. The woman is described in the story as "the murdered woman" (Hebrew, *ha-isha ha-nirṣa-ha*, Judges 20:4). The root (*RṢḤ*) is the same as the root of the word for murder in the Decalogue.

The crime is described by the author-editor as the worst in the history of the commonwealth. "Not has there happened, nor has there been seen anything like this since the day that the Israelites went up from the land of Egypt until this day" (Judges 19:30).

The crime was brutal and appalling by any standards, but it was compounded by the Benjaminites who refused to cooperate with the other tribes in the investigation and resolution of the matter. This led to civil war, the near destruction of a whole tribe (Benjamin) and the near dissolution of the entire Israelite league. In the end, under divine guidance, the forces of Israel triumphed over the Benjaminites, and the nation survived (Judges 20). Restoring Benjamin to the tribal league was a more difficult and delicate task, but this too was accomplished through the timely intervention of dedicated men (Judges 21).

Adultery

We have now reached the eighth book, the Book of Samuel, which deals with adultery. Adultery is often mentioned in the Hebrew Bible, especially in the Latter Prophets (Isaiah, Jeremiah, Ezekiel and the 12 Minor Prophets), but only one example of this crime is spelled out in detail with the names of people and places and specific circumstances. This is the case of King David, who took Bathsheba, the wife of Uriah the Hittite, and subsequently arranged for Uriah to be killed in battle to conceal his original crime. At the climax of the story, the prophet Nathan confronts the guilty king who ultimately repents (2 Samuel 11-12).

To the author-editor of Samuel, David's adultery with Bathsheba was a turning point not only in David's reign, but also in the history of the kingdom. Subsequent trials and ills, rebellions and machinations, are described as stemming from that violation by the king, who compounded adultery with murder, thereby forfeiting the respect and loyalty of his troops and distancing himself from Yahweh, the covenant and the privileged status he had enjoyed as the anointed of Yahweh. The peril for the country is amply documented, as well as the act of divine remission and compassion. Once again, the kingdom escapes its fate, and the dynasty is preserved for the sake of the nation.

False Testimony

The last book in the Primary History is Kings, and it invokes the ninth commandment. Once again, royalty is involved, and the action causes serious consequences for the entire kingdom. The commandment in this case deals with false testimony in a legal proceeding, what we would call perjury. (In our courts, witnesses testify under oath or solemn affirmation, which is required for perjury, whereas in ancient Israel, oaths were invoked only under special conditions and only on the defendant.) The story in Kings involves Ahab, king of Israel, his Phoenician wife, Jezebel, and a man named Naboth. When Naboth refuses Ahab's offer to purchase his vineyard, Jezebel arranges to have false charges brought against Naboth, accusing him of cursing both God and king. As punishment, Naboth is stoned to death, and Ahab takes possession of Naboth's vineyard (1 Kings 21). This is a clear violation of the ninth commandment: "You shall not bear false witness against your neighbor [fellow citizen]" (Exodus 20:16).

Once again, an angry prophet, in this case Elijah, denounces the guilty party and decrees dire punishment: "Have you killed and also taken possession?...In the place where dogs licked up the blood of Naboth shall dogs lick your own blood" (1 Kings 21:19). Once again a king, faced with undeniable facts, is remorseful and repentant. And once again God mercifully postpones the day of judgment (1 Kings 21:27-29).

The final settling of accounts, however, is not long in coming. Before the Book of Kings ends, both Israel and Judah come to a violent end. Their armies are defeated, their countries conquered, their capital cities destroyed and their leading citizens taken into captivity.

We have come to the end of our series as well. Nine books, nine commandments. But what about the tenth: "You shall not covet"?[6]

The tenth commandment is unique, because the emphasis is on motivation or attitude rather than action, as is clearly the case with the other commandments. The tenth commandment functions therefore as a complement or supplement to several of the preceding commandments—stealing, murder, adultery and false swearing—and provides the motivation or explanation for committing the crime. Each of the crimes involved in the sixth, seventh, eighth and ninth commandments was motivated by an illicit desire or sinful urge to take something that belonged to another—the booty from Jericho in the case of Achan, who confessed that he saw the various items in the spoil and "desired them" (Joshua 7:21)—the same verb as in the Decalogue; the same can be said of the criminals in the story of Judges, whose desire for the Levite led to the murder of his concubine; in the case of David and Bathsheba, David's lust for another man's wife led to adultery. And in the case of Naboth's vineyard, the king's desire for Naboth's property led to a violation of the ninth commandment, false testimony.

Thus, with a modicum of ingenuity and adjustment, we can correlate the Decalogue and the Primary History and make a dramatic correspondence between commandments and books culminating in the collapse of the two kingdoms, the end of national history and the Babylonian Exile.

Could this sustained pattern have been sheer coincidence (buttressed by the ingenuity of a modern analyst looking for such correlations)? Or did a creative redactor deliberately construct a history of his people on the framework or scaffolding of the Decalogue? Did he deliberately preserve the overall unity of the heterogeneous elements by strategically highlighting particular themes to bring out the central story of the covenant between God and Israel, the consequences of the relationship and the judgment upon and verdict against the nation?

This particular device or pattern has never been observed before—at least to my knowledge—which should caution against supposing it was the major or central objective of the redactor. It was one of several ways of highlighting the central theme of the history of Israel and reinforcing the unity of the account comprising the nine books of the Primary History. Israel's history could be told on two levels—as the story of a people or the story of successive violations of the commandments, one by one, book by book, until the nation ran out of options and was finally destroyed.

A F T E R W O R D

Rev. Gary H. Lubenow of Basin, Wyoming, offers these refinements to Freedman's "excellent observations":

Deuteronomy 32 is a better candidate for the violation of the fifth commandment (honoring father and mother) than Freedman's choice of Deuteronomy 21:18-21. Professor Freedman himself has observed that the passage in Deuteronomy differs from the passages in the other books of the Primary History he chooses because the passage in Deuteronomy is hypothetical: "If a man has a stubborn and rebellious son...then...." The other episodes involve *narrated* violations of the commandments.

This narrative form seems important to the pattern. Note that the narrative in Leviticus 24:10-23 on which Freedman relies is (except for the pericopes in chapters 8-10) the *only* narrative episode in the whole Book of Leviticus. This suggests that another possibility in Deuteronomy should be considered. And I suggest Deuteronomy 32.

Although the fifth commandment requires honor for father and mother, it is not obvious that only *human* parents are referred to in the commandment. In Malachi 1:6, God issues the challenge: "If I am a father, where is the honor due me?" This imagery is taken up in Deuteronomy 32: "They are no longer his children" (verse 5); "Is he not your Father, your Creator" (verse 6); "He was angered by his sons and daughters" (verse 19); "They are unfaithful children" (verse 20). In Deuteronomy 32:18, God is pictured as both father and mother: "The Rock who fathered you, the God who gave you birth," and, in Deuteronomy 32:11-12, God is pictured as an eagle brooding over her young and encouraging their first attempts at flight.

Nor are human parents out of the picture; Deuteronomy 32:7 reminds the vagrant Israelites to remember the old days, the former generations, to "ask [their] fathers" about God's provision and faithfulness to them. And in verse 17, Israel is accused of worshiping "gods [their] fathers did not fear." So Israel has failed to honor both human and divine parents.

The most explicit clue, however, comes at the conclusion to Deuteronomy 32. Verses 44-47 implore the people to obey "all the words of the law" so that "*you will live long in the land.*" This is an explicit reference to the fifth commandment, where the specific reward for obedience to this commandment is that "*you will live long in the land.*" **BR** *6:6 (1990), p. 48*

Hershel Shanks, editor of BR, suggests an alternative to Freedman's treatment of the tenth commandment, Thou shalt not covet:

With his customary uncanny ability to see patterns in biblical literature that the rest of us can see only after he points them out, Freedman identifies Israel's sequential violation of nine of the Ten Commandments in each of the first nine books of the Hebrew Bible. Some adjustments are required, but not many. Thus, we see the violation of the first two commandments in Exodus (when Israel's national existence begins), rather than in Genesis and Exodus, the violation of the third commandment in Leviticus, the fourth in Numbers, the fifth in Deuteronomy, the sixth, seventh and eighth in Joshua, Judges and Samuel, and the ninth in Kings. Having broken all the commandments *seriatim*, Israel is sent into exile.

What about the tenth sin, coveting? Freedman is aware that he hasn't covered this commandment; that is why he calls his article "The Nine Commandments" instead of "The Ten Commandments." In the text of his article, Freedman explains that the tenth commandment is different from the others—involving motivation and attitude, rather than action. And besides, he says, because coveting was involved in the violation of several preceding commandments—stealing, murder, adultery and false swearing—the tenth commandment has also been violated.

It seems to me there is an explicit violation of the tenth commandment that fits right into the pattern Freedman discovered. The incident involving Naboth's vineyard (which illustrates the violation of the ninth commandment, false swearing) also involves coveting (the tenth commandment), and it does so explicitly. In the episode of Naboth's vineyard, we have the description *par excellence* of covetousness.

Ahab, who has wealth beyond dreaming and is surrounded by the prerogatives that attach to royalty, still covets his neighbor's vineyard. The text elaborates—Ahab goes into his palace vexed and sullen; he lies down on his bed; he turns away his face; he refuses food (1 Kings 21:4). His wife, Jezebel, implores him, "After all, you are a king," she tells him. "Be cheerful; I will get you the vineyard." Thus she relieves his condition. Nowhere else in the Bible do we find such a description of covetousness.

Freedman says that covetousness is also involved in the incidents illustrating stealing, murder and adultery. But in the case of Achan, we have only a single statement that he desired the booty from Jericho (Joshua 7:21), unlike the full description of Ahab's covetousness. The men who raped and murdered the Levite's concubine (Judges 19) apparently wanted to have sex with the Levite, but that desire is never made explicit. The case of David and Bathsheba offers a special opportunity to depict desire, but we are told only that Bathsheba was very beautiful; David's desire for Uriah's wife is expressed only implicitly (2 Samuel 11:2-4).

Only in the case of Ahab, the last violation in what Freedman calls Israel's Primary History (Genesis through Kings), does the text give a detailed description of covetousness. Moreover, we also have a double violation in this episode—false swearing and covetousness. Just as we opened the sequence in Exodus with a double violation—the golden calf involved both apostasy and making a graven image—so we have a double violation at the end. Beginning and ending with double violations creates a classic "envelope" structure. And with the violation of the tenth commandment, the sequence is complete. Not nine commandments, but ten commandments.

I suggested this idea to Freedman before we published his article, but he rejected it. In the Achan episode, the word for covet is actually used, he said, but not in the other episodes, not even in Ahab. This may detract somewhat from my argument, but, I submit, not much. As Freedman himself wrote, "Because the [biblical] editor [redactor] is working with existing literary works and not just a collection of bits and pieces, he is naturally limited as to how much he can arrange or rearrange, organize and reorganize, or manipulate his material. Hence we can expect certain deviations and adjustments." **BR** *6:2 (1990), p. 8*

Freedman replies:

When it comes to the tenth commandment, there is clearly a difference of perception, as this is a commandment (against coveting) that can not be violated by itself in the form of a punishable crime, as the others can. So almost by definition, if the tenth commandment is violated in a criminal fashion, it has to be connected with breaking at least one other commandment. Shanks and I both have shown that there is at least one other commandment violated to demonstrate that the tenth commandment has been violated at the same time. I have suggested that that is the case with all four of the last commandments. The same word is used in the sixth commandment, and covetousness is clearly a motivational factor in the other episodes. And I would agree that this is also true in the case of the ninth commandment. Perhaps even more so, as Shanks says. But coveting is certainly not exclusive to the ninth commandment. Shanks emphasizes that the violation of the tenth commandment ties in better with the ninth commandment than with any of the others. As long as we agree that the tenth is significantly different from the other nine commandments (and Shanks, a lawyer, should be the strongest advocate of the qualitative difference), and that it is a—or the—motivating factor in the violation of at least four other commandments, then we have nothing to quarrel about.

If Shanks wants to say, in spite of these two points, that the author-compiler really wants to connect the tenth commandment solely (?) with breaking the ninth, who is there to stop him? Shanks may know more about the author's mind than I do. But certainly his view is not incompatible with my overall position, and mine differs from his only in that I don't want to go the extra step and say that the author intended to combine the ninth and tenth commandments. I don't think it is the same as the combination of commandments one and two, where there is much more precedence for combining them (numbers one and two in Jewish and Catholic counting are, by my reckoning and by that of Protestants generally, really one commandment). By contrast, no one counts numbers nine and ten as one commandment. And in the case of numbers one and two, we have a previous book, Genesis, to account for, whereas in the case of numbers nine and ten, there is, explicitly, and I think deliberately, no tenth book to reckon with.

At the same time, I think Shanks' insight into the psychological connections between commandments nine and ten is excellent, and his description of Ahab and his greed is a literary masterpiece. His argument is an exceptionally worthy spin-off of my observations. I think my statement of the case can easily and fully accommodate his observations. However, I am not sure his understanding is really the same as mine or even compatible with it. **BR** *6:5 (1990), p. 12*

CHAPTER 4

The David and Goliath Saga

Emanuel Tov

In contrast to the unity found by Freedman, Emanuel Tov demonstrates that not all editors did neat work. Many scholars have argued that the Septuagint version of 1 Samuel 16-18 is an abridgment of the much longer received Hebrew text. Tov argues that the Hebrew text is a combination of two shorter versions of the story, one of which is preserved in the Greek translation. Only such a conflation, he says, can explain the internal contradictions in the Hebrew, for example the introduction of David in chapter 17 after he has already figured in chapter 16. The implications of Tov's argument are far-reaching: "The fact that the redactor...created a text displaying such inconsistencies is precisely what is supposed to have happened in other cases throughout the Bible, where texts underwent conflation, expansion and interpolation."–Ed.

Jeffrey H. Tigay of the University of Pennsylvania sets the stage for the article that follows:

Since the rise of biblical criticism in the 17th century, scholars have concluded that the books of the Hebrew Bible, like many other ancient literary classics, have not reached us in their original form but are the products of lengthy evolution. Many parts of the Bible are thought to include new material composed by revisers or variant accounts of the same events interpolated into the original text by editors who wished to present information not found in any one account.

These conclusions were reached by critics reading between the lines of the traditional text of the Bible. Phenomena such as inconsistencies, redundancies and thematic and stylistic variants were read as clues that a given text was the combined work of more than one author or age or that it had been revised. Following these clues, scholars tried to analyze texts into their original components. Although they marshaled powerful arguments, the "analysts" were in effect arguing for the existence of lost documents, which none of them had ever seen and for which there were no known sources. Because copies of the presumed earlier stages of these books were rarely available for consultation, the analyses were perforce confined to the traditional text, with few references to external controls. The "analysts" could never demonstrate that inconsistencies and the like necessarily resulted from revision or interpolation, and, with few exceptions, they could not show that ancient compositions had undergone the kind of evolution they hypothesized. Consequently, the results of biblical criticism, though impressive, have remained largely hypothetical.

Today, we are in a position to introduce empirical perspectives into this theoretical structure. Many literary compositions from ancient Mesopotamia and post-Exilic Israel are known in several versions from different periods. Such texts as the Gilgamesh Epic and the Samaritan version of the Torah can be shown to have reached their final forms in ways remarkably similar to the ways biblical critics believe the books of the Bible developed.[1] There are even cases where earlier versions of parts of the Bible are available, and by comparing them with the final versions we can see that the Bible developed in ways similar to those postulated by biblical critics. In many cases, it can be seen that inconsistencies and the like really are the results of the editing process, as the analysts supposed. These cases do not in themselves prove the theories correct, but they do confirm that they are plausible.

In the following article, Professor Emanuel Tov argues on the basis of the Septuagint that the story of David and Goliath, as it appears in the Hebrew text of the Bible, is one such case.

B iblical critics try to get behind biblical texts as they have come down to us to determine their history and prehistory, to find out if they were formed by combining two or more different texts or strands, to determine what was left out or added along the way and, perhaps, even to understand why.

Occasionally, we have more than one text of a passage or even of a book that provides us with real evidence—something besides theoretical clues—which allows us, more or less, to trace the step by step development of the final text. In this way, we can test, in particular instances, whether the theoretical procedures of transmission that scholars hypothesized actually occurred. Such a case involves not just textual transmission, but also presumably the *different* texts that were created at a very early stage, when the biblical book was still in the process of being created.

One such instance concerns the episode of David and Goliath in 1 Samuel 16-18, in which the youthful David slays the Philistine strongman in his mighty armor. In this instance, we have, in fact, two different versions of the story. The version preserved in our Hebrew Bibles is known as the Masoretic text, or MT as scholars call it. Although this version has come down to us in a medieval form, it actually goes back to a much earlier period and is already attested in a few verses of a pericope found among the Dead Sea Scrolls. The other version of the David and Goliath story is preserved in the oldest manuscripts of the Septuagint, or LXX as scholars refer to it. The LXX is a Greek translation of the Hebrew Bible made for the Jews of Alexandria in the third or second century B.C.E. According to legend, 72 scholars working independently produced identical translations. The number was later rounded off to 70, hence the abbreviation LXX.[2]

The David and Goliath episode in the MT is a surprising 80 percent longer than the same episode in the LXX!

In the box on the following pages, the MT of 1 Samuel 16:17-18:30 is reprinted. The parts that appear in the MT but not in the LXX ("minuses," as they are called) are printed in italics.[3]

Besides the minuses of the LXX, there are other differences between the two versions. Sometimes one word is used in the LXX and another in the MT. And in 17 instances there are "pluses" in the LXX, that is, things that appear in the LXX but not in the MT. The pluses range from single words to complete sentences. How can we account for all these differences? We cannot tell *a priori* which version of the episode is earlier because both versions may be based on traditions much earlier than their actual date.

In the past, scholars have suggested two theories to explain the differences between the two versions of the David and Goliath episode. The first is that the LXX translators abridged the Hebrew text to eliminate some contradictions and discrepancies. The second is that the LXX translators were working from a shorter Hebrew text. Both explanations, however, focus only on the large minuses in the LXX and disregard the shorter minuses, the variant readings and the pluses in the LXX.

By examining these neglected details, I believe we can demonstrate that both explanations are wrong, or at least oversimplified. We can now show that the LXX translators did work from a shorter Hebrew version of the David and Goliath story, which represented an earlier stage in the literary development of the story. I believe we can also reconstruct the way the different versions were combined in the longer Hebrew text preserved in the MT as part of the literary development of the Book of Samuel. We may consider ourselves "lucky" to have these insights into the history of the development of the book through the preservation of these ancient traditions.

The key to affirming that the LXX translator worked from a shorter Hebrew text is the assumption that the LXX version is a *literal* translation, that the technique of translation, we might say, was literal rather than free. The next assumption, which is probably a reasonable one, is that a translator committed to a literal translation of a text would not have felt free to omit 44 percent of the original, which is what the LXX translator must have done if he started from the same basic Hebrew text as the one preserved in the MT. Therefore, he must have been working from a shorter Hebrew text, which he translated literally.

How do we know that the LXX translators produced a literal translation if we don't have the Hebrew text from which they worked? There are four different kinds of clues. (1) The translators used the identical Greek equivalent for single Hebrew word-elements (particles like a *waw*, for example, which means *and* or *but* depending on the context), despite differences in context; the result is often so-called "Hebraisms" in the Greek language. An example of one Hebraism in the story of David and Goliath follows. In Hebrew *between* is expressed by repeating the word *ben* before the words on either side, as if to say between Scylla and between Charybdis. The second *between*, used in Hebrew, is incorrect in Greek (as it is in English). Yet in the LXX translation of the David and Goliath story, the Greek equivalent of *between* is repeated as it is in Hebrew. Previous investigators have pointed out other Hebraisms in the Greek translation of the David and Goliath story. (2) The LXX translators followed the Hebrew word order even when this was awkward in Greek. (3) Quantitatively, the LXX translators tried to use one Greek word for each Hebrew word. (4) Frequently, though not always, the Greek translator used the same Greek word for a single Hebrew word.

For all these reasons, we conclude that the Greek translation of the David and Goliath episode in the LXX is a relatively literal one. If this conclusion is correct, then it is unlikely that the translators would have omitted 44 percent of the text they were translating. The Greek translators have shown that they were unwilling to take many liberties with the text. We can, therefore, assume that the LXX translators were working from a Hebrew text that was much shorter than the MT that has come down to us.

Some scholars have suggested that the LXX version is an abridgment of the MT version because the shorter version eliminates some inconsistencies and contradictions in the MT version. For example, in 1 Samuel 17:55-58, when the young David approaches Goliath, King Saul asks his general, Abner, to identify the boy. Abner says he doesn't know him. After David kills Goliath, David is brought to Saul and introduced to him. Yet in the scene preceding the battle between David and Goliath, Saul and David had a lengthy conversation about David confronting Goliath (1 Samuel 16:17-23). Why do Saul and Abner fail to recognize him later, and why is it necessary to introduce David a second time to King Saul? It has been suggested that the passage in which Saul and Abner claim not to know David was omitted by the LXX translators in order to eliminate this inconsistency.

Standing alone, this is a reasonable suggestion, although it presupposes that the translator allowed himself considerable liberty with the text. But this explanation is weakened by the fact that scores of other contradictory passages have been left in the LXX translation, including many in the Book of Samuel. Moreover, the elimination of inconsistencies in the Hebrew text would explain only a small percentage of the alleged omissions from the LXX translation. Lengthy passages are omitted where leaving out short sections would have been

The Different Stories of David and Goliath in the Hebrew Bible and the Greek Bible
1 Samuel 16:17-18:30

The words in italic type are found only in the Hebrew version (MT); all other words are found in both the Hebrew version and the Greek version (LXX).

16:17 So Saul said to his courtiers, "Find me someone who can play well and bring him to me." **18**One of the attendants spoke up, "I have observed a son of Jesse the Bethlehemite who is skilled in music; he is a stalwart fellow and a warrior, sensible in speech, and handsome in appearance, and the Lord is with him." **19**Whereupon Saul sent messengers to Jesse to say, "Send me your son David, who is with the flock." **20**Jesse took an ass laden with bread, a skin of wine, and a kid, and sent them to Saul by his son David. **21**So David came to Saul and entered his service; Saul took a strong liking to him and made him one of his arms-bearers. **22**Saul sent word to Jesse, "Let David remain in my service, for I am pleased with him." **23**Whenever the [evil] spirit of God came upon Saul, David would take the lyre and play it; Saul would find relief and feel better, and the evil spirit would leave him.

17:1 The Philistines assembled their forces for battle; they massed at Socoh of Judah, and encamped at Ephes-dammim, between Socoh and Azekah. **2**Saul and the men of Israel massed and encamped in the valley of Elah. They drew their line of battle against the Philistines, **3**with the Philistines stationed on one hill and Israel stationed on the opposite hill; the ravine was between them. **4**A champion of the Philistine forces stepped forward; his name was Goliath of Gath, and he was six cubits and a span tall. **5**He had a *bronze* helmet on his head, and wore a breastplate of scale armor, a bronze breastplate weighing five thousand shekels. **6**He had bronze greaves on his legs and a bronze javelin slung from his shoulders. **7**The shaft of his spear was like a weaver's bar, and the iron head of his spear weighed six hundred shekels; and the shield-bearer marched in front of him.

8He stopped and called out to the ranks of Israel and he said to them, "Why should you come out to engage in battle? I am the Philistine champion, and you are Saul's servants. Choose one of your men and let him come down against me. **9**If he bests me in combat and kills me, we will become your slaves; but if I best *him* and kill him, you shall be our slaves and serve us." **10**And the Philistine ended, "I herewith defy the ranks of Israel. Get me a man and let's fight it out!" **11**When Saul and all Israel heard these words of the Philistine, they were dismayed and terror stricken.

12*David was the son of a certain Ephrathite of Bethlehem in Judah whose name was Jesse. He had eight sons, and in the days of Saul the man was already old, advanced in years.* **13***The three oldest sons of Jesse had left and gone with Saul to the war. The names of his three sons who had gone to the war were Eliab the firstborn, the next Abinadab, and the third Shammah;* **14***and David was the youngest. The three oldest had followed Saul,* **15***and David would go back and forth from attending on Saul to shepherd his father's flock at Bethlehem.* ▶

¹⁶The Philistine stepped forward morning and evening and took his stand for forty days.

¹⁷Jesse said to his son David, "Take an ephah of this parched corn and these ten loaves of bread for your brothers in camp. ¹⁸Take these ten cheeses to the captain of their thousand. Find out how your brothers are and bring some token from them." ¹⁹Saul and the brothers and all the men of Israel were in the valley of Elah, in the war against the Philistines.

²⁰Early next morning, David left someone in charge of the flock, took [the provisions], and set out, as his father Jesse had instructed him. He reached the barricade as the army was going out to the battle lines shouting the war cry. ²¹Israel and the Philistines drew up their battle lines opposite each other. ²²David left his baggage with the man in charge of the baggage and ran toward the battle line and went to greet his brothers. ²³While he was talking to them, the champion, whose name was Goliath, the Philistine of Gath, stepped forward from the Philistine ranks and spoke the same words as before; and David heard him.

²⁴When the men of Israel saw the man, they fled in terror. ²⁵And the men of Israel were saying, "Do you see that man coming out? He comes to defy Israel! The man who kills him will be rewarded by the king with great riches; he will also give him his daughter in marriage and grant exemption to his father's house in Israel." ²⁶David asked the men standing near him, "What will be done for the man who kills that Philistine and removes the disgrace from Israel? Who is that uncircumcised Philistine that he dares defy the ranks of the living God?" ²⁷The troops told him in the same words what would be done for the man who killed him.

²⁸When Eliab, his oldest brother, heard him speaking to the men, Eliab became angry with David and said, "Why did you come here, and with whom did you leave those few sheep in the wilderness? I know your impudence and your impertinence: you came down to watch the fighting!" ²⁹But David replied, "What have I done now? I was only asking!" ³⁰And he turned away from him toward someone else; he asked the same question, and the troops gave him the same answer as before. ³¹The things David said were overheard and were reported to Saul, who had him brought over.

³²David said to Saul, "Let no man's courage fail him. Your servant will go and fight *that* Philistine!" ³³But Saul said to David, "You cannot go to that Philistine and fight him; you are only a boy, and he has been a warrior from his youth!" ³⁴David replied to Saul, "Your servant has been tending his father's sheep, and if a lion or a bear came and carried off an animal from the flock, ³⁵I would go after it and fight it and rescue it from its mouth. And if it attacked me, I would seize it by the beard and strike it down and kill it. ³⁶Your servant has killed both lion and bear; and *that* uncircumcised Philistine shall end up like one of them, for he has defied the ranks of the living God. ³⁷The Lord," *David went on*, "who saved me from lion and bear will also save me from the Philistine." "Then go," Saul said to David, "and may the Lord be with you!"

³⁸Saul clothed David in his own garment; he placed a bronze helmet on his head *and fastened a breastplate on him.* ³⁹David girded his sword over his garment. Then he tried to walk; but he was not used to it. And David said to

Saul, "I cannot walk in these, for I am not used to them." So he *David* took them off. ⁴⁰He took his stick, picked a few smooth stones from the wadi, put them in the pocket of his shepherd's bag and, sling in hand, he went toward the Philistine.

⁴¹*The Philistine, meanwhile, was coming closer to David, preceded by his shield-bearer.* ⁴²*And the Philistine looked* and he saw David; he scorned him, for he was but a boy, ruddy and handsome. ⁴³And the Philistine called out to David, "Am I a dog that you come against me with sticks?" The Philistine cursed David by his gods; ⁴⁴and the Philistine said to David, "Come here, and I will give your flesh to the birds of the sky and beasts of the field."

⁴⁵David replied to the Philistine, "You come against me with sword and spear and javelin; but I come against you in the name of the Lord of Hosts, the God of the ranks of Israel, whom you have defied. ⁴⁶This *very* day the Lord will deliver you into my hands. I will kill you and cut off your head; and I will give the carcasses of the Philistine camp to the birds of the sky and the beasts of the earth. All the earth shall know that there is a God in Israel. ⁴⁷And this whole assembly shall know that the Lord can give victory without sword or spear. For the battle is the Lord's, and He will deliver you into our hands."

⁴⁸When the Philistine began to come *and advance* toward David, *David quickly ran up to the battle line to face the Philistine.* ⁴⁹David put his hand into the bag; he took out a stone and slung it. It struck the Philistine in the forehead; the stone sank into his forehead, and he fell face down on the ground. ⁵⁰*Thus David bested the Philistine with sling and stone; he struck him down and killed him. David had no sword.* ⁵¹So David ran up and stood over the Philistine, grasped his sword *and pulled it from its sheath;* and *with it* he dispatched him and cut off his head.

When the Philistines saw that their warrior was dead, they ran. ⁵²The men of Israel and Judah rose up with a war cry and they pursued the Philistines all the way to Gath and up to the gates of Ekron; the Philistines fell mortally wounded along the road to Shaarim up to Gath and Ekron. ⁵³Then the Israelites returned from chasing the Philistines and looted their camp.

⁵⁴David took the head of the Philistine and brought it to Jerusalem; and he put his weapons in his own tent.

⁵⁵*When Saul saw David going out to assault the Philistine, he asked his army commander Abner, "Whose son is that boy, Abner?" And Abner replied, "By your life, Your Majesty, I do not know." ⁵⁶"Then find out whose son that young fellow is," the king ordered. ⁵⁷So when David returned after killing the Philistine, Abner took him and brought him to Saul, with the head of the Philistine still in his hand. ⁵⁸Saul said to him, "Whose son are you, my boy?" And David answered, "The son of your servant Jesse the Bethlehemite."*

¹⁸:¹When he finished speaking with Saul, Jonathan's soul became bound up with the soul of David; Jonathan loved David as himself. ²Saul took him [into his service] that day and would not let him return to his father's house.— ³Jonathan and David made a pact, because he loved him as himself. ⁴Jonathan took off the cloak and tunic he was wearing and gave them to ▶

David, together with his sword, bow and belt. ⁵David went out, and he was successful in every mission on which Saul sent him, and Saul put him in command
of all the soldiers; this pleased all the troops and Saul's courtiers as well. ⁶When
they came home [and] David returned from killing the Philistine, the women
of all the towns of Israel came out *singing and dancing to greet King Saul* with
timbrels, shouting, and sistrums. ⁷The women sang as they danced, and they
chanted: Saul has slain his thousands; David his tens of thousands! ⁸*Saul was
much distressed* and greatly vexed about the matter. For he said, "To David they
have given tens of thousands, and to me they have given thousands. *All that he
lacks is the kingship!"* ⁹From that day on Saul kept a jealous eye on David. ¹⁰*The
next day an evil spirit of God gripped Saul and he began to rave in the house, while
David was playing [the lyre], as he did daily. Saul had a spear in his hand,* ¹¹*and
Saul threw the spear, thinking to pin David to the wall. But David eluded him twice.*
¹²Saul was afraid of David, *for the Lord was with him and had turned away from
Saul.* ¹³So Saul removed him from his presence and appointed him chief of a
thousand, to march at the head of the troops. ¹⁴David was successful in all his
undertakings, for the Lord was with him; ¹⁵and when Saul saw that he was successful, he dreaded him. ¹⁶All Israel and Judah loved David, for he marched at
their head.

¹⁷Saul said to David, "Here is my older daughter Merab, I will give her to you
in marriage; in return, you be my warrior and fight the battles of the Lord." Saul
thought: "Let not my hand strike him; let the hand of the Philistines strike him."
¹⁸David replied to Saul, "Who am I and what is my life—my father's family in
Israel—that I should become Your Majesty's son-in-law?" ¹⁹But at the time that*

---

enough to remove the inconsistencies. And not all the inconsistencies have been
eliminated in the LXX. In 1 Samuel 16:18, David is called "a man of valor and
a man of war" (*gibbor ḥayil we-iš milḥama*); later he is called a mere "lad"
(*na ʻar*). Both references appear in the LXX translation.

In short, the argument that the LXX translators abridged the text they were
working from is not convincing. Moreover, we find nothing like the alleged
abridgment in the David and Goliath story elsewhere in Samuel where there
are contradictions and inconsistencies.

We must conclude, therefore, that the episode as related in the LXX was
an independent, cohesive version of the David-Goliath story and that the MT
story was created by combining two previously independent accounts,
a process scholars call conflation. One of these accounts is preserved in the
LXX. We know the other account only as it is embedded in the conflate MT.

One indication that the MT version is a conflate account is that some parallels or duplicates of what were originally two separate versions of the same
episode are included. In both accounts, David is introduced to Saul. In the conflate account in the MT, he is introduced twice, once in 16:17-23 and a second
time in 17:55-58 (the latter is missing from the LXX). In both accounts, Saul

Merab, daughter of Saul, should have been given to David, she was given in marriage to Adriel the Meholathite. ²⁰Now Michal, daughter of Saul, had fallen in love with David; and when this was reported to Saul, it *the matter* was pleasing for him. ²¹Saul thought: "I will give her to him, and she can serve as a snare for him, so that the Philistines may kill him." *So Saul said to David, "You can become my son-in-law even now through the second one."* ²²And Saul instructed his courtiers to say to David privately, "The king is fond of you and all his courtiers like you. So why not become the king's son-in-law?" ²³When the king's courtiers repeated these words to David, David replied, "Do you think that becoming the son-in-law of a king is a small matter, when I am but a poor man of no consequence?" ²⁴Saul's courtiers reported to him *saying,* "This is what David answered." ²⁵And Saul said, "Say this to David: 'The king desires no other bride price than the foreskins of a hundred Philistines, as vengeance on the king's enemies.'"—Saul intended to bring about David's death at the hands of the Philistines.—²⁶When his courtiers told this to David, David was pleased with the idea of becoming the king's son-in-law. *Before the time had expired,* ²⁷David went out with his men and killed two hundred Philistines, *David* brought their foreskins *and they were counted out* for the king, that he might become the king's son-in-law. He *Saul* then gave him his daughter Michal in marriage. ²⁸When Saul saw *and knew* the Lord was with David and that Michal daughter of Saul loved him, ²⁹and he *Saul* grew still more afraid of David; *and Saul was David's enemy ever after.*

³⁰*The Philistine chiefs marched out to battle; and every time they marched out, David was more successful than all the other officers of Saul. His reputation soared.*

offers one of his daughters to David. In 18:20-27 (MT), he offers his daughter Michal; in 18:17-19 (MT), which is missing from LXX, he offers David his eldest daughter, Merab.

The two accounts combined in the MT are not completely parallel and often contain different elements and different details. As a result, the conflate version preserved in the MT not only contains inconsistencies, but also some misplaced events.

One instance on which all scholars agree concerns Saul's attempt to kill David. As it appears in 1 Samuel 18:10-11 (MT), it is surely misplaced. The passage is repeated verbatim in 1 Samuel 19:9-10 (MT). In the earlier appearance (1 Samuel 18:10-11 MT), Saul's attempt to kill David undercuts the gradual intensification of his envy and suspicion of David. Indeed, in the LXX account the sequence of events is more logical than in the combined version in the MT. In the LXX, Saul is at first envious of David (18:8-9), then suspicious (18:12), then frightened because of David's success (18:13-15). Then, he wants David killed by the Philistines; and when that fails, Saul tries to kill David himself (19:9-10). In the combined MT version, Saul's progressive antagonism to David is interrupted by his premature attempt to kill David.

Moreover, the conflate account in the MT contains a number of inconsistencies. We have already referred to the most conspicuous one. After David is introduced to Saul and appointed armor-bearer (16:17-23 MT), he disappears from the battlefield and reappears as a shepherd who had been tending his father's sheep; neither Saul nor Saul's general, Abner, knows him, and David is reintroduced to Saul (17:55-58 MT).

And there are other inconsistencies in the MT:

• In 17:12, David and his father Jesse are introduced to the reader, although they had already been identified in chapter 16 of the MT.
• David is depicted in more than one way in the composite MT narrative. In 16:21, he is Saul's armor-bearer, and in that capacity he fights Goliath. In 17:12-31 and 55-58, he is an unknown shepherd boy who happens to be visiting his brothers when Goliath challenges the Israelites to a duel.
• In 18:13, David is made an officer in Saul's army, although he was already made an officer in 18:5.
• According to 17:25, whoever defeats Goliath will be given with King Saul's daughter in marriage as a reward. But in 18:20ff., Saul looks for pretexts to convince David to marry his daughter, and David insists that he is unworthy.
• According to 18:20-27, Saul offers David Michal, but in verses 17-19, he offers David his eldest daughter, Merab, in accordance with his promise to marry his daughter to the man who defeats Goliath.

Why the editor or redactor created this conflate version is a matter of conjecture. It stands to reason that he wanted to preserve certain traditions and details from another version of the David and Goliath account that were not included in the short Hebrew text on which the LXX translation was based. It is especially hard to understand why he included 17:12-31, where David comes back for a second time as an unknown shepherd, and 17:55-58, in which he is again introduced to Saul after slaying Goliath. Perhaps he simply liked the story; perhaps he wanted to convey a particular idea, namely that God's people can be victorious even through seemingly insignificant figures (in this version David was unknown before the battle).

But the redactor did not entirely ignore the inconsistencies created by juxtaposing the two versions. A few details in the MT have the effect of smoothing out certain inconsistencies.

In 17:12, for example, David's father, Jesse, is identified, although he was already introduced in chapter 16. Therefore, the redactor added the word *ha-zeh* (this one) after the identification in chapter 17, which has the effect of saying "the aforementioned Jesse," as if to say "I know he has already been introduced." In 17:15, we are told that David went back and forth from King Saul's court to tend his father's sheep in Bethlehem, perhaps to smooth over David's second arrival on the battlefield. And in 18:21b, the Masoretic redactor adds, "You can become my son-in-law now through the second [daughter]," a kind

1 SAMUEL 17:44-18:22 in the Septuagint, Codex Vaticanus (LXX^B). In this version almost half of the verses of 1 Samuel 17-18 found in the Hebrew text are absent.

of cross-reference to the change from Merab, Saul's eldest daughter who was referred to earlier, to Michal, Saul's second daughter.

The implications of this analysis of the David and Goliath story go far beyond this particular episode. The redactor who combined the two versions created a text with inconsistencies, which is precisely what is supposed to have happened in other cases throughout the Bible where texts underwent conflation, expansion and interpolation. The only difference is that in this case we can document the existence of two layers of the story because they have been preserved in the LXX; in other cases, the existence of various layers can not be demonstrated and must remain hypothetical.

CHAPTER 5

The Synoptic Gospels
Matthew, Mark and Luke

David E. Aune

*The creative use of sources also informs David E. Aune's explanation of why the
first three Gospels "exhibit striking literary similarities" as well as significant differences. For example, although there were several "oral traditions containing various types of sayings of Jesus and stories about Jesus," Mark was apparently the
first to collect them and place them in a geographical and chronological framework.
His purpose was "not simply to record the facts concerning the life of Jesus, but rather
to argue that...Jesus ought to be regarded as the Messiah." Matthew and Luke
drew on Mark but, "apparently dissatisfied with the way Mark begins and ends,
added material...to produce more lengthy and sophisticated accounts."–Ed.*

"Synoptic Gospels" refers to three of the four Gospels in the New Testament
canon–Matthew, Mark and Luke (but not John). The adjective *synoptic*,
like the noun *synopsis* from which it is derived, is based on the Greek adjective *synoptikos*, meaning "seeing the whole together." The "Synoptic Gospels"
can be printed in three parallel columns and "seen together" because the
sayings and stories are strikingly similar.

This was first done in 1776, when the German New Testament scholar
Johann J. Griesbach (1745-1812) arranged the first three Gospels in parallel
columns in a book with a long Latin title, the first part of which was *Synopsis
Evangeliorum Matthai Marci et Lucae* (Synopsis of the Gospels Matthew, Mark
and Luke). The first three Gospels have been referred to as Synoptic Gospels
ever since.

The Gospel of John was omitted from Griesbach's synopsis, and from most
subsequent synopses of the Gospels, because it is very different from the other
three. About 90 percent of the sayings and stories about Jesus in John have no
parallel in the Synoptic Gospels.

Three Versions: Jesus Cures the Fever

Matthew 8:14-15	*Mark 1:29-31*	*Luke 4:38-39*
"And when Jesus entered Peter's house,	"And immediately he left the synagogue, and entered the house of Simon and Andrew with James and John.	"And he arose and left the synagogue, and entered Simon's house.
he saw his mother-in-law lying sick with a fever;	Now Simon's mother-in-law lay sick with a fever, and immediately they told him of her.	Now Simon's mother-in-law was ill with a high fever, and they besought him for her.
and he touched her hand and the fever left her and she rose and served them."	And he came and took her by the hand and lifted her up and the fever left her; and she served them."	And he stood over her and rebuked the fever and it left her; and immediately she rose and served them."

The box above contains the miracle story of Jesus curing the fever of Simon's mother-in-law, which is found in all three Synoptic Gospels. The texts are arranged in parallel columns to form a synopsis.

Although these three texts are not identical, there are enough similarities to make any teacher suspect plagiarism. The Mark version is the longest with 44 Greek words; Luke is next with 38 words; and then comes Matthew with 30 words.

Obviously, some kind of dependence is reflected in these three passages. But what kind? Did one author copy from another? Or did all of them rely on the same early Christian oral sources and reproduce the story independently of one another? A combination of these two solutions is also possible. One evangelist could have copied from the text of another but could also have introduced changes based on an oral version with which he was familiar.

Finding a satisfactory explanation for the similarities as well as the differences among the first three Gospels is called the Synoptic Problem. Solving the problem requires source criticism, that is, an attempt to determine the sources used by particular authors.

New Testament scholars have proposed various solutions to this problem during the last two centuries. The solution most widely accepted today is referred to as the two-source theory. It is based on the priority of Mark, portions of which were copied by the authors of Matthew and Luke. On the basis of evidence in the box above, it could be argued that Matthew and Luke condensed Mark. It should be noted that although plagiarism is frowned on today, the ancient world had nothing like copyright laws, and authors borrowed freely from earlier writings.

Two Versions: Serving Two Masters

Matthew 6:24	*Luke 16:13*
"No one can serve two masters; for either he will hate the one and love the other, or he will be devoted to the one and despise the other. You cannot serve God and Mammon."	"No servant can serve two masters; for either he will hate the one and love the other, or he will be devoted to the one and despise the other. You cannot serve God and Mammon."

Even though most New Testament scholars accept the hypothesis of the priority of Mark, a strong minority supports the theory of the priority of Matthew, called the Griesbach hypothesis. Advocates of this minority view contend that Matthew was the first Gospel and that Luke (who was dependent on Matthew) appeared next. Mark was written last, they argue, and was based on both Matthew and Luke.

Our sample text could be used to support this argument; Mark seems to have combined material from Matthew and Luke and added some phrases of his own.

In many instances, close parallels in Matthew and Luke do not appear in Mark. A typical example is shown above.

The two texts are identical except for the word *servant* in Luke (Matthew has 27 Greek words, while Luke has 28). This close similarity between Matthew and Luke can be explained in several ways: (1) Luke copied from Matthew (the Griesbach Hypothesis); (2) Matthew copied from Luke; or (3) Matthew and Luke copied from a third source. The third possibility is the one accepted by most New Testament scholars today.

The hypothetical source used by Matthew and Luke—the second source of the two-source theory—is called "Q," an abbreviation for the German word *Quelle*, meaning "source." Since Q primarily consists of sayings of Jesus, it is often called the Sayings Source. The simplest description of Q is that it consists of non-Marcan parallels between Matthew and Luke. Q could have been an oral source, but most scholars think it was a document, now lost, written about 50 C.E. in Palestine. Those who accept the hypothesis of the priority of

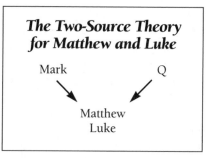

The Two-Source Theory for Matthew and Luke

Mark   Q

Matthew
Luke

Matthew, however, do not believe Q existed because, according to their view, the similarities between Matthew and Luke arose when Luke copied Matthew.

The similarities among the Synoptic Gospels, which permit them to be printed in parallel columns, also mean that they resemble each other in content, theme and structure. They all show that Jesus is the Messiah of Jewish expectation despite the shattering defeat represented in his execution by the Romans. They do this by demonstrating that the suffering and death of the Messiah was predicted in the Old Testament as well as by Jesus himself and by emphasizing the victory represented by the resurrection.

According to the hypothesis of Marcan priority, Mark is the earliest Gospel (often dated to c. 70 C.E.), implying that Matthew and Luke must be later (they are often dated to c. 80 and 90 C.E., respectively). Mark, the shortest of the Synoptics (11,313 words), begins with the story of John the Baptist, who predicts the coming of Jesus, and ends with the story of the empty tomb. According to the Marcan hypothesis, Matthew (18,363 words) and Luke (19,495 words), apparently dissatisfied with the way Mark begins and ends, added material to produce more lengthy and sophisticated accounts. Matthew begins with Jesus' genealogy (traced back to Abraham through David), inserts an account of the virginal conception and birth of Jesus and ends with brief cameo resurrection appearances of Jesus before the women who discovered the empty tomb and his disciples in Galilee. Luke begins with stories of the conception and birth of both John and Jesus and ends with Jesus' ascension to heaven.

Matthew and Luke also appear to have been dissatisfied with the comparatively few sayings of Jesus in Mark. To solve this problem, they borrowed many sayings from Q. They differ, however, in how they incorporated the Sayings Source into their narratives. Matthew radically rearranged Q by placing the sayings into five extensive sermons attributed to Jesus: (1) Sermon on the Mount (Matthew 5-7); (2) On Discipleship (Matthew 10); (3) Parables of the Kingdom (Matthew 13); (4) On Humility and Forgiveness (Matthew 18); and (5) On the End of the Age (Matthew 24-25). Luke, on the other hand, incorporated most of the sayings of Jesus derived from Q into an extensive (and vague) Travel Narrative in Luke 9:51-18:14. Thus, Matthew places the Lord's Prayer in the Sermon on the Mount (Matthew 6:9-13), while Luke inserts it into the Travel Narrative (Luke 11:2-4) rather than into his version of the Sermon on the Mount, often called the Sermon on the Plain (Luke 6:20-49).

Finally, almost all New Testament scholars recognize that the written sources behind the Synoptic Gospels, as well as the Gospels themselves, are based on a large number of oral traditions containing various types of sayings of Jesus and stories about Jesus. Form criticism is the method used to detect the oral "forms" out of which each Gospel was fashioned. These traditions about Jesus were transmitted individually by word of mouth and were not part of a biographical framework of the life of Jesus. Mark was apparently the first to collect these traditions and place them in a geographical and chronological framework within a narrative. Mark's purpose in creating this new type of biography, like Matthew and Luke's after him, was not simply to record the facts of the life of Jesus, but also to argue that, despite evidence to the contrary, Jesus ought to be regarded as the Messiah, the Son of God.

CHAPTER 6

The Baptism of Jesus
A Story Modeled on the Binding of Isaac

William R. Stegner

The authors of the Gospels took raw material and created something new. Stegner notes that the theological significance of Jesus' baptism, which puzzled commentators for centuries, would have been clear to the contemporary audience. He contends that the presentation of the baptism in the Synoptic Gospels includes deliberate echoes—words, images, symbols, structures—of the Binding of Isaac, a story told in Genesis 22. The intention of the authors is to suggest that Isaac, who "was regarded as a kind of original sacrificial offering," prefigures Jesus. "Jesus is like Isaac, except that he was, in fact, sacrificed." To an audience of the time, the verbal and structural similarities between the stories would have suggested immediately that "the shadow of the sacrifice on the cross falls across the baptism story."–Ed.

John's baptism of Jesus is recounted in all three Synoptic Gospels (Matthew, Mark and Luke). Here is how Mark describes it in just 53 Greek words:

> In those days Jesus came from Nazareth of Galilee and was baptized by John in the Jordan. And when he came up out of the water, immediately he saw the heavens opened and the Spirit descending upon him like a dove; and a voice came from heaven, "Thou art my beloved Son; with thee I am well pleased."
>
> Mark 1:9-11; see also Matthew 3:13-17; Luke 3:21-22

Exegetes have puzzled for centuries over the theological meaning of Jesus' baptism, particularly as derived from Mark's account. A new understanding emerges, I believe, when we recognize that this baptism story was modeled on the Old Testament account of Abraham's near-sacrifice of his son Isaac, an episode known to students of the Old Testament as the binding of Isaac.

In the biblical form of the story (Genesis 22), God tests Abraham by telling him to take Isaac, his only son, and offer him to God as a sacrifice. Abraham takes his son to the mountain to which God directs them and prepares an altar on which he lays wood. Abraham then binds his son, lays him on the altar and raises his knife to slay him. At this dramatic moment, an "angel of the Lord call[s] to him from heaven" and tells Abraham to desist, "for now I know that you fear God, seeing you have not withheld your son, your only son, from me." Abraham "lift[s] up his eyes" and sees a ram caught in a thicket. He then sacrifices the ram in place of his son, Isaac.

At first glance, the stories of Jesus' baptism[1] and the binding of Isaac appear to have little connection to one another. Let us look more closely, however.

The binding of Isaac as I have just recounted it is the story as it is told in Genesis 22. But the story was so powerful that it was told and retold over the centuries in various versions from a variety of viewpoints and with a variety of embellishments. Indeed, this was true of many Old Testament stories. That is how the Midrash, a collection of retellings and elaborations of biblical stories written down beginning in about 400 C.E., developed. Many of the exegetical traditions embodied in the Midrash, however, were known much earlier.

Over the centuries, there were many forms of Jewish exegesis and elaboration of scripture besides the Midrash—forms we might call midrashic. One example is the Targums. The Targums are loose translations of the Hebrew Scriptures—paraphrases might be a better word—into Aramaic, produced when Aramaic was the everyday language of the people. The Targums often contain embellishments to and explanations of Hebrew scriptural texts not found in the originals.

One of the most significant changes in later midrashic versions (including the Targums) concerns Isaac, who plays an increasingly prominent part in these versions. One scholar describes the difference this way:

> In Genesis it is Abraham's faith and obedience to God's will even to the offering of his only son, the child of promise, that constitutes the whole significance of the story: Isaac is a purely passive figure. In the rabbinical literature, however, the voluntariness of the sacrifice on Isaac's part is strongly emphasized.[2]

In the account in Genesis, the main character is Abraham; Isaac is portrayed as a mere lad. According to one Midrash, however, he was 37 years old.

The Targums survive, in part, in several manuscripts, known to scholars as Targum Pseudo-Jonathan (also called Yerushalmi I), Neofiti, and the Fragmentary Targum (or Yerushalmi II). The manuscript accounts vary, but the emphasis on Isaac's willingness to be sacrificed is common to all of them.

I believe the targumic versions of the story of the binding of Isaac were the models for the story of the baptism of Jesus. Thus, a version of the Isaac story found in the Targums must have been widely known when the story that lies behind the Gospel account of Jesus' baptism was composed.[3]

When Jesus came out of the water after his baptism, the following things occurred (again I quote from Mark):

1. "He saw the heavens opened and the Spirit descend[ing] upon him."

2. "A voice came from heaven [and said], 'Thou art my beloved Son; with thee I am well pleased.' "

Each of these features of the baptism story has a parallel in the targumic stories of the binding of Isaac:

1. As Isaac lay bound upon the altar, he looked up and saw "the angels of the height."[4] He had a vision and saw "the Shekhinah [the divine essence or spirit] of the Lord."[5]

2. A voice from heaven explains the significance of the scene: "Come, see two chosen individuals in the world; the one sacrificing and the other being sacrificed; the one sacrificing is not hesitating and the one being sacrificed stretches forth his neck."[6]

Bible scholars would say that the two stories exemplify the same form, a form often used by biblical writers to describe a vision. When a vision is described, the narrative frequently mentions the opening of heaven or a voice from heaven. In the Targums, this literary form of the vision is retained, but greater emphasis is placed on the content of the heavenly words than in the biblical visions. The heavenly words stress the significance of the moment in the life of the person who receives the vision.

In both the baptism and the binding stories, however, the voice from heaven describes the significance of the scene, in one instance for Jesus, in the other for Isaac. Both accounts exemplify the same literary form, namely the Old Testament form of a vision with interpretive words from heaven.[7]

The two stories have much more in common than literary form. Within this form, there are striking similarities. Lying on the altar, Isaac looks up and sees "the angels of the height." This seems to be another way of saying that the heavens were opened, in keeping with the ancient world view that God and his angels dwelt above the vault of the heavens. In the Gospel account, the heavens had to be "opened"[8] before the Holy Spirit could be seen.

More significant, the content of the vision is almost the same in both stories. In the Gospels, Jesus sees "the Spirit descending"; in the targumic accounts of the Genesis story, "the Shekhinah of the Lord" is revealed to Isaac.

The similarity between the "Spirit"[9] and the "Shekhinah" is obvious. The Shekhinah, in rabbinic thought, is a "manifestation" of God himself, reflecting "his nearness" to his people.[10] In the Gospel accounts, the Spirit or Holy Spirit indicates the presence and nearness of God. So close are the two terms—Shekhinah and Holy Spirit—that in some texts they are used interchangeably. As one observer has commented:

The two expressions are often interchanged in the old Rabbinic texts. Both are frequently used as synonyms for God....The man who is closely united with the Shekhinah also possesses the Holy Spirit, and the one possessing the Spirit also sees the Shekhinah.[11]

Moreover, the words the heavenly voice addresses to Jesus have a direct relationship to the account of the binding of Isaac: "Thou art my beloved Son; with thee I am well pleased." In the Greek translation of the Hebrew Bible known as the Septuagint (about 300 B.C.E.), Isaac is referred to as "the beloved son." Thus, the heavenly voice echoes the Greek translation of Genesis.[12]

The second half of the message from the heavenly voice, "with thee I am well pleased," is also echoed in the binding of Isaac. In effect, the heavenly voice tells Jesus he is the recipient of God's "elective good pleasure."[13] The Greek word for "pleased" is *eudokeō*; it can also mean "choice," conveying the notion of election. The idea of election is found twice in the targumic accounts of the binding of Isaac. There the heavenly voice applies the Aramaic term for a person elected by God (*yachida*) to both Isaac and Abraham.[14]

Another connection that has frequently been made between the two stories is that Isaac was a near-sacrifice, while Jesus, the lamb of God, was actually sacrificed.[15] In the Targums to Leviticus 22:27, Isaac is referred to as a "lamb who has been elected/chosen." Thus, the concept of God's choice or election is found in both stories.[16]

One of the most enigmatic details in the baptism story is the dove: "The Spirit descend[ed] upon [Jesus] like a dove." Most commentators see the dove as a symbol of Israel. A beautiful Midrash comments on the phrase from the Song of Songs 4:1,[17] "Thine eyes are as doves":

As the dove is chaste, so Israel are [sic] chaste. As the dove puts forth her neck for slaughter, so do [sic] Israel, as it says, "For Thy sake we are killed all the day" (Psalm 44:23). As the dove atones for iniquities, so Israel atone [sic] for the other nations.[18]

The dove shares a remarkable characteristic with Isaac—both stretch forth their necks as sacrifices. As the Targums say: "Come, see two unique individuals [Abraham and Isaac]...the one being sacrificed [Isaac] stretches forth his neck." Note the equation. The dove, a symbol for Israel, makes atonement and stretches forth its neck. Isaac, too, stretches forth his neck on the altar as he makes atonement for Israel. Could the dove, associated with Isaac in later rabbinic literature, have already been associated with him in New Testament times? Could the dove in the baptism story have been a reminder of the similar roles played by Isaac and Jesus? Here is another connection between the figure of Isaac and the story of Jesus' baptism.

In short, the baptism story was told with the story of the binding of Isaac in mind, as is suggested not only by the similar literary forms, but also by similarities and echoes in content. The reader of the baptism story was supposed to recall the story of Isaac.

Telltale verbal similarities between Mark and the Septuagint translation of Genesis 22 also support this interpretation (a fact no other commentator seems to have noticed). Both stories begin with the same introductory phrase, "and it happened." (The Revised Standard Version omits this phrase in translating Mark 1:9.) Jesus *saw* the heavens *being split*, while Abraham *saw* the place where he was to sacrifice Isaac. In Genesis 22:14, Abraham names the place *the Lord will see*. Jesus saw the heavens *being split*, and Abraham *split* the wood for the burnt offering. In Genesis 22:11 and 22:15, the voice calls to Abraham *from heaven* (singular); in Mark 1:11 a voice comes *from heaven* (plural). The cumulative effect of verbal agreements in the short baptism narrative is indeed remarkable.

The author modeled the story of the baptism of Jesus on the story of the binding of Isaac for a reason. He had a point to make, a theological point. The theology of the targumic story of the binding of Isaac is plain. The sins of Israel were forgiven by the continual sacrifices offered in the Temple at Jerusalem. The near-sacrifice of Isaac was regarded as a kind of original sacrificial offering that validated and gave significance to all subsequent sacrifices offered on the same mountain.

In the Targum versions, Mount Moriah, where the binding of Isaac occurred, was in fact the Temple Mount. The relationship between the near-sacrifice of Isaac and the regular sacrifices on the Temple Mount is reflected in Geza Vermés' beautiful translation of the Fragmentary Targum to Genesis 22:14:

> Now I pray for mercy before you, O Lord God, that when the children of Isaac come to a time of distress, you may remember on their behalf the binding of Isaac their father, and loose and forgive them their sins and deliver them from all distress, so that the generations which follow him may say: In the mountain of the Temple of the Lord, Abraham offered Isaac his son....[19]

The theological significance of the baptism story is not stated directly (hence the confusion among contemporary interpreters). The reason for this omission, however, is that the original hearers would have made the association with the Isaac story. Jesus is like Isaac, except that he was in fact sacrificed. They would have understood that the theology of the baptism story was the theology of the cross. Just as Isaac was offered as an expiatory sacrifice, so Jesus would be offered.

The theological point of the Isaac story dovetails with the theology of the cross. If this theory is correct, the shadow of the sacrifice on the cross falls across the baptism story, which introduces the adult Jesus to the Gospel reader. This theory is reinforced by two important words that connect the baptism to the cross. The first is the word *baptism* itself.

In the third prediction of his suffering and death, Jesus, on the road to Jerusalem with his 12 disciples, foretells what will happen to him (Mark 10:32-34). James and John ask to sit at his right and left hand in his glory, but Jesus replies: "You do not know what you are asking. Are you able to drink the cup that I drink, or to be baptized with the baptism with which I am baptized?" (Mark 10:38).

A second connection between Jesus' sacrifice on the cross and his baptism may be found in an occurrence described in a single word. When Jesus breathed his last on the cross, the curtain of the Temple was torn in two (Mark 15:37-38; Matthew 27:50-51). A more literal translation is "split" rather than "torn"; the Greek word is *schizo*.[20] The reader will recall that when Jesus emerged from the water after being baptized, the heavens were opened (Mark 1:10; Matthew 3:16). Again, a more literal translation is "split" rather than "opened"; the same Greek word, *schizo*, is used. In good rabbinic fashion, the scene of the baptism is connected to the scene of the cross by the use of this unusual word.[21] Jesus' baptism is thus connected both to his sacrificial death and to the story of the sacrificial binding of Isaac, on which the baptism story was modeled.

I do not mean to imply that this is the *only* correct interpretation of Jesus' baptism, but surely it is *one* valid interpretation. There is probably no single correct interpretation of the baptism story, which has many layers of meaning. The baptism story was doubtless formulated in the early Aramaic-speaking church. It was not uncommon at that time for there to be more than one approved interpretation of a story. What I have presented is what the rabbis would have referred to as "another interpretation."

AFTERWORD

Rev. Canon J. G. Kohner of Pointe Claire, Quebec, suggests adding resurrection to Stegner's list of parallels between Isaac and Jesus:

Both Isaac and Jesus rose from the dead. There is a rabbinic tradition that Isaac was in fact offered as a sacrifice and died. In Genesis 22:19, Abraham returns alone from the mountain. Isaac is not there to weep over the death of Sarah (Genesis 23:1-3) and only reappears in Genesis 24:62. This tradition, or Midrash, may have been a response to Christian pressure: "Our Jesus died and rose again...." On the other hand, it may have predated Jesus among Pharisees who did believe in life after death.

Second, in the baptism of Jesus, his emergence from the waters of the Jordan has also been interpreted (by Paul, by prayer books in the Anglican communion, etc.) as a resurrection to new life, or at least a hint or foretaste of his rising from the dead.

Thus, I believe that in addition to the points made by William Stegner, resurrection is an element that can be added to the similarities between the stories, although I recognize that the evidence for Isaac's resurrection may be an effect of the baptism account. **BR** *1:4 (1985), p. 16*

Formation of the Canon

The third aspect of biblical composition is canonization, the process by which certain traditions and texts became "the Bible" while others were either ignored or rejected. It is comforting to believe that authentic material was accepted and questionable material rejected—and that the difference was always clear. But this may not have been so.

CHAPTER 7

What Did Jesus Really Say?

Marcus J. Borg

"Scholars Seek to Discredit Christ," screamed the tabloid headline. And this was just one of many misconceptions about the work of the Jesus Seminar, as Marcus Borg explains. Some 40 scholars spent five years in the Jesus Seminar analyzing the words attributed to Jesus in the Gospels and rating them from "almost certainly" to "almost certainly not" authentic. They worked from the assumption that the Gospels are human "memories of Jesus transformed and adapted." Borg notes that the evidence for this assumption can be found in the Gospels themselves, in the differences between the Synoptic Gospels and John, and in differences among the Synoptic Gospels. "The issue is not falsification," Borg explains. The Gospels reflect "the developing tradition of the early Christian community."—Ed.

About 40 scholars, all specialists in the study of the historical Jesus, are seated around a table. They have just completed a discussion of a saying attributed to Jesus in the canonical Gospels and other ancient Christian sources. The time has come to vote on a simple but complex question—do you think Jesus actually said that? Or, to frame the question in semitechnical language, is this saying of Jesus, as reported in one or more of the Gospels, historically authentic to Jesus? Each scholar votes by casting one of four colored balls into a ballot box. Red means "yes, almost certainly"; pink means "more likely yes than no"; grey means "more likely no than yes"; and black means "almost certainly not."

The Jesus Seminar, convened by New Testament scholar Robert Funk in the spring of 1985, was committed to a five-year collective examination of the historical authenticity of all the words attributed to Jesus in the New Testament and other ancient Christian sources. The ultimate goal is publication of *The Five Gospels: The Search for the Authentic Words of Jesus*,[1] in which the words of Jesus will be printed in four colors corresponding to the voting. Such a

SERMON ON THE MOUNT by Franz Guillery. In a famous passage from the sermon, Jesus tells his followers: "If anyone strikes you on the right cheek, turn to him the other also" (Matthew 5:39b). According to the Jesus Seminar, this *is* an authentic saying of Jesus; it is printed in red in the new edition of the Gospels. *Photo: ©Three Lions/Superstock*

systematic and collective study of the sayings of Jesus is without precedent in the history of scholarship and is part of a renaissance of scholarly interest in what Jesus was like as a historical figure before his death.[2]

The question of who Jesus was has recently become news in the broader culture as well. Not only has the Jesus Seminar received considerable national publicity, but major stories about historical Jesus research have also appeared in *The Atlantic* and *The New York Times Book Review*.[3] The release of the Martin Scorcese film *The Last Temptation of Christ* put the question on the cover of *Time* and in *USA Today* and hundreds of other newspapers. People not unalterably opposed to the movie cite its most constructive feature as the stimulation of reflective curiosity—"It makes you think about what Jesus might really have been like."

Many people wonder why there should be any questions at all. The very idea that scholars are voting on the sayings of Jesus strikes many Christians as outrageous or even blasphemous,[4] as does the suggestion that the historical Jesus might have been different from the portraits of him in the Gospels. These people simply identify Jesus, as a figure of history, with what the Gospels say about him; and "faith" to them means believing the Gospels are true, theologically *and* historically.

Many others (within as well as outside the church) may not be outraged but may still wonder why anyone might think Jesus was different from the

Gospel portraits of him. They also wonder how scholars can make judgments about the historical authenticity of traditions attributed to Jesus. How do scholars decide which parts of the Gospels are historical, that is, which parts accurately reflect what Jesus said and did?

To answer these questions, we must begin with a sketch of how the Gospels are viewed by mainstream biblical scholars[5] and how Jesus' image has developed since biblical scholarship began two centuries ago. Briefly, the Gospels are seen as *the developing tradition of the early Christian community*. This simple statement has two immediate implications. First, the Gospels are human documents, and, like all human documents, they are historically conditioned by their time and place. In other words, they reflect the points of view of individual authors and the Christian communities for which they spoke. Second, the Gospels are not straightforward historical reports of what Jesus said and did; they are memories of Jesus transformed and adapted—transformed by the authors' experience of him as a living, spiritual reality in the decades after Good Friday and Easter and adapted to the needs of the particular communities in which they were written. *The Gospels are history transfigured.*

To mainstream scholars, the evidence that justifies this view of the Gospels can be found in the Gospels themselves. A detailed comparison of the Gospel of John, on the one hand, and the Synoptic Gospels (Matthew, Mark and Luke), on the other, reveals two very different portraits of Jesus. In John, Jesus openly proclaims himself with the most exalted titles known in his time; in the Synoptics, Jesus is reticent (even silent) about his identity. Scholars have concluded that the Gospel of John represents a much more developed form of the tradition, one that clearly reflects what the risen Christ had become in the experience of early Christians after Easter. John's portrait of Jesus is very different from the portrait of him in the Synoptics.

Moreover, a careful study of the many parallel accounts in the three Synoptic Gospels of the same incidents or sayings (that's why they're called synoptic) often discloses differences that can most naturally be explained as modifications introduced by the authors in response to developing traditions.[6] A meticulous study of patterns and themes in the Synoptic Gospels reveals that the authors adapted their materials to meet the needs of different situations confronting the early church. In short, a detailed study of the canonical Gospels leads naturally to the conclusion that traditions about Jesus *developed*. Indeed, in an important sense, *everything* in the Gospels is part of the developing tradition of the early church. Jesus' words and the stories about him that have come down to us were preserved and shaped by the memories and experiences of early Christians.

Given this background, the historical question becomes how one decides which elements of the Gospel tradition accurately reflect what the historical Jesus was like. When does the tradition closely reflect his words and deeds, and when does the development of church tradition go considerably beyond what Jesus himself was like? To use the terminology of the Jesus Seminar, when should one vote "red," and when should one vote "black"? For the past 200 years, especially in this century, scholars of the historical Jesus have developed criteria for making these kinds of judgments.[7]

The first criterion is multiple attestations in early tradition. Simply put, it counts in favor of the historical authenticity of a saying (theme, motif or action) if it is found in two or more early layers of the tradition. This criterion is based on the most widely held scholarly view of the development of the Synoptic Gospels. The two earliest sources are the Gospel of Mark and a source scholars call Q, a hypothetical document defined as the common source of about 200 verses found in both Matthew and Luke.[8] To these two early sources (Mark and Q), some scholars now add the Gospel of Thomas, a collection of sayings attributed to Jesus that was recently discovered in Egypt among the documents known as the Nag Hammadi Codices.[9] A unit of tradition found in two or more of these sources must be regarded as multiple attestation in early tradition.

Multiple attestations alone, however, do not establish historical authenticity because even the earliest source—presumably Q—is usually dated some 20 to 30 years after the death of Jesus. In other words, there was still considerable time for development. Moreover, multiple attestation (like the other criteria) does not work alone, that is, in isolation from other criteria. Some material found in early tradition is, as we shall see, historically suspect, whereas some material (especially parables) found in only one later source may be commonly considered historically authentic.

A second criterion requires us to discount tendencies that are demonstrably part of the developing tradition of the church. One of the best (and somewhat controversial) ways of illustrating this criterion is the question of Jesus' self-awareness of his divinity. Did he think of himself as divine or as the Messiah? Or, to put the question in a form that permits historical inquiry, how did he refer to himself? Did he speak of himself as divine or as the Messiah?

According to the tradition in its fully developed form (especially the Gospel of John), Jesus referred to himself with the most exalted titles known in his time—Messiah and the Son of God. In John, there are many other epithets with this same divine denotation (the bread of life, the light of the world, etc.). One might, therefore, think the historical question was settled and that the only question remaining is whether Jesus was speaking the truth or he was deluded.

But a closer look at the tradition reveals a more complex picture. If we arrange the sources chronologically, we discover that in the earliest sources Jesus does not publicly proclaim his messianic or divine status. Jesus' "identity" was not part of his message in these sources. In sayings attributed to Jesus in Q and the Gospel of Thomas, he makes no claims for his divinity. According to Mark, Jesus' exalted status was not mentioned in public preaching during his ministry; it was a secret known only to his disciples (Mark 8:27-30) and became part of the public message about Jesus only after Easter (Mark 9:9). As we move to later tradition, we can see that Matthew and Luke occasionally add exalted titles to passages they took from their sources. In John, the development reaches its peak. There Jesus speaks of himself not only as one with God, but, in the series of great "I am" statements, he also declares himself to be the bread of life, the light of the world, the resurrection and the life (John 6:48, 8:12, 10:30, 11:25), even pre-existent: "Before Abraham was, I am" (John 8:58). In short, there is an observable tendency as the tradition develops to add exalted titles to words attributed to Jesus.

The issue is not one of falsification or exaggeration, as might be supposed. We know that for the early Christians after Easter, Jesus was both Christ and Lord, that is, both Messiah and divine. This conviction, grounded in their own experience, affected the way they told the story of Jesus. In other words, they told the story of who Jesus was in the light of their fuller perception in the decades after Easter. The titles themselves are testimony to their experience of the risen Christ.

Thus, using the criterion of discounting demonstrable tendencies of the developing tradition, one must strongly suspect that the proclamation of Jesus that he was both Lord and Christ was a post-Easter development and not part of Jesus' original message. Within the framework of mainstream biblical scholarship, such texts, which probably reflect later tradition, would properly receive "gray" or "black" votes at the Jesus Seminar.

A third criterion involves the environment reflected in a particular text. Into what environment does the text fit? Does it fit into the Palestinian environment of around 30 C.E., or does it fit into a non-Palestinian or later environment? In order to be judged authentic, the text must fit into the environment of Jesus' time and place; if it fits only in a later environment, it cannot be authentic in its present form. Two examples, one rather minor and the other more significant, illustrate this criterion.

Both Matthew and Luke contain the parable of the wise and foolish builders (Matthew 7:24-27; Luke 6:47-49), but with a small difference in the description of how each one built his house. In both versions, a person who hears Jesus' words and follows them is compared to a man with a strong house that can withstand floodwaters; a person who does not follow them is likened to a man whose house is swept away. In Matthew, the contrast is between a wise man who builds his house on rock and a foolish man who builds his house on sand. In Luke, there is no reference to rock or sand; rather, the contrast is between building on a deep foundation and building with no foundation. What is one to make of this difference? Matthew's version reflects conditions in Palestine, where building on sand meant building in the middle of a dry, sandy streambed (a wadi), which would become a raging stream in the rainy

The Parable of the Wise and Foolish Builders
(verses requiring use of the environmental criterion)

Matthew 7:24-27

"Every one then who hears these words of mine and does them will be like a wise man who built his house upon the rock; and the rain fell, and the floods came, and the winds blew and beat upon that house, but it did not fall, because it had been founded on the rock. And every one who hears these words of mine and does not do them will be like a foolish man who built his house upon the sand; and the rain fell, and the floods came, and the winds blew and beat against that house, and it fell; and great was the fall of it."

Luke 6:47-49

"Every one who comes to me and hears my words and does them, I will show you what he is like: he is like a man building a house, who dug deep and laid the foundation upon rock; and when a flood arose, the stream broke against that house, and could not shake it, because it had been well built. But he who hears and does not do them is like a man who built a house on the ground without a foundation; against which the stream broke, and immediately it fell, and the ruin of that house was great."

reason. Luke's reference to building with or without a foundation reflects building techniques outside of Palestine. In short, Matthew's version is at home in a Palestinian environment, whereas Luke's version is adapted to the broader Mediterranean environment. In this case, scholars would be likely to judge the core of the parable in both Gospels as authentic and Matthew's version closer to what Jesus actually said.

A second text illustrates the environmental criterion applied not only to the form, but also to the substance of a text. According to Mark 7:19b, Jesus "declared all foods clean," thereby abolishing the dietary kosher[10] laws of the Hebrew Bible. But did Jesus really do that? There are reasons to suspect that questioning the validity of the Jewish dietary laws arose only after Easter, when the early church became a movement including both Jews and gentiles. We know from the Book of Acts and from Paul's epistles that the validity of the Torah dietary laws was controversial among early Christians. Although early church leaders struggled with the question, they never appealed to Jesus as having spoken on the issue. Moreover, if Jesus had "declared all foods clean," as Mark says, one would expect the Gospels to report conflict on this issue with Jewish opponents; such conflicts were reported about Sabbath observance, eating with outcasts, tithing, etc. But no conflicts with Jewish authorities about eating nonkosher food are reported. In short, the statement in Mark that Jesus declared all foods clean fits much better into the later environment of the early church than when Jesus lived.

In recent decades, as a result of sustained study of the forms of Jesus' speech as reported in the Gospels, a new criterion—the criterion of "distinctive form"—has emerged. Two forms are especially prominent in the Gospels—the proverb/aphorism and the parable. Both are found in early layers of the tradition, thus satisfying the criterion of multiple attestations. In addition, however, these forms have a distinctive function. They are invitational forms of speech, that is, they invite listeners to take a different view of things. Proverbs and aphorisms are short, pithy sayings that invite or provoke insight: "Figs are not gathered from thorns" (Luke 6:45); "No person can serve two masters" (Matthew 6:24); and "The last shall be first" (Luke 13:30). Parables are narratives or stories that draw listeners in and invite them to see through the lens provided by the story. In the teachings of Jesus, both forms are not only invitational, but also subversive. The insights they invite usually subvert or undermine conventionally accepted ways of looking at things. They invite listeners to see God differently, to see themselves and others differently, to see their own situations differently.

Because of the frequency and distribution of proverbs and parables in the tradition and because of their distinctive function, they are regarded as the most characteristic forms by which Jesus imparted his message. They are the bedrock of the tradition. In short, proverbs and parables are generally judged to be authentic, even if they are found in only one source.

But the criterion of distinctive form also provides a means of making judgments about the historical authenticity of the *applications* and *settings* of the parables in the Gospels. Some illustrate doctrines or teach moral lessons. For example, Matthew sets the parable of the talents (Matthew 25:14-30) in the context of teaching about the second coming of Christ and the last judgment, important doctrines in the early church. And Luke uses the parable of the Good Samaritan (Luke 10:25-37) to teach a moral lesson about what being a good neighbor means. But originally these parables do not seem to have functioned as illustrations of moral or doctrinal principles; rather, their original function was to invite listeners to experience radically new ways of seeing, to reverse conventional ways of seeing. In the invitation to change perception, the authentic voice of Jesus is heard. The settings in the Gospels and the applications were usually added later.[11]

We come now to a criterion about which there has been considerable dispute, controversy and uncertainty—the criterion of dissimilarity. According to this criterion, material in the Gospels that is dissimilar to material in Judaism and in the early church is authentic Jesus material. The reasoning behind the criterion is quite simple. If the preservers and shapers of the text in the early church did not take the text from Jewish tradition or from the emerging convictions of the church, it must have come from Jesus himself.

This criterion can be used in a positive or negative way. In its negative form, it is used to *exclude* everything that does not pass this test as inauthentic.

THE LORD'S PRAYER by the French artist James Jacques Tissot is one of a suite of almost 400 works painted between 1885 and 1895 illustrating *The Life of Christ*. Unlike many European artists of his day who created anachronistic biblical scenes with European costumes and settings, Tissot strove for authenticity. He based his paintings on solid archaeological research and on two extended trips to the Near East.

According to the Jesus Seminar, the first words of the Lord's Prayer, "Our father who art in heaven" (Matthew 6:9b), are "almost certainly not" authentic; therefore, these words will be printed in black. However, the next words, verse 10a, "Hallowed be thy name. Thy kingdom come," will be printed in pink; the seminar voted that Jesus probably did speak these words. (Luke's shorter introduction—"Father" [Luke 11:2]—will be printed in red; the seminar considers this wording to be authentic.) *Photo: John H. Eggers Publications and the Brooklyn Museum/©Three Lions*

For example, any quotation of or allusion to the Hebrew Bible in the Gospels must be excluded from the historically authentic words of Jesus because the Hebrew Bible is manifestly part of the Jewish tradition and was also the sacred Scripture of the early church. Because quotations and allusions to the Hebrew Bible in the Gospels are not "dissimilar," they are excluded from the category of authentic material, according to the negative application of this criterion. Any text in the Gospels that can plausibly be understood as a concern of the early church must also be excluded as inauthentic. All that is left after strict application of this principle is material that is distinctive or without parallel. Not surprisingly, the exclusionary application of this criterion leaves a minimalist picture of Jesus.

The negative application of the principle of dissimilarity makes logical sense in an abstract way, but it is extreme. To suppose that there is no continuity between Jesus and the community from which he came or the community that formed around him is unreasonable. The criterion confirms only things that set Jesus apart from his milieu. What is most distinctive about an individual, however, may not account for much that is characteristic of him. Furthermore, when priority is given to the criterion of dissimilarity, as it frequently is, nothing can be admitted to the category of historically authentic material, no matter how well attested according to other criteria, unless it is also dissimilar.

In its positive form, the criterion of dissimilarity is used to *include*, but not necessarily to exclude. In other words, if material meets the criterion of dissimilarity, it is likely to be included. But if it does not pass this test, it is not necessarily excluded; if it does not pass this test, we look to other criteria to determine inclusion or exclusion. Thus, material that is dissimilar to known emphases of Judaism or the church has a high claim to authenticity, but nothing is implied about material that does not pass this test. For example, the laws of Judaism regarding purity and impurity were a matter of concern in the early church. The negative use of the criterion of dissimilarity would, therefore, exclude sayings about purity from the authentic words of Jesus. But these issues appear in many sources (Mark and Q) as well as in many forms (parables, proverbs, controversy sayings). Thus, there is good reason to think that purity issues were of concern to Jesus. The negative application of the criterion would lead us to an incorrect conclusion in this case. But the positive application of the criterion of dissimilarity would not exclude these materials. Material that does not pass the test of dissimilarity might be accepted on other grounds and would not be excluded automatically.[12]

The final criterion we will consider here is the criterion of coherence. This criterion functions on two levels. First, it can be applied in a "micro" way to judge individual sayings. In other words, a saying may be accepted as authentic if it coheres with an already established core. For example, the Gospel of Thomas includes a brief parable attributed to Jesus known as the Parable of the Assassin:

> Jesus said, "The kingdom of the father is like a certain man who wanted to kill a powerful man. In his own house he drew his sword and stuck it into the wall in order to find out whether his hand would carry through. Then he slew the powerful man."
>
> Gospel of Thomas, Saying 98

THE CALLING OF PETER AND ANDREW, a 19th-century engraving, illustrates Mark 1:16-20. In this passage, Jesus says "Come after me, and I will make you become fishers of men." The vote on this passage was gray; these words did not meet the seminar's criteria for authenticity.

In this parable, Jesus describes an assassin practicing his sword thrust at home to make sure he is strong enough to carry out his mission. Many scholars are willing to accept this parable as authentic because it resembles other parables about making sure one is able to follow through on a planned course of action (for example, Luke 14:28-32) or parables that feature reprehensible characters to make a point (for example, Luke 16:1-8). This is an example of the micro-application of the criterion of coherence.

The criterion of coherence also functions in a "macro" way, namely in the creation of a comprehensive, coherent picture of Jesus. The various elements in the picture must form an intelligible, noncontradictory whole. If the overall picture leaves out elements with a strong claim to historical authenticity, then it cannot be said to make coherent sense of the evidence. At the macro level, the criterion of coherence thus moves toward comprehensiveness. The final test of any historical reconstruction is the degree to which authenticated data can be integrated into a coherent whole. In this sense, the historian's work is very much like that of a detective. The most convincing hypothesis is one that incorporates as many of the clues—as much of the reliable evidence—as possible.

For example, the late 19th-century scholarly portrait of Jesus as primarily a teacher who spoke of the "fatherhood of God" and "the infinite value of the human soul" did not take into account the element of crisis and urgency that runs throughout the Gospel accounts of Jesus. Similarly, the dominant 20th-century scholarly portrait of Jesus as a prophet who proclaimed the imminent end of the world does not take into account the large number of texts that reflect Jesus' concern with the historical direction and future of his people in his own time. And the somewhat eccentric picture of Jesus as a violent political revolutionary[13] disregards texts that indicate he advocated nonviolence. None of these portraits meets the criterion of coherence applied on a macro level because none includes all of the relevant data.

These, then, are the principal criteria by which scholars make judgments about what the historical Jesus was like. Although I have described the criteria separately, they are both complex and interrelated in practice. A computer cannot be taught to make these judgments, even when it is programmed with the criteria and all the available information. Like all historical judgments, these require a discerning eye and a sympathetic ear. They entail not only technical skills, but also imagination. One must be able to imagine a world very different from ours and imagine coherent images of Jesus that draw the data together.

To some, the scholarly quest for the historical Jesus seems a fruitless, wasteful and destructive enterprise that corrodes cherished beliefs.[14] And at excessive and eccentric moments, it has been both fruitless and corrosive. But for anyone curious about the historical Jesus, and not simply about what the early church said about him, historical study is the only avenue open.[15] Moreover, for many of us engaged in this pursuit, the picture of Jesus that emerges is both fascinating and compelling.[16] At its best, the historical study of Jesus gives us a glimpse of what he was like and helps us understand why and how he became the towering figure he is.

AFTERWORD

Robert C. Tompkins of Towson, Maryland, describes Borg's discussion as "interesting and compelling" but worries about the Jesus Seminar voting on the authenticity of sayings attributed to Jesus. Every committee he has served on, he says, "had one great taboo—never was a scientific judgment arrived at by vote."

In the same issue, Charles K. Gordon of Sierra Vista, Arizona, is troubled by the criterion of "dissimilarity"—the idea that sayings must be rejected if they reflect the views of contemporary Judaism or the early church:

Readers will find the criteria listed in the article of considerable value in helping them distinguish the genuine words of Jesus from words put into his mouth by redactors—except for the fifth criterion, which (as Professor Borg points out) is highly controversial (especially in its unwarranted denial of Jesus' Jewish background).

I would be interested in learning Professor Borg's opinion of the following statements, all italicized, which I consider to be genuine words of Jesus. For *obviously*, had these (embarrassing) remarks by Jesus not been widely and firmly established as authentic, they would have been expunged from the Gospels long ago. I begin with the well known plea of the gentile woman who asked Jesus to cure her daughter (Mark 7:25-27; Matthew 15:22-26). Jesus answers: *"I was only sent to the lost sheep of the house of Israel. It is not right to take the children's bread and throw it to the dogs."*

"Go nowhere among the Gentiles...but go rather to the lost sheep of the house of Israel" (Matthew 10:5b-6).

These two statements together satisfy criterion number six; they cohere. And they cohere with Jesus telling his disciples: *"Do not give dogs what is holy; do not cast your pearls before swine"* (Matthew 7:6).

In the first two statements, Jesus refers to the *lost sheep* of the house of Israel, which is consistent with his statement: "The well have no need of a physician" (Matthew 9:12b). In other words, his call is to *lapsed* Jews, urging them to return (repent) to *Judaism*. (He was, of course, not bent on converting them to Christianity.) "Good" Jews, devout Jews, he was saying, have no need of his gospel (good news). **BR** *6:1 (1990), p. 5*

Borg offers the following clarification:

Mr. Gordon helpfully calls attention to passages that Christians often ignore that remind us, in the midst of the Jewish-Christian dialogue, that the Jesus movement was originally a Jewish movement. The passages he cites are probably authentic. In all likelihood, Jesus did restrict his mission to Israel; he did not intend to create a new religion that would come to be known as Christianity.

However, to infer that Jesus simply aspired to restore lapsed Jews to the "established" Judaism of his day goes too far. Rather, he initiated a renewal movement within Judaism for the purpose of transforming the life of his people. His understanding of what it meant to be a Jew radically challenged many Jewish beliefs and practices in his time. His movement was a boundary-shattering movement that redefined boundary-setting notions, such as pure/impure, righteous/sinner, compatriot/enemy, rich/poor and male/female. He moved in the direction of inclusiveness. He did not simply invite wayward people back to an established way of life.

Finally, the inclusion of gentiles in what was originally a Jewish movement was a post-Easter development and probably goes beyond the explicit intention of Jesus. Yet it is plausible to see this development as a natural extension of the boundary-shattering qualities of Jesus' teaching and movement. **BR** *6:1 (1990), p. 5*

Brent Lee Metcalfe of Murray, Utah, raises three questions:

1. Who are the approximately 40 scholars participating in the Jesus Seminar?

2. Will a detailed study be published explaining the method of arbitrating extreme disagreements? (If 20 of the participants, for instance, believe a saying is authentic, and the others do not, how would this appear in *The Five Gospels*?[1] And, as a corollary, how would the reader know how many voted in which direction?

3. Is it possible to find out the verdict on a certain pericope prior to publication? (I am interested in the decisions on the Sermon on the Mount/Plain in general, especially Matthew 5:6, Luke 6:21a[25a] and Thomas 69b; and Matthew 5:39-41 and Luke 6:29.) **BR** *6:2 (1990), p. 9*

Borg replies:

1. The Fellows of the Jesus Seminar are listed on pages 96-97 of *The Parables of Jesus: Red Letter Edition*.[2]

2. Each saying has a "weighted average" calculated in the following manner: each red vote counts as three; pink as two; gray as one; black as zero. The total number of points for each saying is divided by the number of votes, thus producing a weighted average somewhere between three and zero. Sayings with a weighted average of 2.251 or more are printed in red, 1.501 to 2.25 in pink, 0.751 to 1.50 in gray and 0 to 0.75 in black. Thus, a saying about which there was an almost even division of opinion would be at the low end of the pink spectrum or the high end of the gray spectrum. Weighted averages and vote totals will be published.

3. Weighted averages and vote totals for the parables of Jesus and for the sayings of Jesus in Mark are available in the first two installments of the multi-colored version of the Gospels: *The Parables of Jesus*, referred to above, and *The*

Gospel of Mark: Red Letter Edition.[3] Most of the sayings you ask about have a high authenticity rating. Weighted averages follow: Matthew 5:6-1.76 (pink); Luke 6:21-2.36 (red); Luke 6:25a-.533 (black); Thomas 69b-1.60 (pink); Matthew 5:39b-40-2.63 (red); Matthew 5:41-2.50 (red); Luke 6:29a-2.63 (red); Luke 6:29b-2.43 (red). **BR** *6:2 (1990), p. 9*

Of course, the work of the Jesus Seminar presupposes studying Jesus vis-à-vis a specific time and culture, as Borg does in his book, Jesus: A New Vision.[4] *Reviewer Adela Yarbro Collins had this to say about Borg's book:*

Professor Borg advocates a new image of Jesus as a person filled with the Spirit whose goal was to transform the social world of his people. In presenting this image, Borg makes use of two organizing principles, Spirit and culture. His notion of Spirit is informed not only by the biblical tradition, but also by social, scientific and history-of-religions studies of ecstatic or paranormal experiences. His notion of the relation of Spirit to culture is shaped by H. Richard Niebuhr's classic *Christ and Culture.*[5] In his presentation of Jesus, Borg makes use of four social types, healer, sage, prophet and founder of a renewal or revitalization movement.

Borg argues that Jesus followed the ecstatic, mystical tradition of biblical and Jewish religion, comparable to the traditional images of Moses, Elijah, the writing prophets of Israel and the charismatic rabbis, Honi the circle-drawer and Hanina ben Dosa. Exorcisms and healings performed by Jesus are taken as historically credible and indicative of Jesus' spiritual power.

In his discussion of Jesus' relation to culture, Borg portrays him as both radical and subversive. Jesus called on his people to center themselves in God, rather than in the triple snare of wealth, honor and religion. The way taught by Jesus was metaphorical death followed by new life issuing from a new heart.

As the leader of a revitalization movement and a prophet, Jesus challenged the dominant politics of holiness and called instead for a politics of compassion. In place of a politics that divided pure and impure, Jew and gentile, observant and unobservant, male and female, righteous and sinner, Jesus lived out of and called for an experience of Spirit that would relativize social distinctions and support the way of peace rather than violence. Jesus was killed because he tried, in the name and power of the Spirit, to transform his own culture and threatened the conventional wisdom and power structures....

The major weakness of Borg's book is that he eliminates the eschatological dimension (relating to the fulfillment of God's promises) from the life and teaching of Jesus. Eliminating this dimension distorts the record just as much as ignoring the healings and exorcisms does. Borg feels justified in disregarding the eschatological dimension because his notion of eschatology is outdated and simplistic. He thinks that to say that Jesus was an eschatological prophet means that he believed the world would come to an end in his life-time and that he called on people to repent before it was too late. Perhaps this is how scholars at the turn of the century understood eschatology in relation to Jesus, but it certainly does not represent the current interpretation of escha-tological and apocalyptic texts. Only a few texts actually depict the dissolution of the created world. Even in those cases, one can debate whether they were meant to be taken literally. In other words, eschatology has a broader and richer range of meaning and significance than the simple belief in the end of the physical world.

So erosion of the consensus that Jesus expected the end of the world in his generation does not necessarily imply erosion of the image of Jesus as an eschatological prophet, as Borg claims. Further, it is a logical fallacy to say that, if Jesus did not expect the imminent end of the world, then the kingdom of God in his teaching must have a noneschatological meaning.

Borg is right to take seriously the evidence for charismatic Judaism, namely the stories in rabbinic literature about Rabbi Honi and Rabbi Hanina. But his failure to take into account the evidence for ecstatic and mystical experience in apocalyptic literature is a glaring omission. Unfortunately, Borg perpetuates the old scholarly bias regarding the admirable prophets and the degenerate apocalypticists.

Another weakness of the book is Borg's confusion between what he calls the conventional wisdom of Jesus' culture and the politics of holiness. Borg claims that the politics of holiness was responsible, in large part, for the Jewish conflict with Rome. He also claims that all the renewal movements of Jesus' time connected holiness with resistance. Indeed, he says that this connection was made by the culture as a whole. Borg oversimplifies the relation between religious ideas and historical events and obscures the differences among var-ious Jewish groups. He also claims that the politics of holiness played a role in Jesus' death. It is clear that the conventional wisdom of the time led to Jesus' death. It is not clear what role the politics of holiness played, especially considering that, as Borg admits, the Pharisees, who were the primary advocates of such politics, had little or nothing to do with enforcing them.

Although I differ with Borg in substantial ways, I believe his book is a step in the right direction and helpful for a general audience. It is helpful because Borg presents a marvelously lucid synthesis of much recent work on Jesus and because he relates the results of historical research to the contemporary situ-ation. With regard to ongoing scholarly work on Jesus, he moves in the right direction by taking Jesus' life into account, as well as his teaching.
BR *5:5 (1989), p. 12*

CHAPTER 8

Does the Gospel of Thomas
Contain Authentic Sayings of Jesus?

Helmut Koester
Stephen J. Patterson

Have previously unknown sayings of Jesus been recently discovered? Is it possible at this late date for authentic teachings to come to light? Two of the earliest sources for the Synoptic Gospels are the Gospel of Mark and a hypothetical document called "Q," from the German word Quelle *(source). Helmut Koester and Stephen J. Patterson suggest that the noncanonical Gospel of Thomas may resemble Q. Discovered in Nag Hammadi, in Upper Egypt, the Gospel of Thomas is a collection of sayings with no narrative framework, more like Proverbs than Mark, Matthew or Luke. If these sayings were collected because some early Christians believed that "these very words of Jesus" were the source of salvation, then they may actually be closer to the "voice of the historical Jesus" than parallels in the canon. And sayings with no canonical counterparts may indeed be authentic.–Ed.*

Scholars have long theorized that collections of Jesus' sayings were circulated in the decades after his death and that, therefore, they would be among the earliest witnesses to his message. Modern critical scholars have even been able to reconstruct one of these collections of sayings—we'll tell you how later. In the scholarly jargon, this collection of sayings is called simply "Q," from the German word *Quelle*, meaning "source." But no copy of Q has ever been found.

Now let your imagination roam. What if? What if an ancient collection of sayings of Jesus were discovered? Suppose it had many parallels to Q, as well as some differences. That would certainly support the idea that collections of Jesus' sayings were, in fact, available to the authors of the canonical Gospels—provided, of course, that we could demonstrate that our imagined

NAG HAMMADI CODICES. At the foot of the rugged cliffs of Jabal al-Tarif, overlooking the fertile Nile valley at Nag Hammadi, a small town more than 300 miles south of Cairo, two farmers looking for fertilizer made an astounding discovery in 1945. Sealed in a large earthen jar were 13 leather-bound books that have come to be known as the Nag Hammadi Codices. Buried by monks around 400 C.E., this monastic library consists of Coptic translations of Greek versions of more than 50 Christian, Jewish and pagan tractates, some dating as far back as the fourth century B.C.E. One of the tractates is the Gospel of Thomas. *Photo: Institute for Antiquity and Christianity, Claremont, California*

collection of sayings was an early composition and not written in the second or third century.

Even more startling, such a collection would probably contain sayings plausibly attributable to Jesus that had not been preserved anywhere else. In short, our imagined collection of sayings might enable us to recover sayings attributed to Jesus that have been lost for more than a thousand years.

Is this beginning to sound like Indiana Jones?

A little before the year 400, a group of monks from a monastery established by Pachomius, the founder of Egyptian monasticism, gathered their small library of 13 leather-bound volumes of religious writings and carefully placed them in a large earthen jar. They closed the mouth of the jar with a shallow red bowl, sealed it with bitumen and buried it at the bottom of a cliff face known as Jabal al-Tarif, which skirts the Nile as it bends its way past the modern town of Nag Hammadi in Upper Egypt.

We cannot be sure why they buried this small library. We do know that the books contained secret knowledge and told about heavenly journeys and mysterious rituals, liturgies and prayers. Books like these could not be kept without risk. Athanasius, the powerful bishop of Alexandria and an uncompromising defender of orthodoxy, had just (in 367 C.E.) published an Easter letter condemning certain unorthodox Christian books as heretical:

> They are fabrications of the heretics, who write them down when it pleases them and generously assign to them an early date of composition in order that they may be able to draw upon them as supposedly ancient writings and have in them occasion to deceive the guileless.[1]

In December 1945, Muhammed and Khalifa 'Ali left their home in al-Qasr, a tiny village near Nag Hammadi, and drove their camels the few kilometers to the Jabal al-Tarif to search for deposits of nitrogen-rich soil that collects at the base of the cliff. The farmers of al-Qasr use this soil to fertilize their fields. That day, as the brothers dug and poked around the boulders that had fallen from the cliff above, they came upon a large earthen jar sealed by a shallow red bowl. When Muhammed 'Ali smashed the jar with his mattock, out tumbled 13 books, which would soon prove to be the single most important archaeological find of the 20th century for the study of the New Testament and the origins of Christianity. In all, the 13 leather-bound volumes—known as the Nag Hammadi Codices—contained more than 50 Christian, Jewish and pagan tractates, most of them hitherto unknown, dating from the fourth century B.C.E. to the fourth century C.E.

After years of being bought, sold, traded and smuggled,[2] the 13 codices were finally reassembled in the Coptic Museum in Cairo, where scholars began the laborious process of transcribing, translating and publishing them.[3] Before that, in the spring of 1948, when 11 of the 13 codices were still in the hands of a Cairo antiquities dealer, a French scholar named Jean Doresse had photographed some of the manuscripts. Among the pages he photographed was the second tractate in Codex II. At the end of this tractate, the following words had been inscribed in titular fashion in the middle of the page: *Peuangelion Pkata Thomas*—The Gospel according to Thomas. However, nothing of the contents was made known at the time.

In the ensuing years, political events frustrated attempts to organize a team of scholars to publish the codices. The prime minister of Egypt was assassinated, a revolution erupted, the government fell and, finally, the Suez Crisis of 1956 shook the country. Not until 1970 was an international team of scholars, under the auspices of UNESCO, organized to publish all of the texts.

But in 1957, Pahor Labib, the director of the Coptic Museum in Cairo, published photographs of some leaves from the codices, among them the pages containing the Gospel of Thomas.[4] Thus began the scholarly effort to understand this mind-boggling text.

Scholars had known of a gospel attributed to Thomas, whose legendary journeys to the East are still regarded as foundational by the old Christian churches of India. A snippet from this gospel is even quoted by a third-century Christian apologist and philosopher named Hippolytus. This reference indicates that the Gospel of Thomas was used by a suspect heretical Gnostic group;

therefore, most scholars assumed that it could hardly have preserved words of Jesus from an early tradition.

But when the full text of the Gospel of Thomas suddenly became available in Labib's photographs, it was discovered that the Gospel of Thomas did *not* primarily contain mysterious Gnostic speculations. Instead it was a collection of sayings of Jesus, each one introduced by the phrase "Jesus said"; moreover, many of the sayings had parallels in the canonical Gospels.

Scholars were also able to connect the Gospel of Thomas with three fragmentary texts[5] found between 1897 and 1904 at another now-famous Egyptian site, Oxyrhynchus, where a huge hoard of ancient papyri was discovered. The three fragmentary texts found among the Oxyrhynchus papyri contained sayings of Jesus, but it was not clear whether they belonged to a particular gospel. When the photographs of the Gospel of Thomas were published, it became evident that the three fragments from Oxyrhynchus were portions of the Gospel of Thomas.[6] The Oxyrhynchus fragments were written in the original Greek; the Nag Hammadi text was a Coptic translation. The discovery of the full Coptic text, however, made it possible to reconstruct the entire Greek text.[7]

In the years following publication of the Gospel of Thomas, several scholarly positions were staked out. Some scholars said it was a late composition and therefore worthless for the purpose of recovering material from the earliest traditions of sayings of Jesus. Other scholars, however, opted for an early date and argued that the Gospel of Thomas represented an early and trustworthy tradition. Such highly regarded scholars as Robert M. Grant of the University of Chicago[8] and Ernst Haenchen of the University of Münster[9] were among those who regarded the newly discovered gospel as a heretical fabrication, nothing more than an unoriginal attempt to distort the sayings of Jesus, whose more authentic voice was to be found in the canonical Gospels. Among the first to see the Gospel of Thomas as an independent witness for the tradition of the sayings of Jesus were the eminent Dutch scholar Gilles Quispel,[10] the famous Alsatian Patristic scholar Oscar Cullmann[11] and the British scholar Hugh Montefiore.[12] In recent years, more and more scholars have adopted the latter view. Increasingly, the Gospel of Thomas is seen as an independent, reliable witness to the tradition of the sayings of Jesus.

Before any gospels were written, and contemporaneous with the earliest written Christian documents, Christians knew and transmitted the words of Jesus orally. Later these sayings were written down in collections. Sometimes parts of a collection were embedded in a narrative framework, as in Matthew and Luke, and edited or altered to fit the new literary context.

Using techniques of critical analysis, scholars have identified the peculiar features of editorial changes and alterations in each of the canonical Gospels. If the collection of sayings in the Gospel of Thomas had come from a canonical Gospel, we should have found traces in Thomas of these peculiar editorial elements (introduced by the author of the canonical Gospel) in the wording,

"THE GOSPEL ACCORDING TO THOMAS" say the two lines standing alone at lower center. Written in the Coptic (late Egyptian) language in Greek letters, the "gospel" begins with a heading that identifies the purported author more precisely: "These are the Secret Sayings which the Living Jesus spoke, and which Didymus Judas Thomas wrote down." In three passages in the Gospel of John, we are told that the disciple Thomas "was also called Didymus," a Greek word meaning "twin." Since the name Thomas is actually a transcription of an Aramaic word meaning "twin," the canonical Gospels do not really tell us Thomas' given name. But the Gospel of Thomas reveals that his given name was Judas, thus making an identification possible. Of the people named Judas in the New Testament, Judas the brother of Jesus (Mark 6:3; Matthew 13:55)—Jesus' twin according to the apocryphal Acts of Thomas—is the most likely identity of Thomas and hence of the purported author of the Gospel of Thomas. *Photo: Institute for Antiquity and Christianity, Claremont, California*

order or composition of sayings of Jesus. For example, if the order of the sayings in the Gospel of Thomas were the same as the order in which the author of the Gospel of Matthew had deliberately composed them, we could be sure that the author of the Gospel of Thomas had used the Gospel of Matthew. But scholars who argue that the Gospel of Thomas is dependent on the canonical Gospels have yet to show that the Gospel of Thomas follows any canonical Gospel version of the tradition of the sayings. This raises the possibility, at least, that the Gospel of Thomas is quite early.

In the canonical Gospels, the sayings of Jesus are often embedded in narratives, but there is no trace of a narrative framework in the Gospel of Thomas. This, too, suggests an early date.

In many cases, a saying or parable in the Gospel of Thomas is preserved without secondary expansion or allegorizing, that is, in a form that is not only shorter and more concise, but also evidently more nearly original than the canonical parallels. This suggests not only that the Gospel of Thomas represents an independent tradition, but also that the sayings derive from a time even earlier than the composition of the canonical Gospels. Therefore, when reconstructing the historical beginnings of the religious movement initiated by Jesus of Nazareth, the Gospel of Thomas must be given equal weight with the canonical Gospels.

Let us look more closely at the contents of the Gospel of Thomas to illustrate these contentions and to flesh out the argument. Then we will consider some of the implications.

The "Gospel of Thomas," the designation by which we call the document, appears at the end of the manuscript. It was added later by the scribe who copied it. The heading at the beginning of the book says, "These are the Secret Sayings which the Living Jesus spoke, and which Didymus Judas Thomas wrote down." This is the real title of the work, which designates it as a book of sayings. There are no references to the story of Jesus or his birth, life, death or resurrection. He is referred to simply as the "Living One." Occasionally disciples ask questions, to which the reply is a saying or parable.

The author of Thomas was certainly not trying to compose a "gospel" like the canonical Gospels. Stringing sayings together into a written document is, however, a kind of composition often found in "wisdom" literature. The Book of Proverbs in the Hebrew Bible is one example. Other examples are the Wisdom of Ben Sirah and the Wisdom of Solomon, which are preserved in the so-called Old Testament Apocrypha. There are also early Christian examples of this type of literature. The Epistle of James in the New Testament is one; another is the first six chapters of the early Christian manual known as the *Didache* or *Teaching of the Twelve Apostles*. But we have already mentioned the most important Christian collection of sayings, Q, which is the reconstructed book of sayings that was an important source used by both Matthew and Luke. We will return to Q later.

The Gospel of Thomas fits nicely into the tradition of this Jewish literary genre as it was adapted by early Christians. Wisdom books were customarily ascribed to particular authors, often worthy ancients, as in the case of the Wisdom of Solomon. But in the case of the Gospel of Thomas, the authority came from ascribing the sayings to Jesus, rather than from the collector of the sayings, Didymus Judas Thomas. Who was he? Was additional authority– reliability–based on the name of the collector given in the title? The answer is clearly yes, but who he was is not entirely clear.

A person named Thomas appears in lists of the Twelve, or the Twelve Apostles, in Matthew, Mark, Luke and Acts (Matthew 10:3; Mark 3:18; Luke 6:15; Acts 1:13), but none of these references says anything about him. A Thomas is also mentioned several times in the Gospel of John, twice asking questions (John 11:16 and 14:5), and again in the story of the Unbelieving Thomas (John 20:24-28). He is also listed as one of seven disciples in John 21:2. In three of the passages in John, the phrase "who was also called Didymus" is added.

Actually, Thomas is not a proper name; it is a transcription of the Aramaic word for twin. The Greek word *didymus* also means twin. So from the canonical Gospels we learn only that this fellow was a twin. The Gospel of Thomas, however, preserves his given name, Judas.

Several people in the New Testament are named Judas: (1) Judas Iscariot, who betrayed Jesus by identifying him to the authorities with a kiss (Mark 14:44-45); (2) Judas, the son of James, who appears in a list of apostles (Luke 6:16 and Acts 1:13; Thomas also appears in this list, so Thomas and this Judas were two different persons); (3) Judas, the brother of Jesus (Mark 6:3; Matthew 13:55).

Whoever collected the sayings in what we call the Gospel of Thomas attributed them to Judas the twin undoubtedly as a kind of guarantee of reliability or authenticity. The most likely Judas would seem to be the third alternative listed above, Judas, the brother of Jesus.

If this is correct, the Eastern Church may be the source of the Gospel of Thomas, because in the Eastern Church there was a tradition that Judas, the apostle and brother of Jesus, was in fact the twin brother of Jesus (so stated in the apocryphal Acts of Thomas).[13]

The sayings collected in the Gospel of Thomas consist, for the most part, of aphorisms, proverbs, wisdom sayings, parables, prophetic sayings about the "Kingdom of the Father" and community rules. The sayings are delivered one after another. Each saying is introduced by the formula "Jesus said."

The general theme is wisdom. Wisdom sayings express the truth about God and about the essence of the human self. They address questions of human nature and destiny and, by extension, the nature of the world and a person's proper relationship to the world. The wisdom sayings in the Gospel of Thomas are typical of the early Christian-sayings tradition to which Thomas, as well as Matthew, Mark and Luke, was heir.

Printed below are two examples of wisdom sayings from the Gospel of Thomas,[14] which, like other Jewish and Christian sayings collections of this type, reveal what is fundamental about people and their behavior. Beside each is a parallel saying from Q, as cited in the Gospel of Luke. The absence of the addresses "You Pharisees" and "You fools!" from sayings of the Gospel of Thomas may indicate that Thomas' version of the first saying is earlier than Luke's.

Gospel of Thomas Saying 89	**Luke 11:39-40**
Jesus said, "Why do you wash the outside of the cup?	And the Lord said to him, "Now you Pharisees cleanse the outside of the cup and the dish, but inside you are full of extortion and wickedness?
Do you not realize that he who made the inside is the same one who made the outside?"	You fools! Did not he who made the outside make the inside also?"

Gospel of Thomas **Saying 45**	**Luke 6:44b-45**
Jesus said, "Grapes are not harvested from thorns, nor are figs gathered from thistles, for they do not produce fruit. A good man brings forth good from his storehouse; an evil man brings forth evil things from his evil storehouse which is in his heart, and says evil things."	 "Figs are not gathered from thorns, nor are grapes picked from a bramble bush The good man out of the good treasure of his heart produces good; and the evil man out of his evil treasure produces evil; for out of the abundance of the heart the mouth speaks."

Other sayings in the Gospel of Thomas address the wisdom theme from a more mythological standpoint. In Judaism of this period, wisdom was not a concept but an actual being, a supernatural messenger from God. In sayings like the one below (with a parallel from Matthew), Jesus speaks with the voice of Wisdom, the heavenly messenger, inviting people to take up his yoke.

Gospel of Thomas **Saying 90**	**Matthew 11:28-30**
Jesus said, "Come unto me, for my yoke is easy and my lordship is mild, and you will find repose for yourselves."	 "Come to me, all who labor and are heavy-laden, and I will give you rest. Take my yoke upon you and learn from me; for I am gentle and lowly in heart, and you will find rest for your souls. For my yoke is easy, and my burden is light."

Some of the sayings in the Gospel of Thomas contain a prophetic element:

> His disciples said to him, "Twenty-four prophets spoke in Israel, and all of them spoke of you." He said to them, "You have omitted the one living in your presence, and have spoken (only) of the dead."
>
> Gospel of Thomas, Saying 52

The reign of God in the Gospel of Thomas, in contrast to most of the New Testament books, is not a future catastrophic event but is already under way. But, even though this view is not common in the New Testament, there are traces of it that show it was not unique to Thomas. The following saying, with its parallel from Luke, illustrates the point:

Gospel of Thomas **Saying 113**	**Luke 17:20-21**
His disciples said to him, "When will the	Being asked by the Pharisees when the kingdom

kingdom come?" Jesus said, "It will not come by looking for it. It will not be a matter of saying, 'Here it is,' or 'There it is.' Rather, the kingdom of the Father is spread out upon the earth, and people do not see it."

of God was coming, he answered them, "The kingdom of God is not coming with signs to be observed; nor will they say, 'Lo, here it is,' or 'There,' for behold, the kingdom of God is in the midst of you."

Thomas, however, sees the coming of the kingdom primarily as an event that takes place when the disciples gain a new understanding of themselves, and thus gives the concept a peculiar wisdom flavor.

> Jesus said, "If those who lead you say to you, 'See, the kingdom is in the sky,' then the birds of the sky will precede you. If they say to you, 'It is in the sea,' then the fish will precede you. Rather the kingdom is inside of you, and it is outside of you. When you come to know yourselves, then you will be known, and you will realize that it is you who are the sons of the living Father. But if you will not know yourselves, you dwell in poverty, and it is you who are that poverty."
>
> Gospel of Thomas, Saying 3

Let us look now at some parables, stories which, like parables in the canonical Gospels, disclose a new reality to those who are willing to listen.[15] Parables depict unusual or problematic situations that are resolved in often surprising ways that open a fresh understanding of the world into which the listener is invited.[16] Comparing these parables with their counterparts in the canonical Gospels, one often finds that, in Thomas, the persons acting in the parables abandon common sense, ignore the dictates of prudence and lunge for a single object discovered at an unexpected moment.

Here is a parable that involves catching fish. Matthew, in his version, interprets sorting the fish as a symbol for the last judgment; in the Gospel of Thomas, however, the fisherman chooses one highly prized fish.

Gospel of Thomas
Saying 8

The man is like a wise fisherman who cast his net into the sea and drew it up from the sea full of small fish. Among them the wise fisherman found a fine large fish. He threw all the small fish back into the sea and chose the large fish without difficulty. Whoever has ears to hear, let him hear.

Matthew 13:47-50

The kingdom of heaven is like a net which was thrown into the sea and gathered fish of every kind; when it was full, men drew it ashore and sat down and sorted the good into a vessel, but threw away the bad. So it will be at the close of the age. The angels will come out and separate the evil from the righteous and throw them into the furnace of fire; there men will weep and gnash their teeth.

Here is a parable about a merchant who sells everything to buy a fascinating pearl, again with a parallel from Matthew. Discovering our true identity as "sons of the living Father" results in such enthusiasm, in such fixation on the newly discovered, highly prized thing, that the world and normal values are suddenly and dramatically reduced in importance.

Gospel of Thomas **Saying 76**[21]	**Matthew 13:44-46**
The kingdom of the Father is like a merchant who had a consignment of merchandise and who discovered a pearl. That merchant was shrewd. He sold the merchandise and bought the pearl alone for himself. You too, seek this unfailing and enduring treasure where no moth comes near to devour and no worm destroys.	The kingdom of heaven is like treasure hidden in a field, which a man found and covered up; then in his joy he goes and sells all that he has and buys that field. Again the kingdom of heaven is like a merchant in search of fine pearls, who, on finding one pearl of great value, went and sold all that he had and bought that pearl.

Some of the sayings tell of the "mysteries" (Gospel of Thomas, Saying 62), which scholars refer to as Esoteric Wisdom. These sayings speak of hidden truths about human existence, heavenly origins, separation from the world and liberation of the soul from the body. In the sequence quoted below, devoted followers are told about their divine origins and given secret passwords to facilitate the return journey to their heavenly home:

> Jesus said, "Blessed are the solitary and the elect, for you will find the kingdom. For you are from it, and to it you will return."

> Jesus said, "If they say to you, 'Where did you come from?' say to them, 'We came from the light, the place where the light came into being on its own accord and established [itself] and became manifest through their image.' If they say to you, 'Is it you?' say, 'We are its children, and we are the elect of the living Father.' If they ask you, 'What is the sign of your Father in you?' say to them, 'It is movement and repose.' "
>
> Gospel of Thomas, Sayings 49-50

The religious perspective reflected in sayings like these is often associated with Gnosticism. Gnostics believed that their origin and their destiny lay in the supreme deity who dwells in heavenly remove from the evil world; this evil world is the creation of a rebellious angel or demiurge who means to keep humans sleepy and intoxicated, thus ignorant of their true identity; a divine messenger will come and wake the initiates and release them from the bonds of ignorance by bringing them true knowledge (*gnosis*) about themselves. In the following saying, Jesus speaks with the voice of this heavenly messenger:

> Jesus said, "I took my place in the midst of the world, and I appeared to them in the flesh. I found all of them intoxicated; I found none of them thirsty. And my soul became afflicted for the human beings, because they are blind in their hearts and do not have sight; for empty they came into

the world, and empty too they seek to leave the world. But for the moment they are intoxicated. When they shake off their wine, then they will repent."

Gospel of Thomas, Saying 28

The moment of return, however, requires preparation. One must cultivate a proper understanding of the world to be ready to leave its confines when the time comes:

> Jesus said, "Whoever has come to understand the world, has found (only) a corpse, and whoever has found a corpse is superior to the world."
>
> Gospel of Thomas, Saying 56

Understanding the world as something dead leads inevitably to a proper understanding of the body and corporeal existence. Becoming superior to the world involves depreciating the flesh in favor of the spirit.

Separating the soul from corporeal existence does not mean that the soul will henceforth exist as a disembodied spirit wandering through the cosmos without form or identity; rather, the soul freed from its bodily prison enters a new kind of corporeal existence that awaits it in the heavenly realm. This new "body" is often spoken of as the heavenly "image" that awaits the soul but is guarded and enclosed in the safety of the godhead until it can be properly claimed. Thus, Thomas speaks of images concealed in the Father until their splendor will be revealed to the utter astonishment of those by whom they will be claimed.

> Jesus said, "The images are manifest to man, but the light in them remains concealed in the image of the light of the Father. He will become manifest, but his image will remain concealed by his light."

> Jesus said, "When you see your likeness, you rejoice. But when you see your images which came into being before you, and which neither die nor become manifest, how much will you have to bear!"
>
> Gospel of Thomas, Sayings 83-84

But Thomas' rejection of the world is not a purely intellectual exercise. It has a practical side as well. At the heart of the Christian lifestyle as reflected in the Gospel of Thomas is social radicalism that rejects commonly held values. Much of the social radicalism in the sayings in the Gospel of Thomas is, of course, shared with the canonical Gospels.

The Gospel of Thomas urges Christians to reject the ideal of a settled life; the true Christian life requires itinerancy:

> Jesus said, "Become passers-by."
>
> Gospel of Thomas, Saying 42

> Jesus said, "[The foxes have their holes] and the birds have their nests, but the son of man (= the human being) has no place to lay his head and rest."
>
> Gospel of Thomas, Saying 86
compare Matthew 8:20; Luke 9:58

Even family bonds must be rejected:

> Jesus said, "Whoever does not hate his father and his mother cannot become a disciple to me. And whoever does not hate his brothers and sisters and take up his cross in my way will not be worthy of me."
>
> Gospel of Thomas, Saying 55
> compare Matthew 10:37-38; Luke 14:26-27

Shrewd business practices are also rejected, as they are in the canonical Gospels (see Matthew 5:42; Luke 6:34, 12:13-15):

> [Jesus said], "If you have money, do not lend it at interest, but give [it] to one from whom you will not get it back."
>
> Gospel of Thomas, Saying 95

Rejecting the world means accepting those whom the world has rejected. Thus, as they are in the canonical Gospels, the poor are blessed (Gospel of Thomas, Saying 54 = Luke 6:20), as are the suffering (Gospel of Thomas, Saying 58), the persecuted (Gospel of Thomas, Saying 68 = Matthew 5:11-12; Luke 6:22-23) and the hungry (Gospel of Thomas, Saying 69 = Luke 6:21).

As we noted earlier, some scholars have argued that the Gospel of Thomas is a compendium of sayings based on the canonical Gospels and that Thomas' interpretation of Jesus' sayings is an attempt to gnosticize the canonical tradition of Jesus' words. However, the Gnostic element in Thomas cannot be used as a basis for arguing either that it is late or that it is derivative of the canonical Gospels. Recent scholars have demonstrated that the rise of Gnosticism must be dated much earlier than the second century C.E.; Gnosticism can no longer be viewed as a relatively late Christian phenomenon. Indeed, among the tractates discovered at Nag Hammadi are a number of texts that reveal a rich legacy of Jewish Gnosticism, which probably predates the beginnings of Christianity.[17] Thus, Thomas' religious perspective, even if it is "Gnostic," would have been right at home in the first century.

One striking feature of the Gospel of Thomas is that the sayings make no reference to Jesus' death or resurrection—the keystone of Paul's missionary proclamation. Does this suggest a late date of composition? The answer is clearly no. In the collection of sayings known as Q, which was used as a source by both Matthew and Luke, Jesus' death is not part of the Christian message either. Q, like Thomas, is not interested in stories or reports about Jesus' resurrection and his subsequent appearances as the risen Lord. Reflections on Jesus' death and resurrection may well have occurred in the early church, as is reflected in Paul's letters, but the early church leaders were not unanimous that resurrection was the fulcrum of Christian faith. In both Q and Thomas, Jesus' significance lay in his words, and in his words alone.

Q, as noted earlier, is a reconstructed document. We do not have an actual copy of it. Q is a critical element in the so-called two-source theory of the composition of the three Synoptic Gospels—Matthew, Mark and Luke. The many parallels between these three Gospels indicate that there must be a relationship between them. The most commonly held scholarly view is that Matthew and Luke both used Mark, the oldest and shortest of the three, as one principal source. Matthew and Luke then added accounts of the early life of Jesus and accounts of his post-resurrection appearances. But scholars also noted that there were many parallels between Matthew and Luke that are not in Mark; these must have come from another common source—Q. The parallels between Matthew and Luke (that are not found in Mark) constitute what we know of Q.

Q, as reconstructed in this way, is primarily a collection of sayings. The Gospel of Thomas is an example of an actual collection of sayings like Q has been presumed to be.

Another striking feature of the Gospel of Thomas is the almost total absence of Christological titles, such as Christ/Messiah, Lord or Son of Man. In this way it differs from Q; in Q, the title Son of Man plays a significant role as a designation of Jesus as the one who will appear from heaven at the end of time. But a recent study has demonstrated that Q was composed in two successive stages.[18] In the earlier stage, the understanding of Jesus as the Son of Man was not yet present. At that stage, Jesus was presented as a teacher of wisdom and a prophet who announces the presence of the kingdom in his words.

In this respect, the early Q is consistent with the Gospel of Thomas and suggests an early date for the sayings collected in the Gospel of Thomas. Like the early Q, much of the material in the Gospel of Thomas—especially those passages with parallels in the early Q—was probably written within ten or twenty years of Jesus' death.

The parallel passages in Thomas and early Q are concentrated in the sayings of Q preserved in Luke's Sermon in the Field (Luke 6:20-49) and Matthew's Sermon on the Mount (Matthew 5-7). Interestingly enough, those passages in the Sermon in the Field and the Sermon on the Mount that are regarded by scholars as the authentic core of these sermons are the same passages found in the Gospel of Thomas. Some of these remarkable parallels are given in the following box. The sayings shared by Matthew, Luke and Thomas are among the sayings that were circulated orally among Christians at a very early time, before they were collected to form the basis for the sermons in Matthew and Luke.

It is also striking that what is missing in the Gospel of Thomas of the materials now included in Luke's Sermon in the Field (for example, curses against the rich in Luke 6:24-26) are passages that scholars agree were added by Luke to material he drew from Q.

This analysis suggests an early date for the original composition of the Gospel of Thomas. Indeed, these sayings derive from roots as ancient as those of the canonical Gospels.

Another similarity between Q and the Gospel of Thomas reinforces the conclusion that both were collections that circulated (among Christians for

whom the words of Jesus had exclusive saving power) during the years immediately after Jesus' death. This similarity involves prophetic sayings. The sayings we have just looked at involving parallels between Q and the Gospel of
Thomas were mostly sayings of secular wisdom. But both collections also contain prophetic sayings, and here the parallels are even closer and more

---

Parallels Between Thomas and Q

Gospel of Thomas, Saying 54
Blessed are the poor, for yours is
the kingdom of heaven.

Q 6:20[28] = Matthew 5:3
Blessed are you poor, for yours is
the kingdom of God.

Gospel of Thomas, Saying 69
Blessed are the hungry, that the
stomach of the one in want may
be filled.

Q 6:21 = Matthew 5:6
Blessed are you that hunger now,
for you shall be filled.

Gospel of Thomas, Saying 68
Blessed are you when you are
hated and persecuted, and no place
will be found, wherever you have
been persecuted.

Q 6:22 = Matthew 5:11
Blessed are you when people hate
you, and when they exclude you
and reproach you, and cast out
your name as evil, on account of
the Son of Man.

Gospel of Thomas, Saying 6
Do not lie and do not what you
hate (to be done to you).

Q 6:31 = Matthew 7:12
And as you wish that people would
do to you, do so to them.

Gospel of Thomas, Saying 34
If one blind person leads another
blind person, both of them will fall
into a hole.

Q 6:39 (Matthew 15:14)
Surely a blind person cannot lead a
blind person? Will they not both
fall into a pit?

Gospel of Thomas, Saying 26
You seek the speck that is in your
brother's eye, but you do not see
the beam that is in your own eye.
When you take the beam out of
your own eye, then you will see
well enough to take the speck out
of your brother's eye.

Q 6:41-42 = Matthew 7:3-5
Why do you see the speck that is in
your brother's eye, but do not
notice the beam that is in your own
eye? How can you say to your
brother, "Brother, let me remove
the speck that is in your eye," when
you yourself do not see the beam
that is in your own eye? You hypocrite, first remove the beam that is
in your own eye, and then you will
see clearly to remove the speck that
is in your brother's eye.

complete.[19] These parallel passages teach that salvation is in Jesus and his words. Here is one example:

Gospel of Thomas **Saying 79a**	**Q 11:27-28**
A woman in the crowd said to him, "Blessed are the womb that bore you and the breasts that fed you." He said to her, "Blessed are those who have heard the word of the Father and have truly kept it."	...a woman from the crowd raised her voice and said to him, "Blessed is the womb that bore you, and the breast that you sucked!" but he said, "Blessed rather are those who listen to the word of God and keep it."

Thus, the materials that the Gospel of Thomas and Q share come from several oral or written collections of sayings of Jesus that included prophetic passages and parables as well as wisdom sayings and that can be dated to the earliest followers of Jesus.

The Gospel of Thomas gives us some insight into the beliefs of Jesus' followers in the first three decades after his death. These were the people who first collected Jesus' sayings because they believed that these very words were the source of life and salvation. Jesus was dead, but he remained "the Living One" even after his death; understanding his words of wisdom and his prophetic announcement of the presence of the kingdom would continue to give eternal life.

By contrast, Paul did not care at all what Jesus had said; to Paul, Jesus' death and resurrection were the turning point of the ages, the first fruits of the coming of the kingdom. If Paul had been completely successful, very few of the sayings of Jesus would have survived. Only a few sayings are contained in Paul's letters. But there were Christians besides Paul who believed Jesus' words were the primary source of understanding and salvation, and they preserved and developed the tradition of his sayings. Most of these traditions were eventually incorporated into the Pauline conception of Christianity, that is, they became sayings uttered by the one who died on the cross for our salvation—important words, but not indispensable for understanding the Christian faith.

The Gospel of Thomas is the most important surviving document of Jesus' followers who did not share the Pauline message. The only thing that mattered to them was what Jesus said. Here, and only here, did they find their true identity as "sons of the living Father."

The most surprising aspect of this analysis of the Thomas tradition is that this understanding of Jesus' message is not a late development but is, perhaps, the oldest and most nearly original understanding of Jesus, dating back to the very beginnings of the Jesus movement.

The Gospel of Thomas, of course, reinforces what we have learned from the reconstruction of Q. But the Gospel of Thomas also goes beyond Q. All we know of Q is what was preserved by incorporation in Matthew and Luke. Thomas also preserves parallels, as we have seen, but contains other sayings and parables that may be equally old.

In fact, although it is notoriously difficult to prove that this or that saying in the Jesus tradition actually comes from Jesus himself,[20] some have argued that several of Thomas' sayings have a claim to authenticity in this literal sense. For example, the famous parable scholar Joachim Jeremias[21] has argued that Saying 82 of the Gospel of Thomas comes from Jesus: "He who is near me is near the fire, and he who is far from me is far from the Kingdom."

The German scholar Johannes Bauer[22] has argued that Saying 58 is an authentic Jesus saying: "Jesus said, 'Blessed is the man who has suffered and found life.'" Bauer also thought that Saying 52 may have come from Jesus:

> His disciples said to him, "Twenty-four prophets spoke in Israel, and all of them spoke of you." He said to them, "You have omitted the one living in your presence and have spoken (only) of the dead."

Many have argued that Thomas' parables are likely to have come from Jesus himself. Many of the parables in the Gospels attributed to Jesus are preserved in Thomas in more primitive forms than their canonical counterparts, and thus may help us eventually to recover the authentic voice of the historical Jesus. But a cluster of parables in the Gospel of Thomas (Sayings 96-98), two of which have no canonical parallels, may be just as old. Clustered together with no apparent thematic connection, they probably derive from an ancient parable collection lost to us but known to Thomas:

> Jesus [said], "The Kingdom of the Father is like a certain woman. She took a little leaven, [concealed] it in some dough, and made it into large loaves. Let him who has ears hear."

> Jesus said, "The Kingdom of the [Father] is like a certain woman who was carrying a jar full of meal. While she was walking [on] a road, still some distance from home, the handle of the jar broke and the meal emptied out behind her on the road. She did not realize it; she had noticed no accident. When she reached her house, she set the jar down and found it empty."

> Jesus said, "The Kingdom of the Father is like a certain man who wanted to kill a powerful man. In his own house he drew his sword and stuck it into the wall in order to find out whether his hand could carry through. Then he slew the powerful man."

No one has yet explained these parables. But the early church leaders knew what they meant and valued them as sayings of Jesus. Scholars have yet to decide if these or any other sayings from the Gospel of Thomas do in fact come from Jesus. But one thing is certain. No discussion of Jesus and the origins of Christianity can be complete unless due consideration is given to the witness of Thomas.

AFTERWORD

Considerable controversy swirls around the suggestion by Koester and Patterson that the Gospel of Thomas represents a version of Christianity that put the words of Jesus above the resurrection. Pastor Ryan Ahlgrim of Peoria, Illinois, faults the reasoning behind this theory:

I fully agree with [Koester and Patterson's] conclusion that the Gospel of Thomas contains several sayings that go back to the earliest church, possibly even to the historical Jesus, but I believe the authors overextend themselves when they say that "the early church was not unanimous in making the resurrection the fulcrum of Christian faith. For both Q and Thomas, Jesus' significance lay in his words, and in his words alone."

This sweeping conclusion is based on the fact that Q and Thomas are collections of sayings rather than narratives of Jesus' ministry or passion. Does one necessarily exclude the other? Source criticism has shown that the miracle stories in the Gospels once circulated as a separate collection. Are we to deduce from this that for some early Christians Jesus' significance lay in his miracles only and not in his resurrection?

That Q and Thomas are collections of sayings only gives evidence that Jesus' words were treasured for their own sake by many early Christians but *not* that they considered Jesus' resurrection insignificant. On the contrary, the fact that the Gospel of Thomas refers to Jesus as "the Living One" seems to assume some sort of belief in Jesus' resurrection.

Earliest Christianity certainly was greatly diverse theologically. Paul's letters amply prove this. But the claim that one branch of the earliest church disregarded belief in Jesus' resurrection (in favor of his words alone) seems highly unlikely.

Perhaps I am mistaken, but their article appears to have an ulterior motive. The authors seem to be catering to people who want to justify calling themselves Christians even though they do not believe the message of the resurrection. Such people should be honest enough to stop calling themselves Christians and use a more accurate label, such as "People Who Like Jesus' Sayings." **BR** *6:4 (1990), p. 6*

Jim Roth questions the underlying principles used by the authors for determining authenticity. He calls them "assumptions":

For example: Of any two possible alternative versions of the same statement, the shortest is presumed to be the most original, all other things being equal. Here is another example: An antisupernatural bias is an indicator of authenticity (supernatural images are automatically assumed to be later accretions to the original text). A final example: The absence of an advanced Christology is proof of uncontaminated, primitive witness.

Why do we see so little discussion of these assumptions and their attendant philosophies? I do not mean to be unkind, but are these sacred cows that are beyond the realm of public debate? Are there no opposing views? I wonder if there is any real substance underlying these hermeneutical principles. **BR** *6:6 (1990), p. 48*

Patterson replies:

Everyone engaged in research brings to his/her work both assumptions and presuppositions; Professor Koester and I are no exceptions. Unchallenged and unexamined assumptions may, in fact, be devastating to scholarly work. We must always be on the lookout for them and attempt to bring them to consciousness so that they may be debated.

Presuppositions, however, are another matter. All researchers must attempt to proceed on the basis of previous work, provided it is sound and convincing. Progress in scholarship could scarcely be achieved otherwise. All three of the issues Mr. Roth raises are, more or less, presuppositions (not assumptions) firmly grounded in the history of New Testament scholarship. They are born of years of careful analysis of the texts, not a philosophical or ideological position.

Much of the critical study of the Gospels since the turn of the century has been devoted to the question of how the Jesus tradition gradually developed. I would refer the reader to two landmark works in that history—Rudolf Bultmann's *History of the Synoptic Tradition*[1] and Joachim Jeremias' *The Parables of Jesus*.[2] A brief discussion of results can be found in Marcus Borg's article "What Did Jesus Really Say?" (reprinted on pp. 74-84 in this volume). **BR** *6:6 (1990), p. 48*

And Gerson H. Brodie of Denver, Colorado, writes to ask:

...if there are polemics against "the Jews" (like the ones in the canonical Gospels and Acts) in the sayings of Jesus cited by Thomas. "If they are not present, I think that would argue for a very early date, before the political struggle between the early Church and the Pharisees had begun." **BR** *6:4 (1990), p. 7*

Koester responds:

There are very few references in the Gospel of Thomas to the Jews. In Saying 43, Jesus answers a question of the disciples, "Who are you that thou should say these things to us?" by saying "[Y]ou have become like the Jews, for they either love the tree and hate its fruit or love the fruit and hate the tree."

The Pharisees are referred to twice. Saying 39 refers to the "Pharisees and scribes who have taken the keys of knowledge"; Saying 102 pronounces a "woe" against the Pharisees, "for they are like a dog sleeping in a manger of oxen, for neither does he eat nor does he let the oxen eat."

There is no systematic polemic in the Gospel of Thomas such as we find in Matthew 23. The Gospel of Thomas belongs to an early stage in the development of the tradition of Jesus' followers, in which the controversy between Christianity and the new establishment of Judaism after the First Jewish Revolt against Rome (which ended in 70 C.E.) had not yet developed. The Gospel of Thomas does reflect debates between the followers of Jesus and some leaders of the Jewish community, but within the framework of the community of Israel.
BR *6:4 (1990), p. 7*

CHAPTER 9

How the Books of the Hebrew Bible
Were Chosen

Marc Brettler

Brettler rejects the widely held claim that a rabbinic "Council of Jamnia" in the first century C.E. established the canon of the Hebrew Bible. He maintains that "the canon reflects the judgment of popular rather than rabbinic groups" and that canonization "did not occur at a single moment under the auspices of some religious power group." He believes that the tripartite division of Hebrew Scriptures into Torah (Law), Nevi'im (Prophets) and Kethubim (Writings) indicates that groups of books were accepted as privileged at different times. Moreover, the reason Daniel, a prophetic book, and Chronicles, a historical book, appear among the Writings is that they were too late to be admitted into sections that had already been closed by canonization.–Ed.

The canonical books of the Bible are those books included as opposed to those excluded. The English word *canon* derives from a Greek word meaning measuring rod. Canon thus refers to the books that measure up, or meet certain criteria, for being included in a particular literary corpus. By definition, canonization implies a process by which various books are judged and suggests that certain books are excluded as noncanonical. As a result, books that are included in a canon have much greater prestige and authority than those that are excluded.

Most Jews and Christians have grown up with the notion of canonical scriptures, but the idea was radically new in the context of the ancient Near East. To the best of our knowledge, no other ancient Semitic civilization attempted to sort through the literature, raise some works to a higher status by deeming them canonical and relegate others to a lower status by declaring them unworthy of being admitted into the canon.

Why did the notion of canon develop specifically in Israel? Unfortunately, the process by which the 24 books of the Hebrew Bible were canonized is not clearly described either in biblical or rabbinic literature. All we can do is reconstruct the process on the basis of hints and clues.

Clearly the canonization of the Hebrew Bible did not occur at a single moment under the auspices of a particular religious power group. This is obvious from the tripartite structure of the Hebrew Bible: (1) Torah (the Pentateuch—Genesis, Exodus, Leviticus, Numbers and Deuteronomy); (2) Nevi'im (literally the Prophets, but actually the historical books of Joshua through Kings—called in Jewish tradition the Former Prophets—and the prophets Isaiah through Malachi, called in Jewish tradition the Latter Prophets); and (3) Kethubim (Writings, that is, sundry material). This order is probably reflected in Luke 24:44, which refers to "the law of Moses [Torah] and the prophets [Nevi'im] and the psalms," meaning Kethubim, designating the Kethubim by the first and largest book in the collection.

Certain books in the Hebrew canon do not seem to fit the category to which they are assigned. Kethubim includes Daniel, which is really a prophetic book, and Chronicles, which parallels the historical books of Samuel and Kings in the Nevi'im section. If the Bible had been canonized at a single moment, Daniel would have been placed adjacent to a prophetic book such as Ezekiel, and Chronicles would have been next to Kings, which is where they belong thematically. (In most English Bibles, which follow the order in the Greek translation of the Bible known as the Septuagint, that is where these books appear.) Chronicles and Daniel are both late books (probably fourth century and second century B.C.E., respectively), and the best explanation for why they were not incorporated into Nevi'im is that the Nevi'im section of the canon was closed by the time they were composed. This inconsistent ordering suggests that Nevi'im was canonized before Kethubim. Generally, we have deduced that the Torah was canonized first, then Nevi'im and finally Kethubim.

It is difficult to assign dates to each stage of this process. According to some scholars, the texts now incorporated in the Torah were completed before the Babylonian Exile of 587/6 B.C.E.; others claim that the latest Torah texts were composed during the Babylonian Exile or after the return to Zion in 538 B.C.E. Probably the experience of being exiled or of living through the Exile or of reconstituting a community in the land of Israel after the return to Zion necessitated religious consolidation, including authorizing certain legal and historical traditions. Establishing the "correct" legal traditions must have been especially pressing for the exilic community because several prophets had predicted that destruction or exile would result from abrogation of the law (see, for example, Amos 2:4-5). Upon their return, therefore, when the catastrophe of Exile had come to an end and the community in Israel was reconstituted, the leaders had to establish which texts incorporated the laws that had to be observed. These texts were chosen from a multiplicity of legal and historical traditions, which various groups in ancient Israel claimed were authoritative, divine revelation. Several were chosen and ultimately became canonized as Torah, "(the) teaching," which became the legal yardstick for the community in crisis.

Although canonization involved rejecting certain traditions, which were ultimately forgotten, the chosen texts did not produce a uniform, monolithic work. Different conceptions of creation exist side by side in Genesis 1-2; different slave laws are legislated in Exodus 21, Leviticus 25 and Deuteronomy 15; and different celebrations of the fall ingathering festival, Sukkot, are described in Exodus 23:16 (compare 34:22), Leviticus 23:23-43 and Deuteronomy 16:13-15. This suggests that canonization was an inclusive process intended to enfranchise several groups within ancient Israel. At the time of canonization, no one group had enough power to foist its texts on the others as the only legal teaching. As a result, the canonized texts created a diverse and sometimes contradictory work that incorporates several traditions.

A similar process must have transpired with Nevi'im (Prophets). Surely there were more prophets in ancient Israel than the 15 who have their own books in the Bible (Isaiah, Jeremiah, Ezekiel and the 12 Minor Prophets). The biblical text refers to other prophets and their prophecies; for example, Jeremiah 28 mentions a prophet named Hananiah, son of Azzur. At some point, a selection must have been made from among the works and oracles of these prophets. Given that the Torah had already been canonized, the criterion of Deuteronomy 18:22, that a true prophet could be recognized by the fulfillment of his oracle, was probably central to deciding which prophetic works to include in the canon. Prophets whose prophecies had not been validated were excluded. This process probably occurred some time between the fifth century B.C.E. (the date of Malachi, the latest prophetic book) and the second century B.C.E. (the accepted scholarly date of Daniel, a prophetic book not included in the Hebrew canon of Nevi'im). The canonization of Nevi'im required compromises similar to the ones for canonizing the Torah; Nevi'im incorporated diverse conceptions of God and a variety of theological notions about such basic concepts as theodicy (the problem of unexplained evil in a world created by a just God), retribution and repentance.

It is difficult to know precisely when the Kethubim section (Writings) was canonized. The latest book in the division is probably Daniel, which can be dated to the middle to late second century B.C.E. The earliest mention of 24 books (counting Samuel, Kings, the 12 Minor Prophets, Ezra-Nehemiah and Chronicles each as one book) as comprising the entire Bible is from the apocryphal book known as the Fourth Book of Ezra, which dates to the late first century C.E. The Jewish historian Josephus in the late first century C.E. seems to corroborate this. Josephus claims that the Bible contains 22 books; he probably counted Ruth and Judges as a single book and Jeremiah and Lamentations (traditionally believed to have been written by Jeremiah) as a single book; thus his 22 books are the same as the 24 in Fourth Ezra. This suggests that the Hebrew Bible as a whole, including Kethubim, was canonized sometime between the second century B.C.E. and the first century C.E.

The Kethubim section is as diverse as the Torah and Nevi'im sections. Job, Proverbs and Ecclesiastes present radically different views of how God rules the world. Psalms and Song of Songs, both beautiful and poetic, set forth different notions of the relationships central to human existence. These multiple perspectives were incorporated in the canon because they were important to different groups.

Although the evidence allows for canonization of the entire Hebrew Bible between the late second century B.C.E. (when Daniel was written) and the late first century C.E. (when Fourth Ezra and Josephus mention the complete canon), most scholars claimed that the final canonization took place in the first century C.E. at the "Council of Jamnia (or Jabneh)." But no such council was ever convened to discuss the canonicity of biblical texts. The existence of the council is based on misunderstandings of several second-century C.E. rabbinic texts, in which the rabbis debate whether or not particular biblical texts, such as Ecclesiastes and Song of Songs, "defile the hands" (with ritual impurity). The phrase "to defile the hands" refers to whether or not a book is divinely inspired and not to its canonical status. The rabbinic debates concern inspiration, not canonicity. There are also several discussions about "hiding away" the books of Ezekiel, Proverbs, Ecclesiastes and Song of Songs. However, these are theoretical discussions reflecting theological problems raised in these texts, which were problematic enough that one could *imagine* decanonizing them. The rabbinic discussions are not full-fledged debates; no one seriously considered removing Ezekiel or Proverbs from the canon. Thus, the rabbinic texts do not prove that the Hebrew Bible was canonized by a group of rabbis in the first century C.E. More likely, the Hebrew Bible was canonical, that is, authoritative, before the late first century C.E. Furthermore, the canon reflects the judgment of popular rather than rabbinic groups.

Particular works might have been excluded from the canon for various reasons. Perhaps they did not reflect the legal practices of a predominant social group or the prophecies were not verified or they were written recently. This last factor, that books of recent vintage were not usually canonized, precipitated the appearance of Pseudepigrapha, or "false writings"—books that claimed to be written much earlier than they were by attributing authorship to important biblical personalities.

This fiction first appeared during the biblical period. For example, clear linguistic and historical evidence suggests that Daniel was written in the second century B.C.E., but certain passages in the text imply that it was written three centuries earlier. The author of Daniel made this false claim so his book would become an instant, ancient classic—and he succeeded! Other books from the second century B.C.E. in which no attempt was made to falsify the date of origin, such as the Wisdom of Ben Sirah, were not canonized in the Hebrew Bible. Several of these (the Wisdom of Solomon as well as the Wisdom of Ben Sirah), however, are considered canonical in the Catholic Church and are included in Catholic Bibles. Texts that are preserved in the early church canon but not in the rabbinic canon are called Apocrypha.

What was the fate of books that did not make it into the canon? Although they were not burned or forcibly removed from circulation, many rejected books were eventually abandoned and forgotten. But some of them from the late first millennium B.C.E. and the early first millennium C.E. escaped oblivion by being preserved as Apocrypha and Pseudepigrapha.

AFTERWORD

The Most Reverend John F. Whealon of Hartford, Connecticut, disagrees with Brettler that the Book of Daniel belongs in Prophets:

The literary form of Daniel was not prophecy but apocalypse. Its literary form means that the proper place for this book, recognizable to the ancients as an apocalypse, would have been among the Writings and not the Prophets [in the Tanakh]. **BR** *5:6 (1989), p. 39*

Brettler explains:

I agree with the Most Reverend Whealon that much of Daniel should be considered apocalypse. However, to the best of my knowledge, in rabbinic circles apocalypse was not differentiated from prophecy (in contrast to the early Christian community, in which the Book of Revelation played a major role). Thus, there are several examples of apocalypse in typical prophetic books, such as Isaiah and Zechariah. Furthermore, in rabbinic literature, Daniel was often called *Daniel ha-Navi* (Daniel the Prophet). This reflects the notion that, from the ancient rabbinic perspective, the book bearing Daniel's name should have been canonized as part of Nevi'im (Prophets). That it was canonized among the Writings suggests that this book was not extant when the section known as Prophets was canonized. **BR** *5:6 (1989), p. 39*

Citing Edward J. Young's An Introduction to the Old Testament[1] *and Gleason Archer's* A Survey of Old Testament Introduction,[2] *Rector William Holiman of New York City questions Brettler's statement that "the accepted scholarly date" for the composition of Daniel is the second century* B.C.E. *Brettler responds:*

The general scholarly consensus that Daniel dates from the second century C.E. is supported by evidence that seems incontrovertible to me. Daniel betrays a clear knowledge of the Greek language; for example, the word usually translated "bagpipes" in Daniel 3:5 and elsewhere is *symphonyah*, a Greek loan word, cognate to English *symphony*. Greek words in this verse and elsewhere in Daniel suggest that Daniel was not written in the early post-Exilic period, as is claimed in the text, but much later, after the conquest of the land of Israel by Alexander the Great when Greek began to influence the Hebrew language spoken in Israel. Furthermore, the author of Daniel has knowledge of specific events of the second century that goes far beyond the general predictions typical of the prophetic genre. In fact, the "predictions" may not have been prophetic at all, but may have been written when the events took place in the second century. In that sense, the Book of Daniel should be characterized as Pseudepigrapha, or false writing. **BR** *5:6 (1989), p. 40*

CHAPTER 10

How the Books of the
New Testament Were Chosen

Roy W. Hoover

Hoover also describes a canonization process that took several centuries. Although we do not know exactly when and how Christian leaders decided which works to canonize, quotations and references in the works of church fathers show that Paul's letters were held in great esteem by the end of the first century, the gospel tradition somewhat later, and a variously defined "New Testament" by the end of the second century. Some works were included because they were "consistent with established orthodoxy"; others were rejected because they were too "recent." The present New Testament canon was authoritatively defined by Athanasius, bishop of Alexandria, in the second half of the fourth century. Hoover notes that "none of the canonical lists mentions inspiration as a criterion," leading him to the provocative conclusion that the motivation for creating the canon was not religious but political.–Ed.

How did church leaders decide which books to include in the New Testament? When was the decision made? By whom? The surviving evidence, unfortunately, does not provide answers in the detail we would like, but it does document a number of developments that eventually led to the New Testament as we know it.

At a very early stage (by the end of the first century C.E.), several churches had collected some of Paul's letters. Clement, who is traditionally regarded as the third bishop of Rome, although this is uncertain, wrote a letter from Rome to the church in Corinth exhorting them to read part of Paul's first letter to the Corinthians (*1 Clement* 47.1-3).[1] It thus appears that the church at Rome had a copy of Paul's letter less than half a century after he wrote it. The author of 2 Peter also seems to know of a collection of Paul's letters (2 Peter 3:15-16).

Ignatius, the second-century bishop of Antioch, wrote letters to seven churches while he was en route to Rome, where he suffered martyrdom.

Ignatius frequently attempts to elaborate Paul's ideas in these letters, and when he tells the Ephesians that Paul mentions them "in every letter" (*Letter to the Ephesians* 12.2), Ignatius shows that he knows at least several of Paul's letters.

But a collection of Paul's letters is not a canon. And the question we are examining is when and how the canon was determined. *Canon* is the Greek term for norm or rule. It is the standard by which things can be measured. A canon of scriptures is a collection of books that are accepted as authoritative. The New Testament canon accepted by most Christians today consists of 27 books.[2]

Within a century of Jesus' death, Christians had produced a small but diverse library of writings in addition to Paul's letters. We know of two collections of Jesus' sayings. The full text of one, the Gospel of Thomas, was recently found at Nag Hammadi;[3] the other, known as Q, is a hypothetical source that accounts for the nearly identical sayings found in the Gospels of Matthew and Luke for which there are no parallels in Mark (the primary source for both). There was also a so-called Signs Gospel, a collection of wondrous deeds ascribed to Jesus, which scholars believe underlies the Gospel of John. In addition, there were dialogues and revelations attributed to Jesus, various accounts of his birth, several accounts of acts of the apostles, homilies and more. All of these were candidates for what was to become the New Testament, but at this early date none could be called canonical.

The first proposal for a canon for the Christian movement was made in the middle of the second century by Marcion, the owner of a successful shipping business and the son of a bishop of the church in Asia Minor. Marcion proposed that the church reject the Jewish Scriptures and embrace a canon of its own, composed of one gospel, Luke, and the letters of one apostle, Paul. Marcion argued that, for the sake of unity and the truth of the gospel, the church ought to identify its own normative writings and stop relying on Jewish Scriptures. He contended that references to the God worshiped by the Jews in Luke and Paul were corruptions of what Luke and Paul originally wrote. Therefore, Marcion expunged these references from the versions of Luke and Paul that he included in his proposed New Testament.

Marcion's radical ideas ignited a controversy that led ultimately to his excommunication, but his heretical proposal forced the church to make a case for the value and status of the Jewish Scriptures, and, more relevant here, the episode prompted the church to consider which writings ought to be regarded as canonical, or normative, and why.

The many attempts by the church to resolve this now-unavoidable question can most readily be appreciated in various lists of books to be approved for reading in churches and books to be rejected.

The oldest extant list of New Testament writings, at least in the opinion of some scholars, is known as the Muratorian Canon, which is named for Lodovico Antonio Muratori (1672-1750), an 18th-century scholar who discovered the list in a Milan library. The Muratori fragment contains 85 lines in Latin and dates to the eighth century. But scholars believe this is a translation from Greek, the original of which may have been written as early as the late second or third century.[4] The Muratorian Canon is an annotated list of writings, which, according to the anonymous author, were accepted by the Catholic Church. Included in the list of rejected writings are some works that reflect the views of various heretical individuals and groups, including Marcion.

Although the specific situation addressed by the Muratorian Canon is not identified, the tone of the list is clearly polemical. If it was written in the late second century, as some scholars think, it is the earliest known response to Marcion's challenge to the church to define the canon of scriptures.

The Muratorian Canon lists as authoritative the four Gospels,[5] Acts, 12 letters of Paul (neither Philemon nor Hebrews is mentioned), Jude, 1 and 2 John, and the Wisdom of Solomon (part of the Old Testament Apocrypha for Protestants and considered deuterocanonical—one of a second group of authoritative writings added to the canon later—by Catholics). The Apocalypse of John—Revelation—and the Apocalypse of Peter are on the list, but the author notes that these two books were not accepted by everyone in the church. The Apocalypse of Peter is not in the modern canon; Revelation is. The Muratorian Canon does not include the following books, which are also in the modern canon: James, 1 and 2 Peter, and 3 John. The document known as the *Shepherd of Hermas*, written in an apocalypse form but concerned with repentance and moral instruction, is mentioned but rejected because it is late.

Two other sources close to the time of the Muratorian Canon, if we assume it dates from the late second century, shed further light on the status of the canon in the aftermath of Marcion's bold initiative. One is Irenaeus, bishop of Lyon in Gaul (France). In works written about 185, Irenaeus quotes extensively from some 20 books as authoritative—the four Gospels, Acts, Paul's letters (excluding Hebrews), 1 John, 1 Peter, Revelation and the *Shepherd of Hermas*.[6] The other source is the scholar and theologian Origen of Alexandria (c.185-254); Eusebius, bishop of Caesarea, compiled a list of authoritative books cited by Origen similar to the list mentioned by Irenaeus.[7]

The most illuminating of these early lists was drawn up by Eusebius himself in a multivolume history of the church published in 325. Eusebius, like his predecessors, divided books into three categories—accepted, disputed and rejected. In the *accepted* category are all 20 books endorsed by Irenaeus. Hebrews, which is not mentioned in any of Eusebius' three categories, may be included among the (unspecified) letters of Paul. Eusebius was uncertain about the appropriate status of Revelation, so he tentatively placed it among both the *accepted* and the *rejected* writings. Five general letters constitute his list of *disputed* works, and seven are named in the *rejected* category, including, tentatively, Revelation.

When Eusebius' list of authoritative books is compared with the lists of Irenaeus and Origen, it is apparent that 25 or 30 years after Marcion proposed that the canon be limited to one gospel and probably ten letters of Paul, Irenaeus had taken a position on the canonical status of 20 books; his list was augmented but never altered—the four Gospels, the Acts of the Apostles, 13 letters of Paul (including 1 and 2 Timothy and Titus, omitted by Marcion), 1 John and 1 Peter. All of the later lists include these writings. About the other seven writings included in the New Testament as we know it (Hebrews, James, 2 and 3 John, 2 Peter, Jude and Revelation), opinions differed. As late as 325 C.E., when Eusebius drafted his list, no known list included all of them as canonical.

Irenaeus, in an earnest argument, contended that the gospels must number four. He noted a perfect correspondence between the four points of the compass, the four principal winds and the fourfold gospel intended for all the world. Further, in Revelation 4:7 John records four living creatures surrounding the throne of God. To Irenaeus, they correspond to attributes of the four gospels. The first is like a lion, corresponding to Mark (royal power); the second, a calf, to Luke (sacrificial and sacerdotal order); the third, with a human face, to Matthew (advent as a human being); and the fourth, an eagle, to John (gift of the Spirit).[8] On the basis of this symbolic cosmological argument, Irenaeus concluded that the gospel canon was complete, authentic and unalterable. Fanciful though these considerations may appear to modern readers, for Irenaeus they confirmed that the fourness of the gospels was sacred.

Before Irenaeus' spirited affirmation of the canonicity of the four gospels, some had argued that four gospels compromised the unity of the message. Marcion's proposal of a single gospel at least had the advantage of eliminating discrepancies and inconsistencies. Around 165, Tatian in Syria had produced the *Diatessaron* (literally "one through four"), a single composite gospel combining and harmonizing the texts of Matthew, Mark, Luke and John. The complete text of this innovative work has not survived, but it reveals another impulse, apart from Marcion's, to make unity a fact. The church rejected such impulses, however, and elected to understand the four gospels as four testimonies to a single gospel story, a single saving message.

When Eusebius drew up his list in 325 C.E., he relied on less fanciful criteria than Irenaeus had more than a century earlier. Eusebius noted whether writings had been mentioned by earlier generations of church leaders (a historical criterion), whether the style was consistent with the style of writings known to have been written early in the history of the church (a literary criterion) and whether the content was consistent with established orthodoxy (a doctrinal or theological criterion).

Interestingly, none of the canonical lists mentions inspiration as a criterion for determining which writings should be included in the canon. The reason, apparently, is that all Christians were filled with the spirit, so inspiration could not be used to distinguish canonical from extracanonical Christian writings. It is often noted that the one writing in the New Testament claiming to be

The Emergence of the New Testament
Shifting Canonical Lists from the Second to the Fourth Centuries

(The order of books in each list has been rearranged to simplify comparison.)

Marcion c. 140	Irenaeus** c. 180	Muratorian Canon c. 200	Eusebius c. 325	Athanasius 367 (canon of the Western church)
	Matthew	[Matthew	Matthew	Matthew
	Mark	Mark]†	Mark	Mark
Luke	Luke	Luke	Luke	Luke
	John	John	John	John
	Acts	Acts	Acts	Acts
Romans	Romans	Romans	Romans	Romans
1 Corinthians	1 Corinthians	1 Corinthians	1 Corinthians	1 Corinthians
2 Corinthians	2 Corinthians	2 Corinthians	2 Corinthians	2 Corinthians
Galatians	Galatians	Galatians	Galatians	Galatians
Ephesians*	Ephesians	Ephesians	Ephesians	Ephesians
Philippians	Philippians	Philippians	Philippians	Philippians
Colossians	Colossians	Colossians	Colossians	Colossians
1 Thessalonians	1 Thessalonians	1 Thessalonians	1 Thessalonians	1 Thessalonians
2 Thessalonians	2 Thessalonians	2 Thessalonians	2 Thessalonians	2 Thessalonians
	1 Timothy	1 Timothy	1 Timothy	1 Timothy
	2 Timothy	2 Timothy	2 Timothy	2 Timothy
	Titus	Titus	Titus	Titus
Philemon				Philemon
				Hebrews
	James (?)			James
	1 Peter		1 Peter	1 Peter
				2 Peter
	1 John	1 John	1 John	1 John
		2 John		2 John
				3 John
		Jude		Jude
	Revelation of John	Revelation of John	Revelation of John (?)	Revelation of John
	Shepherd of Hermas	Wisdom of Solomon		
		Revelation of Peter		

---

* Called Laodiceans by Marcion.

** Compiled from references in his writings.

† The first part of the list has not survived. The first writing listed, Luke, is called the third Gospel.

inspired is the Revelation of John, and this is the book that was most often disputed.

The next list after Eusebius' that survives from antiquity is the list of Athanasius, bishop of Alexandria, published in 367. He names the same 27 books that constitute the modern New Testament. Sometime in the years between Eusebius (325 C.E.) and Athanasius (367 C.E.), the New Testament canon assumed its present form.

What happened between the time of Eusebius and the time of Athanasius to account for the consensus? How did church leaders finally decide what to include and what to exclude? Unfortunately, our sources are mute on this issue. The Council of Nicea in 325 did not address the question, nor did Eusebius, Athanasius or any other writer of the period.

One event suggests an intriguing and plausible explanation. In 331, the Roman emperor Constantine sent a letter, the text of which has survived,[9] to Bishop Eusebius in Caesarea asking him to arrange for the production of 50 Bibles. The books were to be skillfully executed copies of "the divine scriptures" on fine parchment for use in the churches of the new capital of the empire, Constantinople. Constantine not only promised to pay all of the expenses incurred in this project, but he also provided two carriages to ensure the timely delivery of the completed Bibles for his personal inspection.

Eusebius was an advisor to and confidant of the emperor. He is widely regarded as the principal architect of the political philosophy of Constantine's reconstituted empire. A trusted ally of the emperor, who advocated and implemented the policies of the newly Christianized state, he knew that Constantine was concerned about the unity of the church and the unity of the state. He also knew that the Bibles prepared for the capital city would play an important role in unifying the church. The inclusiveness of Athanasius' canonical list in 367 has the look of political accommodation. It resolves disagreements between churches in the East and churches in the West about the canonical status of Hebrews and Revelation by including both. It therefore seems plausible to conjecture that the last seven books (Hebrews, James, 2 Peter, 2 and 3 John, Jude and Revelation) were added to the list not as a result of historical or theological argument but to satisfy needs of the state. In other words, for all practical purposes, the New Testament canon was settled when Constantine ordered the 50 Bibles. Their publication was palpable evidence of the unity of the church and symbolized the unity of the empire.

The fourth-century canon has been durable, but it has never been universally accepted. Among Eastern Orthodox churches, the diversity in evidence before Constantine continued. The Syrian church canon, for example, is the Peshitta, a Syriac version of the New Testament dating from the fifth century, which does not include 2 Peter, 2 and 3 John, Jude or Revelation.

Martin Luther, in the 16th century, thought James, Jude and Revelation unfit to be included among the canonical books. He placed Hebrews and these three books last in his translation of the New Testament because he doubted their claims to canonical status. The Gustavus Adolphus Bible (Stockholm, 1618), apparently a Swedish translation published during the reign of Gustavus Adolphus (1611-1632), and the Tyndale Bible (c.1525), compiled by William Tyndale, "the father of the English Bible," also placed these four books at the end, probably for similar reasons.

The Roman Catholic Church did not issue an authoritative statement about the contents of the Bible until 1546 when the Council of Trent, by a vote of 24 to 15 with 16 abstentions, declared the writings in Jerome's fourth-century Latin Vulgate version to be the official church canon. Although the New Testament canon is the same as the one used in Protestant churches, the Old Testament includes what Protestants refer to as Old Testament Apocrypha, a group of intertestamental books that were not included in the Protestant canon (or the Hebrew Bible).

In short, no single canon has ever been accepted by all Christians. In fact, the status of the New Testament canon today is similar to what it was in Eusebius' day—an issue on which there is both considerable consensus and continuing debate.

AFTERWORD

In his review of Ron Cameron's The Other Gospels: Non-Canonical Gospel Texts,[1] *Charles W. Hedrick sketches the history of the gospel tradition and summarizes the 16 earliest competitors to Mark, Matthew, Luke and John:*

The four canonical Gospels were not the only gospels produced by the church. The Book of Mark is generally regarded as the earliest narrative gospel (about 70 C.E.). But even Mark competed with an anonymous "sayings" collection written some years earlier. Both Mark and this early sayings collection were later used as sources by Matthew and Luke, who incorporated these earlier works into their gospels. Matthew and Luke, however, edited them to produce versions that were more acceptable and versatile than Mark's. For example, Matthew arranged large sections of material in six discourses of Jesus that were used as instructional handbooks. Thus, Matthew and Luke—the new editions of the early gospel tradition—are different in literary form and theological stance from their predecessors, although these differences seem minor compared to the strikingly different Gospel of John.

The fourfold canonical Gospel tradition—Matthew, Mark, Luke and John—came to dominate the church in the second and later centuries C.E. But these were not the only gospel texts produced in the early period of church literary activity. The evidence for other first-century C.E. gospels is meager but clear. Indeed, Luke tells his readers (1:1-4) that his work was preceded by the work of *many* others, whose narratives, he suggests, were somewhat deficient. Luke, unfortunately, did not give the names of his predecessors and early competitors. Nevertheless, some of these first-century texts have survived. We know the names of others from later sources, even though, unfortunately, the texts themselves have succumbed to the ravages of time or the censor's pen. Some of these were once cited as authoritatively as the four canonical Gospels were. Others were rejected and suppressed as spurious....

Many of the documents Cameron includes are called gospels, although they are often quite different from the Gospels of Matthew, Mark, Luke and John. In the early period before the canonical Gospels exerted a dominant influence over the life of the church, the term *gospel* was more fluid. Initially, it was used to describe a joyous oral announcement in both Christian and non-Christian contexts (see Mark 1:14, 10:29; Galatians 1:6-9). Indeed, the application of the term to the four canonical Gospels demonstrates that the word *gospel* did not imply a set literary form because the formal characteristics as well as the theological stances of the canonical Gospels are quite different from each other....

A brief description of the noncanonical gospels will give a general idea of their contents. The first clear reference to the Gospel of Thomas is a citation by Hippolytus, an early third-century Christian writer. Cameron dates the original composition of this gospel to the second half of the first century C.E. Only a few fragments from various Greek versions of Thomas have survived. A complete Coptic translation, however, was discovered in 1945 at Nag Hammadi in Upper Egypt. This Coptic translation included sayings of Jesus similar to sayings in the canonical Gospels. The Gospel of Thomas is based on a sayings tradition similar to, but independent of, the Synoptic Gospels. The complete Nag Hammadi corpus, a collection of heretical Christian literature, has been available in English only since 1977.

Another discovery from Nag Hammadi is *The Dialogue of the Savior*. Originally written in Greek, this document has survived in a single fragmentary Coptic text. It purports to be a dialogue between Jesus and his disciples, Judas, Matthew and Mariam, but is actually a collection of diverse sayings concerned mainly with eschatology, the end of the world. In the text, the salvation associated with the end times is interpreted paradoxically as a future event that is also available in the present. The dialogue source of the text dates from the second half of the first century and has parallels with the canonical Gospels and the Gospel of Thomas.

The *Gospel of the Egyptians*, not to be confused with the Nag Hammadi Gospel of the Egyptians, survives only in a few quotations by Clement of Alexandria, a Christian writer who lived at the end of the second century C.E. The text, which was popular among certain ascetic groups, is quoted by Clement, who used brief sections of it to refute his opponents. The composition of the document is dated by Cameron to the late first century or early second century. The text advocates extreme sexual asceticism as the means of overcoming the distinction between the sexes and returning to the original androgynous (male/female) state of the first man, Adam. The ideal human state is understood to be that of Adam, who was originally created as a being both male and female. Later, these principles were separated into Adam and Eve. This text rejects sexual intercourse as a correct way of regaining the original condition (compare, for example, 1 Corinthians 6:15-17). Only through asceticism can one regain the original androgynous state.

All that remains of the gospel known as Papyrus Oxyrhynchus 840 is one tiny parchment leaf discovered in 1905 in Oxyrhynchus, Egypt. The date of composition, according to Cameron, is the second half of the first century C.E. The text consists of a debate between Jesus and a Pharisee about Jewish purification rites. The controversy is similar to the debates in Mark 7:1-23. Cameron believes the narrative derives from an oral tradition rather than from the canonical Gospels.

Originally written in Greek, the Apocryphon of James survives in a single Coptic translation found in the Nag Hammadi library. The text is a dialogue between Jesus and his disciples Peter and James, in which the disciples ask short questions and Jesus replies with lengthy speeches. These speeches are, however, composed principally of discrete sayings, some of which appear in the New Testament. But none reflects a dependence upon the canonical Gospels.

Apparently, they came from an independent source. Indeed, it has been argued elsewhere that two of the parables in this text are genuine sayings of Jesus, although they are not known in the canonical Gospels. Cameron dates the composition of the text to the first half of the second century C.E.

Discovered as recently as 1958, the *Secret Gospel of Mark* appears as a fragmentary quotation in a hitherto unknown letter of Clement of Alexandria. The fragmentary quotation comes from an early edition of the Gospel of Mark used by the Carpocratians, a libertine Gnostic group known from the second century. The fragmentary quotation consists of a narrative account of Jesus raising a young man from the dead, an initiation rite and an encounter between Jesus and three women. The new material quoted from the *Secret Gospel of Mark* occurs between verses 10:34 and 35 and after 10:46a of canonical Mark. Cameron surmises that the original Mark, composed around 70 C.E., is no longer extant. Our canonical Mark appears to be an abridgment of *Secret Mark* and was composed around the beginning of the second century C.E.

Papyrus Egerton 2 is a gospel consisting of three fragmentary papyrus leaves of a Greek codex originally composed, according to Cameron, in the latter part of the first century C.E. It consists of sayings, controversy stories and miracles of Jesus. An examination of close parallels with John 5:39,45 and 9:29 leads Cameron to the conclusion that it is either the source of the narrative in John or an independent witness to that source. Papyrus Egerton 2 was discovered in Egypt in 1935.

The Gospel of Peter is a fragmentary Greek gospel text containing a passion narrative, an epiphany story, an empty tomb narrative and an introduction to a resurrection story. It was discovered in Upper Egypt in 1886 or 1887. The passion narrative is based on oral tradition; there is no evidence of dependence upon the canonical Gospels. Indeed, it is possible that this gospel antedates the four canonical Gospels and may have been a source for them. Cameron dates the composition of the Gospel of Peter to the second half of the first century C.E.

The Gospel of the Hebrews, known since the second century C.E., has been preserved in a few fragmentary quotations by Christian writers of the second century and later. This is a Jewish-Christian document narrating the pre-existence, birth, baptism and temptation of Jesus, some sayings, and an account of a resurrection appearance to James. The Gospel of the Hebrews does not appear to have been dependent on the canonical Gospels. Cameron dates its composition to the middle first to middle second centuries C.E.

"John's Preaching of the Gospel" is an independent piece of traditional gospel material in a text entitled the Acts of John. This part of the text, "John's Preaching of the Gospel," exists in a manuscript that was discovered in 1886, although part of it was also quoted by Augustine in the fifth century C.E. The oldest portion of the "Preaching" is a hymn that has parallels to the prologue of canonical John. The understanding of Jesus is docetic; that is, although

Jesus assumed human form, he was really pure spirit. Cameron dates the composition of this homiletic section of the Acts of John to the early second century.

The Gospel of the Nazareans is preserved in fragmentary quotations by certain early Christian writers and in the margins of certain medieval manuscripts. An expanded version of the canonical Gospel of Matthew, the Gospel of the Nazareans was known as early as 180 C.E. and is probably the gospel text used by a group of Jewish-Christians in western Syria. Although the text appears to have been a translation of the Gospel of Matthew into Syriac or Aramaic, it nevertheless introduces new sayings of Jesus.

The Gospel of the Ebionites (a group of early Jewish-Christians) is a gospel harmony of which only a few fragments are preserved in quotations by Epiphanius, a Christian writer of the fourth century C.E. The gospel has been known since the second century C.E. It begins with John the Baptist and apparently omits the birth and infancy narratives because the Ebionites did not believe in the virgin birth. Cameron dates the composition of the harmony to the middle of the second century C.E.

The Protoevangelium of James, known since the first half of the third century C.E. from the writings of Origen, survives in numerous Greek manuscripts dating from the tenth century C.E., although in 1958 a third-century Greek manuscript was discovered. The Protoevangelium of James is a composite document reflecting both oral material and written sources (that is, Matthew and Luke). From the oral tradition come legends of Mary's parents, her childhood and betrothal to Joseph, Joseph's previous marriage and the birth of Jesus. Cameron dates the composition of the text to the middle of the second century C.E.

The Infancy Gospel of Thomas is a collection of miracle stories performed by Jesus before he turned 12 years of age. The oldest manuscript dates from the sixth century C.E., but scholars usually identify the text with an unnamed writing quoted by Irenaeus at the end of the second century C.E. The sources used by the author of the text are the Gospel of Luke and oral tradition. These legendary miracle stories parallel similar accounts of other "divine men" in antiquity. Cameron dates the composition of the text to the middle to late second century C.E.

The *Epistula Apostolorum* purports to be a letter from the apostles to a group of "catholic" Christians and includes a revelation of Jesus that validates the catholic teaching. The letter speaks against Simon and Cerinthus, Christian Gnostics of the second century and opponents of the catholic position. Discovered in 1895, it survives in Ethiopic and also in Coptic, which is the oldest translation made from the Greek original. The discourse/dialogue style is developed out of creedal formulas, catechetical instruction and excerpts from dogmatic writings, all of which are employed in the service of emerging orthodoxy. Cameron dates the composition of the text to the middle to late second century C.E.

The *Acts of Pilate* has been known since the fourth century C.E. from the works of early church writers, and it survives in several medieval manuscripts dating from the 12th century C.E. It is an apologetic writing that introduces certain theological beliefs of an early Christian community in a narrative of Jesus' trial before Pilate, his crucifixion and burial, the empty tomb and a discussion of Jesus' resurrection by a Jewish council. The sources for the text are the Jewish Scriptures and the New Testament Gospels. Cameron dates the composition of the text to the middle second to third centuries C.E.
BAR *10:1 (1984), p. 14*

CHAPTER 11

Don't Let Pseudepigrapha Scare You

Hershel Shanks

One category of books rejected by both normative Judaism and Christianity is the Pseudepigrapha, that is, Bible-like writings attributed to "ancient figures who are not actually the authors." Hershel Shanks surveys James H. Charlesworth's monumental two-volume collection of Pseudepigrapha, describes them and explains why "you can't understand Christian origins unless you understand Old Testament Pseudepigrapha." Enoch, for example, is quoted in the New Testament and "reflects a number of conceptual similarities to early Christianity." Such similarities have led Charlesworth to argue that Christianity "did not evolve out of a dying mother, but out of a highly sophisticated and phenomenologically complex Jewish 'religion' and culture."–Ed.

You can't understand Christian origins unless you understand the Old Testament Pseudepigrapha. So says Professor James H. Charlesworth of Princeton Theological Seminary, and he is clearly riding the crest of modern scholarship.

Nobody understands the Old Testament Pseudepigrapha better than Charlesworth. He is, indeed, Mr. Pseudepigrapha—the editor of a massive two-volume collection of these documents published in 1983 and 1985 under the title *The Old Testament Pseudepigrapha*.[1] The reviewer for *Biblical Archaeology Review* called *The Old Testament Pseudepigrapha* a "classic" from the day it was published. Volume 1 was the winner of a 1984 Biblical Archaeology Society (BAS) publication award; volume 2 won special recognition from the judges for the 1986 BAS publication awards.

Nothing about the Pseudepigrapha is easy, however. Even defining the word can be tricky. According to Charlesworth, the definition given in the distinguished 1971 *Encyclopaedia Judaica* is "misleading and uninformed... anachronistic and distorted." I believe him.

Actually, the word *pseudepigrapha* is plural. The singular is *pseudepigraphon*. A pseudepigraphic work is a writing (an *epigraphon*) attributed to an ancient figure who is not actually the author (hence, *pseud-*)—such as Adam, Enoch, Moses, Abraham, Solomon, Elijah, Ezra, etc. The Old Testament Pseudepigrapha are Bible-like Jewish writings, mostly from about 250 B.C.E. to 200 C.E., that were not canonized in the Hebrew Scriptures. These writings are as varied in form as the books of the Bible. The Pseudepigrapha include apocalypses, prayers, psalms, visionary literature, oracles, apocalyptic (relating to God's final act in history sometime in the future) and eschatological (relating to the end of time, the *eschaton*) literature, wisdom literature, philosophy, testaments, odes and histories, to name just some of the overlapping categories. Charlesworth's collection of Old Testament Pseudepigrapha contains 52 documents (plus 13 works in the supplement of volume 2), some of which are only fragmentary.

Understanding Christian origins

With this new collection, the Old Testament Pseudepigrapha takes its place beside two other collections of ancient documents that are also critical for understanding the origins and early development of Christianity—the Dead Sea Scrolls and the Nag Hammadi Codices. (In English, *codex* refers to an early handmade book; in Latin, *codex* means book.)

The Nag Hammadi Codices are a collection of more than 50 treatises found by two Egyptian peasants in a pottery jar on the bank of the Nile in 1945 near the village of Nag Hammadi. The Nag Hammadi Codices in their present form date to the middle fourth century C.E., although of course they incorporate a great deal of older material.

The Nag Hammadi Codices differ from the collection of Old Testament Pseudepigrapha in several respects. For the most part, the Old Testament Pseudepigrapha date from 250 B.C.E. to 200 C.E. (although the extant copies are usually much later). On the whole, then, the Old Testament Pseudepigrapha are older than the Nag Hammadi Codices. The latter are chiefly important for the study of early church history and the development of early church doctrine, especially in Egypt. The Old Testament Pseudepigrapha are more pertinent to the study of Christian origins. Unlike the Nag Hammadi Codices, many of the Pseudepigrapha are contemporaneous with, or even earlier than, the documents in the New Testament.

The designation "Dead Sea Scrolls" refers to a large collection of scrolls and scroll fragments recovered since 1947 from 11 caves on the northwestern shore of the Dead Sea overlooking the Wadi Qumran. Because the community that hid the scrolls in the caves was destroyed by the Romans in 68 C.E., no scroll dates later than this. The earliest community (or sectarian) document in the collection dates to about 150 B.C.E.

Both the Dead Sea Scrolls and the Nag Hammadi Codices are narrower collections than the Old Testament Pseudepigrapha. The Nag Hammadi Codices are Christian documents committed to Gnostic beliefs that differed radically from what emerged as orthodox Christianity. (*Gnostic* refers to the beliefs and practices of a variety of religious groups that relied on secret knowledge revealed to a select few. *Gnosis* is the Greek word for this nonempirical insight.) The Dead Sea Scrolls reflect the commitments of a group of sectarian Jews, probably Essenes, who were violently opposed to the Jewish establishment that controlled the Jerusalem Temple. The Old Testament Pseudepigrapha, on the other hand, are mostly Jewish documents that must be taken to reflect widespread Jewish attitudes and beliefs inside and outside Palestine during Jesus' lifetime and the early development of Christian doctrine.

All of the Nag Hammadi Codices have been published—a superb accomplishment achieved under the direction of James M. Robinson at the Institute for Antiquity and Christianity and the Claremont Graduate School in Claremont, California.[2] By contrast, the failure to publish thousands of Dead Sea Scroll fragments is a major scholarly scandal that—we all hope—will soon be corrected.

In contrast to these two collections of documents, which were unknown before they were discovered in the 1940s and 1950s, the Old Testament Pseudepigrapha have long been known and consist of documents preserved in a variety of ways over the millennia.

Interest in Old Testament Pseudepigrapha before the 18th century arose almost exclusively from the mistaken belief that they *were* written by the biblical heroes to whom they were attributed. Scholars and intellectuals during the European Enlightenment in the 17th and 18th centuries, however, achieved a new appreciation of man's intellectual accomplishments in antiquity. In 1722 and 1723, J. A. Fabricius published the first major collection of Old Testament Pseudepigrapha, a two-volume collection of Jewish documents translated into Greek and Latin.

In the first half of the 19th century, after the defeat of Napoleon at Waterloo in 1815, large crates filled with ancient manuscripts and books were sent from the Middle East to the great European libraries. These crates contained a number of Old Testament Pseudepigrapha previously unknown in the West. One of the most sensational was the Book of Enoch,[3] which is actually quoted in the New Testament and which reflects a number of conceptual similarities to early Christianity.

In the early 20th century, two great collections of Pseudepigrapha were published—one in German in 1900 by C. Kautzsch and the other in English in 1913 by R. H. Charles. Until the Charlesworth collection of the 1980s, R. H. Charles' collection of 1913 was the standard English reference work on the subject.

Then came World War I and a period of neglect that lasted through World War II. The Pseudepigrapha were considered sectarian writings on the fringes of Jewish orthodoxy that ultimately evolved into normative rabbinic Judaism.

Just as the synagogue and the church rejected them from the canon, so too did the learned elite.

The search for the *biblical theology*

Encouraged by the discovery of the Dead Sea Scrolls and the Nag Hammadi Codices, scholars have rediscovered—or redirected their attention to—the Pseudepigrapha. Interest has been heightened by the fact that fragments of several pseudepigraphic works—Enoch, Jubilees, a version of the Testaments of the Twelve Patriarchs and Melkizedek—were found in the Dead Sea caves. These fragments can thus be confidently dated to before 68 C.E.

Professor Charlesworth contends there is another important reason for renewed interest in Old Testament Pseudepigrapha. It is what he calls the "Bankruptcy of Biblical Theology." The most influential exponent of the Biblical Theology School was the New Testament scholar Rudolf Bultmann, who contended that the proper subject of study for New Testament scholars was the *kerygma*, the redemptive message reflected in the New Testament texts, rather than the facts of history. Bultmann and his school focused on the theological understanding of early Christian communities, rather than the historical tools for understanding the text of the New Testament. After World War II, there was a shift away from this point of view; the search for *the* biblical theology proved unavailing.[4] At the same time, a number of prominent scholars suggested independently that the Gospels, if properly examined, could be understood as historical documents and that the pursuit of history is theologically legitimate. Once the idea that history in the Gospels is important has been accepted, it is a short step to affirming the importance of other sources of historical information that might shed light on the period when Jesus lived and Christian doctrine developed. Today, as Charlesworth says, "almost all biblical scholars recognize that a study of the New Testament must include the sources contemporaneous with it."

Interest in early Judaism in the post-World War II period was also renewed. The Jewish writings in the Pseudepigrapha represent the cherished traditions and beliefs of many early Jews.

An international team of scholars was ultimately convened to produce a new edition of the Old Testament Pseudepigrapha. The team of scholars included, as Charlesworth tells us, "white and black, male and female, Christian and Jewish, and even a Falasha. They are specialists who work in the United States, Canada, England, Scotland, Holland, Germany, Poland, Greece, Israel and Australia." Fifty-two scholars in all participated in the project, which culminated in the new English edition of the Old Testament Pseudepigrapha. At the same time, translations into other languages either have appeared or will appear—Danish, modern Greek, Italian, German, French, Spanish and Japanese.[5] In order to produce these new translations, scholars must master not only Hebrew, Aramaic and Greek, but also Coptic, Syriac, Latin, Ethiopic, Old Church

Slavonic and Armenian, because these are the languages in which the Pseudepigrapha have been preserved.

The new English edition of the Pseudepigrapha includes 52 documents, compared with 17 in Charles' edition of 1913. Moreover, even the documents previously translated in Charles' collection have now been adorned by more recent scholarship, and emendations in Charles' translations, which were made to clarify difficult passages, have been eliminated.

After completing his work on the Pseudepigrapha in 1985, Charlesworth published a short monograph "to assess the significance of the Old Testament Pseudepigrapha for a better understanding of Early Judaism, Christian origins and especially the writings of the New Testament."[6] Most of the material in this article comes from, or, more accurately, is lifted from, Charlesworth's monograph.

The juxtaposition of early Judaism and Christian origins makes it clear that Christian origins cannot be understood except in the context of early Judaism. As Charlesworth explains, "The origins of Christianity are inextricably rooted in Early Judaism." By early Judaism, Charlesworth means Judaism from about 300 B.C.E. to 200 C.E. Early Judaism "denotes the beginnings of synagogue (modern) Judaism," the transition from biblical Israelite society and religion to rabbinic Judaism.

Early Judaism and metaphysical speculations

Although Charlesworth is ultimately concerned with understanding Christian origins and early Christianity, he repeatedly emphasizes the need to study early Judaism for its own sake—on its own terms—and thus to study the Pseudepigrapha for their own sake and on their own terms. Charlesworth criticizes those who use the Pseudepigrapha "only to illustrate a theme, like the messianic kingdom and its banquet, a term, like the son of man, or a concept, like the belief in the bodily resurrection of the individual after death." He castigates those who treat the Pseudepigrapha as "writings not to be understood, but to be mined."

Early Jewish literature as reflected in the Old Testament Pseudepigrapha, he asserts:

> ...must be read thoroughly, sympathetically and reflectively before any attempt is made to compare [it] with so-called Christian documents....Any comparison between two very similar "religions"—such as Early Judaism and Early Christianity—must compare ideas, symbols and words in their full living context....[E]ach religion [Judaism and Christianity] must be understood holistically and compared as a whole with the other, also understood as a whole. Both religions must be treated in precisely the same way, with the same justice and empathy. Each is to be understood on its own terms.

This means that scholars studying Christian origins and early Christianity must intersect extensively with scholars studying early Judaism *per se*. Since the dramatic discovery and revelations of the Dead Sea Scrolls, interest in early Judaism has soared.

Lest it be thought that early Judaism—and therefore early Christianity—can be studied only on the basis of one collection, Charlesworth reminds us not only of collections like the New Testament, the vast rabbinic corpus, the Dead Sea Scrolls, the Nag Hammadi Codices, writings of the historian Josephus and the philosopher Philo, and the Pseudepigrapha, but also collections of documents from the pagan-Hellenistic world. Just as non-Jewish elements were significant in the development of early Judaism, they were also significant, both derivatively and directly, in the development of early Christianity. Both early Judaism and early Christianity were greatly influenced by foreign cultures.

The scholarly task has become impossibly burdensome. As Charlesworth concedes, "No scholar today can claim to be a master of more than one ancient collection." Indeed, Charlesworth questions if it is possible "really [to] digest all that is in the Pseudepigrapha." Thus are we prepared for the paradox: "Yet limiting oneself to one collection is a fatal flaw."

Having declared the impossibility of the undertaking, there is no alternative but to undertake the task. Naturally, Charlesworth emphasizes the Pseudepigrapha.

He concludes that early Judaism, especially as reflected in the Pseudepigrapha, was erudite and sophisticated, alive and full of highly developed metaphysical speculations and introspective perceptions into the psychological complexities of being human. "Early Judaism was characterized by amazing erudition and by brilliantly articulated and highly advanced concepts and perceptions."

Josephus, the first-century Jewish historian, described four different Jewish sects—Pharisees, Sadducees, Essenes and Zealots—which are sometimes thought to be the only Jewish groups of the time. The pseudepigraphic writings undercut this notion:

> Seeing Early Judaism through four sectarian windows is myopic and unperceptive. A sensitive investigation of Early Judaism leads to the discernment of other groups; we must include in our description (at least) also the Hasidim, the Hellenists, the Nazarenes, the Samaritans, the Boethusians, the Herodians, the Hemerobaptists, the Masbothei, the Galileans, the mystics, the apocalyptic groups, the baptist movements led by John the Baptist, and others, perhaps including Jesus of Nazareth at the beginning of his public ministry and the early followers of Jesus.

Early Jewish sects

Both Philo and Josephus tell us that the vast majority of Jews did not belong to any sect. And as Charlesworth notes, "Secular Jews probably did not write literature; they wrote legal and economic documents that almost always have not survived." Charlesworth concludes:

> I am convinced that our customary sectarian approach to Early Judaism
> is inappropriate, and that reference to four major sects is no longer
> adequate if we want to portray sensitively religion and daily life in
> Early Judaism.

The appreciation of the complexities in early Judaism has led to a "corresponding hesitation to attribute any early Jewish document to one of the four great sects." In Charlesworth's edition of the Pseudepigrapha, not a single document is assigned, for example, to the Pharisees—or to any other sect. As Charlesworth observes:

> We know far too little about the sects. The only sources for the Pharisees
> are the New Testament writings, Josephus, and a few paragraphs in the
> Mishnah; and certainly we all agree that these are tendentious and heavily edited. The Pharisees were far more latitudinarian than either our
> publications portray or the debates between Hillel and Shammai convey.
> A legalistically oriented Pharisee, for example, may have been closer in
> many ways to a Sadducee than to an apocalyptically-inspired fellow
> Pharisee. The Essenes likewise were subdivided into separate groups:
> some were celibate and monastic, others married and raised families.
> The Zealots, the last sect to appear of the popularly conceived "four
> sects," may have arisen only around 66 C.E. and they need to be
> distinguished from the brigands and the *sicarii*.

The more we appreciate the complexities of early Judaism, the more we are forced to understand that the idea of normative Judaism in this period must be abandoned; nor can we hope to find the "essence" of early Judaism because an essence "does not allow for the fundamental diversities in Early Judaism." It is impossible, Charlesworth says, "to extract from the extant documents a systematic theology of Early Judaism. The old portrait of a normative Judaism has been shattered by the vast amount of new literary evidence from Early Judaism, especially the documents gathered together in the *Old Testament Pseudepigrapha*." As Charlesworth succinctly explains:

> The concept of a normative Judaism result[ed] primarily from a tendency
> to read back into pre-70 Judaism [before the Roman destruction of
> Jerusalem in 70 C.E.] the "religion" found in much later, heavily edited
> rabbinic texts, and secondarily from the incorrect impression that Paul
> inaccurately portrayed a Judaism with a normative system. Most
> scholars have come to discard the concept of normative Judaism for
> pre-70 phenomena, but a few scholars linger on with this and other
> anachronistic models.[7]

We must be careful not to read post-70 circumstances (after the Roman destruction) back into the period of Christian origins.

> Far too often New Testament scholars have claimed to have painted an
> accurate picture of Early Judaism, when in fact they have read back into
> the period before 70 much of the tension and the distasteful anti-Jewish
> polemic that we have all, perhaps reluctantly, come to admit is characteristic of Paul's polemical utterances, and of the *Tendenzen* in Matthew

and John. If a New Testament scholar wishes to understand Early Judaism, he or she must listen sensitively to *all* of the extant literature.

Palestinian Christianity was never "primitive"

What does all this tell us about Christian origins? In the broadest sense, we must abandon a concept like "primitive Christianity," which has long been favored by scholars to describe early Palestinian Christianity. Charlesworth rejects the term because of what it implies:

> [Christianity] did not evolve out of a dying mother, but out of a highly sophisticated and phenomenologically complex Jewish "religion" and culture. Christianity was the heir of over a thousand years of traditions, both written and oral. Christianity arose in a cosmopolitan Jewish culture which was impregnated after the Exile repeatedly by influences from Babylon, Egypt, Persia, Syria, Greece, Parthia and Rome.

In short, from the beginning, Christian theology was highly sophisticated. It is not necessary to posit later development in the Hellenistic world outside Palestine.

> The first generation of Jews converted to "Christianity" was proficient in developed and sophisticated thoughts;...the earliest followers of Jesus, who were Jews, brought with them into the new Jewish movement that would be called "Christian" this sophistication. The greatest development of thought in Early Christianity would probably have occurred in Palestine and in the decades from 30 to 75 and not elsewhere from 75 to 150.
>
> Early Christian thought did not have to move outside Palestine to be significantly affected by Greek and Roman ideas.
>
> Christology did not evolve, with unexpected jumps and mutations, but it developed out of pregnant elements ready for maturation. Without undermining the obvious significant development of Christian thought and Christology from 30 to 150, in the 30s, and even during Jesus' public ministry, there were highly developed ideas. What was needed was not so much more development, as *transference* and *specification*. The transference to Jesus of many of the ideas already highly developed about the Lord God and his messengers; the specification of Jesus as the one-who-was-to-come; for example, as the Messiah, as the Son of God, and as the Son of Man.

After the Roman destruction of Jerusalem and the burning of the Temple in 70 C.E., Judaism moved in a new direction; Judaism as it emerged after 70 C.E. was very different from Judaism before the Roman destruction. In the post-70 period, rabbinic Judaism triumphed. But it is anachronistic to try to understand Christian origins in terms of rabbinic Judaism, even though New Testament documents written after 70 C.E. sometimes reflect a monolithic rabbinic Judaism that did not obtain at the time of Jesus.

In a recent study, Alan F. Segal of Columbia University emphasizes that two new religions emerged in the first century—Judaism and Christianity:

The time of Jesus marks the beginning of not one but two great religions of the West, Judaism and Christianity. According to conventional wisdom, the first century witnessed the beginning of only one religion, Christianity. Judaism is generally thought to have begun in the more distant past, at the time of Abraham, Moses, or even Ezra, who rebuilt the Temple destroyed by the Babylonians. Judaism underwent radical religious changes in response to important historical crises. But the greatest transformation, contemporary with Christianity, was rabbinic Judaism, which generally became the basis of the future Jewish religion.

So great is the contrast between previous Jewish religious systems and rabbinism that Judaism and Christianity can essentially claim a twin birth. It is a startling truth that the religions we know today as Judaism and Christianity were born at the same time and nurtured in the same environment.[8]

Early Judaism and apocalyptic speculations

When searching for Christian origins, we must be careful to look for them in pre-70 Judaism rather than post-70 rabbinic Judaism. The roots of rabbinic Judaism can also be found in pre-70 Judaism; the differences between what Charlesworth calls early Judaism (pre-70 Judaism) and rabbinic Judaism as it emerged after the Roman destruction of the Temple are profound. In the post-70 period, Judaism developed "into a more systematized, organized, so-called normative structure of Judaism."

"What is missing in the rabbinic writing and so pervasively characteristic in Early Judaism, is the thoroughgoing, categorically eschatological form and function of thought and life." In short, pre-70 Judaism, or early Judaism as Charlesworth calls it, was filled with apocalyptic speculations and apocalypticism of which there is relatively little evidence in later rabbinic literature but which is abundantly in evidence in the pre-70 literature—certainly for the Essenes in the Dead Sea Scrolls, but also for Judaism in general in the Pseudepigrapha.

As Charlesworth says, "The Pseudepigrapha open our eyes to a cosmos full of activity." The apocalypticism that pervades so many New Testament writings is also present in much contemporaneous Jewish literature.

An earlier generation of scholars considered Christian apocalypticism *sui generis* or, perhaps, related to Hellenistic religions outside of Palestine. Charlesworth muses: "How odd it is to be told [as a previous generation of scholars told us] that Early Christianity is so different from Early Judaism because the Christian doctrine cannot be extracted from it." We are just beginning to penetrate this relationship—especially since the discovery of the Dead Sea Scrolls and the renewal of interest in the Pseudepigrapha. "We are entering a new phase in research in Early Judaism and Christian Origins." The Christian inheritance from early Judaism is not only "rich," but also complex.

At the outset, we are faced with the problem of dating the Pseudepigrapha. Dating is not as great a problem with respect to the Dead Sea Scrolls because the community that preserved them was destroyed by the Romans in 68 C.E. This so-called *terminus post quem* is not available for the Pseudepigrapha. The extant manuscripts are all later—much later (except for fragments of Pseudepigrapha found among the Dead Sea Scrolls). And their compositional history is complex. Scholars are attempting to "get behind" the texts that have survived, to strip away the layers and establish by whom and when each Pseudepigraphon was written and then determine textual influences.

Dating each pseudepigraphic document must be done separately. Sometimes there is simply not enough evidence to date the original composition at all. Often it is difficult to determine if a document is of Jewish or Christian origin. Most early followers of Jesus were Jews, and labelling them Christians may be a distortion. Moreover, Jewish compositions may have been edited later and interpolations added from a Christian point of view. Yet on occasion, it may be possible to reconstruct, at least tentatively, the Jewish substratum of some documents.

Despite textual difficulties, scholars have been surprisingly successful in unscrambling the history of many pseudepigraphic works. Charlesworth lists eight works that are "clearly" pre-Christian Jewish documents and ten more that "probably" fit into this category. Another 14 compositions are later but contemporaneous with New Testament writings of the second century and should enhance our understanding of the background of these writings.

Pre-Christian Jewish documents

The three principal pre-Christian Jewish documents are 1 Enoch, some of the Testaments of the Twelve Patriarchs and Jubilees, which is the clearest case. Fragments from 14 different copies of Jubilees were found in the Dead Sea caves. Jubilees is free of Christian interpolations and redactions and was probably written shortly before 150 B.C.E., antedating the establishment of the Essene community at Qumran.

The case of 1 Enoch is more complicated. Fragments of this text were also found among the Dead Sea Scrolls. These fragments are clearly Jewish and pre-Christian, but they are only fragments. Because 1 Enoch is a composite document that may combine six separate works, including a lost Book of Noah, each part of the work must be assessed separately. Nevertheless, Charlesworth tells us:

> The results of labours by scholars throughout the world have moved us far away from a level of exasperation or frustration when working with 1 Enoch....It is now clear that specialists on 1 Enoch at present affirm not only its Jewish character but also its pre-Christian, or pre-70 date; and that judgment pertains to all segments of this composite work.

There is more debate about the Testaments of the Twelve Patriarchs. In its present and final form, it is a Christian document. Nevertheless, according to Charlesworth, it is "not a *Christian composition* but a *Christian redaction* of earlier Jewish testaments." Indeed, fragments of the Testament of Levi and the Testament of Naphtali *in Hebrew* were found in the Dead Sea caves, confirming that at least these two of the twelve are Jewish and pre-Christian. (Charlesworth complains that the editor who was assigned publication rights to these fragments, J. T. Milik, has not published them, so the texts themselves are not yet available to scholars.) Charlesworth concludes:

> I have no qualms about stating boldly that it is highly probable that behind each one of the twelve testaments in the Testaments of the Twelve Patriarchs there is a Jewish substratum which can be reconstructed tentatively once the clearly Christian redactions and interpolations have been identified.

Thus, pseudepigraphic documents like these can be helpful for reconstructing Christian origins and the history of early Christianity. This is especially important because only two collections of ancient Jewish documents are quoted in the New Testament—the Old Testament and the Old Testament Pseudepigrapha.

We may close with two examples of how pseudepigraphic writings are used in New Testament research. The letter of Jude is one of the so-called general epistles of the New Testament, epistles not addressed to a particular Christian community. The author of this epistle challenges the reader to strive for true faith and inveighs against the inroads of heretics who "set up divisions"—perhaps a reference to an early Gnostic sect—and here, in verses 14-15, the author quotes from the Book of Enoch to show that these things had been prophesied.

Enoch for a Christian audience

We can confirm that Jude quotes from Enoch by consulting a late Ethiopic version of Enoch. Moreover, we can be confident that this part of Enoch is Jewish and pre-Christian because a fragment of this very passage, in Aramaic, not Ethiopic, was found in the Dead Sea caves; and the handwriting of this fragment allows us to date it to the first century B.C.E.

In Jude's quotes, however, there are significant changes in the text. Jude alters the text of Enoch so that the prophecy of the coming of the Lord—which Jude takes to be a prophecy of the coming of Jesus—*has been fulfilled*, rather than, as it appears in Enoch, *will be fulfilled*. According to Jude, Enoch prophesied: "Behold *the Lord came* with his holy myriads, to execute judgments against all." But in fact, Enoch prophesied: "Behold *he will arrive* with the myriads of the holy ones to execute judgment upon all." As Charlesworth says, "For Jude, Christ came and accomplished his task; in the light of this he will return, as Enoch had prophesied about God." Jude freely alters the original text within what were considered acceptable bounds to prove his point.

Moreover, not only does Jude change the future tense in Enoch to the past tense,[9] but he also uses *Lord* (*Kurios*) instead of *he*. Thus, Jude "has made a decidedly Christian adaptation of 1 Enoch." By changing *he* to *Lord* (*Kurios*),

Jude may be applying a prophecy of the eschatological coming of God to Christ's first coming, as well as to the Parousia, his anticipated imminent second coming. In addition, Jude refers to *his* holy ones, where Enoch actually says *the* holy ones.

Comparing the Texts

The following chart contains three columns. The first column is the text of a fragment from 1 Enoch found in the Dead Sea caves. Although it is just a scrap with fewer than ten complete words, it is enough to show that this text is the same as the passage in a much later document of 1 Enoch, shown in the second column. The Dead Sea cave fragment is in Aramaic; the later document is in Ethiopic. Thus, the Dead Sea cave fragment demonstrates that the later Ethiopic document preserves a pre-Christian Jewish text. This may be compared with the text of Enoch as quoted in the New Testament Letter of Jude (verses 14-15), which is shown in the third column. Notice that in the original Enoch, the text reads that the Lord "*will arrive.*" As quoted in Jude, the passage is taken to refer to the Christ, "the Lord *came.*" Moreover, in Jude the "holy myriads" supposedly referred to in Enoch are "his" (Christ's), a possessive not found in the original Enoch. According to Professor Charlesworth, these changes were made for Christological purposes—"Christ is the Lord."

Aramaic Enoch from Dead Sea Cave	Ethiopic Enoch 1:9	Jude 14-15
		And Enoch prophesied about these things seven generations after Adam, saying:
	Behold, he *will arrive*	"Behold (the) Lord [*Kurios*] came
[with the myri]ads of the holy one[s],	with the myriads of the holy ones	with his holy myriads,
[...]	in order to execute	to execute
[...]	judgment upon all.	judgment against all,
[...]	He will destroy the wicked ones	and to convict
[all f]lesh, regarding	and censure all flesh on account of everything	all the ungodly ones of all their
the works [of...]	that they have done,	ungodly deeds which
[...]	that which the sinners	they did godlessly,
[...all] the boastful and hard [things...]	and the	and of all the hard things which
	wicked ones	the ungodly sinners
[...]	committed	spoke
[...]	against him.	against him."

In short, Christ possesses the holy legions; they are *his*. Charlesworth tells us:

> As most interpolations are alterations by Christians of Early Jewish writings, the alteration is caused by Christology. He—that is Christ—is "the Lord"....In most cases, as in Jude 14-15, the alteration of an earlier Jewish quotation is precisely because of the belief in the advent of the one-who-was-to-come. The commitment to Jesus as the Christ, the Messiah, shifted inherited parallel verbs and nouns according to the light shown upon the text, altering these traditions like light passing through a prism.

Thus we see how early Jewish theology was transformed into Christology.

One more point should be noted. Jude calls this passage from Enoch a prophecy. Hence, "it is certain the author of Jude considered the document [Enoch] inspired." Charlesworth wonders: "How can Christians discard as insignificant, or apocryphal, a document that is clearly pre-Christian, Jewish, and quoted as prophecy by an author [Jude] who has been canonized?"[10]

The example we have just considered is precise and detailed. The second, and last, example is more general and specifies, in one respect, the growing recognition of the Jewish background of some terms that took on significant Christological meanings for early Christian communities. The most prominent of these is the title *Son of Man*, which the early church accorded Jesus (e.g., Mark 8:27; Matthew 16:17 et al.). The term is frequently used in the Old Testament but without the messianic implications in the New Testament, except, most notably, in Daniel. To understand when and why the "son of man" took on Christological connotations, we must look not only to Daniel, but also to Enoch. It is now accepted that the phrase as it appears in 1 Enoch is not an emendation but is part of the original composition. The phrase there refers to a celestial figure. Moreover, as Charlesworth says, it is clear in the text that Enoch himself is said to be the Son of Man.

Just how Enoch influenced the early followers of Jesus is not yet clear, but it seems likely that it did. One scholar, George Nicklesburg, has suggested that Luke may have been personally acquainted with the man who translated Enoch into Greek; indeed, so close are some of the parallels that Luke himself may have translated Enoch into Greek. In ways such as these Pseudepigrapha make their impress felt, and modern scholars ignore them at their peril.

A F T E R W O R D

When the first volume of Charlesworth's The Old Testament Pseudepigrapha[1]
appeared, Jacob Neusner wrote this appreciation:

The publication of this book constitutes the single most important event in the
last year (and, I suspect, in the last decade) in the study of the Hebrew Scriptures
and ancient Judaism. This magnificent volume should take its place, on the day
it is published, on the shelf of every person interested in the Hebrew Scriptures
(Old Testament). It replaces a classic of biblical studies, R. H. Charles'
The Apocrypha and Pseudepigrapha of the Old Testament in English,[2] and today
becomes a classic itself.

What has Charlesworth wrought? Why is it important? Let us begin by identifying the kind of ancient writings collected here. Jews in ancient times wrote
many holy books; only a few attained sufficient status to be included in the
canon of scripture. Many other writings, although claiming divine inspiration,
were not canonized. These noncanonical, or pseudepigraphic, writings were
preserved either by accident (for example, in the dry sands of the desert) or
by choice (for example, in the diverse churches of early Christianity). Not
until the early 18th century did scholars, beginning with Johannes Fabricius,
collect and identify these writings and study them in connection with
the Bible.

When R. H. Charles published the great collection I referred to above, he
selected from a vast and scattered literature.

In this new volume of Pseudepigrapha, Charlesworth and his coworkers
have improved upon the past in two significant ways. First, they collected,
translated and annotated a great many more documents than Charles did.
Second, and more important, Charlesworth and his colleagues take these writings seriously on their own terms. This is in marked contrast to earlier scholars who were interested in pseudepigraphic writings only because they might
illuminate the life and times of Jesus; for these scholars, the Pseudepigrapha
were simply part of the Jewish background of what really mattered.

Charlesworth and his colleagues thus present a vast repertoire of ancient
Jewish writings—much as the Dead Sea Scrolls have done—in order to illuminate that world for its own sake. A truly liberal spirit animates the excellent
scholars who translated the ancient works in this collection. Most of the specialists who worked on the project are, in fact, believing Christians; it is with
no small measure of pride that we observe that ours is an age in which
Christianity allows ancient Judaism to come to center stage and speak in its
own terms and through its own writings. In the future, I hope, faithful Jews
will study the earliest phases of Christianity with equal liberality of spirit and
equal respect for the spiritual treasures of others.

A pseudepigraphic work is a writing attributed by the author to some other
person—hence the prefix *pseud-.* In the writings in this collection, from whom

do we hear? No lesser personalities than Enoch, Shem, Ezekiel, Zephaniah, Ezra (many times!), Baruch, Abraham, Elijah, Daniel, the Twelve Patriarchs, Moses, Solomon and even Adam. This is a catalogue of the great figures in ancient Israelite life who made deep impressions on the imaginations of later writers. The later writers speak in the name of past heroes. We ourselves sometimes compose this way in our minds: "What would I say in such and such a situation if I were George Washington?"

In ancient times, imaginative fiction was not considered a significant literary genre. People believed that God governed human affairs (Israel's in particular), and they therefore wanted messages from God to be delivered by figures worthy of receiving and handing on divine messages. Hence we hear not from a second-century B.C.E. writer himself but from Adam of Eden, Moses of Sinai, Ezra of the restoration and equivalent prophets and holy men. (None of the writers or the people through whom they speak is female.)

The writings in this collection were composed from about the second century B.C.E. to the seventh century C.E. Most are dated by the translators to between the second century B.C.E. and the second century C.E., but the dates are difficult to fix exactly. Some are dated simply "prior to ninth century C.E." or similar vague notations. No one is to blame. The evidence is what it is.

Charlesworth has brought together nearly 30 documents, some of them brief, most of them quite long. The collection is divided into two parts according to literary genre. The first part is called "apocalyptic literature and related works," the second, "testaments (often with apocalyptic sections)." Each entry introduces an ancient document with an introduction, a synopsis—that is, a narrative and a description of the main ideas. We are told about the text, the original language, the date and point of origin, historical significance, theological significance, relation to canonical books, relation to apocryphal books and cultural significance. Each introduction is followed by a fully annotated translation. Each document is outlined in subheads, so that we have something clearer than long columns of undifferentiated type (such as we find in most translations of the rabbinic classics, for example). At the end of the volume is a select bibliography, including texts, translations and other studies. The annotations provide divergent readings or possibilities other than the ones in the text. Down the side run parallel references, so that we can study the text at hand with all possible cross-references. ***BAR** 10:1 (1984), p. 48*

PART II

Transmission of Biblical Texts

Introduction

After the sacred texts were composed, they were copied by hand and circulated. Although the original autographs had long since worn out, copies of these sought after documents were in turn copied and circulated, first separately, then in small collections, and finally in the single book called the Bible. If a copy differed from the original exemplar (because a scribe made an error or updated the language or expanded a passage), the changes were copied as well. Thus text "families" arose. As time passed, some, then all, of the biblical books were translated, creating "versions" of different text families in Aramaic, Greek, Latin and other languages. On several occasions, the texts were systematically reviewed and revised to establish definitive editions, or "recensions." The process of copying and translating would then start with the new branch of the tradition. Thousands of manuscripts, many discovered in the last half century near the Dead Sea and Nag Hammadi in Egypt, tell the story of how the texts were transmitted.

The generally accepted form of the Hebrew Bible is called the Masoretic text, a label derived from the Hebrew verb meaning "to hand over" or "to transmit." The term reflects the belief that this text was handed down from generation to generation in uncorrupted form. Printed Hebrew Bibles follow Masoretic manuscripts dating from the tenth and eleventh centuries C.E. Although produced a thousand years after the canon was closed, the best of these manuscripts, like the Aleppo Codex and others by the Ben Asher school of Tiberias, were produced by scribes who inherited a rigorous *masorah* (tradition) for preserving the written form and oral recitation of the text—rules for spelling, punctuation, layout, phrasing, intonation and liturgical chanting.

The Masoretic text differs in many places from corresponding passages in ancient "witnesses" such as the Greek Septuagint, Syriac Peshitta and Samaritan Pentateuch, and from quotations in the New Testament. Sometimes "witnesses" agree with each other, and sometimes they do not; for instance, the Samaritan Pentateuch, as preserved in the Abisha Scroll, shares some 2,000 variant readings with the Septuagint but also exhibits unique revisions, such as a long, eclectic tenth commandment. Each witness has a separate transmission history, of course, and differences have been variously explained as polemical alterations, scribal errors and recensions.

Because manuscripts, by definition, are written by hand, variations can be introduced in a number of ways. For example, a scribe may omit letters, words or phrases if his eye jumps from the word he is copying to a similar word, letter or phrase later in the passage. The Septuagint text of 1 Samuel 14:41 reads:

> Saul said to the Lord, God of Israel, "Why have you not responded to your servant today? If the iniquity was due to my son Jonathan or to me, Lord, God of Israel, let the lot show Urim; and if you say it was due to your people Israel, let it show Thummim."

In the Hebrew text, however, everything between the first and last occurrence of the word *Israel* is missing: "Saul said to the Lord, God of Israel, 'Let it show Thummim.'"

In the other direction, a scribe may add material by slipping backward and repeating letters or words he has already copied. This may have happened in Matthew 27:17, for example, where the name of the prisoner who is released is given in some manuscripts as Jesus Barabbas. Or the copyist may transpose the order—the farewell at the end of Romans 16 appears in various manuscripts after verses 20, 23 and 27. When texts were read aloud to several copyists working side by side, words could be misheard or homonyms confused; the alternate readings of Romans 5:1—"we are at peace" and "let us have peace"—may have been caused by the similar pronunciation of these Greek verbs. And the difference between "so that you might have a double pleasure" and "so that you might have a double favor" in 2 Corinthians 1:15 is the difference between the Greek words *chara* and *charis*.

When a copyist corrects or clarifies the text, variations may be deliberately introduced. For example, in Midrash Tanḥuma and Midrash Rabbah, the idea of *tikkun soferim*, the "scribal emendation" of phrases, which might otherwise have been interpreted in disrespectful or misleading ways, is discussed. For example, the Midrash on Genesis 18:22 notes that the clause "Abraham stood before the Lord" should logically have been "the Lord stood before Abraham," but this would have implied that God was serving Abraham. And in Ezekiel 8:17, God's complaint that "they have thrust the branch to my nose"—which the rabbis interpreted as an obscene gesture—was changed to "their noses." And in 1 Kings 21:10,13 and Job 1:5,11, the euphemism "bless God" is written instead of the unacceptable "curse God."

In the Talmud (Soferim 1.8), differences between the Masoretic text and the Septuagint are also attributed to well intentioned scribes who emended the latter text. In Greek, the first verse of Genesis reads "God created in the beginning" instead of following the Hebrew literally, "In-the-beginning created God," so that "In-the-beginning" would not be mistaken for the creator of God. The hare is omitted from the list of unclean animals in Leviticus 11:6 so as not to offend a member of the Ptolemaic court whose name meant "hare." And so on.

Among New Testament manuscripts, a copy of John from about the year 200 already shows words crossed out and replaced. In some manuscripts, the first part of the quotation in Mark 1:2-3—"Behold, I am sending my messenger before you, and he will prepare your way"—is identified as coming from Malachi, although in the canonical text the entire passage is ascribed to Isaiah. And Christian scribes sometimes harmonized parallel stories or "corrected" passages from the Hebrew Bible to coincide with the quoted form in the New Testament. Sometimes a scribe even inserted his own comments, as in Romans 16:21-22, where Tertius—"who took down this letter"—added his greeting to the greetings of Paul, Timothy, Lucius, Jason and Sosipater.

It has been suggested that, unlike the Qumran sectarians, whose huge library attests to a literary ethos, early Palestinian Christians stressed face-to-face preaching because of the urgency of their message that the second coming and new age were at hand. Only after the generation that had known Jesus passed from the scene and the gospel was carried to distant lands did writing become important, although the written word did not immediately replace the oral tradition. Perhaps because writing was used to validate or explain doctrines that already existed rather than as the source of doctrine, sacred texts were fluid, and writers treated them in ways that we might now consider fast and loose.

Even in Marcion's canon (second century), which was limited to Luke and some Pauline epistles, the texts were purged of all traces of Jewish belief, perhaps because Marcion believed these ideas had been inserted by polemicists in the first place. For example, the marriage allegory in Ephesians 5:21-33 comparing Christ and the Church to husband and wife ends with "For this reason a man shall leave/ his father and mother/ and be joined to his wife,/ and the two shall become one" (Genesis 2:24). But Marcion, who had no use for the Hebrew Bible, converted the allegory into a defense of celibacy: "For the sake of the church, a man shall leave his father and mother, and the two shall be one flesh."

There are, then, many reasons for textual variations. But just identifying differences in a group of manuscripts does not tell us if the variations are scribal errors, corrections, additions or deletions. Scholars who subscribe to one school of textual criticism are now trying to peel away the layers of change and recover the original text of the Bible, a text sometimes thought of as the *ur*-text, the true original, or, as C. A. Briggs called it, "the real Bible." Until the middle of the 20th century, this approach to the Hebrew text was mostly based on hypothetical reconstructions from late manuscripts and ancient witnesses.

As is evident from *Understanding the Dead Sea Scrolls*[1] and other recent studies, however, new material from the Dead Sea Scrolls dramatically challenged the previous view of standardization and transmission. For example, in a controversial theory, opposed by James A. Sanders in *The Dead Sea Scrolls: After Forty Years*,[2] Frank Moore Cross proposes that there were three Old Testament text types—Egyptian, Palestinian and Babylonian. Based on the differences between two groups of manuscripts, Cross places adoption of the Babylonian type as the standard between the middle of the first and the middle of the second centuries C.E.

Cross and others argue that the Qumran texts necessitate reformulating our ideas about the development of biblical religion, especially relations among Pharisaic, Sadducean, Essenian and rabbinic Judaism, and between Christianity and Judaism. In addition, until the discovery of the Dead Sea Scrolls, readings in the ancient witnesses that differed from the Masoretic text were ascribed to errors in translation or later transmission. The Qumran library, however, includes Hebrew texts that sometimes share these differences, thereby proving to some scholars the antiquity, if not authenticity, of these readings.

In his article, Marc Brettler warns that not all ancient manuscripts are necessarily better than recent copies of Masoretic manuscripts. Because transmission of the Masoretic text was done very carefully, the biblical texts of the Ben Asher school still retain their importance. And Alan D. Crown believes that, in some places, the Samaritan Pentateuch preserves a text that dates between the third century B.C.E. and the first century C.E., but he suspects that it has been tampered with.

Textual historians of another school try to discover which texts existed at various stages of evolution and how they were understood by the faith communities of the time. After all, these scholars observe, numerous religious, philosophical and literary works were written—and have disappeared. In Numbers 21:14-15, there is a quote from the now lost Book of the Wars of the Lord. And the text of 1 and 2 Kings repeatedly refers the reader to the royal chronicles of Judah and Israel. In Ephesians 5:14, Paul quotes a couplet he assumes his audience will recognize, but we can no longer identify it.

We have biblical texts because various religious communities valued, copied and preserved them. Why these particular texts? New manuscript discoveries may provide the answers. A twofold question that has long puzzled Bible scholars is why there are four Gospels, and why these four. Ancient authors mention many other narratives about Jesus, some of them also called "gospels." What set the four canonical Gospels above the others? What function did they serve that the others did not?

Like the Dead Sea Scrolls, the manuscripts found in 1945 at Nag Hammadi suggest new theories. In *The Gnostic Gospels*,[3] Elaine Pagels theorizes that the Nag Hammadi documents were rejected by emerging orthodox Christianity because they favored spiritual, instead of bodily, resurrection; personal mystical experiences, Pagels argues, undermined the centralized authority of the church.

Moreover, Gnosticism, like Marcion's theology, was based on a dualistic idea. Gnostics distinguished God the Creator from God the Father of Jesus, and, as is reflected in the Qumran documents, they saw the world as a battleground of light against darkness. In contrast, such language does not figure prominently in the Pauline letters. In this respect, 2 Corinthians 6:14-18 seems to be an out-of-context insertion of just such dualistic language:

> ...what has righteousness to do with wickedness?
> Or what fellowship has light with darkness?
> What accord has Christ with Belial?
> Or what has a believer in common with an unbeliever...

Perhaps further study of the Nag Hammadi documents and the Dead Sea Scrolls will provide clues as to who wrote them and when and why they were hidden.

Scholars revel in the arcana of manuscript studies, but these discoveries do not usually touch the average person until they influence translations. The Vulgate—the Latin version of the Bible by the fourth-century church father Jerome—was until recently the primary biblical text of Catholicism. In his pioneering modern English version published in 1945-1949, Ronald Knox translated Jerome's Vulgate translation. The New Jerusalem Bible (1986), on the other hand, incorporates the findings of the latest Hebrew and Greek scholarship.

The New Jewish Publication Society translation claims simply to follow the traditional Masoretic text. The New English Bible, however, incorporates so many readings from the Septuagint, Dead Sea Scrolls and other witnesses that a separate companion booklet was issued, *The Hebrew Text of the Old Testament: The Readings Adopted by the Translators of the New English Bible.*[4] And, although the editors state in the introduction to the New English Bible that variations in New Testament manuscripts rarely make an "appreciable difference to the meaning so far as it could be represented in translation," the translators also created an eclectic text, which was later published as *The Greek New Testament.*[5]

In *Early Manuscripts and Modern Translations of the New Testament,*[6] Philip W. Comfort describes changes to the New English Bible as well as the influence of Greek papyri discovered in the 20th century on the Revised Standard Version, Today's English Bible, the New American Standard Version, the New International Version and the New Jerusalem Bible.

Evolution of the Text

The study of how the Bible was transmitted from the past to the present involves determining how the text evolved and identifying the characteristics of various manuscripts. Until recently, the evolution of the Hebrew text was deduced by comparing late manuscripts of the Masoretic text to "witnesses" like the Samaritan Pentateuch, the Greek Septuagint, the Aramaic Targums and other ancient translations. But two almost undreamed of discoveries in the middle of the 20th century radically changed the situation. Among the Dead Sea Scrolls were manuscripts of the Hebrew Bible a thousand years older than the manuscripts previously available to scholars. And the Nag Hammadi Codices provided textual evidence of the struggle between emerging Christian orthodoxy and competing heresies.

CHAPTER 12

The Text behind the Text of the Hebrew Bible

Frank Moore Cross

*Frank Moore Cross explains how the Dead Sea Scrolls illuminate the early trans-
mission of biblical books, the fixation of the text and the procedure by which the canon
was established–in other words, "what the biblical materials were like before they
became 'biblical.'" He contends that differences between two groups of Dead Sea
Scrolls allow us to date and understand why the Hebrew Bible was standardized.
The Qumran manuscripts vary significantly from the Masoretic text, whereas variations in a second group of manuscripts from Wadi Murabba'at, Nahal Hever and
Masada are minor. Cross concludes that the Qumran texts, which date from about
250 B.C.E. to 68 C.E., were written at a time when different versions of biblical books
were still widely circulated; however, by the second century C.E., when most of the manuscripts in the second group were written, standardized texts had been adopted.*

*Cross believes that Palestinian, Babylonian and Egyptian text types also exist-
ed but that when an independent Judean state was established under the
Hasmoneans, a "fixed, authoritative text" to mediate between competing parties
debating doctrine and law became a necessity. Hillel and his followers, who represented the "intellectual influence of the powerful Babylonian community," established a "conservative, often pristine" Pentateuch, rejecting even the paleo-Hebrew
script used by the ruling priests for Temple inscriptions and coins. Unlike other
ancients, such as the Greek scholars who worked on Homer, the rabbis did not choose
eclectically from many texts or combine variant readings; they selected a single
textual tradition.–Ed.*

Almost 40 years have passed since the fateful spring day in 1947 when a
young Bedouin shepherd threw a stone into a cave in a cliff on the northwestern shore of the Dead Sea and heard the sound of pottery shattering
inside. When he and a companion later summoned the nerve to crawl into the
cave (now known as Qumran Cave 1), they found seven decaying leather rolls.

These were the original "Dead Sea Scrolls." William Foxwell Albright, the most distinguished Near Eastern archaeologist and Hebrew epigraphist of his generation, immediately hailed the finds as the greatest manuscript discovery of modern times.

In the ensuing years, both archaeologists and Bedouin have explored hundreds of caves in the great wadis that, like the Wadi Qumran, cut through the towering cliffs that mark the Jordan Rift. In the competition between clandestine Bedouin diggers and archaeologists, the laurels have most often gone to the intrepid and patient shepherds. In any case, leather and papyrus manuscripts were eventually found in ten more caves in the vicinity of Khirbet Qumran, the ruins of a community of Essenes—Jewish sectaries—to whose library the documents once belonged. So we now have manuscripts from Qumran caves numbered 1 through 11. From Cave 11 came the great Temple Scroll acquired by the late Yigael Yadin in 1967.[1]

More manuscripts and papyri were discovered in large caves in the wadis south of Qumran—the Wadi Murabba'at, the Naḥal Ḥever and the Naḥal Ṣe'elim. In 1962, the oldest documents from the Jordan Rift were found in the Wadi ed-Daliyeh, north of Jericho. These are the Samaria legal papyri from the fourth century B.C.E.[2] In 1963-1964, Yadin uncovered manuscripts in excavations of the ruins of Herod's fortress at Masada, a diamond-shaped mountain overlooking the Dead Sea.

Any *one* of these finds would have been regarded as nothing short of sensational. Together, they have been overwhelming—in two senses. First, the magnitude of these discoveries can hardly be comprehended. Second, the labor of piecing together hundreds of thousands of fragments, along with editing, interpreting and assimilating the manuscripts, have often overwhelmed the scholarly community, whose responsibility is both glorious and oppressive.

Nearly 40 years of discovery and research have now passed. I suspect that another 40 years will pass before the first exploratory investigation of these "treasures of darkness" will be completed. Almost every year a large new volume of unpublished material comes into print, and this will continue for many years to come. I am myself in the process of completing three volumes of unpublished manuscripts and papyri. The impact of these discoveries and of this research will be enormous.

I should like to explore here several important areas of historical study from which new insights and conclusions are emerging. First, I shall discuss the bearing of new studies upon our understanding of the history of the biblical text. From the Dead Sea Scrolls, we have learned a great deal about the early transmission of biblical books, the fixation of the texts of biblical books, and even the procedure by which the canon of the Hebrew Bible came into being. In short, we now know in some detail what the biblical materials were like before they became "biblical," as well as the process by which the texts were fixed and chosen as "biblical."

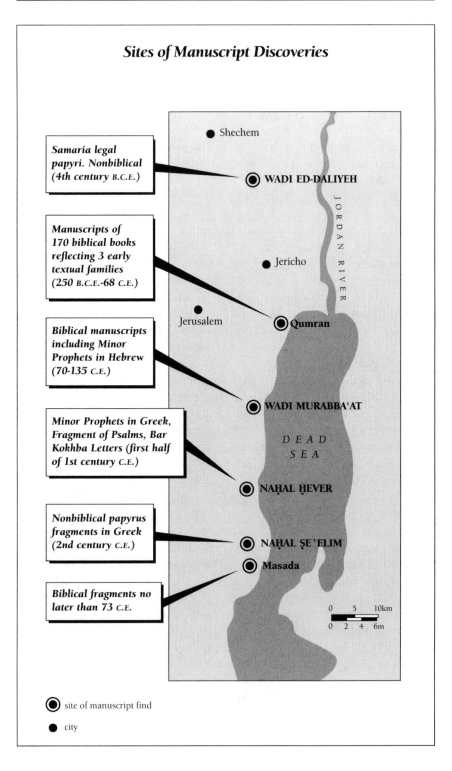

Sites of Manuscript Discoveries

Samaria legal papyri. Nonbiblical (4th century B.C.E.)

Manuscripts of 170 biblical books reflecting 3 early textual families (250 B.C.E.-68 C.E.)

Biblical manuscripts including Minor Prophets in Hebrew (70-135 C.E.)

Minor Prophets in Greek, Fragment of Psalms, Bar Kokhba Letters (first half of 1st century C.E.)

Nonbiblical papyrus fragments in Greek (2nd century C.E.)

Biblical fragments no later than 73 C.E.

Shechem

WADI ED-DALIYEH

JORDAN RIVER

Jericho

Jerusalem

Qumran

WADI MURABBA'AT

DEAD SEA

NAHAL HEVER

NAHAL ŞE'ELIM

Masada

0   5   10km

0   2   4   6m

⊙ site of manuscript find

● city

To place the new evidence in context, it will be useful to review briefly the status of the study of the textual history of the Hebrew Bible prior to the discovery of the manuscripts on the shore of the Dead Sea.

The Bible survives in many Hebrew manuscripts and in several ancient versions translated from the Hebrew. In medieval Hebrew manuscripts, there are hundreds, even thousands of variations, most of them minor, a few major. In the old versions, especially in the Old Greek version (which was written beginning in the third century B.C.E. and is commonly called the Septuagint), there are thousands of major and minor variations. Even before the discovery of biblical manuscripts in the caves of Qumran and elsewhere in the Jordan Rift, these manuscripts and versions provided a rich body of resources for textual critics attempting to reconstruct the history of the biblical text. At the same time, the history of the text of the Hebrew Bible has been confused and obscured by an assumption, or rather a dogma, on the part of the ancients—rabbis and church fathers alike—that the Hebrew text was unchanged and unchanging. These texts, they believed, were not subject to the usual scribal realities that produced families of texts and different recensions (a recension is an edition of an ancient text involving a more or less systematic revision of an earlier text form) in other works that survived long periods of transmission.

This dogma of the *Hebraica veritas* may be found as early as the late first century C.E. in Josephus' *Contra Apionem*:

> We have given practical proof of our reverence for our scriptures. For, although such long ages have now passed, no one has ventured to add, or to remove, or to alter a syllable; and it is an instinct with every Jew, from the day of his birth, to regard them as decrees of God, to abide by them, and if need be, cheerfully to die for them.[3]

Josephus evidently regarded the Hebrew Bible, in theory at least, as immutable.[4]

Origen, the church father, ordinarily used the Old Greek version of the Bible. But he, too, apparently assumed that his Greek Bible was translated from a Hebrew textual base that was the same as the rabbinical Hebrew text used in his day. Hence, in his monumental Hexapla,[5] he carefully corrected his Greek manuscripts to agree with the *Hebraica veritas*—incidentally, with catastrophic results for the subsequent transmission of the Greek Bible.

Writing in the fourth century, Jerome applied the principle of "correcting to the Hebrew" to the Latin Bible, displacing earlier Latin translations (based on the Old Greek Bible) with a new Latin translation that has come to be called the Vulgate, a Latin version translated from the standard rabbinic recension of the Hebrew Bible in use in Jerome's time.

The search for the early stages in the history of the text of the Hebrew Bible began to be pursued scientifically in the late 18th century, but the extant manuscripts were all medieval, and the results were disappointing for those who hoped to find traces of archaic forms of the text. Sifting through the medieval manuscripts yielded a mass of variant readings but no evidence of alternate textual families or text types. The variants were secondary and recent, the errors of medieval scribes that crept in after the text had been fixed. Indeed, it could be argued that the theory of a fixed and unchanging Hebrew text was supported by evidence from the collections of medieval manuscripts.

The more astute textual scholars, however, argued that all medieval Hebrew manuscripts derived from a single recension fixed early in the Christian era and that this recension alone survived in the Jewish communities. Direct access to the early development of the text of the Hebrew Bible (prior to the recensions) was thus effectively blocked.[6] Accordingly, the variations in the great collections of manuscripts then available were of little or no help in recovering ancient readings behind corruptions in the *textus receptus*, that is, the received or traditional text. It could be, and was, argued that the medieval text was based on a single archetype or single manuscript of each biblical work, which already contained the pattern of errors found in the medieval text.[7]

The fact is, however, that in the 19th century, there was little hard evidence to determine the procedure by which the rabbinic recension found in all medieval manuscripts came into being and was promulgated. In the end, the vigorous scholarly debates of the 19th century subsided, and although research and theorizing continued, no major advances were made until the discovery of Hebrew and Greek manuscripts in the wilderness of Judah—the Dead Sea Scrolls.

The discovery of ancient manuscripts in the 11 caves of Qumran provided the first unambiguous witnesses to an ancient stage of the Hebrew text of the Bible.[8] These caves have yielded some 170 manuscripts of biblical books, most of them fragmented, and their publication is still in progress.[9]

Although all the evidence has not yet been published, we can compare these Qumran manuscripts with a dozen or so biblical manuscripts, also fragmentary and some still unpublished, that were recovered from the Naḥal Ḥever, the Wadi Murabbaʿat and Herod's fortress at Masada. The two groups of manuscripts—the Qumran manuscripts and the manuscripts found in the southern caves and at Masada—differ in two critical respects. The manuscripts of the Qumran group are earlier, ranging from about 250 B.C.E. to 68 C.E., at which time the Essene community at Qumran was destroyed by the Romans during the suppression of the First Jewish Revolt (66-70 C.E.). On paleographical grounds, then, we can date most of the Qumran biblical manuscripts to no later than the first half of the first century of the Common Era. The second, "southern group"—from the caves of the Wadi Murabbaʿat, the Naḥal Ḥever and Masada—are from a later period. The most important manuscripts of the southern group are the great Hebrew Minor Prophets Scroll[10] from a cave in the Wadi Murabbaʿat and the Greek Minor Prophets Scroll from the Naḥal Ḥever.

The Minor Prophets Scroll from the Wadi Murabbaʿat can be dated paleographically to the second half of the first century of the Common Era, and the biblical fragments from Masada to no later than 73 C.E., when the Romans stormed the bastion and destroyed the fortifications. A number of the biblical fragments from the southern caves date to the interval between the First and Second Jewish Revolts, that is, between 70 and 135 C.E., and once belonged to followers of Bar Kokhba, the messianic leader of the Second Revolt (132-135 C.E.).

The two groups of biblical manuscripts differ not only in date but also in another important way. Manuscripts in the southern (later) group do not deviate significantly from the archetypal rabbinic recension—that is, the recension that is ancestral to the Masoretic text,[11] our traditional Hebrew Bible.[12] This is a marked contrast to the Qumran documents, which reveal other text types.

The data drawn from the southern manuscripts enable us to conclude that before the end of the first century of the Common Era, a recension of the text of the Hebrew Bible had been promulgated that had overwhelming authority, at least in Pharisaic circles, and that came to dominate the Jewish community in the interval between the fall of Jerusalem to the Romans in 70 C.E. and the Roman suppression of the Second Jewish Revolt in 135 C.E.

The textual situation at Qumran was entirely different. The Qumran manuscripts show no traces of the standardization that marks the rabbinic recension. At Qumran, we find evidence of discrete and, indeed, recognizable families of textual tradition, including text types that are different from the rabbinic recension. These variant streams of tradition have been called "recensions" or "families" or "local texts."[13]

Sometimes a text type is strikingly different from the traditional text that has come down to us. In extreme instances, a textual tradition is preserved in a manuscript that derives from an edition of a biblical work broadly different in content and length from the edition used in the rabbinic recension. For example, there are two editions of Jeremiah reflected in manuscripts from Qumran—a long version known from our traditional Bible, and a short version, in which the order of the prophetic oracles is also different. There are two editions (or collections) of the Psalter, one Persian in date, one Hellenistic. There is a whole Daniel literature, of which the Book of Daniel is only a single part. Different editions of biblical books, however, are relatively rare. For the most part, the textual families detectable in extant biblical manuscripts are marked by variants in individual readings—grammatical changes, alternate vocabularies, omissions or additions of words, phrases, and even, on occasion, paragraphs.

The text types of most biblical books appear to be the products of natural growth or local development; changes were made in the process of scribal transmission and were not the result of a controlled or systematic recension, revision or collation at a given place or time. But the different texts do have traits, some more or less systematic, by which they can be classified into different families. The common traits of a textual family include, for example,

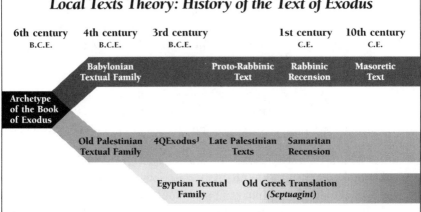

Local Texts Theory: History of the Text of Exodus

LOCAL TEXTS THEORY. This chart shows how the text of one book of the Bible, Exodus, developed. From a lost sixth-century B.C.E. archetype, three textual families evolved—a Babylonian text, a Palestinian text, then, branching off from the latter, an Egyptian text. The Babylonian text ultimately developed into the Masoretic text. The Palestinian text family, a fragment of which was found in Cave 4 at Qumran, developed into the Samaritan recension. The Egyptian text developed into the Greek Septuagint.

A similar development occurred in the text of the Book of Samuel. A fragment of the Palestinian text of Samuel was found in Cave 4 at Qumran. Because the Samaritan recension contains only the Hexateuch (the Pentateuch plus the Book of Joshua), the text of Samuel was not preserved in the Samaritan recension. Otherwise the development of Samuel followed the same outline as Exodus.

"bad genes," an inherited group of mistakes or secondary readings perpetuated by copyists generation after generation. Other distinguishing traits may be particular orthographic (spelling) styles, distinctive scripts, the repeated appearance of peculiar chronologies or numeral calculations (arising often from attempts to resolve apparent or real errors in traditional numbers), the systematic introduction into the text of parallel readings (especially in legal sections with parallel sections in other books), and the repeated use of archaizing or "modernized" grammatical and lexical features.

The Qumran manuscripts not only provide evidence of early textual traditions; perhaps even more important, the data drawn from the Qumran discoveries have enabled us to identify and delineate other textual traditions from before the Common Era—including the Hebrew textual base of the Old Greek translation, the textual background of the Samaritan recension of the Pentateuch, and the text type that was used in the rabbinic recension. In this great complex of textual materials, as many as three textual families have been identified in certain biblical books (the pentateuchal books and the books of Samuel), two textual families in other books (notably in Jeremiah and Job), and in many other books only one textual tradition (for example, Isaiah and Ezekiel). Textual critics are confronted with the task of organizing this evidence: the existence of a plurality of early textual types; a limited number of distinct textual families; and the relative homogeneity of variant textual traditions over several centuries.

I have proposed a theory of "local texts" to satisfy the requirements of these data. As applied to the books with three textual families, namely in the Pentateuch and Samuel, this theory may be sketched as follows. Three forms of the text appear to have developed slowly between the fifth century B.C.E. and the first century B.C.E. in the Jewish communities in Palestine, Egypt and Babylon, respectively. The Palestinian text family is the dominant one in the Qumran manuscripts. The earliest witness is found in the Chronicler's citations of the Pentateuch and Samuel. The Palestinian text was also used in the Samaritan recension of the Pentateuch.

In its late form, the Palestinian text can be characterized as an expansionistic text, marked frequently by conflation (two variant readings combined into one text), glosses (brief explanatory notes in the margins or between the lines), synoptic additions (inserted readings from parallel passages from other sources) and other intense scribal activity. Omissions from scribal lapses are relatively infrequent. To this family belong the pentateuchal manuscripts inscribed in the paleo-Hebrew script, a derivative of the old national script of pre-Exilic Israel.[14]

The second textual family, which we label Egyptian, is found in the Old Greek (Septuagint) translation of the Pentateuch and Reigns (the Greek version of Samuel and Kings) and in the short edition of Jeremiah found in one Hebrew manuscript at Qumran. In some respects, the Egyptian family resembles the Palestinian family, especially the earliest Palestinian witnesses, and may be regarded as a branch of the Old Palestinian family.

The third family we designate "Babylonian," although we are not sure where it originated. As we shall see, the intellectual influence of the powerful Babylonian community played a decisive role in the emergence of the authoritative rabbinic recension. This third text type, known thus far only in the Pentateuch and Samuel, was the basis of the rabbinic recension. The "Babylonian" Pentateuch text is conservative and often pristine. There is little evidence of expansion, and there are relatively few traces of revision or modernization.

Thus at Qumran, and in traditions of the biblical text that broke off from the main Jewish stream before the turn of the Common Era, we find several textual families. None, including the text type ancestral to the rabbinic recension, shows evidence of systematic recension or stabilization.

In the southern caves and at Masada, however, we find only a single text type that shows every evidence of the external controls that fixed the text, which we call the rabbinic recension. The southern group of manuscripts are very close in time to the archetype of this recension. We are led, therefore, to the conclusion that the rabbinic recension of the Hebrew Bible—what we may also call the authoritative Pharisaic text—was fixed by the time of the Roman destruction of Jerusalem in 70 C.E. This recension became regnant only in the interval between the two Jewish Revolts, when the Pharisaic party came to dominate the surviving Jewish community and rival parties diminished and disappeared. Sects like the Christians and Samaritans continued to exist but only as separate communities isolated from Pharisaic influence. Rabbinic Judaism survived and with it the rabbinic recension.

The rabbinic recension was a response to a textual crisis that developed in late Hellenistic and early Roman times. After the Maccabean Revolt, initiated in 167 B.C.E., an independent Jewish state was reestablished, the first since the Babylonians destroyed Jerusalem and the First Temple in 587 B.C.E. In the wake of Maccabean victories that led eventually to the full independence of Judea under the rule of Simon the Maccabee (140-134 B.C.E.), was a Zionist revival. Augmented by Parthian expulsions of the Jews, a flood of people returned to Jerusalem from Babylon, Syria and Egypt.[15] By the first century before and the first century after the Common Era, competing local texts and editions were circulating in Judah, causing considerable confusion, as is reflected in the library at Qumran.

The uncontrolled development of the texts of individual textual families precipitated a crisis when the urgent need for precise doctrinal and legal (halakhic) exegesis arose in Hellenistic Judaism. Party strife began in earnest in the middle second century B.C.E. with the emergence of the Sadducean, Pharisaic and Essene parties. Subsequent religious disputes increased the need for a fixed, authoritative text. By the beginning of the first century of the Common Era, when the main parties splintered into smaller sectarian groups, there were intense intraparty as well as interparty and sectarian disputes and contentions.

These data provide the general time and historical context of the rabbinic recension. The time frame in which we must place the promulgation of the rabbinic recension is hinted at in the history of the Greek recensions.[16] The rabbinic recension was promulgated in the first half of the first century C.E. At the same time, the hermeneutical rules (logical principles used to interpret a text, or guides to exegesis) were fixed, and there are accounts of Pharisaic discussions between the schools of Hillel and Shammai, which presume a more or less fixed text. I think we can go even further and attribute the initiation of the recensional labors that fixed the text of the Pharisaic Bible to the great sage Hillel himself (early first century C.E.)—or at least to the school of rabbinic scholars he inspired.

Hillel, it should be remembered, came to Palestine from Babylon and became the dominant and most creative spirit of his day; he was a giant whose influence on Pharisaism cannot be exaggerated, and his direct descendants were the principal leaders in the normative Jewish community for many generations.

If Hillel and his circle were responsible for the selection of the proto-rabbinic manuscripts on which the rabbinic recension was based, that would explain a number of textual peculiarities. For example, the texts of the Pentateuch and Samuel chosen for the rabbinic recension appear to be of Babylonian origin rather than the prevailing late Palestinian texts that were readily available.[17] At the time of the recension, the rabbis also rejected the paleo-Hebrew script and orthographic style, which was used in the most elegant pentateuchal manuscripts inscribed in Palestine. They chose instead the common Jewish script, which was in general use in Palestine and throughout the diaspora Jewish communities. The choice of the common Jewish script is particularly striking in view of the official use of the old national script by the ruling high priests for temple inscriptions and for coins.

When Pharisaic scholars fixed the text, they followed a pattern unusual in the textual history of ancient literary documents. Instead of producing an eclectic text by choosing preferred readings and rejecting obvious glosses or additions (as Greek scholars in Alexandria did in establishing a short, if artificial, recension of the text of Homer), or combining variant readings from different textual traditions, the recensional technique that produced conflate recensions of the Septuagint and the New Testament, the rabbis selected a single textual tradition, which we term the proto-rabbinic text, a text that had been in existence in individual manuscripts for some time.[18] For each biblical book of the Hebrew Bible, the rabbis chose exemplars of one textual family or even a single manuscript as a base. They did not collate the wide variety of text types available; on the contrary, in some instances they firmly rejected the dominant late-Palestinian text.

And they did not select texts with a common origin or local background. In the Pentateuch, they chose a short, relatively unconflated text—a superb text from the point of view of the modern critic—that we believe derived from a conservative Babylonian textual tradition. In the Major Prophets, on the other hand, they chose the relatively late and full Palestinian texts of Isaiah, Ezekiel, and Jeremiah. In Jeremiah, in fact, they selected the long edition in preference to the shorter, and in some ways superior, edition.

The choice of a non-Palestinian text of the Pentateuch is of particular interest. The books of the Torah (the Pentateuch) were considered authoritative by all Jewish parties. Indeed, the Sadducees and the Zadokite priests of the separatist Samaritan community regarded the Pentateuch alone as the basis of religious doctrine and practice. The Samaritans, unlike the rabbis, chose for their sectarian recension of the Pentateuch a late Palestinian text inscribed in paleo-Hebrew, also known from the finds at Qumran.

We may speculate that Hillel's personal preference was responsible for the surprising choice of the Babylonian textual base for the Pharisaic Pentateuch. In this case, the conservative Torah scrolls that he knew and to which he was accustomed became, at his urging, the basis of the new rabbinic recension. It is possible that an old saying embedded in the Babylonian Talmud preserves a memory of Hillel's role in events leading to the fixation of the Hebrew text and canon: "When Israel forgot the Torah, Ezra came up from Babylon and reestablished it; and when Israel once again forgot the Torah, Hillel the Babylonian came up and reestablished it."[19]

This much is certain. Throughout Jewish history, the vigorous religious community in Babylon repeatedly developed spiritual and intellectual leaders who reshaped the direction of Palestinian Judaism and defined its norms. Such was the case in the Restoration after the Exile, again in the person of Hillel, and finally in the rise of the Babylonian Talmud.

So far we have talked almost exclusively about fixation of the text as opposed to stabilization of the canon. In the remarks that follow, we shall focus on the latter, specifically fixation of the Pharisaic canon of the Hebrew

---

The Canon of the Hebrew Bible and the Excluded Books

The Canon of the Hebrew Bible

UNDISPUTED INCLUDED BOOKS		LATE/MARGINAL BOOKS INCLUDED
Pentateuch (B, P, E)	**Prophets**	Ecclesiastes (*Qohelet*)
Genesis	Joshua	Song of Songs
Exodus	Judges	Esther
Leviticus	Samuel (**B, P, E**)	Ezekiel (**P**)
Numbers	Kings	Daniel
Deuteronomy	Isaiah (**P**)	
	Jeremiah (**P, E**)	
Twelve Minor Prophets		
Hosea	Nahum	**Writings**
Joel	Habakkuk	Psalms
Amos	Zephaniah	Proverbs
Obadiah	Haggai	Job
Jonah	Zechariah	Ruth
Micah	Malachi	Lamentations
		Ezra/Nehemiah
		Chronicles

EXCLUDED LATE/MARGINAL BOOKS ATTRIBUTED TO PRE-MOSAIC PATRIARCHS	EXCLUDED LATE/MARGINAL BOOKS
Pseudepigrapha	Ben Sira
Enoch literature	Maccabees
Vision of Amram	Tobit
Testaments of the Twelve Patriarchs	Judith
(*Sons of Jacob*)	Baruch
	Wisdom of Solomon
	Epistle of Jeremiah
	Additions to Daniel

TEXT FAMILIES. The tentative identification of the textual families (Babylonian, Palestinian, Egyptian) by Frank Moore Cross is based on all of the data, old and new, including Qumran fragments, the Masoretic text and the Old Greek versions. Most of the Qumran material is Palestinian (P). In the case of Jeremiah, both the Palestinian and Egyptian families are represented by manuscripts from Qumran.

Bible. We shall use the term *canon* in the strict sense—a fixed list of books of scripture that was deemed unvariable, not to be added to or subtracted from. Originally the term *canon* meant a rule; in the usage of the church fathers, a canon was a closed list of books defined as authoritative for religious faith and practice.

The earliest definition of the "closed" Hebrew canon is found in Josephus in his apologetic work, *Contra Apionem*, written in Rome in the last decade of the first century C.E. He asserted that there was a fixed and immutable number (22) of "justly accredited" books.[20] Their authority was based on their derivation from a period of uncontested prophetic inspiration beginning with Moses and ending in the era of Nehemiah.

> [W]e do not possess myriads of inconsistent books, conflicting with each other. Our books, those which are justly accredited, are but two and twenty, and contain the record of all time. Of these, five are the books of Moses, comprising the laws and the traditional history from the birth of man down to the death of the lawgiver....From the death of Moses until Artaxerxes, who succeeded Xerxes as king of Persia, the prophets subsequent to Moses wrote the history of the events of their own times in thirteen books. The remaining four books contain hymns to God and precepts for the conduct of human life. From Artaxerxes to our own time the complete history has been written, but has not been deemed worthy of equal credit with the earlier records, because of the failure in the exact succession of prophets.[21]

Josephus' "canon" specifically excludes works of Hellenistic date and, by implication, works attributed to pre-Mosaic patriarchs. In the paragraph subsequent to the one cited, he adds that the precise text of the 22 books was fixed to the syllable. What is the origin of Josephus' doctrine of a fixed text and a fixed canon? Josephus was a Pharisee, and I believe he draws upon his Pharisaic tradition and, ultimately, the work and teachings of Hillel.

There is no evidence in non-Pharisaic Jewish circles before 70 C.E. of a fixed canon or a fixed text. The Essenes at Qumran exhibit no knowledge of a fixed text or canon. The same is true in the Hellenistic Jewish community in Alexandria and in the early Christian communities. Until recently there has been a scholarly consensus that the acts of inclusion and exclusion that fixed the canon were completed at the "Council of Jamnia (Yabneh)" about the end of the first century of the Common Era.[22] But after sifting the rabbinic evidence, scholars have now concluded that the rabbis did not fix the canon in the proceedings of the academy of Yabneh. At most, they discussed marginal books, notably Ecclesiastes (Qohelet) and the Song of Songs, and declared that both Ecclesiastes and the Song of Songs "defile the hands," i.e., are holy books and should be included in the canon. This decision ratified the dicta of the house of Hillel in the case of Ecclesiastes, and probably in the case of the Song of Songs as well.[23] Moreover, it must be insisted that the proceedings at Yabneh should not be called a "council," certainly not in the late ecclesiastical sense of the word.

Whatever decisions were taken at Yabneh, they were based on earlier opinions, and they did not settle the disputes over marginal books—Song of Songs, Ecclesiastes and Esther of the "included" books, Ben Sira among the "excluded" or apocryphal books.

In any case, it is clear that Josephus in Rome did not take his cue from contemporary or later proceedings at Yabneh. Nor did he manufacture a theory of canon from whole cloth. Thinly concealed behind Josephus' Greek apologetics is a clear and coherent theological doctrine of canon that came, we believe, from the canonical doctrine of Hillel and his school.[24]

We cannot date the fixation of the Pharisaic canon earlier than the time of Hillel, as occasional scholars have attempted to do. Our evidence comes from the so-called Kaige recension (see note 16). At the end of the first century B.C.E., the Greek Bible was revised to bring it into line with the proto-rabbinic text, not with the later fixed rabbinic recension. The revised Greek text was called the Kaige recension. Similarly, the revision embodied in the Kaige recension extended to the Book of Baruch and the longer edition of Daniel, works that were excluded from the rabbinic recension. The effort to "update" Baruch and the longer edition of Daniel would be difficult to explain if, at the time the Kaige recension was prepared, the Book of Baruch and the additions to Daniel had already been excluded from the Pharisaic canon. Since the Kaige recension can be dated to about the turn of the Common Era, and its Pharisaic bias is clear, it follows that as late as the end of the first century B.C.E., even in Pharisaic circles, there was no authoritative, canonical list, at least not in final form.

I am persuaded by the accumulation of evidence that the same circumstances that brought on the textual crisis that led to the fixation of the Hebrew text—varied texts and editions, party strife and sectarian division, the systematization of hermeneutic principles and halakhic dialectic (the mode of legal reasoning by which religious law was derived from scripture)—also brought on a "canonical" crisis that necessitated fixing a Pharisaic canon. I am also persuaded that Hillel was the central figure who sharpened the crisis and responded to it. The fixation of the text and the fixation of the canon were thus two aspects of a single, complex endeavor. Both were essential to erecting "Hillelite" protection against rival doctrines of cult and calendar, alternate legal dicta and theological doctrines, and speculative systems and mythological excesses of certain apocalyptic schools and proto-Gnostic sects. To promulgate a textual recension, moreover, there must be a limit on the number of books to be authorized. By selecting one text of a book over another—in the case of Jeremiah or Chronicles or Daniel—decisions were made that were at once textual and canonical. Ultimately, the strategies that initiated the fixation of the biblical text led to the *de facto*, if not *de jure*, fixation of a canon.

The principles by which works were excluded from the Pharisaic canon are reflected in Josephus' notices and no doubt were used to eliminate works offensive to Hillel and the house of Hillel. A host of pseudepigraphical works written in the name of Enoch, Melchizedek, the sons of Jacob, Amram and the like, which became popular in Hellenistic times and which fill the library of Qumran, were excluded from the canon. The prophetic sequence began with Moses. There can be little doubt, moreover, that the rabbis recognized the recent date of certain apocryphal and pseudepigraphic works (cycles such as Enoch and the Testaments of the Patriarchs were still in the creative, fluid phase of composition well into the Roman Period). The principle of excluding "post-Prophetic" works meant the propagandistic Book of Maccabees, certain Hellenistic novellas and Ben Sira were also suppressed, although Pseudepigrapha written in the name of the "Prophets," especially the Jeremianic Apocrypha, Baruch and the Letter of Jeremiah, must have caused difficulties and disputes. In all probability, Ezekiel, Song of Songs and Ecclesiastes were controversial because of their content but were sufficiently old and recognized to prevent their being excluded from the canon.[25] Most mysterious is the selection of an edition of Daniel from the Maccabean Age or later, although it also contains earlier material, and of Esther. In general, however, the rabbis chose works or editions that, in fact, had reached final literary form (that is, compositional activity had ceased) by the end of the Persian Period (late fourth century B.C.E.).

If I am correct in perceiving the hand of Hillel in the promulgation of a Pharisaic text and canon and in recognizing a reference to this achievement in the rabbinic saying, "When Israel once again forgot [the Torah], Hillel the Babylonian came up and reestablished it," I must nevertheless acknowledge that this canon and text did not immediately supplant other traditions or receive uniform acceptance even in Pharisaic circles. The ascendancy of the Hillelite text and canon came with the victory of the Pharisaic party and the Hillelite house in the interval between the two Jewish Revolts against Rome. Since then, the text and canon of the Hebrew Bible—despite rabbinical queries about marginal books from time to time—have remained fixed and are guarded to the present day.

CHAPTER 13

Original Biblical Text
Reconstructed from Fragments

Frank Moore Cross

In the following article, Cross shows how the variant readings in Qumran manuscripts allow "the reconstruction of the original text of the Bible." For example, the Masoretic version of 1 Samuel 11 records an attack on Jabesh-Gilead by King Naḥash of Ammon, but the reasons for the attack and for the demand that surrendering Israelites be blinded were not stated. In a Qumran text, however, an additional paragraph describes events preceding the attack and provides the explanation.

Although this passage might be dismissed as a later insertion, Cross believes it is authentic. He notes that the first appearance of "Naḥash the Ammonite" in the Masoretic text is the only instance of 20 or so examples in Samuel and Kings when a reigning foreign king is not introduced with the title "So-and-so, king of So-and-so." In the passage in the Qumran manuscript, Naḥash is introduced with his full title. The standard text, Cross concludes, must once have included this passage.

Cross believes that by studying the Qumran texts we can correct false notions about the development of biblical religion. Apocalypticism, for instance, has traditionally been considered a late, transient phenomenon in Judaism. Since the extensive Enoch literature was discovered, however, scholars have pushed back the origin of apocalypticism to the late Persian period, that is, the fourth century B.C.E. "The movements of John the Baptist and of Jesus of Nazareth must now be redefined as apocalyptic rather than prophetic," Cross says. And echoing Charlesworth and Sarna, Cross asserts that old school Christian scholars overlooked early evidence of apocalypticism because they were intent on contrasting an "enslaving and static" Judaism with the "free and gracious spirit of prophecy" in Christianity. He argues that "there can be no question that the apocalyptic movement was one of the ancestors of both Pharisaic Judaism and Jewish Christianity."–Ed.

The manuscripts from Qumran that differ from received texts not only provide data for the history of the biblical text, as I described in the previous article, but, on occasion, they also provide readings of exceptional interest for reconstructing the original text of the Bible. Let me give an example of one such reading. In the received text of Samuel, we read about a critical confrontation between Saul and Naḥash, king of the Ammonites. Saul is victorious and, as a result, is confirmed as Israel's first king.

As it has come down to us in the biblical account in 1 Samuel 11, Naḥash besieged the Israelite city of Jabesh-Gilead. The men of Jabesh-Gilead asked Naḥash for surrender terms. Naḥash's terms were harsh. Besides the Israelites becoming servants of the Ammonites, the victors would gouge out the right eye of every man in the city. Before agreeing to these terms, the men of the town asked for a one-week respite to see if their fellow Israelites would come to their aid. When Saul heard of their plight, he rallied the militia of Israel, crossed the Jordan and met Naḥash and the Ammonites in battle. Saul was overwhelmingly victorious and delivered Jabesh-Gilead, thereby demonstrating his leadership. He was promptly confirmed as king.

Why did Naḥash suddenly attack Jabesh-Gilead, an Israelite city allied with the house of Saul? We are not told. The question is especially puzzling because Jabesh-Gilead was far north of the boundary claimed by the Ammonites. And the question is particularly interesting because Naḥash not only brought defeat down on his own head, but more serious for Ammon's future, the attack proved to be the catalyst that united Israel and set in motion forces that led to the rise of the Israelite empire under Saul's successor, David. In the end, Ammon became subject to the Israelite empire. Naḥash's attack on Jabesh-Gilead was a pivotal event in both Israelite and Ammonite history.

A first-century B.C.E. manuscript of the Books of Samuel found in Qumran Cave 4 contains a long passage, not found in our Bible, at the beginning of chapter 11 of 1 Samuel. This manuscript (designated 4QSam[a] in the technical literature) is the best preserved biblical manuscript from Cave 4. When fully published, it will consist of more than 25 printed plates of fragments. The manuscript belongs to a Palestinian textual tradition that varies from the text type used in the rabbinic recension. The received text of Samuel is, in fact, notorious for scribal lapses, especially omissions; the present example is one of a number of instances (perhaps the most dramatic) where 4QSam[a] preserves lost bits of the text of Samuel.

The lost-and-now-recovered passage gives the background for Naḥash's attack on Jabesh-Gilead. Naḥash,[1] at the head of a resurgent Ammonite nation, had earlier reconquered land long claimed by both Ammon and the Israelite tribes of Reuben and Gad east of the Jordan River. In his own view, Naḥash resubjugated people who had occupied his land. He therefore punished his old Israelite enemies (and sometime subjects) with a systematic policy of mutilation—gouging out the right eye of every able-bodied man. In ancient times,

THIS LONG-LOST PASSAGE from 1 Samuel does not appear in the version of the Old Testament we know today. One of thousands of manuscript fragments found in the famous Qumran caves near the Dead Sea, this passage solves a mystery in chapter 11 of 1 Samuel. It explains that the Ammonite king Naḥash attacked the Israelite city of Jabesh-Gilead because the city had harbored fugitives from the conquered tribal lands of Reuben and Gad. Until the discovery of this scroll fragment, the rationale for Naḥash's attack and his threat to blind the men of the city had been a mystery. *Photo: Israel Antiquities Authority*

mutilation was standard treatment for rebels, enemies of long standing and treaty violators. Examples of rebels or arch-foes being blinded include Samson blinded by the Philistines (Judges 16:21) and Zedekiah blinded by the Babylonians (2 Kings 25:7; Jeremiah 39:7, 52:11). Blinding as a punishment for rebels is also documented in Assyrian annals. Mutilation and dismemberment for violation of a treaty are also well documented in biblical and extrabiblical sources.[2]

Mutilation by blinding was not, however, the treatment meted out to newly conquered subjects in a city outside the conqueror's domain, like Jabesh-Gilead. The mutilation as recounted in the received text of Samuel has always been puzzling for this reason.

From the newly recovered passage, we learn that some 7,000 Israelite warriors of Reuben and Gad who had survived defeat by Naḥash's forces fled and took refuge north of the traditional border of Ammon (at the Jabbok River), in the Gileadite city of Jabesh. A month or so after their escape, Naḥash resolved to subjugate Jabesh-Gilead for sheltering his escaped "subjects." This was Naḥash's motivation, or excuse, for striking at Jabesh-Gilead, which was far north of his claimed borders and was allied with Benjamin and Saul.

Now we know why Naḥash attacked Jabesh-Gilead and why he insisted on mutilation as a term of surrender. Partial blinding was the punishment he had inflicted on the Israelites of Gad and Reuben. People who harbored enemies deserved the same punishment inflicted on the enemy.

But Naḥash unknowingly sealed his own fate. Saul of Benjamin, enraged by news of the affair and "seized by the spirit," rallied the western tribes, crossed the Jordan with an Israelite militia and "slaughtered the Ammonites until the heat of the day." Saul's victory over Naḥash at Jabesh-Gilead consolidated support for Saul's kingship over all Israel and, in the end, sealed the fate of the Ammonites.

Here is the account of the episode, with the additional passage retrieved from Qumran in italics. (Brackets indicate lacunae in the manuscript reconstructed by the writer.) The reader might try reading the unitalicized portion first, then the italicized portion, to appreciate how the added text illuminates the background of the received text.[3]

> *Naḥash, king of the children of Ammon, sorely oppressed the children of Gad and the children of Reuben, and he gouged out a[ll] their right eyes and struck ter[ror and dread] in Israel. There was not left one among the children of Israel bey[ond the Jordan who]se right eye was no[t put o]ut by Naḥa[sh king] of the children of Ammon; except that seven thousand men [fled from] the children of [A]mmon and entered []]abesh-Gilead. About a month later* Naḥash the Ammonite went up and besieged Jabesh-Gilead. All the men of Jabesh-Gilead said to Naḥash, "Make a treaty with us and we shall become your subjects." Naḥash the Ammonite replied to them, "On this condition I shall make a treaty with you, that all your right eyes be gouged out, so that I may bring humiliation on all Israel." The elders at Jabesh said to him, "Give us seven days to send messengers throughout the territory of Israel. If no one rescues us, we shall surrender to you."

The missing paragraph was lost probably as a result of a scribal lapse—the scribe's eye jumped from one line break to the other, both beginning with Naḥash.

It has been suggested that the extra paragraph in this manuscript of Samuel is not part of the original composition but a late addition, a haggadic expansion,[4] but I see no evidence whatever for this. (The term *haggadah* is used by the rabbis for the interpretation of scripture except for legal exposition.) The added text gives rather flat historical "facts," with no edifying element, theological bias, theory to prove or hortatory motif. In short, I perceive no haggadic elements in the passage.

On the contrary, a number of telltale signs suggest the additional passage was in the original. Consider, for example, that in the received text of Samuel, the king of the Ammonites is introduced simply as "Naḥash the Ammonite."

This is extraordinary. In Samuel and Kings, there is an otherwise invariable pattern; when the reigning king of a foreign nation is introduced for the first time, his full or official title is given, "So-and-so, king of So-and-so." There are some 20 examples of this. The omission of Naḥash's full title is the sole exception to this rule. Indeed, the pattern obtains for the whole of the Deuteronomistic history (Deuteronomy, Joshua, Judges, Samuel and Kings) and is violated in the received text only here. However, if the paragraph from 4QSamᵃ is original, Naḥash is introduced first as "king of the children of Ammon," his full title, precisely in accord with the Deuteronomistic historian's unvarying practice. This is a strong argument for the originality of the passage in Samuel. Incidentally, the Ammonite king's official title as given in the newly found passage, "king of the children of Ammon," also appears on a recently discovered Ammonite inscription from Tell Siran.[5]

Now that we have this additional paragraph in our text of Samuel, we can recognize that the same paragraph was present in Josephus' Bible. In *Antiquities of the Jews* (6.68-70), Josephus vividly describes the background of the attack on Jabesh-Gilead, a description that must have been based on a biblical passage identical with the passage from Samuel that has now been recovered from Qumran Cave 4:

> However, a month later, he [Saul] began to win the esteem of all by the war with Naas [Naḥash], king of the Ammonites. For this monarch had done much harm to the Jews who had settled beyond the river Jordan, having invaded their territory with a large and warlike army. Reducing their cities to servitude, he not only by force and violence secured their subjection in the present, but by cunning and ingenuity weakened them in order that they might never again be able to revolt and escape from servitude to him; for he cut out the right eyes of all who either surrendered to him under oath or were captured by right of war...Having then so dealt with the people beyond Jordan, the king of the Ammonites carried his arms against those called Galadenians [Gileadites]. Pitching his camp near the capital of his enemies, to wit Jabis [Jabesh], he sent envoys to them, bidding them instantly to surrender on the understanding that their right eyes would be put out: if not, he threatened to besiege and overthrow their cities: it was for them to choose, whether they preferred the cutting out of a small portion of the body, or to perish utterly.

Obviously, Josephus is paraphrasing the lost passage from Samuel. This is just one example of how the Dead Sea Scrolls may help us restore a more complete biblical text.

Another area of study that will be greatly affected by the manuscript discoveries in the Jordan Rift is the history of biblical religion—or perhaps we should say the *development* of biblical religion. For example, we are now in a better position to compare the psalms of the canonical Psalter with the corpus of later Hellenistic hymns found at Qumran, especially the collection of psalms from Cave 11; or we can describe the development of slave law in Persian Palestine on the basis of Samarian papyri.

The impact of the discovery of the Qumran manuscripts has nowhere been greater than on our understanding of the place of the apocalyptic movement in the history of late biblical religion.[6] The term apocalyptic usually conjures up the Book of Daniel, a late, full blown exemplar of apocalyptic literature. The Bible also contains a much earlier apocalypse in the Book of Isaiah (chapters 24-27), the date of which has been debated by several generations of biblical scholars. From Qumran, we now have an immense apocalyptic literature as well as works colored by apocalyptic eschatology.[7]

As reflected in the Qumran literature, apocalyptists saw world history in terms of warring forces, God against Satan, the spirit of truth against the spirit of error, light against darkness. The struggles of God with man and man with sin, evil and death were objectified into cosmic struggles. Dualistic themes from archaic myths were transformed into historical myths. The world, which was captive to evil powers and principalities that had been given authority in the era of divine wrath, could be freed only by Divine Might. Apocalyptists saw— or believed they saw—the dawning of the day of God's salvation and judgment. The old age had come to the end of its allotted time, and the age of consummation was at hand, the age when the world would be redeemed and the elect vindicated. Apocalyptists saw signs of the approaching end of days. They believed the final war, Armageddon, had begun and the Messiah "bringing the sword" was about to appear. Satanic forces, brought to bay, had already lashed out in a final defiant convulsion that was manifested in the persecution, temptations and tribulations of the faithful. In short, apocalyptists lived in a world in which the sovereignty of God was the sole hope of salvation. In the earnestness of their faith and the vividness of their hope, they were certain that God was about to act.

Apocalypticism has generally been regarded as a late, short-lived phenomenon in Judaism. This view is changing, however, in light of the mass of new data and careful research on old and new data. The earliest portions of the Enoch literature, for example, were dated a generation ago to the Roman period (after 64 B.C.E.) or, at the earliest, to the late Hellenistic period (second or early first centuries B.C.E.). Those dates must now be pushed back to the late Persian period (fourth century B.C.E.). We actually have an Enoch manuscript—not an autograph of the original—from about 200 B.C.E. Studies of early biblical apocalyptic (or proto-apocalyptic) literature, notably the Isaianic apocalypse (Isaiah 24-27), have shown that it dates from the sixth century B.C.E. Indeed, the first strains of apocalyptic dualism and eschatology arise, I would argue, with the decline of classical prophecy in the sixth and fifth centuries B.C.E. And we must now recognize that proto-apocalyptic works, together with later apocalyptic works, reflect a religious development that spans more than half a millennium.

In the 19th and early 20th centuries, apocalypticism figured little or not at all in scholarly descriptions of the history of Israelite religion. Apocalypticism was treated as a fringe phenomenon, an idiosyncratic product of a few Jewish seers.

Christian scholars of the older view (who largely disregarded apocalypticism) believed biblical religion developed according to a dialectic in which the "free, ethical and historical spirit" of prophetic religion was frozen in legalism whose "enslaving and static modes" marked post-Exilic religion. According to this view, the free and gracious spirit of prophecy reemerged *only* in New Testament Christianity. Hence, Christian scholars were inclined to bypass apocalyptic works in an attempt to trace continuities between prophecy and primitive Christianity.

Older Jewish scholars shared the prevailing distaste for apocalyptic literature; they considered apocalyptic literature sectarian, even though a bit of it had slipped into the Hebrew canon. Influenced by the anti-apocalyptic and anti-Gnostic reactions of rabbinic Judaism, Jewish scholars read back into Hellenistic-era and even Persian-era Judaism the prevailing ethos of rabbinic Judaism. As late as 1929, George Foot Moore wrote in his influential study of Judaism:

> ...inasmuch as these writings [the apocalypses] have never been recognized by Judaism, it is a fallacy of method for the historian to make them a primary source for the eschatology of Judaism, much more, to contaminate its theology with them.

Thus, Christian and Jewish scholars joined in a conspiracy of silence on the subject of apocalypticism.

In the last generation, the special import of apocalypticism for the study of Christian origins was rediscovered, so to speak. The rich resources from Qumran confirm and reinforce these new insights. Indeed, the study of Christian origins has been transformed by data from the Qumran library. The pace of new research is sure to accelerate as new manuscripts are published.

The movements led by John the Baptist and Jesus of Nazareth must now be redefined as apocalyptic rather than prophetic in their essential character. Gershom Scholem shocked my generation with his demonstration of the survivals of apocalyptic mysticism in the era of Rabbi Akiba (late first and second centuries C.E.). Younger scholars, I venture to say, will confirm and extend insights into the importance of apocalypticism for both early Judaism and primitive Christianity.[8]

The apocalyptic communities of the last centuries before the Common Era played a major role in the complex matrix out of which both Christianity and rabbinic Judaism were born. We are now beginning to recognize the enormous changes Judaism underwent between the origins of the Pharisees in the multihued religious milieu of the Hellenistic era and the oral codification of the Mishnah (about 200 C.E.). This should not be surprising if we remember that in even less time the Christian community moved from Jewish sectarian origins in Jerusalem to Nicene orthodoxy in Constantine's Byzantium.

In my judgment, the apocalyptic movement will be recognized in the years ahead as a major phase in the evolution of biblical religion that flourished between the end of prophecy in its institutionalized form in the sixth century B.C.E. and the rise of rabbinic Judaism, gentile Christianity, and Gnosticism in the first and second centuries C.E. In this interval of more than 500 years, Jewish apocalypticism was a mainstream of religious life as well as speculation. Nonapocalyptic strains also existed, of course. But there can be no question that the apocalyptic movement was one ancestor of both Pharisaic Judaism and Jewish Christianity, as well as of the Gnostic syncretism that characterized both movements in the first centuries of the Common Era.

I venture to predict that future descriptions of the Jewish parties of the Hellenistic and Roman periods will be far more complex and nuanced than the simple, neat images of the past. The Sadducees, whom we have pictured as religious conservatives and worldly bureaucrats, now are known to have spawned a radical apocalyptic wing at Qumran. The Pharisees also appear to have been less than homogeneous within their communes (*ḥabûrôt* in Hebrew). They accepted in their canon some apocalyptic works, such as Deutero-Zechariah and Daniel, although they rejected others, such as Enoch and the Testaments of the Twelve Patriarchs. By and large, the Pharisees appear to have been dominated by moderates. The radical elements broke off and joined the Zealot movement. Later the conservative members were overwhelmed by the school of Hillel.

The discoveries in the Jordan Rift, especially at Qumran, have initiated a new era in the study of the history of late biblical religion and Jewish sectarianism. Assimilation of the new data will be slow. Older scholars will probably prefer to ignore the new materials, which will be too strong for their stomachs. I remember the late Yigael Yadin reading diatribes against his colleagues for ignoring the Temple Scroll he published. Of course, it is uncomfortable to be told, "Here is a new scroll—go rewrite all your books." Or, "Here is a new Jewish library of the third to first centuries; examine all your old presuppositions, retool, and start afresh." New directions in research will rest largely on the shoulders of young scholars. I envy those who will live to read the new syntheses.[9]

A F T E R W O R D

In The Dead Sea Scrolls: After Forty Years,[1] *James A. Sanders is skeptical about Cross' theory of text families: "The earliest scrolls do seem to exhibit some relative fluidity. There have been theories about how to account for that. Text critics tend to want to talk about families of texts, so that is standard in text criticism and there are those, such as our colleague at Harvard, Professor Frank Cross, who believe they see families of texts–Babylonian, Palestinian and Egyptian. Most scholars do not see that as clearly as Frank does, but nonetheless we all have to observe this relative fluidity."*

Cross contends that new manuscript discoveries will necessarily lead to a new explanation of Christian origins amidst a multivalent Judaism. The form of this explanation is one of many issues addressed by Father Andrew Greeley and Rabbi Jacob Neusner in The Bible and Us: A Priest and a Rabbi Read Scripture Together.[2] *In an exchange in* BR *Rabbi Neusner wrote:*

Based on invalid assumptions, the dialogue between Judaism as a religion and Christianity as a religion has been a surface conversation that covers over profound mutual incomprehension.

The prevailing theory of the dialogue is that Jesus was a Jew and that, therefore, in order to understand Christianity, Christians must come to terms with Judaism. An important school of New Testament studies, for example, tries to identify authentic sayings of Jesus in the Gospels (as opposed to sayings only attributed to him by the later church) by *excluding* sayings that they deem un-Judaic. Other, even more important circles of New Testament scholars look to Jewish texts as a principal source of the hermeneutics, or interpretive principles, of Christian Scripture. Theologically, a distinction is made between the historical Jesus–who was born, lived and died as a Jew–and the Christ of theology.

The connection to the dialogue between Judaism and Christianity is then simple. The two religions can speak comprehensibly with one another because Christianity derives from Judaism through the person of the historical Jesus. If we wish to understand Christianity, we simply peel back the layers of "inauthentic" theology and reach back into the core, the Judaism of Jesus at the heart of authentic Christianity. But for this to work, Judaism must be represented in such a way as to reject the Judaisms of that time and place that do not fit this picture; Jesus, admittedly, vastly reformed what was.

The necessary conclusion of this line of thought is that Christianity is what Judaism ought to have become. The upshot of a dialogue with Judaism based on this kind of analysis is an apologetic for Christianity and a condemnation of Judaism as we know it–not much better than the medieval disputations–hardly a model of genuine interchange between religions attempting to take one another seriously.

Nor has Judaism contributed a more suitable example of how to take another religion seriously in terms of one's own....

According to Jewish apologetic, since the prophets did not prophesy about Jesus Christ, Judaism conveys the authentic faith of ancient Israel. The beam in the hermeneutical eye of this "inauthenticizing" of Christian interpretation is that the same hermeneutic used in Matthew is also used in the Midrash, the collection of ancient Jewish expansions of Scripture that impart a rich contemporary meaning to the already ancient text, the result being that the ancient text has no more the plain sense of the ancient writer in the Midrash than it has in the Christian interpretation by Matthew.

From all of this, a rather radical conclusion follows. Only when Christianity sees itself as the church fathers did—as new and uncontingent, a complete revision of the history of humanity from Adam onward, and not as subordinate or heir to Judaism—and only when Judaism sees itself as the sages of the oral Torah did—as the statement of God's Torah for all humanity—will the two religions recognize the simple fact that they really are totally alien to one another....

In the currently fashionable Jewish-Christian dialogue, it is common to read the New Testament, especially the Gospels, in the context of the Judaism of that time and place. But much of what is taken for granted in the Gospel narratives will surprise Jewish readers. For example, someone recently asked me about burial practices in the first century. I replied that I have no evidence from the rabbinic sources that pertains to that time, but, in general, a few centuries later, men cared for the bodies of men and women for the bodies of women. Yet the Gospels tell us women tended the body of Jesus. As a Jew, what am I to make of this? It seems completely surprising; I wonder if anyone found it so before. But the fact is we find Christianity truly surprising whenever we accord to Christian Scriptures their proper, autonomous standing. Christianity came into being as a surprising, unprecedented and entirely autonomous religious system, not as a child, legitimate or otherwise, of Judaism.
BR *6:6 (1990), p. 32*

Andrew Greeley replies:

Professor Neusner and I share the position that rabbinic Judaism (the Judaism of the oral and written Torah) and Christianity are two distinct religious traditions, both of which emerged in the early centuries of the Common Era out of the pluralistic religious culture of Second Temple Israel. Rather than mother and daughter, they are sister traditions with a common mother. They are, to use Neusner's terminology in a sense I think he would approve, two different "Judaisms."

As I worked with Professor Neusner on our book, I came to exactly the opposite conclusion from his in answer to the question I believe underlies the issue of ecumenism between the two traditions. That question is if, besides being distinct traditions, rabbinic Judaism and Christianity also, because of their common ancestry, are in some sense one tradition. It seems to me they are. He disagrees.

I note that the passionately committed Holy One of the Exodus is the Christian God as well as the Jewish God. I note that the story of the pathos of God, told by the prophets,[3] is a Christian story, too. I note that our common spring festivals—Passover and Easter—are festivals of the same promise and the same new birth of freedom. I note that both Jews and Christians can and do claim Moses as "our rabbi" and that we read some of the same sacred books. I suggest that a sociologist of religion from Mars would have a hard time thinking of the two traditions as totally different religions.

Thus, contrary to Neusner, I conclude that dialogue between the two traditions is not only possible but necessary. This dialogue is of two kinds. First, we must converse about the things we already share. In this dialogue, we—Christians and Jews—must explore what we both inherited from our common mother, Israel. Second, we must also discuss the unity we do not have. For the fracture line between us cannot be the will of the Holy One.

The issue in the second dialogue is obviously Christology. Is it possible to formulate—or even begin to formulate—a theory of the role of Jesus that both traditions can live with?

The problem here is not, I submit, the messiah question. In a book edited by Neusner,[4] Jewish and Christian authors agree that there were different Jewish and Christian definitions of the term "messiah" in the Second Temple period and immediately after, but none of the meanings overlapped. Jesus was the Messiah by some Christian definitions of the term, but not by any Jewish definition. Hence the traditions mean different things by the same word.

In a brilliant essay (in a collection of essays in my honor),[5] Neusner pointed the way to a tentative first step in a dialogue that may lead to a Christology that Judaism and Christianity might share, a dialogue that presumably could go on for centuries, if not millennia.

Many will say that Christianity and Judaism can never achieve a mutually satisfactory Christology. To which I respond with Harry Truman, never say never because never is a hell of a long time! **BR** *6:6 (1990), p. 39*

CHAPTER 14

Nag Hammadi Codices Shed Light on Early Christianity

James Brashler

The tandem development of text and religion is explored by James Brashler in his analysis of The Gnostic Gospels, *by Elaine Pagels. Pagels describes "the complex picture of early Christianity and Judaism during the first two centuries of this era" in order to uncover "the social milieu and ecclesiastical politics...that led to the rejection of the ideas they contain...." She believes leaders of "emerging orthodox Christianity" felt threatened by the views expressed in these gospels. For example, belief in a "spiritual" resurrection of mystical experiences threatened the "hierarchy...through whose authority all others must approach God." Refusal to accept the monotheistic "God the creator" implied "rejection of his representative, the bishop, and the clergy of the church." And the belief in a divine trinity of Father, Mother and Son implied accepting women as equals.*

Brashler feels that Pagels' "linkage between theological views and social/political practices is asserted rather than demonstrated" but concludes that she has done a "masterful job" of summarizing manuscripts important to understanding the history of early Christianity and Judaism.–Ed.

It is a long way from the Nile Valley of Egypt to the front page of *The New York Review of Books*, but the fascinating story of *The Gnostic Gospels*[1] by Elaine Pagels has traveled that far.

Books written by good scholars seldom achieve best-seller status. When the book is about a little known collection of manuscripts associated with heretical religious sects and written in a dead language that few people have even heard of, best-seller status is even more unlikely. It is a tribute to the skill and ingenuity of Professor Elaine Pagels (soft g as in gelatin), formerly of Barnard

College and now on the faculty of Princeton University, that her book, *The Gnostic Gospels*, has been so well received by the publishing establishment and the reading public. Summarized in a series of articles in *The New York Review of Books*, offered as a Book-of-the-Month Club alternate selection and translated into several languages, *The Gnostic Gospels* is a lucid account of the significance of the Coptic Gnostic[2] documents found in 1945 near Nag Hammadi, Egypt.

The story behind the discovery and eventual publication of the Nag Hammadi manuscripts has all the ingredients of a spy thriller. The discoverers, Mohammed Ali and his brother Khalifah, lived in a village named el-Kasr in Upper Egypt. While digging for mineral-rich soil called *sebakh* at the base of the cliffs along the Nile near the village of Homra Dom, they discovered a large sealed pottery jar. Hoping for buried treasure, they broke open the jar only to find a collection of old books written in a language they could not read. They carried the books back to their home, where their mother reportedly used some of the pages to light the fire in her oven.

Not long after the discovery of the manuscripts, it was rumored that Mohammed Ali and his brothers murdered the son of the sheriff of Homra Dom in reprisal for the death of their father some six months earlier. One result of this feud was that Mohammed Ali was afraid to return to the site of the discovery. Fearing that the books would be found by the police, Mohammed Ali placed them in the care of a Coptic priest. The priest gave one to a relative, who brought it to Cairo. The rest were gradually sold to other residents of the village for small sums of money, and they in turn sold the manuscripts to antiquities dealers in Cairo.

One book was sold to the Coptic Museum; another made its way out of the country and was sold to friends of the psychologist C. G. Jung. They gave it to him as a birthday present, and it became known as the Jung Codex.[3] Ultimately, however, the bulk of the material was confiscated by the Egyptian government after having been photographed by a young French scholar, Jean Doresse. Just when Doresse's reports were alerting the scholarly world to the existence of an important new manuscript discovery, the Suez crisis of 1956 made international cooperation even more difficult than usual. As a result, most of the Nag Hammadi Codices remained inaccessible to scholars. After the codices were declared government property and deposited in the Coptic Museum, an international committee of scholars working under the auspices of UNESCO was appointed, but the committee made little progress toward publishing the documents.

Not until the American biblical scholar James M. Robinson of Claremont Graduate School entered the picture in 1965 and succeeded in gaining the support of other scholars for reorganizing the UNESCO committee did the Nag Hammadi story gradually emerge. Robinson concentrated his considerable scholarly influence, his organizational skills and his seemingly limitless energy on the prompt translation and publication of the Nag Hammadi documents.

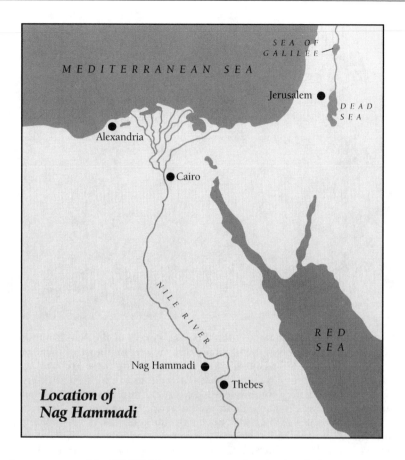

Location of Nag Hammadi

As the secretary of the UNESCO committee, Robinson headed an international team that photographed the manuscripts and conserved them as adequately as possible in their present repository, the Coptic Museum in Cairo. As the director of the Nag Hammadi Library Project at the Institute for Antiquity and Christianity in Claremont, he organized a team of translators, many of them young American scholars, who learned the Coptic language as they worked with the new finds. And as organizer of the Nag Hammadi excavations, he delved into the early history of Christianity in Egypt.

Many other scholars have subsequently joined the growing movement to understand the complicated historical background of early Christianity assumed by the Nag Hammadi documents. Fortunately, the papers used to stiffen the covers of the Coptic codices were legal documents that referred to specific dates; therefore the manuscripts have been solidly dated to the middle fourth century. However, the codices are Coptic translations of documents that were written much earlier. Just how these translations fit into the complex picture of early Christianity and Judaism during the first two centuries of this era is still a matter of considerable scholarly debate.

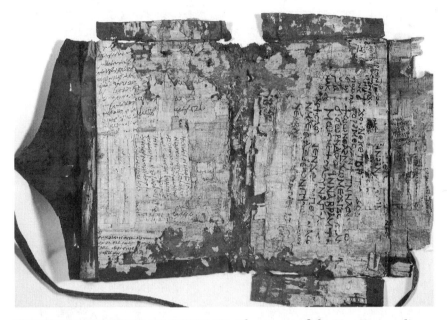

PAPYRUS-LINED COVER OF CODEX VII. The covers of the Nag Hammadi
Codices not only preserved 1,240 pages of text, keeping most of them intact
for 1,600 years, but they also provided a key to dating these archaeological
treasures. Each leather cover had been stiffened and reinforced with layers of
papyrus, many of which were discarded personal and business documents of
monks from the nearby Pachomian monasteries. These documents often contained specific names and dates. This particular codex cover was made partly
of business documents belonging to a monk named Sasnos, who was in
charge of the monastery herds. The years 333, 341 and 348 are cited, indicating that Codex VII was put together in the middle of the fourth century.
    Like the other 12 codices, or books, of the Nag Hammadi library, Codex
VII is made up of separate tractates or essays written in Coptic (an ancient
Egyptian language). The 52 tractates of the entire Nag Hammadi collection
reflect the world view of the Gnostics, a heretical Christian sect in direct conflict with orthodox Christian authorities. The texts often highlight the antago-
nisms between the two groups. *Photo: Institute for Antiquity and Christianity,
Claremont, California*

Elaine Pagels' book is an attempt to answer this exceedingly difficult
question. Pagels makes it clear that she approaches these writings as a church
historian, and her special interest is in uncovering the social milieu and ecclesiastical politics reflected in the Nag Hammadi Codices that prompted leaders of emerging orthodox Christianity to reject the ideas they contain. An
analysis of the new texts from Nag Hammadi together with the previously
known early Christian sources will make it possible, she says, to see "how politics and religion coincide in the development of Christianity....We can gain
a startlingly new perspective on the origins of Christianity."

Pagels begins with a pivotal Christian doctrine, the resurrection of Jesus. Christian tradition is clear about this doctrine. Jesus of Nazareth died on a cross and arose bodily from the grave as a result of God's miraculous intervention. The church father Tertullian, among many others, emphasized the necessity of believing in the physical resurrection of Jesus and labeled anyone who denied the bodily resurrection a heretic. The reasons were not purely theological, Pagels suggests, but also political. She asserts that consolidation of the religious and political authority of the orthodox bishops was a major factor in the development of the orthodox doctrine of the resurrection of Jesus. Faced with a bewildering variety of opinions and reports about the nature of the resurrected Jesus, church leaders turned to the accounts of the apostles as authoritative and rejected accounts that did not reinforce this view.

The Nag Hammadi documents have preserved some of the differing views on the resurrection. They tell us that opponents of the orthodox bishops believed in a spiritual resurrection, which made Jesus alive to them through visions and mystical experiences. From the resurrected Jesus, the Gnostics received revelations of heavenly secrets and insights into the nature of ultimate reality.

The leaders of emerging orthodox Christianity rejected Gnostic revelations as fraudulent. They insisted upon belief in the physical resurrection of Jesus as reported in the four Gospels, Matthew, Mark, Luke and John, which they accepted as the measure (canon) of truth. Gnostic teachers, on the other hand, claimed apostolic authority for their views and criticized orthodox believers for preferring a crude materialistic literalism, which was inferior to their spiritual knowledge. The dispute came down to a matter of authority—the traditional reports accepted by church leaders versus the personal experiences of Gnostic teachers and their followers. The political realities at stake in this dispute, according to Pagels, went far beyond the theological issues. The orthodox view, she concludes, "legitimized a hierarchy of persons through whose authority all others must approach God."

Another basic tenet of orthodox Christianity, the belief in one God, the Father who created heaven and earth, came under strong attack on several fronts, including some represented by the writers of the Gnostic documents from Nag Hammadi. In several of these Gnostic works, the creator God is ridiculed as a blind and ignorant tyrant who was unaware of a higher, purely spiritual deity, the ultimate source of all reality. In the Apocryphon of John, for example, the creator God is said to be weak and "impious in his madness...for he said, 'I am God and there is no other God beside me,' for he is ignorant of his strength, the place from which he had come" (II.1:11,18-22).[4]

Why did orthodox leaders like Irenaeus reject the view of God the creator as blasphemous? Pagels' answer is, again, that political and social realities were involved. A corollary to the belief in one creator God was belief in one earthly representative of this God, a single monarchical bishop. Behind the

Gnostic rejection of the orthodox, monotheistic creator God was an implicit rejection of his representative, the bishop, and the clergy of the church that represented the bishop's authority in the congregations. Pagels finds clear evidence of Gnostic anticlericalism in the Apocalypse of Peter from Nag Hammadi, where the author states, "Others...outside our number...call themselves bishops and also deacons, as if they had received their authority from God. Those people are dry canals" (VII.3:79, 22-32). In contrast to hierarchically organized orthodox Christian congregations, Pagels tells us, Gnostic fellowships were led by spirit-filled leaders chosen by lot, with men and women participating as equals.

In a chapter entitled "God the Father/God the Mother," Pagels analyzes traditional Christian language about God and contrasts it with Gnostic imagery and ideas in the Nag Hammadi writings. She concludes that "many of these texts speak of God as a dyad who embraces both masculine and feminine elements." Aware of the diversity of the Nag Hammadi texts, she asserts that they depict God as having a female dimension, often complementing a male dimension. The female side exists in a kind of polarity akin to the *yin* and *yang* in Eastern concepts of ultimate reality. Furthermore, she says, the Gnostic texts depict the deity as a divine mother who is Holy Spirit. A divine trinity made up of Father, Mother and Son is also found in some of the Nag Hammadi documents. The divine mother is sometimes characterized as the personification of wisdom or ultimate truth. In this role she bears the name Sophia, the Greek word for wisdom.

The feminine imagery in the Gnostic writings was suppressed, to use Pagels' terminology, by orthodox church leaders who rejected the social consequences of such ideas, namely the consequences of including women as equals, especially in the life and leadership of the church. According to Pagels, "from the year 200, we have no evidence for women taking prophetic, priestly and episcopal roles among orthodox churches." This is surprising, she says, in light of the openness to women she finds in earlier Christianity and the general cultural trend toward expanded roles for women in later Roman society. Conflicts over the status of women and related questions of sexuality are reflected in the Nag Hammadi writings, Pagels says. Her conclusion is that "The Nag Hammadi sources, discovered at a time of contemporary social crises concerning sexual roles, challenge us to reinterpret history—and to reevaluate the present situation."

Pagels also discusses two other basic Christian theological affirmations, the crucifixion of Jesus and the nature of the church. In both cases, she contrasts the dominant early Christian view that came to be accepted as orthodox with views in the Nag Hammadi Codices. The contrasts are striking. Was Jesus a human being who really suffered, or was he a spirit who appeared to suffer? Is the Christian church a holy, catholic family of believers with a common creed, a recognized canon of sacred scriptures and an apostolic hierarchy headed by the bishop, or is the true church a fellowship of enlightened brothers and sisters united by spiritual experiences and knowledge?

Even more significant, in Pagels' opinion, are the everyday implications of these differing theological views. Those who emphasized the physical nature of Jesus' suffering placed a high value on the suffering of Christians who were persecuted for their faith. Thus, the cult of martyrs and saints who died at the hands of Roman persecutors became part of orthodox Christian belief. Some Gnostics, who also placed a high value on the sufferings of Jesus, saw him as a model of one who triumphed over physical oppression. But others emphasized Jesus' spiritual nature and minimized the significance of his suffering. They identified themselves with the spiritual Jesus who never actually died. Logically, from this point of view, they rejected the value of martyrdom and considered the eagerness of some Christians to suffer persecution as misguided enthusiasm. In its most extreme form, this enthusiasm was turned against the Gnostics themselves, Pagels suggests, when zealous orthodox Christians later persecuted them for their heretical views.

In a concluding chapter entitled "Gnosis: Self-knowledge as Knowledge of God," Pagels summarizes the Gnostic view that human suffering is the result of *ignorance* rather than *sin*. Salvation, then, is to be found in knowledge (*gnosis*), and knowledge is to be understood as liberating insight into ultimate reality and personal identity rather than factual data. According to the Gnostic documents, such insight comes from the Gnostic revealer, the Savior—usually Jesus, but other figures are sometimes named—who is described as a heavenly messenger. His message is of internal illumination, self-understanding and symbolic truth and is often cast in mythological language. Inner confusion and contradictions give way to inner peace and mystical ecstasy when gnosis replaces ignorance and light replaces darkness. Such a religion, says Pagels, understandably appealed only to a few and "was no match for the highly effective system of organization of the catholic church."

The effective organization led by the bishops accounts for the survival and character of Christianity, Pagels concludes. She readily acknowledges her appreciation of the theological and political acumen of the winners in the struggle for dominance in early Christianity. Nevertheless, her sympathy for the losers in the struggle to define orthodox Christianity is apparent. She admires "those restless, inquiring people who marked out a solitary path of self-discovery" and implies that they embodied more of the values of Jesus of Nazareth than their orthodox opponents were willing to admit. But she does not advocate a revival of Gnosticism or take a Gnostic stand against orthodox Christianity. Instead, as a historian, she has examined the evidence—especially the newly discovered and newly published evidence—pertaining to the origins of Christianity.

As a popular presentation of a difficult and complex topic, *The Gnostic Gospels* has enjoyed success rarely achieved by such books. Pagels has demonstrated that she is a gifted writer as well as a technically proficient scholar. It takes courage to tackle such an assignment and do it well; she has succeeded where few others have dared to try. As a scholar who is familiar with the documents as well as the historical and theological complexities, I applaud her book as a provocative contribution to serious religious writing.

As one might expect, Pagels has her critics. They tend to be scholars who challenge the accuracy of details or dispute what one of them has called her tendency toward "the greening of the Gnostics." Roman Catholic scholars in particular have suggested that she has put the Gnostics in much too favorable a light, while, at the same time, putting the orthodox church fathers in a correspondingly bad light. Others suggest that she has not examined her sources with full rigor and has extracted from them only those passages that fit her feminist biases or the biases of the book-buying public. To some extent, such criticism may reflect bruised piety or sour grapes. It may also be the result of expecting more from a popular book than a book of that genre can deliver.

Pagels' work is certainly not beyond criticism. My own view is that she has promised more than she can deliver. The revolutionary insights promised at the beginning of the book are reduced by the end of the book to provocative questions Pagels only begins to explore. At times she seems to move, almost unwittingly, from a possibility suggested in the subjunctive mood or a rhetorical question to a probability or an assumption of the same idea.[5] To me, the linkage between theological views and social/political practices is asserted rather than demonstrated in the book. Of course, such a connection is extremely difficult to establish conclusively, especially when our historical sources are incomplete and are the products of people who were personally involved in the complex process of doctrinal development. Pagels' use of the term "political" will strike some readers as unusual because she means ecclesiastical politics for the most part rather than governmental or civic activities.

For anyone interested in biblical archaeology, Elaine Pagels has done a masterful job of describing and summarizing a major manuscript discovery that is extremely important in the history of early Christianity and contemporaneous Judaism. Gnostic writers were clearly indebted to both traditions and have preserved elements of early traditions that were relegated to the periphery or excluded altogether from orthodox Christianity and rabbinic Judaism. Traditions about Jesus from the Nag Hammadi writings, especially collections of his sayings like the Gospel of Thomas, provide new and potentially significant material for New Testament studies and may provide clues to authentic words of Jesus not preserved in the New Testament.

Interpretations of the early chapters of the Book of Genesis according to Gnostic writers may help illumine Jewish and Christian interpretations of those same chapters by the Jewish philosopher Philo of Alexandria, for example, as well as the apostle Paul. The Nag Hammadi documents have also shed light on the Gospel of John and the epistles of Paul. In Pagels' doctoral dissertation at Harvard University (published in 1973)[6] and another book on Paul in 1975,[7] she investigated the relationships between John and Paul, on the one hand, and the ideas of Gnostic teachers like Valentinus and Basilides, on the other. Scholars are still trying to resolve these complex questions with the help of the Gnostic writings.

The Nag Hammadi Codices surely help us understand the tendency toward mystical piety based on revelation or ecstatic experience as one variety of religious experience in the Greco-Roman world of late antiquity. These writings also provide new material for understanding the many types of ancient Gnosticism. Interactions between Greek philosophical thought and early Christianity, in both the Gnostic and emerging orthodox forms, can also be illumined by these new writings.

Attempts to uncover the circumstances surrounding the burial of the Nag Hammadi manuscripts have not been as successful as the archaeological excavations that were helpful in shedding light on another major manuscript discovery, the Dead Sea Scrolls. An excavation carried out by the Institute for Antiquity and Christianity in Claremont, California, under the leadership of Dr. James Robinson and Dr. Bastiaan Van Elderen, has uncovered significant remains of early Christian monastic communities near the discovery site. But direct links with the Nag Hammadi Codices have not been found, and even the exact location of the original find is not known. The broader question of how a collection of mostly Gnostic texts came to be buried near the center of early Christian monasteries considered to be bastions of orthodoxy has yet to be answered. The interactions between Gnostic and orthodox leaders in the development of Christianity in Egypt and other centers of Christianity such as Alexandria and Rome is one of the concerns of a new project being undertaken by Dr. Birger Pearson and several associates under the auspices of the Institute for Antiquity and Christianity.

For now, Pagels' *The Gnostic Gospels* is the best popular introduction to the difficult but fascinating subject of early Christianity and Gnosticism.

A F T E R W O R D

Brashler further explores the promise and problems of the Nag Hammadi documents in reviews of two books published in 1988.[1] In a review of the third revised edition of The Nag Hammadi Library in English, *edited by James M. Robinson and Richard Smith, he surveys a decade of scholarship and compares different approaches to translating these difficult texts:*

How has our understanding of the Gnostic texts changed in the past decade? Do improvements in the third edition of translations show that at least some of the difficulties presented by the Coptic texts have been resolved by advances in understanding Coptic syntax and vocabulary? Do new introductions to the texts help the reader penetrate the complex and abstruse content of these ancient writings? Or are those who greeted the original publication as heretical gibberish supported by the new translations?...

Turning to James Robinson's introduction, we find, without significant change from the 1977 edition, the idea that Gnosticism is best understood not as a Christian heresy but as a multifaceted Hellenistic religion with pre-Christian, or at least non-Christian, Oriental roots. There is no reference to Bentley Layton's recent argument that Gnostic texts constitute a heretical countercanon, opposing both Christian and Jewish canons. One looks in vain for major shifts or advances in the scholarly understanding of Gnosticism and Gnostic texts....One of the few new developments reflected in the introduction concerns the putative link between early Judaism and the emergence of so-called Sethian Gnosticism. This is allegedly a strain of Gnosticism attested in texts in which the biblical figure Seth, the third son of Adam, plays an important role.

...The highly abstract, verbose and ambiguous Coptic style has been reproduced in what passes for English. In return for diligent attempts to wrestle meaning from these translations of translations, modern readers often find themselves inundated by a befuddling cascade of words, phrases, clauses and even sentences that defy rational analysis.

It may be that modern translators have done the best they can with inferior Coptic translations. The blame for incomprehensibility should, perhaps, be placed on the anonymous ancient Copts who tried to translate from Greek to Coptic. I am sure this is an appropriate explanation for tractates like VI.5, the excerpt from Plato's *Republic*. After all, this small fragment came from a difficult philosophical masterpiece that requires special knowledge of both Platonic Greek style and ancient philosophy to render it accurately.

But this tractate is an exception in the Nag Hammadi corpus. Far more typical, I believe, is tractate I.4, "The Treatise on the Resurrection." Bentley Layton demonstrated, in his Harvard dissertation and in his anthology, *The Gnostic Scriptures*,[2] that these texts require a different method of translation than the literal, word-for-word equivalence method generally used by translators on the Claremont team. Layton's approach to translation differs from theirs in two crucial ways. First, he assumes that a coherent Greek original was the basis for the existing Coptic translation and that problems in the Coptic can be better understood and perhaps overcome when the underlying Greek text is taken into account. Layton's aim, then, is "to be flexible in translating from the ancient Coptic, taking account of the text's original composition in Greek as a product of Hellenistic-Roman culture."[3] He then applies his impressive knowledge of Greek syntax and Hellenistic philosophical and religious rhetoric to the Coptic texts with exceedingly helpful results. The Coptic texts begin to make better sense, and the translations are more readable when such an approach is taken.

The second methodological difference between the Claremont translators and Layton lies in translation policy; Layton more adequately reflects the provisional state of our knowledge of Coptic. While the Claremont translators diligently follow standard works like Walter Till's *Koptische Grammatik*[4] and Walter Crum's *Coptic Dictionary*,[5] Layton goes beyond these to understand the grammar of the particular tractate he is translating. The detailed grammatical appendices at the end of Layton's translation of "The Treatise on the Resurrection" are evidence of the meticulous care with which he has analyzed the grammatical and lexicographical peculiarities of that text. "As the new texts appear," Layton writes, "it becomes ever clearer how much research in Coptic grammar lies before us and how rich and rewarding these labors will be." Unfortunately, the revised edition of the Claremont translations shows little progress along these lines. **BR** *6:1 (1990), p. 10*

CHAPTER 15

Truth and Legend about the Septuagint

Leonard J. Greenspoon

The original Holy Scriptures of Christianity consisted of the Jewish Bible–in the Greek version of the Septuagint. The inferiority or superiority of the Septuagint to the Hebrew Masoretic text thus became a matter of bitter polemical dispute between Jews and Christians. Even before that, however, Jews had debated the pros and cons of this Hellenistic translation, as Leonard J. Greenspoon explains.

According to the Letter of Aristeas, Ptolemy II Philadelphus asked the Jewish high priest in Jerusalem to send wise men to translate the Pentateuch for his library in Alexandria. Seventy-two eminent scholars worked for 72 days to produce a divinely inspired version, the perfection of which so impressed the Jewish audience at a public reading that "they commanded that a curse should be laid...on anyone who should alter the version by any addition or change." The author of the letter goes into detail about the qualifications of the translators, the nature of their reception and the general approval of their work, but very little attention is paid to the translation itself. Greenspoon believes that this indicates that the true purpose of the letter was to "defend the authority of this Greek translation....For the author of the Letter of Aristeas, the Greek translation constituted Holy Writ as authentic and binding as the Hebrew text associated with Moses." This defense may have been necessary, he believes, because the Septuagint, which often differs from the Masoretic text, may have come under attack.–Ed.

It often comes as a surprise to laypeople that ancient copies of the Bible vary, sometimes in minor ways, but sometimes in important ways. There are always variations between any two manuscripts of the Bible, even if they are written in the same language. But apart from minor variations among ancient manuscripts, when all the evidence from antiquity is compared, two important textual traditions emerge. They are the Masoretic text and the Septuagint. The Masoretic text (MT) is the Hebrew text as standardized by Jewish scribes in the tenth century C.E. Although our oldest extant copy of the MT is about a hundred years later, the texts these scribes worked with were obviously much older than the tenth century C.E. and were directly linked to even earlier texts, as we now know from the Dead Sea Scrolls.

The Septuagint, often referred to as LXX, is a translation of one form of the Hebrew Bible into Greek. In this article, we will be concerned with the source of this version. The earliest surviving complete copies of the Greek Septuagint date to the fourth and fifth centuries C.E. As we shall see, the translation was made in the third century B.C.E., and the Hebrew manuscripts on which the translation was based are even earlier. Moreover, it is clear that the Hebrew texts on which the Septuagint was based varied considerably from the Hebrew Bible that has come down to us in the MT. Sometimes, scholars prefer the reading in the MT; sometimes the reading in the LXX seems more reliable.

Our interest here, however, is not in the MT or even the LXX per se, but rather in a famous document called the Letter of Aristeas, which tells how the Septuagint came into being.

The Letter of Aristeas purports to be written in the Egyptian metropolis of Alexandria by a certain Aristeas and is addressed to a certain Philocrates, whom he calls his "brother." The subject is how the Pentateuch—in Hebrew, the Torah, the Five Books of Moses—happened to be translated from Hebrew into Greek. According to the letter, the intellectually curious Ptolemy II (Philadelphus, 285-247 B.C.E.), who ruled from Alexandria, wanted his librarian, Demetrius, to assemble a library containing a copy of every book in the world. When Demetrius had collected more than 200,000 books, he so advised the king, adding that he hoped to increase the number to 500,000. Among the books still missing were "the lawbooks of the Jews [which] are worth translation and inclusion in your royal library" (verse 10).[1]

The king replied, "What is there to prevent you from doing this? Everything for your needs has been put at your disposal" (verse 11). Demetrius replied, "Translation is needed. They use letters characteristic of the language of the Jews, just as Egyptians use the formation of their letters in accordance with their own language."

The king then ordered that a letter be written in his name to Eleazar, the high priest of the Jews in Jerusalem. At the same time, the king ordered the release of more than 100,000 Jews who had been forcibly removed to Egypt some years earlier by his father. In Ptolemy's letter, the high priest Eleazar was requested to dispatch 72 men skilled in the Law (six from each of the 12 tribes) to Alexandria to make an accurate translation of the Law into Greek. The translators were to be "elders of exemplary lives, with the experience of the Law and ability to translate it." In reply, Eleazar wrote:

> Eleazar the high priest to King Ptolemy, dear friend, greeting. Good health to you and to Queen Arsinoe, your sister and to your children...On receipt of your letter we rejoiced greatly because of your purpose and noble

> plan...we selected elders, honorable men and true, six from each tribe, whom we have sent with the Law in their possession.
>
> verses 41-42, 46

When the translators arrived in Alexandria, they were accorded unusual honor:

> The king was anxious to meet the members of the deputation, so he gave orders to dismiss all the other court officials, and to summon these delegates. The unprecedented nature of this step was very clear to all, because it was an established procedure that important *bona fide* visitors should be granted an audience with the king only four days after arrival, while representatives of kings or important cities are [were] rarely admitted to the court within thirty days. However, he deemed the present arrivals to be deserving of greater honor, having regard to the preeminence of him who had sent them. So he dismissed all the officials whom he considered superfluous and remained walking among the delegates until he had greeted the whole delegation.
>
> verses 174-175

The translators showed the king the Hebrew scrolls they had brought with them, "fine skins on which the Law had been written in letters of gold in Jewish characters; the parchment had been excellently worked, and the joining together of the letters was imperceptible" (verse 176). In response, the king did obeisance about seven times, and said, "I offer to you my thanks, gentlemen, and to him who sent you even more, and most of all to the God whose oracles these are" (verse 177).

The king then held a week long series of banquets for the translators and set them up in "the finest apartments...near the citadel" (verse 181). Three days later the librarian Demetrius took the 72 translators across a jetty to an island a mile out in the Mediterranean Sea. There they were installed in a sumptuous building to begin their labors. They completed their work in exactly 72 days (verses 301-307).

The resulting translation was then read to the local community of Jews, who acclaimed it with a great ovation (verse 308). The king rejoiced greatly because his purpose had been accomplished (verse 312). When the translation was read to him, "he marveled profoundly at the genius of the lawgiver" (verse 312). On the departure of the translators, he gave "each one three robes of the finest materials, two talents of gold, a cup worth a talent, and complete furnishing for a dining room" (verse 319).

Before asking how reliable this account is, we should first ask if we are working from an accurate copy of Aristeas' letter. The Letter of Aristeas has survived in about two dozen medieval manuscripts. The earliest of these is from the 11th century C.E., more than a millennium after it was written. To bridge that gap, scholars have sifted through the works of ancient Jewish authors (such as Philo, Josephus and rabbinic sources) and Christian writers (Justin, Jerome and Eusebius, for example) for authentic fragments of the Letter of Aristeas. They have also carefully compared the medieval manuscripts of the letter. In this way, they have arrived at a Greek text that approaches, if it does not precisely duplicate, the original letter of Aristeas.

Although Aristeas claims to be an eyewitness to, even a participant in, the events he describes (which would mean he lived and wrote about 270 B.C.E.), virtually no scholar today would uphold that claim. Dates anywhere from the late third century B.C.E. to the first century C.E. have been proposed. Most scholars, however, now agree on the middle second century B.C.E. as the most likely period for the composition of the letter.

The entire letter, now divided into 322 verses, is not long—about the size of the Gospel of John. Although the subject of the letter is, broadly speaking, the translation of the Law for the king's library, very little space is devoted to the translation itself (only verses 9-11, 28-50 and 301-317). The rest is more or less tangentially related to the translation. For example, verses 51-82 contain a detailed description of the gifts sent by the king to the high priest Eleazar, and about a third of the work (verses 187-294) is given over to a display of each translator's wisdom.

The third-century Christian leader Eusebius called the letter "Concerning the Translation of the Law of the Jews," which may have been the original title.[2] At the very least, Eusebius' title refers to the topic of greatest interest to most ancient and modern readers.

Note that Aristeas claims that the impetus for the translation came not from the Jews but from royal Egyptian authority. In support of this claim, some contemporary scholars refer to Ptolemy's documented interest in all kinds of literature, especially the literature of subject peoples like the Jews. In addition, in Greek translation, the Law could have served as a sort of constitution for the semiautonomous Jewish community of Alexandria.[3]

Other scholars—who are now in the majority—disagree.[4] They contend that it is much more likely that the Jews instigated the translation to serve their own liturgical and pedagogical needs. When the evidence is reinvestigated from this point of view, Ptolemy's interest in a Greek translation of Jewish Law begins to evaporate. Moreover, it seems unlikely that a translation instigated by an outside force could have gained as authoritative a position within the Jewish community as the Septuagint did.

But if we accept, as most modern researchers do, that the Letter of Aristeas was composed by a Jew for a primarily Jewish audience, what possible motive could he have had to invent the story that Ptolemy instigated the project? Probably Aristeas put this story in the letter because it was too well known to be omitted. On this important issue, the scholarly jury is still out.

What about the actual process of translation described in the letter? Does it have the ring of probability, or does it seem farfetched and unrealistic? A careful examination of the passages dealing with this question suggests that the procedure is not only probable, but also eminently workable. The 72 translators were given excellent working conditions.

> [Demetrius]...assembled them in a house which had been duly furnished near the shore—a magnificent building in a very quiet situation—and invited the men to carry out the work of translation, all that they would request being handsomely provided....The business of their meeting occupied them until the ninth hour [3:00 p.m.] of each day.
>
> verse 303

They worked from Hebrew manuscripts that had the approval and authority of the chief Jewish religious functionary, the high priest in Jerusalem. The translators were distinguished and knowledgeable:

> Eleazar selected men of the highest merit and of excellent education due to the distinction of their parentage; they had not only mastered the Jewish literature, but had made a serious study of that of the Greeks as well. They were therefore well qualified for the embassy, and brought it to fruition as occasion demanded; they had a tremendous natural facility for the negotiations and questions arising from the Law, with the middle way as their commendable ideal; they forsook any uncouth and uncultured attitude of mind; in the same way they rose above conceit and contempt of other people and instead engaged in discourse and listening to and answering each and every one, as is meet and right. They all observed these aims, and went further in wishing to excel each other in them; they were, one and all, worthy of their leader and his outstanding qualities.
>
> verses 121-122

The work was apparently divided up, for we are told that the translators compared results with one another: "They set to completing their several tasks, reaching agreement among themselves on each by comparing versions" (verse 302). When they could not reach agreement by consensus, the majority ruled; we are told in the librarian Demetrius' memorandum to the king (quoted in the letter) that 72 translators (six from each tribe) would be used and that the "text [would be] agreed [to] by the majority" (verse 32). In this way, Demetrius concluded, the "achievement of accuracy in the translation" would be assured, and "we may produce an outstanding version in a manner worthy both of the contents and of your purpose" (verse 32).

This procedure—individuals working separately and then comparing their work in order to produce a finished product—is, in general, the way translation committees operate to this very day. Only the palatial surroundings and the uninterrupted work schedule differentiate the Alexandrian translators from their modern counterparts! "Handsomely provided" with "all that they would require," the Jewish elders maintained a rapid pace. "The outcome was such that in 72 days the business of translation was completed" (verses 301, 307).

Such an accomplishment in 72 days was certainly no mean feat, but, lest there be any misunderstanding, it is important to point out that they translated only the Torah, the Five Books of Moses. The letter repeatedly refers to "the lawbooks of the Jews" (verse 10), "the Law of the Jews" (verse 30), "legislation, as could be expected from its divine nature, [that] is very philosophical and genuine" (verse 31). This is unambiguous evidence that only the Pentateuch was involved. On this point, the author of the letter and modern scholars agree.

At a later date, the rest of the books of the Hebrew Scripture, as well as the Apocrypha, were translated into Greek, and today references to the Septuagint often include the entire collection. Early Christian writers were the first to use the term Septuagint with this expanded meaning. Among them, Jerome (best known for the Vulgate, or Latin translation of the Bible) was virtually alone in maintaining the original Jewish understanding that only the Pentateuch was the subject of the Letter of Aristeas.

Returning to the Letter of Aristeas, the author apparently realized that it was more than a coincidence that 72 translators completed their task in exactly 72 days. It is, he says, "as if such a result was achieved by some deliberate design" (verse 307). The Letter of Aristeas goes no further. Later sources—both Jewish and Christian—do. In them, we find numerous embellishments. Philo, a first-century C.E. Jewish philosopher who lived in Alexandria, identified the island where the translators worked as Pharos and referred to the translators as "prophets and priests of the mysteries," who, as they worked, "became as it were possessed, and, under inspiration, wrote, not each...something different, but the same word for word, as though dictated to each by an invisible prompter."[5] To commemorate this event, Philo tells us, an annual festival was held, for Jews and non-Jews alike, on Pharos. Unfortunately, popularized accounts of the Letter of Aristeas often incorrectly attribute Philo's embellished version to Aristeas.

On the Christian side, we also find numerous embellishments. Epiphanius, writing in the fourth century, tells us that the 72 translators were divided into 36 pairs. Each pair was assigned a single book of the Old Testament or Apocrypha to translate. When they completed their rendering of that book, they were assigned another, so that each book was translated 36 times. When this mammoth task drew to an end, all of the copies were compared. The result? "There was found no discrepancy!" The translations were identical!

Although the description of the translation process itself in the Letter of Aristeas is plausible and attractive, it is, unfortunately, contradicted by internal evidence in the Septuagint Pentateuch itself. Careful examination of the Greek text of the five books of the Torah reveals differences in style, grammar and word choices that are incompatible with the contention that the entire body of material was translated at one time by one cohesive group.[6] One recent study, for example, concluded that "Numbers and Deuteronomy are the product of different translators."[7]

Although the Jewish tradition continued to ascribe the Greek text to 72 translators, in Christian tradition the number 70 predominates. The name Septuagint (seventy) is based on this Christian tradition. It is sometimes suggested that the name simply rounds off the number of translators to 70, but this is incorrect.

The number 72—six representatives from each of the 12 tribes of Israel—was not meaningful for Christians. They took their lead from the 70 elders who were with Moses at Mount Sinai and from the reference to the 70 whom Jesus commissioned in Luke 10.[8]

There may be reasons to question many of the details in the Letter of Aristeas, but a great many scholars agree with the contention that the Septuagint translation of the Pentateuch was produced in the early third century B.C.E. in Alexandria. An examination of manuscript material now available, especially the large caches of papyri that have been unearthed in Egypt in the past hundred years, establishes the first half of the third century as a congenial environment for the production of the Greek translation of the Pentateuch.[9] Moreover, scholars who recently studied the names of the translators given in the letter have concluded that they can all be dated to the early third century B.C.E. These individuals may not have been the actual translators of the Septuagint, but their names are authentic in the temporal context presupposed by the letter.

In addition, the author's accurate descriptions of customs and conditions indicate his familiarity with life in early Ptolemaic Egypt. In this respect, the letter can be compared to the novella about Joseph at the end of Genesis or the Book of Esther. All three are set in milieus drawn from historical reminiscences into which the author has placed characters and events of a "legendary" or paradigmatic nature.

The purpose of the Letter of Aristeas was much broader than the specific questions we have been considering. The comparatively little space the author devoted to describing the translation process underlines this. Nor was he interested in simply providing miscellaneous data about the Septuagint. The author's real purpose was to establish and defend the authority of the Greek translation of the Pentateuch. That purpose is implicit in much of the letter. It emerges, near the end, in the description of the public reading and ratification of the translation:

> Demetrius assembled the company of the Jews in the place where the task of the translation had been finished, and read it to all, in the presence of the translators, who received a great ovation from the crowded audience for being responsible for great blessings....As the books were read, the priests stood up, with the elders from among the translators and from the representatives of the "community," and with the leaders of the people, and said, "Since this version has been made rightly and reverently, and in every respect accurately, it is good that this should remain exactly so, and there should be no revision." There was general approval of what they said, and they commanded that a curse should be laid, as was their custom, on anyone who should alter the version by any addition or change to any part of the written text, or any deletion either. This was a good step taken, to ensure that the words were preserved completely and permanently in perpetuity.
>
> verses 308-311

This episode is a close parallel to the Israelite ratification of the Torah at Mount Sinai as described in Exodus 19 and 24:

> Moses went and repeated to the people all the commands of the Lord and all the norms; and all the people answered with one voice, saying, "All things that the Lord has commanded we will do!"...Then he took record of the covenant and read it aloud to the people. And they said, "All that the Lord has spoken we will faithfully do."
>
> Exodus 24:3,7

To the author of the Letter of Aristeas, the Greek translation constituted Holy Writ as authentic and binding as the Hebrew text associated with Moses. Just as the Hebrew text was divinely inspired, so too was the Greek translation we call the Septuagint.[10]

There is a contemporary parallel to this in the way the King James Version, despite many errors, is regarded as sacred by many believers. One writer recently described what he called the "still widespread belief that the King James Version is the original Word of God and that any translation that differs from it is a perversion, a devil's masterpiece produced by people with a low view of Scripture."[11] The same attitude often plagues modern translators who attempt to improve Bible translations.

Perhaps the author of the Letter of Aristeas, who was writing a hundred years or so after the Greek translation of the Pentateuch, felt the need to defend the Septuagint against a rival translation or revision.[12] Perhaps a "rival" Greek text was produced by Jews for whom the Hebrew text retained a unique sanctity and authority. When they read the Septuagint, they may have noted—as modern readers do—that many passages differed from the Hebrew text. And they may have felt it was their duty to revise the Greek to reflect this Hebrew truth.

Rival Greek texts eventually led to a series of Jewish revisions of the Septuagint, culminating in the Greek recensions attributed to Aquila, Theodotion and Symmachus. Although these three Jewish revisers were not active until the second century C.E., similar revisions can be traced back to pre-Christian times. The appearance of one or another of these "antecedents" may have stimulated the author of the Letter of Aristeas to defend an older, more original form of the Pentateuch, a defense that was later expanded to cover the earliest Greek translation of the entire Old Testament.

Today, when scholars are confronted with differences between the Septuagint and the received, or Masoretic, Hebrew text, they seriously consider the possibility that the Greek reading may be superior because the earliest Greek translators may have used a different Hebrew *Vorlage* (underlying text). This explanation, however, was far from the minds of the Jews described here.

It would be nice if we knew more about the Letter of Aristeas and who wrote it. But perhaps the fascination lies in these enigmas. In any event, the letter is our chief ancient witness to the origins and nature of the Septuagint, the earliest translation of the Bible.

Major Septuagint Manuscripts— Vaticanus, Sinaiticus, Alexandrinus

Readers of Bible commentaries and articles on the Bible are often informed by learned authors that particular words or phrases are found in the Septuagint—and that, therefore, the Septuagint substantiates the learned author's argument. Readings from this ancient Greek translation are often cited to support modern researchers who feel they may have discovered a more authentic wording than the wording in the traditional Hebrew Masoretic text.

Unsuspecting readers may assume that the Greek text of the Septuagint has been transmitted in only one form and that it is a simple matter for scholars to determine the original wording. Unfortunately, as is true of any written work from antiquity, the text of the Septuagint has been subjected to innumerable changes, both deliberate and accidental, as it was copied and recopied

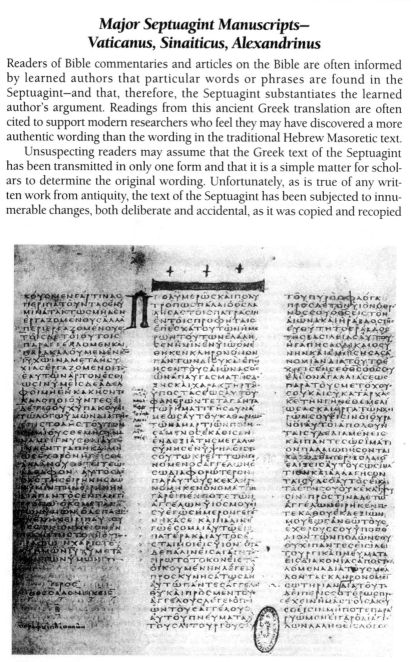

CODEX VATICANUS, Ecclesiastes 4:3–5:2

Photos: Bruce M. Metzger, **Manuscripts of the Greek Bible,** *Oxford University Press*

CODEX ALEXANDRINUS, the first page of the Book of Amos.

over the centuries. Textual critics must collect and evaluate the thousands of variant readings thus produced in an effort to arrive at the earliest recoverable reading for each verse of the Greek Old Testament.

Textual critics of the Septuagint are confronted with hundreds of manuscripts, some almost complete, others extant only in fragments. When they find distinctive readings in several manuscripts, they are able to join them together to form textual "families," which can be described in terms of origin and text type. Individual manuscripts may also be characterized in this way, but scholars must be careful about making generalizations. Today we recognize that the character of any manuscript may vary considerably from book to book or even from section to section of the Bible. Moreover, an authentic, original reading of the Septuagint may sometimes be preserved in a late manuscript of generally poor quality.

In the study of Septuagint manuscripts, pride of place has traditionally been given to a few old copies that are relatively complete and beautifully ▶

CODEX SINAITICUS, Esdras B 14:1-15:5 (=MT Nehemiah 4:1-5:55; in the LXX Ezra and Nehemiah are combined in one book called Esdras B).

written. The most famous of these are Codex Vaticanus, Codex Sinaiticus and Codex Alexandrinus. The first two date to the fourth century and the third to about a century later. All three appear to have a common Egyptian origin. They also have several other common characteristics. They are all codices, or leaf books, a form made popular (if not invented) by Christians; they are all written on vellum, specially prepared lamb skin; all three are written in uncial script (a modification of the all-capital letter formations used primarily in inscriptions); finally, they have all been subjected to numerous alterations and corrections through erasures, interlinear markings and marginal notations.

The scribes who copied these manuscripts made only sporadic use of many features we take for granted in modern printed texts—punctuation marks, word divisions, verse and paragraph divisions, initial capital letters for proper names, breathing marks (for Greek texts), quotation marks and so forth. The absence of these features (and they are missing in virtually all manuscripts of the Septuagint) doubtless caused confusion in antiquity and continues to allow for considerable differences of opinion among researchers.

Interestingly enough, the three so-called greater uncial manuscripts are not copies of each other. They vary in external format and text type, and their origins are largely a matter of scholarly guesswork. We are somewhat better informed of their histories, at least from the early modern period on. We know, for example, that Codex Alexdandrinus was sent to England in the early 17th century by one Cyril Lucar, patriarch of Alexandria (and later of Constantinople). Before that, it had belonged to the Patriarchate of Alexandria, hence its designation as Alexandrinus. The Codex Alexandrinus has been housed in the British Museum since 1757.

It is not clear exactly how and when Codex Vaticanus reached the Vatican (from which it takes its name). This codex is catalogued in some early 15th-century lists of prized possessions of the Vatican Library where it has been housed, except for a brief sojourn in Paris as a prize of war during the Napoleonic period.

Codex Sinaiticus became known to Western scholars in the mid-1800s, much later than the other two. The honor of discovery, in the Convent of Saint Catherine at the foot of Mount Sinai (hence its designation, Sinaiticus), belongs to Konstantin von Tischendorf, a colorful German scholar and adventurer. There is still some controversy and rancor over the means by which he obtained this important ancient witness to the Septuagint, which is now on view in the British Museum.

Earlier generations of textual critics tended to rely almost exclusively on these impressive uncial manuscripts. And there can be no doubt that they retain many original readings in text or corrections. Critics today, however, also study the texts of many later cursive manuscripts (written in smaller script). Cursive manuscripts number more than 1,500 (including fragmentary remains) and are found in museums and libraries throughout the world. But scholars recognize, as their predecessors often did not, that the age or condition of a manuscript is not an infallible guide to the age or condition of the text. Late copies may preserve early readings.

Modern critics also have the advantage of access to material even older than the fourth- and fifth-century uncials. Included in this material are large numbers of fragments written on papyrus discovered over the past century or so, mostly in Egypt. Although the papyrus fragments vary considerably in age and quality, some date back to the pre-Christian era, around the time of the original Greek translation of some parts of the Bible. Fragmentary remains in Greek have also been found among the Dead Sea Scrolls.

Finally, the Septuagint was translated into other languages. A full exploration of the Septuagint text requires taking into account manuscripts translated from Greek into other languages. But that is a complex story for another time.

AFTERWORD

Sidney Sherman of Merrit Island, Florida, raises two questions about the Septuagint and the Letter of Aristeas:

1. Is it not possible or even probable that one of the ancient Targums, the translations of the Scriptures from Hebrew into Aramaic, predated the Septuagint?

2. Greenspoon quotes the Letter of Aristeas reporting on a request by King Ptolemy to the high priest Eleazar for "the dispatch of 72 men skilled in the law (six from each of the 12 tribes) to Alexandria to make an accurate translation of the Law into Greek." This event occurred sometime in the third century B.C.E. Is it not true that ten of the Israelite tribes had lost their identity, mostly as a result of the destruction of Israel by Assyria in the eighth century B.C.E., and that remnants of the ten tribes had been thoroughly merged and were indistinguishable from the tribe of Judah by the third century B.C.E.? Besides Judah, only the Levites maintained a separate tribal identity. **BR** *5:6 (1989), p. 40*

Greenspoon replies:

There is reason to suggest, as Mr. Sherman does, that some form (oral or written) of Aramaic translation of at least a portion of the Hebrew Bible was already in existence when the Septuagint translation was prepared. There is, however, no firm evidence of this. Some scholars have detected an Aramaic rather than a Hebrew *Vorlage* (underlying text) in a few passages of the Septuagint. However, the case for such an early date for a written Aramaic translation of scripture is far from "proven" at this point. Thus, I prefer to retain the standard designation of the Septuagint as the first Bible translation, although I will not be unduly disappointed if further evidence dislodges me from this position.

Mr. Sherman is correct, of course, that there is an element of artificiality in the Letter of Aristeas when the author refers to the 12 tribes long after they had ceased to exist. However, in fairness to our author, we should note that he does not name the tribes but contents himself with "first tribe," "second tribe" and so forth. **BR** *5:6 (1989), p. 40*

Manuscripts

The history of the canon calls attention to how fluid Sacred Writ once was; as ongoing discoveries of manuscripts attest, that fluidity did not end with canonization.

Because they were dependent on available technology, manuscripts varied in material structure as well as language. Scrolls made from papyrus, a plant fiber, were more fragile and less durable than parchment scrolls, which were made of thin leather. Because parchment scrolls were expensive, they were often scraped clean and reused. Comparing manuscripts—even different parts of a single manuscript—can be a lesson in the history of writing (paleography), as well as the evolution of a text.

Transmission of the New Testament differed from transmission of the Hebrew Bible both in time and in writing technologies. Scrolls were made from sheets of writing sewn end to end, the preferred Jewish format and the one required for public reading of the Torah even today. Codices were made from sheets folded and sewn down the middle, the preferred Christian format and ancestor of the modern book. The Bible as we know it could not fit on a single scroll, which rarely exceeded 40 feet in length, but it could be made into a single "book" or codex.

CHAPTER 16

Old Testament Manuscripts
From Qumran to Leningrad

Marc Brettler

Written over a period of more than a thousand years, Hebrew biblical manuscripts embody the evolution of the Hebrew writing system. As Marc Brettler explains, the "major distinction among texts of the Hebrew Bible is whether they are vocalized or unvocalized." The earliest texts show only consonants. Starting probably in the eighth century B.C.E., certain consonants were used as vowel letters–matres lectionis (mothers of reading). After 500 C.E. separate vowel signs were added. Brettler explains that, although some Dead Sea Scroll texts differ from the Masoretic text, modern printed texts are still based on the Masoretic text because the Dead Sea Scrolls are fragmentary and because transmission of the Masoretic text was done very carefully.

The Ben Asher school of Tiberias produced the most reliable Masoretic manuscripts, among them the Aleppo Codex, which was completed in the tenth century but was damaged in a fire in 1947; printed Hebrew Bibles, notably a manuscript in the Leningrad Public Library dating from about 1008, are based on this "family." Other families and versions preserve traditions useful for reconstructing the ancient biblical text.–Ed.

Ancient texts are different from modern books. Today, copyright laws not only assure the author a fair share of royalties, but also that the printed text is the one the author wanted to print. Before the introduction of copyright laws, many different texts of single works were circulated. Some publishers copied the base text exactly, some shortened it, some expanded it. In addition, different copyists used different manuscripts as bases for their editions. All of these things happened to the text of the Bible. The most important manuscripts of the Hebrew Bible are hundreds of years old, and, not surprisingly, they are not identical. Studying various manuscripts is important, both for understanding how one text relates to another and for deciding which version or text is closest to the original.

The texts of the Hebrew Bible and the New Testament have very different histories. The Hebrew Bible contains material written in the course of a millennium, while the entire New Testament was composed within a century. Transmission of the Hebrew Bible began long before the New Testament was written. It is, therefore, not surprising that the history of manuscripts of the Hebrew Bible is not parallel to the history of New Testament manuscripts.[1]

The major distinction among texts of the Hebrew Bible is whether or not they are vocalized. This distinction is based on certain peculiarities of the Hebrew writing system. In the earliest written stage only the consonants of Hebrew words were written down; there were no signs for the vowels. For example, the word for *word* would be written דבר, *dbr*, and read as *davar*. The same consonants, however, could also be read as *dibber* (he spoke), *devar* (word of) or *dever* (pestilence). Context was the guide to proper pronunciation and meaning, much as context helps us decide whether to read the English word *read* to rhyme with *seed* or with *head*. Context, however, is not always enough to establish the meaning of a word.

Starting probably in the eighth century B.C.E., certain consonants (י,ו,ה,א) were used as vowel letters. For example, the Hebrew letter ה at the end of a word would suggest not the *h* sound but the vowel sound *ah*. This system of vowel letters (known as *matres lectionis,* literally "mothers of reading") was an incomplete vowel system that created its own ambiguities.

In the second half of the first millennium C.E., a tradition developed of adding separate vowel signs to biblical texts. For example, the ambiguity of the written word דבר (*dbr*) was resolved by writing דָבָר (*davar*, word), דִּבֶּר (*dibber*, he spoke), דְּבַר (*devar*, word of) or דֶּבֶר (*dever*, pestilence).

The vocalized texts are usually called Masoretic texts, after the Masoretes, a group of scholars who introduced the vowel system and other innovations to safeguard the traditional reading of the text. The term Masoretic derives from the Hebrew root *msr* (מסר; to hand over, to transmit or to count); the Masoretes tried to ensure accurate transmission of the Hebrew text through the precise counting of letters. After a manuscript was copied, the number of letters in the copy was compared to the original; if the numbers did not match, they knew an error must have crept in.

Unvocalized manuscripts, which predated the rise of the Masoretic schools, are called pre-Masoretic texts. Most pre-Masoretic texts have been found in the last half-century in the caves at Khirbet Qumran near the Dead Sea. Some of the Dead Sea Scrolls from Qumran and elsewhere closely resemble the consonantal skeleton of later Masoretic texts. These are called Masoretic-type texts or proto-Masoretic texts.

The Qumran manuscripts are the oldest substantial biblical texts. They include at least portions of every book in the Hebrew Bible except the Book of Esther. Most of the scrolls, however, are either fragmentary or contain only a few sections of a few chapters. One exception is the manuscript called 1QIsaᵃ,[2] which is 54 columns long, an almost complete manuscript of the entire Book of Isaiah. Even though some scrolls from Qumran are more than a thousand years older than the oldest fully vocalized Masoretic texts, printed texts of the Bible are still based on the Masoretic texts because the manuscripts from Qumran are so fragmentary.

Because pre-Masoretic manuscripts of the Hebrew Bible are for the most part fragmentary and Masoretic manuscripts are comparatively recent, ancient translations of the Hebrew Bible have played a major role in the reconstruction of the biblical text. These translations, collectively called the (ancient) versions, are translations of the Hebrew Bible into Greek (the Septuagint and others), Latin (the Vulgate and others), Aramaic (the Targums), Syriac (the Peshitta) and other languages. Translation began in the latter part of the first millennium B.C.E. when Jews in certain communities became more familiar with Greek and Aramaic than with Hebrew.

The earliest written translation we know of was Greek and was made for the Jewish Hellenistic community in Alexandria, Egypt.[3] This translation, the Septuagint, was probably begun in the third or second century B.C.E. Relatively complete manuscripts of the Septuagint written in the fourth and fifth centuries C.E. still exist. To the extent that these are accurate, literal translations, the Septuagint manuscripts are extremely important because they may be the earliest evidence of the continuous text of the Hebrew Bible. The Torah text of the Samaritan community, called the Samaritan Pentateuch, is also an important tool for reconstructing an early biblical text. It differs in many places from the Masoretic text; these differences sometimes reflect sectarian biases but sometimes accurately preserve ancient non-Masoretic readings.

The Dead Sea Scrolls are important not only because they contain variant readings; they have also played an important role in the evaluation of ancient translations. Before the scrolls were discovered, people could claim that the Hebrew Masoretic text, which was known from the end of the first millennium C.E. and later, was the only text worth interpreting. Some scholars claimed that the places where the ancient translations differed from the Masoretic Hebrew text were mistranslations. They refused to consider the possibility that ancient translations might have been based on non-Masoretic texts. But some Hebrew texts found among the Dead Sea Scrolls are close to the text from which the Septuagint must have been translated. One of these Dead Sea Scroll texts is reproduced at right.

This fragment, which was found in Qumran Cave 4 and is called 4QExᵇ (formerly known as 4QExᵃ), is a short section of Exodus 1:1-5. In these three lines, there are two differences from the Masoretic text that agree with the Septuagint. In verse 1, the word for *their father* has been added, as it is in the Septuagint. In verse 5, the number of Jacob's descendants is 75, which is the same as in the Greek translation but different from the Masoretic text, where the number is 70. This fragment and others indicate that differences between the Septuagint and the Masoretic text were not all errors by Greek translators. In fact, as 4QEx^b and other manuscripts demonstrate, translators sometimes worked from Hebrew texts other than the ones on which the Masoretic text is based.

Ancient manuscripts are not always superior to more recent ones. The quality of a manuscript depends on how accurately the scribes copied the manuscript before them and whether they preserved outdated features or updated them. At Qumran, a variety of text types were found—some of which are nearly identical to the consonantal text that appears later as the Masoretic text and some that diverge greatly from it. For instance, the text of the Great Isaiah Scroll was modernized to conform to contemporaneous grammatical standards.

The evidence from Qumran suggests that until 68 C.E., the year Khirbet Qumran was destroyed by the Romans, there was no single, unified biblical text. We find diverse

A DEAD SEA SCROLL FRAGMENT of Exodus 1:1-5, called 4QEx^b, records the move to Egypt of Jacob's household. The three partial lines read "with Jacob their father," "Issachar, Zebulun and Joseph" and "seventy-five persons." Though brief, this late first-century B.C.E. to early first-century C.E. fragment varies in two places from the traditional text of the Old Testament known as the Masoretic text and agrees with the older, third- or second-century B.C.E. Greek translation, the Septuagint. In the fragment, the word "their father" is added and the number of people is 75 instead of the traditional 70. This teaches us that differences between the Septuagint and other translations from the Masoretic text should not be dismissed as mistranslations; the translators may have been working from non-Masoretic manuscripts. *Photo: Courtesy of Frank M. Cross*

readings of equivalent biblical texts at Qumran, as well as in sectarian commentaries called Pesher texts,[4] which sometimes contain comments on two different versions of the same biblical text. This suggests that, at that time, a text could be considered holy and authoritative even though a definitive version did not yet exist.

Exactly when and how the biblical text was stabilized is not known. By the second century C.E., a method of close reading expounding unusual spellings had been developed. This method of interpretation, which is one of the characteristics of the rabbinic Midrash, seems to presuppose a fixed form for the

THE NASH PAPYRUS, a version of the Decalogue and parts of Deuteronomy 6:4-5, this text, dates to the second century B.C.E. and is probably a liturgical fragment. Until the discovery of the Dead Sea Scrolls, the Nash Papyrus was the oldest known biblical fragment. The papyrus text varies in places from the Masoretic text, as in the order of the "Thou shalt not" commandments; some of the variations agree with the Septuagint. *Photo: By permission of the Syndics of Cambridge University*

biblical text. Second-century C.E. biblical manuscripts discovered in Wadi Murabba'at (between Jericho and Ein Gedi) and elsewhere included evidence of texts very close to what we know as the Masoretic text. Thus, the biblical text had probably been stabilized in a form closely resembling the Masoretic text by the second century C.E. Some scholars claim that a silver amulet found in Jerusalem that dates from about the seventh century B.C.E. is an important piece of evidence for the early stages of the biblical text. The tiny rolled scroll contains a text similar to the priestly blessing in Numbers 6:24-26: "May the Lord bless you and keep you; may the Lord cause his countenance to shine upon you, and be gracious to you; may the Lord favor you, and grant you peace." The amulet text is somewhat shorter than the Masoretic version. The amulet text, however, should not be considered a quotation from the Bible; it is probably a quote from a precursor of the priestly blessing that was later preserved in Numbers 6:24-26.

Another source of evidence for an early biblical text is the Nash Papyrus, probably a liturgical fragment dating from the second century B.C.E., which contains a version of the Decalogue (the Ten Commandments) and part of the *Shema* prayer (Deuteronomy 6:4-5). In several places in the Nash Papyrus, the order of the "Thou shalt not" commandments of the Decalogue differs from the order in the Masoretic text; some of these variations resemble the wording in the Septuagint. Before the Dead Sea Scrolls were discovered, the Nash Papyrus was the oldest biblical fragment known.

Many *tefillin* (phylacteries) and *mezuzot* (doorpost inscriptions) excavated at Qumran and elsewhere in the Dead Sea area, including Masada, also contain variations of biblical passages. But these are carelessly written liturgical texts, not carefully copied biblical manuscripts, and are of little value for the reconstruction of biblical texts.

In the second half of the first millennium C.E., the codex—or book form—was introduced for nonliturgical use. Even more significant than the change from scroll to codex in this period was the development of Masoretic Bibles, that is, Bibles with vowels, accents and cantillation marks (notes for chanting the text in liturgical and academic contexts). Some also had marginal (Masoretic) notes to help preserve the integrity of the text. Evidence in texts from the Cairo *genizah* (a storage site for sacred Jewish books no longer fit for liturgical use)[5] shows that these accretions developed gradually and that different systems of notation were developed in different Jewish centers.

The main systems of vowel notation are called Babylonian, Palestinian and Tiberian. The system that ultimately prevailed was the Tiberian system, which was developed in the city of Tiberias in Israel and was closely associated with the Ben Ashers, a famous family of scribes. Today, all printed editions of the Bible use the Tiberian system of vocalization, which places most vowel points or markings below the consonants and most cantillation marks on accented syllables.

The finest of all extant Masoretic Bible manuscripts is the Aleppo Codex, which is named after the city in Syria where it was housed before it was brought to Jerusalem. The beautifully written Aleppo Codex (see photo, page 215) was completed in the late tenth century C.E. in Israel. It was the oldest known manuscript of the entire Hebrew Bible, and it is possibly the first vocalized Hebrew manuscript of the complete Hebrew Bible ever written. Unfortunately, much of the Torah (Pentateuch) and some other sections were destroyed during an Arab pogrom against the Jewish community of Aleppo in 1947.[6] The Aleppo Codex was held in great esteem in the medieval period and was often consulted by scribes to correct other manuscripts. Maimonides, the medieval Jewish philosopher and jurist (1135-1204), considered the paragraph markings in the Aleppo Codex the model that Torah scribes should follow. But because the Aleppo Codex has only recently become available in facsimile edition and because it is now incomplete, the Masoretic manuscript used for most scholarly work today is Leningrad B19[A], a manuscript in the collection of the Leningrad Public Library, which probably dates from 1008. This manuscript is full of erasures and corrections indicating that it has been revised in accordance with the Aleppo Codex or a similar manuscript.

A few extant Masoretic manuscripts of sections of the Bible antedate Aleppo. The Cairo manuscript of the Prophets, written in 896 by Moses ben Asher and housed in the Karaite Synagogue in Cairo, has a slightly different vocalization system than Aleppo. Compared to the differences among the Dead Sea Scrolls of a millennium earlier, however, the variations among Masoretic manuscripts are minuscule. Although many other medieval manuscripts contain readings that diverge from Aleppo or Leningrad, in almost all cases the variations are the products of errors by medieval scribes rather than accurately preserved ancient traditions. Thus, for reconstructing the standard Masoretic text, it is sufficient to use the Aleppo Codex and closely allied manuscripts, such as Leningrad B19[A].

The histories of Hebrew Bible and New Testament manuscripts differ in several respects. Although the Hebrew Bible was composed before the New Testament, the earliest complete manuscripts of the Hebrew Bible—the Aleppo Codex and the Leningrad B19[A]—are 500 years later than those of the New Testament. Because complete manuscripts of the Hebrew Bible are relatively late, ancient translations of the Bible based on Hebrew texts that are no longer extant play a much larger role in textual criticism of the Hebrew Bible than of the New Testament. Finally, the early manuscripts of the New Testament give a complete picture of the pronunciation of the Greek text because Greek writing, like English, specifies both vowels and consonants. In contrast, the manuscripts from Qumran only represent the consonantal shell of the Hebrew Bible with all of its ambiguities, and the pronunciation and meaning of the Hebrew text sometimes depend upon vocalized texts from the end of the first millennium. For these reasons, textual criticism of the Hebrew Bible and of the New Testament have developed, and will continue to develop, as two separate disciplines.

I would like to thank Michael Carasik of Brandeis University for assisting me in writing this article.

CHAPTER 17

New Testament Manuscripts
Uncials, Minuscules, Palimpsests, etc.

Darrell Hannah

The history of New Testament manuscripts is different from the Old Testament because of their different languages and cultural settings. As Darrell Hannah describes, there are more than 5,000 extant manuscripts—that is, handwritten copies—of all or part of the New Testament in Greek and another 10,000 in Latin. Some are ancient and useful for establishing original readings. The oldest are written on papyrus; of the approximately 90 extant papyrus fragments, one or two may date to about the year 100, just 50 to 75 years after the events they describe.

Parchment, which is more long lasting and expensive than papyrus, became available to Christians after Constantine officially adopted Christianity; 274 surviving manuscripts are in uncial—the formal Greek writing style of antiquity—and almost 3,000 are in minuscule—the later cursive hand. Because parchment was durable and expensive, it was sometimes scraped clean and used again, creating a palimpsest, incised writing beneath the new ink. Using chemicals and ultraviolet light, scholars can often decipher the erased text, sometimes with significant results.—Ed.

Every written document before 1456, when Gutenberg's Latin Bible rolled off the press, had to be copied by hand. Copying long works, such as the Bible, was not only a tedious process, but it also resulted in many variations (some major and some minor) in the text. Today, more than 5,000 hand-copied manuscripts of part or all of the Greek New Testament survive, not to mention more than 10,000 manuscripts of the Latin Vulgate New Testament. Much the way archaeologists remove layers of a tell, carefully considering every scrap of evidence, textual critics "dig" through mountains of manuscript evidence and carefully "weight" every variation in the text, searching for the exact wording of the original.

Besides Greek and Latin manuscripts, there are hundreds of manuscripts of other early versions (such as the Coptic and Syriac) and an untold number of quotations from the New Testament in the writings of the early church fathers, all of which can assist textual critics in their search. It should be noted that the principles and tools of textual criticism of the Hebrew Bible differ so markedly from those of the New Testament that only the latter will be dealt with in this article.

Papyri

The oldest manuscripts of the New Testament that have survived are written on papyrus, a material made from a reedlike plant that grows along the banks of the Nile. The plant pith was pressed together to form sheets of "paper." Very few (comparatively speaking) papyrus manuscripts survive the ravages of time; if it were not for the arid climate and hot sand of Egypt, virtually none would exist today. The fragments of approximately 90 different New Testament papyri as well as countless secular documents, deeds, letters, literary works and Old Testament papyri—all of which have come to light in this century—have been found in the Egyptian desert.

Of the New Testament papyri, two collections rank as the most important. The first of these is owned by Sir Chester Beatty and consists of three manuscripts known to scholars as ₱45, ₱46 and ₱47. ₱45 dates from the last half of the third century (250-300 C.E.). Like all New Testament papyri, this one is fragmentary. ₱45 originally contained all four Gospels and the Book of Acts, but today only six leaves from Mark, seven from Luke, 13 from Acts, one from Matthew and one from John survive. ₱46 is much better preserved, with 86 of the original 104 leaves surviving. ₱46 originally contained all the Pauline epistles (except the pastorals, i.e., 1 and 2 Timothy and Titus) and the Epistle to the Hebrews. This important manuscript was thought by most scholars to have been copied sometime around 200 C.E.; however, one text critic has recently suggested, on paleographical[1] grounds, that it dates to around 100 C.E.[2] ₱47, also from the second half of the third century, consists of the middle portion of the Book of Revelation.

The four manuscripts (₱66, ₱72, ₱74, ₱75) in the collection owned by M. Martin Bodmer are equally fragmentary and equally old—and thus as important—as the manuscripts in the Chester Beatty collection. ₱66 and ₱75 are important witnesses to the text of the Gospel of John (₱75 also contains a good portion of the Gospel of Luke), and both date from the third century (₱66 from early in the third century). Remarkably well preserved, the third-century ₱72 contains the whole of 1 and 2 Peter and Jude as well as the apocryphal Nativity of Mary, the 11th Ode of Solomon, a sermon by the church father Melito on the Passover, the apocryphal Third Epistle of Paul to the Corinthians, the fragment of a hymn, the Apology of Phileas (a third-century Egyptian church father) and Psalms 33 and 34.[3] Manuscript ₱74, which was copied much later (seventh century) and has suffered much more from the ravages of time, preserves portions of Acts, James, 1 and 2 Peter, 1, 2 and 3 John, and Jude.

One other papyrus manuscript, ℘52, deserves mention. ℘52 is only a few inches in width and length (2.5 by 3.5 inches) and contains only a few verses from the Gospel of John (18:31-33 and 37-38). But unless ℘46 can be shown to have been copied around 100 C.E., ℘52, which was copied in the first half of the second century C.E., is the earliest extant manuscript of any part of the New Testament.

It should be noted that all the papyrus manuscripts of the New Testament found thus far are in codex (i.e., book) form—as opposed to scroll form. It would seem that, almost from the beginning, the Christian church preferred that sacred writings be in book form, just as the Jewish community preferred the scroll form. Why this was so has never been fully explained, although both economic reasons and the ease of finding specific passages have been suggested.[4]

Uncials

Manuscripts written on parchment have proven to be much more durable than papyri. Although the use of parchment (the treated hide of cattle, sheep, goats or even antelope) dates back to the first century B.C.E., parchment began to replace papyrus as the favored material for New Testament manuscripts around the fourth century. This was probably because of the new status accorded Christianity in the Roman Empire during and after the reign of Constantine. Parchment, which was more expensive than papyrus, was not affordable to Christians on a large scale until after Constantine declared Christianity the officially favored religion.

In antiquity, literary works like the New Testament were written in a formal Greek style known as uncial (or majuscule). By the ninth century, uncial was replaced by minuscule, a "running," or cursive,

UNCIAL GREEK SCRIPT, akin to our capital letters, characterizes the fourth-century vellum Codex Sinaiticus. The passage shown here is from Luke 24. *Photo: Bruce M. Metzger,* **Manuscripts of the Greek Bible,** *Oxford University Press*

form of writing. Uncials are similar to our capital letters and minuscules to our cursive letters.[5]

Because of their age and relatively good state of preservation, the oldest uncial manuscripts are enormously important. All together, 274 uncials survive today and, of these, four or five deserve our attention. The Codex Vaticanus (known to scholars as B or 03) is generally considered the most important. As the name indicates, the Codex Vaticanus is housed in the Vatican Library. It contains not only the New Testament, but also most of the Old Testament, that is, the Greek translation of the Hebrew Bible, the Septuagint. However, the New Testament breaks off in the middle of Hebrews 9:14; the rest of Hebrews and all of 1 and 2 Timothy, Titus, Philemon and Revelation are missing.

Ranking next in importance to Codex B is the Codex Sinaiticus (aleph or 01). Discovered by the German savant Konstantin von Tischendorf in 1859 at Saint Catherine's Monastery on Mount Sinai (thus the name Sinaiticus), it contains most of the Old Testament, all of the New Testament and two early Christian writings—the so-called Epistle of Barnabas and the *Shepherd of Hermas*. Both the Vaticanus (B) and the Sinaiticus (aleph) codices were copied sometime in the fourth century, with the Vaticanus being slightly older. Surviving from the fifth century is the Codex Alexandrinus (A or 02), which also contains both testaments. Textual critics generally regard Codex A as an inferior text of the Gospels. But the rest of the New Testament ranks just below the texts of B and aleph.

A Greek-Latin uncial usually dated to the fifth (but sometimes to the sixth) century, is named for Calvin's successor at Geneva, Theodore Beza (who once owned the manuscript). Codex Bezae (D or 05) contains the four Gospels, the Book of Acts and a small fragment of 3 John. This text differs somewhat—in some places radically—from most other manuscripts. Indeed, in Acts of the Apostles, D is nearly one-tenth longer than B, aleph or A. Although most scholars dismiss the peculiarities of D, they believe it preserves a very ancient form of the New Testament and thus may preserve some correct readings not found elsewhere. Finally, the Codex Claromontanus (D[p] or 06), which dates from the sixth century, is an important witness to the Pauline epistles.

These are without question the most important surviving uncials. There are, of course, many others, but because these are the oldest and best preserved, they are preeminent.

Minuscules

Nearly ten times more minuscule (cursive) manuscripts than uncials have survived—2,795 to be exact. Since minuscule script was not introduced until the ninth century, cursive codices cannot claim the antiquity of most uncials. However, some minuscules were copied directly from very ancient manuscripts and thus preserve much more ancient texts. For example, Codex 33, long known as the "Queen of the Cursives," a manuscript of the entire New

MINUSCULE, or cursive, style of Greek writing is displayed on this 11th-century parchment manuscript of the Letter of Jude. *Photo: Bruce M. Metzger,* **Manuscripts of the Greek Bible,** *Oxford University Press*

Testament except Revelation, contains an excellent text, in many places similar to the texts of aleph and B, even though Codex 33 dates from the ninth century. Another minuscule, Codex 1739, an excellent text of Acts and the Pauline and Catholic epistles, dates from the tenth century and must have been copied from a fourth-century manuscript; in the margins are numerous quotations from the church fathers Irenaeus, Clement of Alexandria, Origen, Eusebius and Basil, all of whom lived before the end of the fourth century.

Minuscules, like uncials, are almost exclusively parchment, although paper, which was introduced in the West from China near the end of the Middle Ages, was also used.

Lectionaries

Heretofore we have discussed only continuous text manuscripts. There are also a large number (2,209)[6] of manuscripts with divided texts arranged according to liturgical use, much like modern lectionaries. Some lectionaries were uncials, but almost 90 percent of those that have survived are minuscules. The vast majority date from the eighth century or later and are generally considered to be of little value for determining the original text of the New Testament.

Palimpsests and Purple Manuscripts

In an age of daily newspapers, weekly and monthly journals and "pulp" novels, it is hard to appreciate how rare writing materials and how valuable books once were. Evidence can be found in palimpsests and deluxe, or "purple," manuscripts.

A PALIMPSEST provides two texts for the price of one. Because writing materials were rare and costly, medieval scribes often scraped the writing from an old manuscript and wrote a new text over it. Above is a parchment palimpsest showing a 13th- or 14th-century Greek Orthodox Church service right side up and a faint underlying ninth- or tenth-century Greek text of Psalm 27 (28 in the Hebrew numeration) upside down. The text is in five columns—a transliteration of the Hebrew and four Greek translations. The first word in each column, preserved in square Hebrew letters, is the tetragrammaton (*yod-heh-vov-heh*), the four-letter name of God transliterated as Yahweh. One tetragrammaton can be easily discerned below and to the left of the top hole in the center of the manuscript. *Photo: Bruce M. Metzger, Manuscripts of the Greek Bible, Oxford University Press*

Because parchment was scarce, the original writing was often scraped off a manuscript, the leaves washed, and another text written on the parchment. But it was impossible to erase the original writing completely. Today scholars, with the help of chemicals, ultraviolet lamps and a good deal of eyestrain, can decipher the "underwriting" of palimpsests. (The word *palim-psest* derives from two Greek words meaning to scrape again or rescrape).

The most famous palimpsest is the important Codex C, or Ephraemi Syri Rescriptus. First copied in the fifth century, Codex C originally contained both the Old and New Testaments. Sometime in the 12th century, it was erased and rewritten with sermons by the Syrian church father Ephraem; thus its name. (As one pundit put it, this was not the only time the Word of God was covered over by sermons!) Codex C was first deciphered by Tischendorf, the discoverer of the Sinaiticus, and is still an important witness to the New

Testament text. All together there are 55 uncial palimpsests of many different varieties. For example, the underwriting of one manuscript is known as the uncial $\mathfrak{p}^{apr}$ or 025; the upperwriting is classified as minuscule 1834. Codex 048 of Acts and the Pauline epistles is a rare double palimpsest, having been rescraped and rewritten twice.

Parchments were often dyed purple and written on with gold and silver inks. These beautiful and expensive books were affordable only to the very wealthy. Deluxe manuscripts were not always appreciated; against such extravagance Jerome wrote: "Parchments are dyed purple, gold is melted into lettering, manuscripts are decked with jewels, while Christ lies at the door naked and dying."[7] A number of purple uncials, such as Codices N, O, sigma and phi, date from the sixth century. Most deluxe manuscripts are textually inferior, but minuscule 565, a ninth-century purple codex, which, according to Metzger, is "one of the most beautiful of all known manuscripts,"[8] contains a very good text. But it is by no means comparable to the great uncials B and aleph.

CHAPTER 18

The Aleppo Codex
Ancient Bible from the Ashes

Harvey Minkoff

According to Maimonides, the medieval philosopher and Bible scholar, the Aleppo Codex, written by the Ben Ashers of Tiberias, was the most respected biblical manuscript of his day. In fact, the Aleppo Codex is the oldest and finest copy of the complete Hebrew Bible "containing vowel signs, punctuation, notes for liturgical chanting, and textual notes." This manuscript is the culmination of 1,000 years of Masoretic scholarship.

The writer explains the what and how of the Masoretic undertaking. The what of the Masorah is accurate transmission of the sacred text–correct pronunciation, phrasing, intonation, word division, spelling, punctuation, poetic layout. The how includes techniques for proofreading and verifying the text–letter counts, word counts, sentence counts. But the how is even more than that. "Though sometimes denigrated as mechanistic, the Masorah actually contributed significantly to biblical exegesis and Hebrew language study." For example, counting words requires knowing what constitutes a word, or, more elusive, what constitutes the "same" word. Deciding these issues required mastering–sometimes even inventing–what we now call grammar and linguistics.

How the Ben Asher Codex found its way from Tiberias to Aleppo and ultimately, although badly damaged, to Israel is also a tale of kidnapping, ransom and international intrigue.–Ed.

The date was December 2, 1947, four days after the United Nations partitioned Palestine into a Jewish state and an Arab state, and Arab mobs in Syria were once again looting, burning, murdering and raping local Jews under the aegis of an anti-Zionist government campaign. Similar pogroms had been staged throughout the country in 1945 to celebrate Syria's independence from France, and they would occur again in 1949 in frustration over the defeat of the Syrian army by the forces of the fledgling state of Israel.

The 2,500-year-old Syrian Jewish community was nearing extinction. The synagogues of Aleppo had been systematically destroyed, every Jewish-owned store had been looted, and 6,000 of the 10,000 Jewish inhabitants had been forced to take refuge in foreign lands.

Rabbi Moshe Tawwil and Asher Baghdadi, the caretaker, watched in horror as flames raged through the Jewish quarter of Aleppo and consumed the ancient Mustaribah Synagogue, an architectural landmark since the fourth century. The building—which had survived for some 1,500 years—shuddered when the intense heat twisted the iron beams and cracked the giant foundation stones. Then the flames engulfed the Cave of Elijah chapel and the shrine where religious relics were stored. Encouraged by the soldiers supposedly sent to protect the synagogue, rioters stormed the building and hurled 40 Torah scrolls into the courtyard, drenched them in kerosene and set them afire, along with thousands of other books and sacred objects.[1]

When the smoldering rubble of Aleppo's main synagogue was searched four days later, biblical scholars around the world were stunned to learn that a priceless treasure—the Aleppo Codex—had been lost. This 760-page parchment manuscript written in the early tenth century was the oldest copy of the complete Hebrew Bible containing vowel signs, punctuation, notations for liturgical chanting and textual notes.

To appreciate the importance of the codex—known in Hebrew simply as Keter Torah (the Crown of the Torah) or Keter Aram Zova (the Crown of Aleppo)—we must go back a few thousand years to the earliest manuscripts of the Bible.

In some ancient manuscripts, there are no spaces between words. With adequate knowledge of prefixes, suffixes and impossible letter combinations, most readers could determine the correct word divisions. But in some cases, alternative word divisions were possible. For example, in Genesis 49:10 the Hebrew (שׁילה) can be read as *šiyloh* (Shiloh) or *šay loh* (tribute to him). The translation in the King James Version is based on the first reading:

> The sceptre shall not depart from Judah,
> nor a lawgiver from between his feet,
> until Shiloh comes.

The New English Bible follows the second:

> The sceptre shall not pass from Judah,
> nor the staff from his descendants,
> so long as tribute is brought to him....

As you may have deduced from the contrasting vowels in *šiyloh* and *šay loh*, the ancient Hebrew alphabet showed consonants but not vowels. Given the nature of Hebrew grammar, anyone fluent in the language can read most words in a running text without ambiguity,[2] just as we know from the context which syllable of *project* to stress in "singers must project their voices" and "the project required funding," even though there are no accent marks in English. But there are some homographs (like the two words spelled *bow* in English); and some names and foreign words (such as words for newly discovered flora and fauna or alien religious practices) that do not conform to the grammatical system. When Aramaic became the everyday language of the Jews, fluency in Hebrew required conscious study, and methods had to be found to preserve the correct pronunciation of the sacred texts.

Among the earliest reading aids were *matres lectionis*, literally "mothers of reading." These are consonants that indicate vowel sounds, for example *h* for *a*, *y* for *i*, *w* for *o*. Thus, *bn* would be pronounced *ben* (son), *bnh* would be *bena* (her son), *bny* would be *beni* (my son) and *bnw* would be *beno* (his son). This practice was not consistently applied even to the same word; a word spelled with a vowel letter was said to be "full" (*plene* in Latin, *male'* in Hebrew); a word with no vowel letter was called "lacking" (Latin *defectivus*, Hebrew *ḥaser*).

Lists of problematic words were also compiled. A few of these words are recorded in the Babylonian Talmud, the 63-volume collection of discussions from the Palestinian and Babylonian rabbinical seminaries of the first to sixth centuries C.E. The rabbis, for instance, commented about words that required special attention because they had two pronunciations (Nedarim 37b-38a) and about which compound words are separated and which connected, for example, the names Ben Oni (son of my pain) versus Benjamin (son of strength), and Beth El (house of God) versus Yisrael (he wrestles with God) (Soferim 5.10-11).

Even though punctuation is a much later invention, the rabbis in the Talmud were aware of the concept of sentences and the importance of intonation. One rabbi suggested that when the Torah is read aloud to listeners who do not know Hebrew, the reader should present the Hebrew one sentence at a time and then wait for the translator to explain it (Megillah 4.4). Another referred to the practice of indicating with hand motions the rise and fall of the voice when reading the Torah (Berakhot 62a),[3] a custom still practiced by some Yemenite and Italian Jews.

We can see, then, that from very early on, transmitting the biblical text from one generation to the next included teaching correct pronunciation, phrasing and intonation. This teaching had to be done orally, of course, because there were no techniques for writing vowels or punctuation.

The entire undertaking of textual transmission—both the *what* and the *how*—is known as Masorah, from the Hebrew verb meaning "hand over." The verb appears in the opening sentence of Mishnah Avot: "Moses received the Torah on Sinai and handed it over (*masar*) to Joshua, and Joshua to the Elders...." In time, a class of teachers arose whose particular skill was Masorah.[4]

THE ALEPPO CODEX was compiled by Aaron ben Asher, the leading Masorete, or biblical textual expert, in tenth-century Tiberias, the center of biblical scholarship at the time. The Aleppo Codex quickly became known as the most accurate text of the Hebrew Bible, and other venerable manuscripts were corrected to agree with Ben Asher's version. "Everyone relied on it," wrote the great medieval Jewish scholar Moses Maimonides, "and I based myself on this for the Torah scroll that I wrote."

Shown here is Judges 9:56-11:2. In addition to the consonantal text, the Aleppo Codex contains vowel marks to indicate vocalization, accents that also serve as a musical notation system to guide the chanting of the Bible during synagogue services, notes on the spelling and meaning of ambiguous words, and cross-references to other appearances of selected words.
Photo: Ben-Zvi Institute/Shrine of the Book/Israel Museum/David Harris

Because they devoted their lives to the book *(sefer) par excellence,* they were called *soferim* in Hebrew,[5] which is now narrowly translated as "scribes"— a term that has unjustly acquired pejorative connotations from the Gospels.

In addition to correct pronunciation, the *what* of the Masorah included maintaining the integrity of the sacred text. The *soferim* determined the correct division of letters into words; they systematized breaking the biblical text into units approximating paragraphs; they distinguished different poetic layouts, for example the two parallel columns of half-lines for the Song of Moses (Deuteronomy 32:1-43) and the "half brick over whole brick, whole brick over half brick" of the Song of the Sea (Exodus 15:1-18) and the Song of Deborah (Judges 5:2-31);[6] and they set standards for the size and shape of letters, the length and width of columns and the writing materials to be used. All of these decisions are so ancient that they are taken for granted as part of the *halakhah* (Jewish law) for writing Torah scrolls, just as we take for granted that the lower case letters *p, q, b* and *d* are distinguished from each other by the relative positions of the circles and stems, and upper case *P, Q, B* and *D* are distinguished from each other in an entirely different way.

But no matter how strict the standards, individual manuscripts were only as good as the copyists who made them. Then, as now, clerical workers could be overworked or careless. Today, proofing a single copy of a book almost guarantees that all copies from the same press run will be identical (although errors at the binding stage might mean pages are omitted or duplicated), but every handwritten text was unique and had to be checked separately for accuracy. The scribes therefore devised techniques for checking manuscripts— the *how* of the Masorah.

Some techniques are still familiar to us. Most modern authors have proofread printer's galleys by reading them aloud to a friend, spelling out words, announcing new paragraphs, calling attention to special features like italics and bold type—all of which must be checked against the original. The scribes also read texts aloud. But when spot-checking or working alone, they used a mathematical technique. They counted the letters, words and sentences in each book of the Bible and listed the middle letter, word and sentence; if the total was incorrect or the wrong letter or word or sentence appeared in the middle position, they knew there was an error somewhere. In fact, the Talmud (Kiddushin 30a) explains: "This is why they were called *soferim,* because they counted (in Hebrew, *hayu soferim*) all the letters of the Torah. They said the *waw* of *ghwn* (Leviticus 11:42) is the middle letter of the Torah, *drš* (Leviticus 10:16) is the middle word, and *whtglḥ* (Leviticus 13:33) begins the middle sentence."

Of course, additions and omissions on both sides of the divide might cancel each other out. So lists were also made of how frequently individual words appeared in the text; spot-checks of vocabulary were used to determine if a manuscript contained errors.

The Masorah is sometimes criticized for being mechanistic, but the *soferim* actually contributed significantly to biblical exegesis and Hebrew language study. For example, the question of what constitutes the "same" word is not always easy to answer. Is the *plene* spelling the same word as the *defectivus* spelling? (For an analogous situation in English, consider whether *draft* is the same word as *draught*.) Is *devoted* the same word in "the money was *devoted* to charity" and "the children were *devoted* to their parents"? Is the *revolution* that corresponds to *revolt* the same word as the *revolution* that corresponds to *revolve*? By trying to answer questions like these, Masoretes—specialists in Masorah—became adept at grammatical analysis and etymology. Their notes often list how many times a word is spelled *plene* or *defectivus* (draught/draft), whether a particular word has two different meanings (devoted) and whether a particular form is really two different words (revolution).

Unlike the details of paragraphing and lettering, which are part of the text itself, proofreading techniques and grammatical comments of the Masorah were written separately. Lest their comments be mistaken for sacred text, the Masoretes did not annotate scrolls used in the liturgy.

The appearance of the codex—or bound book—in the early years of the Christian era presented the Masoretes with a convenient way of distinguishing liturgical texts from other copies of sacred Scripture. Scrolls remained the only acceptable format for public reading of the Bible; books, or codices, however, were acceptable for use in nonliturgical contexts. Using the codex format, therefore, it was possible to write the Masorah notes and explanations next to the text of the Bible.

Typically, the written Masorah takes two forms—short notes, called in Hebrew-Latin *masorah parva* (small masorah), and extended comments, *masorah magna* (large masorah). The *masorah parva* appear as abbreviations in the margin next to and between the columns of text and refer to a word in that column marked with a symbol; for example, using analogous English forms, "draft L B" would mean "this spelling of *draft* is *Lacking* elsewhere in the *Bible*"; "devoted M 3 P" would mean "*devoted* occurs with the *Meaning* it has here 3 times in the *Prophets*."

The *masorah magna* appear on the top and bottom of the page and in appendices after the text. They contain fuller explanations of the *masorah parva*, such as complete cross-references of additional occurrences of words, as well as other comments that Masoretes thought might help scribes or readers. Thus, the answer to our third question above might be "*revolution* from *revolt* here, but from *revolve* in next chapter."

Because scrolls and books were often destroyed by natural deterioration or manmade disasters, many details in the subsequent development of the Masorah have been lost. However, by the ninth and tenth centuries, codices of the Hebrew Bible contained a highly developed system of reading aids.

First of all, there are the *nequdot*, or "points." These are dots and dashes placed above, below and sometimes inside letters to indicate the vowel sounds that follow; for example, a dash below the letter *bet* (ב) would signify *ba*; a dot above (ב) would stand for *bo*. Manuscripts show evidence of three competing systems, called by scholars Palestinian, Babylonian and Tiberian. The Tiberian notation is the most fully developed and is the one in use today.

There is also an elaborate system of *te'amim* (accents), some two dozen symbols (depending on how one counts certain variations) written above and below words to indicate stressed syllables and, in various combinations, subtle distinctions of phrasing and intonation. *Te'amim* are indispensable for analyzing Hebrew grammar. The original purpose, however, may have been to indicate the traditional melody for reading the Bible during religious services, and in this context they are known to most American Jews as the "trope" they had to learn when preparing for bar or bat mitzvah recitals.

Finally, the ninth and tenth century codices of the Hebrew Bible contain extensive *masorah parva* and *masorah magna*. Although emanating from at least two different schools, the best manuscripts are strikingly similar in matters relating to vowels, accentuation and punctuation. The explanatory comments, however, vary, and it is possible to cite the Masorah of a particular scholar. In fact, the *sevirin* (some believe) notation, which some writers used frequently and others rarely, cites opposing views in order to reject them.

Aaron Ben Asher, the scion of a family respected for two centuries as Bible scholars, was the outstanding Masorete in Tiberias during the tenth century. His *Dikdukei ha-Te'amim* (Details of Accentuation),[7] although mainly concerned with correct pronunciation, was one of the earliest analyses of the grammatical behavior of prefixes and suffixes in Hebrew—and, of course, their influence on syllable stress. His Keter Torah, a biblical codex he wrote in the early decades of that century, is considered the finest Masoretic Bible ever produced. Keter Torah is most likely the first manuscript of the complete Hebrew Bible with all the notations for vowels, accents, intonation and melody we have been describing. Aaron Ben Asher also included a fully developed Masorah.

With hundreds of thousands of graphic details, the Ben Asher Codex—380 leaves (760 pages), each measuring 10 by 13 inches, and three columns of text to a page in most places—is the culmination of 1,000 years of Masoretic effort. And it is accurate. Because of scribal errors or inherent flaws, every other extant medieval manuscript of the Hebrew Bible contains numerous discrepancies between the text and the Masorah. Only the Ben Asher Codex is almost perfect in every detail—word counts, cross-references and grammatical notes. It is, as Moshe Goshen-Gottstein says, "the authoritative manuscript within the boundaries of its subtype which, to all intents and purposes, became almost identical with the Tiberian Masoretic text a thousand years ago."[8]

The fame of the Ben Asher Codex was universal. Moses Maimonides, the great 12th-century philosopher and Bible scholar, held it up as a model.

"Everyone relied on it," he wrote, "because Ben Asher worked on it for many years and proofread it many times, and I based myself on this for the Torah scroll that I wrote."[9] And other codices, such as the Leningrad Codex of 1008, were corrected long ago to bring them into line with the Ben Asher manuscript.

How the Ben Asher Codex found its way to Aleppo and the flames of a pogrom is also an instructive story. The veneration of the Jews for the Ben Asher Codex made it valuable to others as well, and the codex was stolen and held for ransom by several kings and conquerors. Maimonides saw it in Cairo after the Jews there ransomed it from the Seljuk Turks, who had looted it from Jerusalem. The codex arrived in the thriving metropolis of Aleppo—where it became known as the Aleppo Codex or Keter Aram Zova—sometime around 1478, after Jewish Aleppines paid off the Ottoman sultan.

Situated in the rocky Syrian mountains 300 miles north of Jerusalem and 70 miles inland from the Mediterranean Sea, Aleppo has been ruled by Hittites, Arameans, Israelites, Assyrians, Persians, Greeks, Romans, Turks, French and Arabs. The city is mentioned in Psalm 60:1 and 2 Samuel 10:6 under the Hebrew name Aram Zova (literally "the Zova district of Syria") as one of the areas conquered by King David. Under the name Ḥalab, the history of Aleppo can be traced back another millennium. According to local legend, the name Ḥalab is derived from the belief that the patriarch Abraham milked (Arabic *ḥalab*) his flocks and distributed food to the poor there.[10]

The Jewish community of Aleppo dates from at least the fifth century B.C.E., when, according to Josephus, the first-century Jewish historian, the Persian king Xerxes instructed Ezra to organize Jewish courts for the area. The close ties between the Aleppine community and Jewish centers in Palestine during the Hellenistic period are apparent in the interesting law of provisional divorce. Because in Jewish law a missing spouse was never presumed dead, a traveler to a foreign land provided his wife with divorce papers that went into effect if he did not return by a certain date; for Palestinian Jews, "foreign" was defined as north of Aleppo.

"The road from every village leads to Aleppo," according to a local saying. And, indeed, situated on the major ancient caravan route between India and Persia to the east, Turkey and Greece to the north and Egypt to the south, Aleppo has long been a center of commerce. Aleppine merchants figured prominently in the economies of Egypt, Iraq and Anatolia; the first Jew to settle in Calcutta, Shalom haKohen by name, was from Aleppo. And Aleppo, in turn, attracted notables in government, commerce and scholarship. *Ḥalabi chalabi*—"a man from Halab is a gentleman"—they used to say in Ottoman Turkish.[11]

After the Arab conquest in the seventh century C.E., the Jews of Aleppo prospered in occupations the Muslims did not want or that their religion banned—banking, dyeing, tanning—as well as medicine and public service. Travelers to Aleppo in the 13th century described a thriving Jewish community with three synagogues and many scholars. In 1225, for example, the head of the community was Joseph ibn Shimon (sometimes called ibn Aknin), the "beloved disciple" for whom Maimonides wrote his famous *Guide for the Perplexed.*

The city was devastated by Tamerlane in 1400, and the Jewish community was rebuilt toward the end of the century. The Jewish population was reinforced at the time by Jews expelled from Spain in 1492 by the Catholic monarchs Ferdinand and Isabella, and Aleppo once again became a center of Jewish scholarship. The Aleppo Maḥzor (Holy Day prayer book) was published by the Hebrew press in Venice in 1527 and is the source of many otherwise unknown religious poems of the Spanish-Jewish liturgy. The main synagogue of Aleppo housed a rabbinical college with an extensive library and many rare manuscripts, including a Maimonides manuscript written in 1236, a Pentateuch dated 1341—and the Aleppo Codex.

Although Aleppo was an important administrative center in the Ottoman Empire, the economic and cultural position of the city declined during the 19th century, along with the empire in general. European powers wrested concessions from the Ottomans. In particular, hundreds of local Arab Christians were granted consular protection, thus creating a class of Ottoman subjects with loyalties to England, France, Holland and a variety of other European patrons. Coupled with the fact that non-Muslim communities—including at least four Christian denominations—had for centuries been allowed to establish autonomous courts, schools, charities and police, the social fabric of Aleppo was torn apart. Previously, for example, although ethnic and religious groups had been concentrated in certain neighborhoods, there were no wholly homogeneous areas. The so-called Kurdish Quarter was predominantly Christian; Muslims lived in the al-Saliba district, home of the Christian elite and their churches; Muslims lived next door to the synagogue and Jews next door to the mosque in Bahsita, the Jewish neighborhood. By the end of the century, however, Jews were living in a ghetto separated from the rest of the city by a gate.[12]

When the Suez Canal was opened, the monopoly of the overland trade route to the East was broken, and Aleppo was no longer the crossroads of the world. Rich merchants emigrated, taking with them high culture as well as their wealth. By 1942, almost 65 percent of the Jewish residents required assistance from communal charities funded from abroad. Even the library of the main synagogue was sold off to raise money—except for the Aleppo Codex.

According to Meir Turner, a rare-book dealer in New York, representatives of the Zionist shadow government in British Mandate Palestine tried to acquire the Aleppo Codex. But the Aleppine Jews were optimistic that they could protect their treasure. Then came the pogroms and the news that the Aleppo Codex had been lost to the flames.

The horror of the loss was twofold. Not only was the Aleppo Codex a priceless artifact, but the promise of its contribution to scholarship had never been fulfilled. In Aleppo, the codex had been stored in the venerable Mustaribah

Synagogue, where it was carefully guarded. For fear that it might be damaged or stolen, visitors had been kept away. Thus, when Jacob ben Hayyim edited the 1525 Bomberg rabbinic Bible, which was the basic text of Christian Hebraists until this century, he had to consult an eclectic version of the text rather than the Aleppo Codex. And when Paul Kahle, one of the most influential Masoretic scholars of this century (who, by the way, was driven from his native Germany by the Nazis in 1938 because his writings were too favorable to the Jews), could not get permission to remove the codex, he used the corrected but less desirable Leningrad Codex for his 1937 revision of Rudolf Kittel's monumental *Biblia Hebraica*. And when Umberto Cassuto—the preeminent historian of Italian Jewry and chief editor of the Hebrew *Biblical Encyclopedia*— examined the manuscript in 1944, he was not even allowed to take notes.

Needless to say, however, Bible scholars longed to see the codex. As Marc Brettler explained in a recent article,[13] although the Qumran documents are 1,000 years older than the codex, they are fragmentary and limited to the consonantal skeleton of Hebrew. Ben Asher's Aleppo Codex is the oldest text of the entire Hebrew Bible with vowels, punctuation and textual notes. Thus, the efforts to remove it to Palestine and the horror that it had been destroyed in the 1947 pogrom.

But the story does not end there. In the 1958 volume of *Sinai*, in a Hebrew article entitled "Ben Asher's 'Keter Torah'—A Brand Plucked from the Fire," Israeli president Yitzhak Ben-Zvi announced that the Aleppo Codex, which had been seriously damaged but was still priceless, had found its way to Israel.

Ben-Zvi did not disclose how the codex was smuggled out of Syria and into Israel. The danger was too great. The 5,000 Jews still in Syria—1,500 in Aleppo— are virtual hostages. As of this writing (1991), their religious schools have been restricted by the government. They have no civil protection against intimidation and violence. They may not hold public jobs, may not meet privately with foreigners, may not travel—and may not emigrate from the country. [Some of these restrictions have been modified or lifted since this article was written. —Ed.]

As years passed and refugees from Aleppo reached safety, the history of the Aleppo Codex has been pieced together. There are still contradictions and unanswered questions, of course—because of the confusion during the riots, the passage of time, the desire of some to exaggerate their role in events and the desire of others to protect family and friends still at risk in Syria.

In general, though, it seems that Rabbi Moshe Tawwil and Asher Baghdadi found the burned codex in the ashes of the destroyed synagogue and gave it to a Christian friend to hide. After being moved from one hiding place to another for almost ten years, the codex was given to Mordecai Fahham, unannounced, the day he was allowed to leave for Turkey, and he smuggled it into Israel at great personal risk. The codex is now in the custody of the Ben-Zvi Institute and the Hebrew University.

A quarter of the original manuscript was destroyed in the fire—all of the Pentateuch up to Deuteronomy 28:17, Ecclesiastes, Esther, Lamentations, Daniel, Ezra and Nehemiah and a few chapters from other books. But the remainder—294 leaves or 588 pages—promises to change our understanding of the Masoretic text.

We have already noted both the opinion of Maimonides that the Aleppo Codex should be a model for Torah scrolls and the belief of Professor Moshe Goshen-Gottstein that the Tiberian Masoretic text is identical to the text in the Aleppo Codex. Absent the codex itself, however, the text for Hebrew Bibles had been based on the Leningrad Codex of 1008, which is a century later and considerably less perfect. It is not surprising, therefore, that immediately after it reappeared, the Aleppo Codex became the centerpiece of the Hebrew University Bible Project, whose goal is publication of a critical edition of the entire Hebrew Bible.

A burst of scholarship followed the reappearance of the codex. A facsimile of the surviving portion (edited by Goshen-Gottstein) was published by the Magnes Press of the Hebrew University in 1976. There have also been studies of accentuation, grammatical notes, relation to other manuscripts and the place of the codex in biblical history.[14]

Since the tenth century, Hebrew manuscripts of the Bible have exhibited only a few minor differences. Thus, we should not expect that examination of the Aleppo Codex will yield headline-grabbing new readings. Goshen-Gottstein puts it well: "I do not foresee that any future evidence could possibly dislodge the Aleppo Codex. Whereas I have no doubt as regards the suitability of this codex as a base text for our text-critical edition, one may have practical hesitations as regards an edition for general and liturgical use."[15]

But the value of the Aleppo Codex to scholars cannot even be predicted yet. Whole generations of Bible scholars have never even seen a fully annotated Masoretic text and have no idea what it may hold. How the Aleppo Codex will change our understanding of the Hebrew Bible, only time—and study—will tell.

I am grateful for the generous assistance of Suzanne Siegel of the Hunter College Library, Rabbi Jerry Schwarzbard of the Jewish Theological Seminary Library and the library staffs of Yeshiva University and Fordham University.

CHAPTER 19

Is the Abisha Scroll 3,000 Years Old?

Alan D. Crown

Does a Torah scroll written by the great-grandson of the high priest Aaron, Moses' brother, still exist? The Samaritans, who separated from Judaism more than two millennia ago, say they have one. This claim is examined by Alan D. Crown. The Samaritan Pentateuch follows a non-Masoretic text, is written in a different script and contains several thousand textual differences, chief among them that Mount Gerizim, rather than Jerusalem, is "the place that the Lord has chosen." If these differences are later sectarian emendations, who made them? The Samaritans have been labeled falsifiers, but they "maintain that the Masoretic text is a falsification and that Jewish scribes deliberately altered many readings to give priority to Jerusalem." Crown believes that "the argument that the Samaritan version of these passages is the older version has considerable force"–although he also believes that the much longer tenth commandment in the Samaritan version was "culled from various parts of the Pentateuch" and added later.

The Samaritan version is one of the witnesses used in reconstructing the original text of the Bible. It "evidences a text of the Pentateuch from the third century B.C.E. to the first century C.E." and in about 2,000 places supports Septuagint readings against the Masoretic text. Crown believes the Samaritan Pentateuch may exemplify a text type "localized in Palestine," in contrast to the Babylonian type that Frank Cross believes became the Jewish standard.–Ed.

A small group of Samaritans–they now number fewer than 300–still lives in ancient Shechem (modern Nablus on the West Bank) at the foot of their holy mountain, Mount Gerizim. They claim to have the oldest Torah (the Pentateuch, or five books of Moses) in existence, written, they say, by Abisha,[1] the great-grandson of Aaron (1 Chronicles 6:50 [6:35 in Hebrew]), 13 years after the Israelite conquest of Canaan—more than 3,000 years ago!

As proof, they cite an almost unforgeable cryptogram embedded in the ancient text—known as the Abisha Scroll.

The Samaritans have lived at Shechem/Nablus for at least 2,300 years. (Another 300 Samaritans live in Holon, south of Tel Aviv.) According to the latest scholarship, they separated from the Jews sometime between the fourth century B.C.E. and the third century C.E. The schism seems to have had two complex phases—first, a political separation in the period of Ezra; second, a religious separation that began in the late fourth century B.C.E. with the Samaritan construction on Mount Gerizim of a rival sanctuary or temple (the site of which has recently been verified by archaeologists). The second phase culminated in the third century C.E. when Baba Rabba, the legendary Samaritan hero, had the Samaritan oral law taught and codified and, apparently, canonized the deviant Samaritan version of the Torah.

At that point, the rabbis changed their minds about the religious identity of the Samaritans. They were no longer regarded as a Jewish sect and were no longer afforded status as Jews or true proselytes to Judaism. For their part, the Samaritans maintained that the Jews had corrupted the Torah, and, until the late 19th century, they maintained an implacable animosity toward Judaism.

The Samaritans themselves reject the name Samaritans or Samarians. These English terms are translations of the Semitic Shomronim, the plural of Shomron (the biblical name for the area we call Samaria). *Shomronim* means people from Samaria. Instead, the Samaritans consider their name to be Shamerim, from *shomrim*, the plural of *shomer* (guardian or watchman). According to their etymology, they are guardians of the Law. This etymology, incidentally, was already known to Jerome, the eminent church father, in the fourth century C.E.[2]

The Samaritan Pentateuch—the Samaritans regard only the first five books of Moses as canonical—differs in some important respects from the Masoretic text, which is the Hebrew *textus receptus* according to Jewish tradition. Perhaps the most significant difference is in Deuteronomy, where the Masoretic text speaks of "the place that the Lord your God *will choose*" for his holy mountain, referring to Jerusalem. In parallel passages in the Samaritan Pentateuch, the text says "the place that the Lord your God *has chosen*," referring to the Samaritan's holy mountain, Mount Gerizim, where the blessings were pronounced (Joshua 8:33-34) when the Israelites entered the Promised Land, as was prescribed by Moses in Deuteronomy 11:29.

The argument that the Samaritan version of these passages is the older version has considerable force. In Deuteronomy 11, Moses addresses the people on the eve of their entry into the Promised Land:

> See, this day I set before you blessing and curse; blessing, if you obey the commandments of the Lord your God which I enjoin upon you this day; and curse, if you do not obey the commandments of the Lord your God, but turn away from the path which I enjoin upon you this day and

follow other gods, whom you have not experienced. When the Lord
your God brings you into the land which you are about to invade and
occupy, you shall pronounce the blessing at Mount Gerizim and the
curse at Mount Ebal.

Deuteronomy 11:26-29

In the next chapter, Moses specifies some of these laws:

You must destroy all the sites at which the nations you are to dispossess
worshipped their gods, whether on lofty mountains and on hills or under
any luxuriant tree....
   Do not worship the Lord your God in like manner but look only to
the site that the Lord your God will choose amidst all your tribes as His
habitation, to establish His name there.

Deuteronomy 12:2,4-5

As the Masoretic text reads, the reference is to Jerusalem, which, however,
was not captured by the Israelites until the reign of King David, 200 years later.

Just before this passage in Deuteronomy 12, Moses refers to the mountain
of the blessing, Mount Gerizim, and immediately upon entering the Promised
Land, the Israelites do in fact pronounce the blessings facing Mount Gerizim
(Joshua 8:33-34). Mount Gerizim was obviously a holy mountain for the
Israelites long before Jerusalem.

In any event, Mount Gerizim remained—and remains to this day—the holy
mountain of the Samaritans, who built their temple there in the late fourth
century B.C.E. The temple was destroyed by the Judean king John Hyrcanus in
128 B.C.E. when he was strengthening his hold on Samaria, but we do not
know if the destruction was complete. The Samaritan chronicles imply that
Hyrcanus later repented of his animosity and restored some religious
privileges, and the Samaritans may have rebuilt an altar on the site of their
destroyed temple. In any case, they continued to worship there until Hadrian's
day (second century C.E.). Hadrian appears to have leveled their *temenos* (sacred
enclosure) and built over it, leaving no clear traces of its existence.

The Samaritans regard themselves as true guardians of the Law. They maintain that the Masoretic text is a falsification and that Jewish scribes deliberately
altered many readings to give priority to Jerusalem over the Samaritan sacred
mountain and the site of their former temple on Mount Gerizim.

Moreover, they say, Mount Gerizim was named in the tenth commandment—
that is, in the large addendum culled from various parts of the Pentateuch that
the Samaritans attach to the commandments. The Decalogues in both Exodus
20:2-17 and Deuteronomy 5:6-21 are followed in the Samaritan Pentateuch by
the following verses indicating the site of the sacred altar, which was to be built
when the Israelites entered the land, and the site of the temple, which would
replace it:

It shall be that when the Lord your God brings you to the land of the
Canaanites which you are to inherit, you shall erect an altar of stones, and

plaster them and write upon these stones all the words of this Torah which I command you this day. You shall erect them on Mount Gerizim and build there an altar to the Lord your God. It shall be a stone altar upon which iron has not been lifted. Of unhewn stone you shall build the altar of the Lord your God and you shall offer up burnt offerings to the Lord your God. You shall slaughter whole offerings and eat and rejoice there before the Lord your God. That mountain is on the other side of the Jordan towards the west in the land of the Canaanites who dwell in the Arabah, near Gilgal, adjacent to Elon Moreh which is before Shechem.[3]

To prove their point, the Samaritans remind skeptics that they have in their possession the oldest Torah scroll in the world, the one on which all later copies of the Samaritan Pentateuch are based. This, of course, is the Abisha Scroll. The Abisha Scroll is not only extraordinarily important to modern Samaritan self-esteem, it is also the principal support for their claim that they are the true B'nai Israel (children of Israel), the so-called lost tribes that disappeared after the Assyrians conquered the northern kingdom of Israel in 721 B.C.E. and deported much of the population and replaced them with immigrants from foreign lands.[4] The Samaritans believe they, not the Jews, are the true guardians of the holy Torah.

Like the Jews, the Samaritans use scrolls in the synagogue for readings during Sabbath and festival services and codices (or books) for study and individual liturgical use. The Samaritans also use a scroll, rather than a codex, during the Samaritan Hag (festival)—the pilgrimage up the holy mountain. The Samaritan high priest carries the Torah scroll in his hands and exhibits it at stopping points along the ancient route. It is hardly surprising to learn that the Samaritans have a number of ancient Torah scrolls. Even so, a Torah written by Abisha does seem a bit extreme, although we know from the Dead Sea Scrolls, which are more than 2,000 years old, that it is possible for ancient scrolls to survive for thousands of years under the right conditions.

According to their own chronicles, the Samaritans have three ancient scrolls, which they use on different festive occasions. By any standard, these would be of considerable interest to scholars. All three scrolls were shown to King Edward VII when, as Prince of Wales, he visited Nablus in 1860.[5] According to a cryptogram in one scroll, it was written about 1441 C.E., in the time of the Samaritan high priest Pinhas the Sixth.[6] This scroll is used on the Day of Atonement and during Sukkot and is often fobbed off on visitors as the Abisha Scroll. The second scroll, the date of which I cannot trace, is used for reading the Sabbath portions.

Of the three ancient scrolls, however, the Abisha Scroll is clearly the most sacrosanct. According to the *Tolidah*, the Samaritan priestly genealogy, the Abisha Scroll was used on Yom Atseret, that is, the Sabbath during Sukkot. This scroll is rarely shown to visitors, even scholars. I have written three books and 39 articles about the Samaritans and have visited them at Nablus many times, but despite my humble requests, I have never been shown the Abisha Scroll.

Like other visitors, I have been shown the Pinhas Scroll and told it was the Abisha Scroll.

Since the existence of the Abisha Scroll became known to Western scholars, it has been the object of curiosity. The first traveler known to have seen it was the bishop of Armagh, Robert Huntington, who saw it in 1690. It was seen again in 1861, this time by the Reverend John Mills during his long residence with the Samaritans. Even after spending three months with them, he was first shown other scrolls; the day before he left, however, he was allowed to see the Abisha Scroll, and he left a brief description of it.[7] Three months later, also in 1861, three travelers had the good fortune to be in the Samaritan synagogue when the Abisha Scroll was transferred to a new metal case. They were able to view the entire manuscript laid out at full length on the synagogue floor, and their notes on their experience were given to the German consul.[8]

As word of the scroll spread, a visit to Nablus became an accepted part of the itinerary of 19th-century travelers to the Holy Land. Usually, they were shown one of the other old scrolls in the synagogue.

The first known photographs of the Abisha Scroll were taken sometime before 1918 by John Whiting, the American vice-consul in Jerusalem, who was asked by an American millionaire, E. K. Warren, to photograph the scroll on his behalf. Warren had purchased several manuscripts from the Samaritans at a time when they were in desperate need of money, so they wished to oblige him. Thus, they gave Whiting permission to photograph the scroll, although they complained later that they were never properly paid.[9] In any event, several sets of photographs were taken and offered for sale; one complete set found its way to the Mugar Library at Boston University. Paul Kahle, the German biblical scholar, was able to acquire a partial set from an unknown source, but he spent many years trying to get better photos.[10]

In 1926, under the British Mandate for Palestine, attempts were made to set up a register of all manuscripts in Palestine that were deemed to be of national interest. A complete set of photographs of the Abisha Scroll was sent to Sir Frederic Kenyon at the British Museum. A copy of this set was eventually made available to Edward Robertson, the librarian of the John Rylands Library in Manchester, but the current whereabouts of both sets of photographs are unknown. At an earlier time, the Palestine Exploration Fund had attempted to obtain a photographic copy of the scroll but had been supplied with photographs of a different Torah.[11]

Our current edition of the scroll was published by Father Federico Perez Castro, a Spanish scholar who was able to have a complete set of photographs taken in the 1950s. After lengthy negotiations by both Castro and the Spanish consul in Jerusalem, Castro photographed the scroll. After a fairly thorough examination of the text, he decided to publish only the older part of the scroll, that is, from Numbers 35 to the end of Deuteronomy. Although he recognized that even this part was conflated from several even older fragments, it became

---

The Importance of the Samaritan Pentateuch

The Samaritan Pentateuch evidences a text of the Pentateuch from the third century B.C.E. to the first century C.E., and perhaps earlier. Along with the Septuagint (LXX—a Greek translation from the Hebrew, dating to the second century B.C.E.) and the Masoretic text (MT—the traditional Jewish version, created in the tenth century C.E. but obviously based on earlier texts), the Samaritan Pentatuech is an important ancient witness.

In approximately 2,000 places, the Samaritan Pentateuch supports Septuagint readings against the Masoretic text and shows that texts other than the Babylonian recension of the Pentateuch, which is incorporated in the Masoretic text, were available. The Samaritan Pentateuch may well be illustrative of a text type that was localized in Palestine, some traces of which can also be found in the paleo-Hebrew texts of Exodus and Leviticus found in the Dead Sea Scroll caves at Qumran.

The Samaritan Pentateuch also provides evidence of polemics between Judah and Ephraim in an earlier age and suggests that not all of the readings in the Samaritan Pentateuch that differ from the Masoretic text are late changes made by the Samaritans to emphasize their point of view but are residual readings of a much earlier text. The Samaritan Pentateuch readings are evidence that the schism between Judah and Israel, which was rooted in early history, was reflected in sacred writ.

In other places, the Samaritan Pentateuch text supports Samaritan sectarian hermeneutics. This text is, therefore, a guide to religious differences between Samaritans and Jews.

---

apparent that only a few small segments in the first part of the scroll, from Genesis to Numbers 35, were old. The rest was very recent and not worth publishing in full. The older parts were published in Castro's book, *Sefer Abisa*.[12]

The cryptogram in the Abisha Scroll that identifies Abisha as the scribe is embedded in the Book of Deuteronomy, chapters 6:10-13:19. Unlike the Jews, the Samaritans allow extraneous markings to be inserted into their Torah scrolls. Especially common are acrostic-cryptograms known as *tashqil* (pronounced tesh-UL). A *tashqil* conveys when the scroll was written and for which synagogue, details about the scribe and, sometimes, how many scrolls or codices he had previously written.

If written in the authentic way adopted by the Samaritans, the cryptogram, or *tashqil*, is difficult, perhaps impossible, to forge *in toto*. A whole work would have to be written to create the forgery.

This is how a *tashqil* is created. With two rules, usually about a centimeter (.39 inch) apart, a bed or column for the cryptogram is created on the parchment. It is always vertical down the center of the page. In the Abisha Scroll the cryptogram follows the normal tradition. Thus, the first two words of the cryptogram, which are read vertically from top to bottom, are picked out of the words הארץ (Deuteronomy 6:10), נטעת (Deuteronomy 6:11), הוציאך

(Deuteronomy 6:12), אתו (Deuteronomy 6:13), ובאת (Deuteronomy 6:18), איביך (Deuteronomy 6:19), ישאלך (Deuteronomy 6:20), לפרעה (Deuteronomy 6:21), which fall beneath each other in the center of the written column. The first two words read אני אבישע (*ani Abisha*, I [am] Abisha). In the Samaritan script they appear as shown at right. (For the sake of clarity, the letters that form the cryptogram have been enlarged; normally they are the same size as the rest of the text. The end of each word in the cryptogram is marked with a short horizontal stroke, shown here after the words *ani* [I] and *Abisha*.)

Some of the words of the *tashqil* in the Abisha Scroll have been subject to dispute. Parts of some words are difficult to read. Some words have been re-inked. On at least one column, the ruled *tashqil* bed has disappeared in the various restorations to which the scroll has been subjected so that it is not clear which letters are to be read as part of the cryptogram. But the basic message is clear.

The version of the *tashqil* in the Abisha Scroll favored by most scholars is quoted by a Samaritan chronicler, Abu'l Fath, who wrote in the latter half of the 14th century. According to Abu'l Fath, the scroll had been missing but was rediscovered during the priesthood of his master, Pinhas ben Joseph, who encouraged him to write his chronicle. As Abu'l Fath observed the cryptogram in the *tashqil* bed, it read as follows:

> I am Abisha, the son of Pinhas, son of Eleazar, son of Aaron the Priest, on them be the favor of the Lord and his glory—I wrote this holy book in the door of the tent of meeting on Mount Gerizim in the thirteenth year of the dominion of the Children of Israel over the land of Canaan to its boundaries round about. I praise the Lord.[13]

Contemporary scholars who have examined the scroll, particularly Yitzhak Ben-Zvi[14] and Father Castro, noted some variations that may provide information about the milieu in which the cryptogram was written, but they do not dispute the basic thrust of the *tashqil* cryptogram. On the face of it—if we accept the fact that a cryptogram like this cannot be forged—this scroll is approximately 3,300 years old, making it the oldest Torah scroll in the world! But, alas, there are problems.

If this scroll was truly written by the hand of Abisha, we would expect to find some references to it in old Samaritan chronicles. Perhaps we would also find at least some allusions to it in the accounts of pilgrims and travelers who passed through Shechem/Nablus in the course of the centuries. But there are none.

Some early church fathers—Jerome, Origen, Eusebius and Cyril of Alexandria—refer to an ancient Hebrew Pentateuch that existed among the Samaritans, implying the existence of a Samaritan version older than anything owned by the Jews. They do not even hint, however, that it may have been

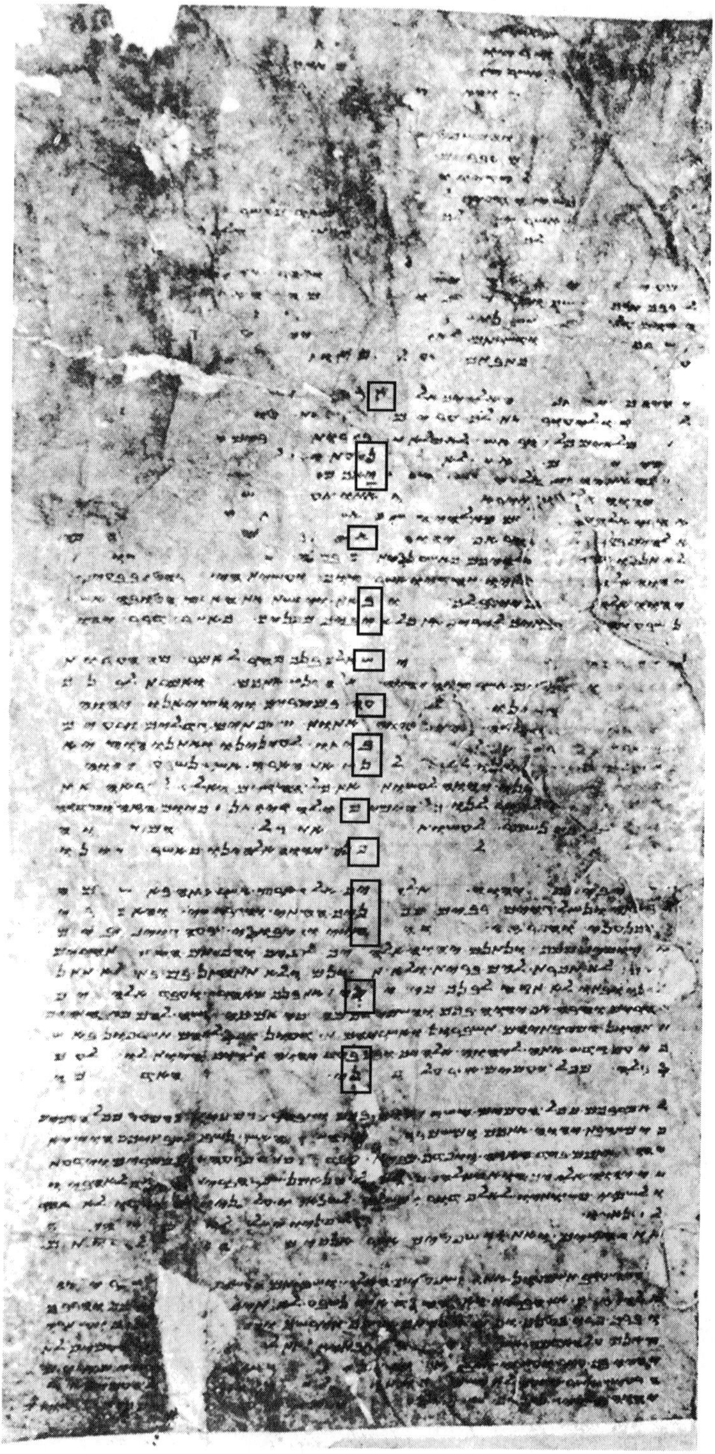

THE ABISHA SCROLL CRYPTOGRAM. The portion of the Abisha Scroll, seen at left in an early 20th-century photo by G. Eric Matson, contains a secret message concealed as an acrosticon in the text of Deuteronomy. The message proclaims: "I am Abisha, the son of Pinhas, son of Eleazar, son of Aaron the Priest, on them be the favor of the Lord and his glory—I wrote this holy book in the door of the tent of meeting on Mount Gerizim in the thirteenth year of the dominion of the Children of Israel over the land of Canaan to its boundaries round about. I praise the Lord."

The letters that form this secret message appear in the words of the text of Deuteronomy, from 6:10 to 13:19. The scroll has been written in such a way that these letters align vertically in the center of each column of text to spell out the message. The full cryptogram runs through five columns of text beginning with the one shown at left, on which we have highlighted some of the letters of the cryptogram. This form of cryptogram, known as a *tashqil*, often appears in Samaritan scrolls and usually includes the name of the scribe and information about the writing of the scroll.

Far from pristine, the Abisha Scroll is a patchwork of repairs and re-inking. Experts have identified six different scribal hands with writing styles spanning 800 years. The portion of the scroll from the end of Numbers through Deuteronomy (including Abisha's cryptogram) is written in the oldest writing style, which was used in Nablus about the first half of the 12th century C.E. *Photo: Plate 7, Sefer Abisa, by F. Castro*

written by someone referred to in the Bible. After the fifth century, we hear no more about an old Samaritan text, despite the fact that numerous pilgrims and historians—Jewish and Muslim—passed through Nablus and wrote accounts of their visits to the Samaritans. Even the Samaritan chronicles are silent on this score.

The Samaritan Book of Joshua[15] differs considerably from the edition in our Bibles. It is much longer, with 50 chapters compared to our 24; it contains considerable traditional Samaritan material not found in our edition. In view of the fact that this work is clearly ancient—it was composed no later than the 11th century C.E.—and drew on older Greek and Samaritan sources of first-millennium C.E. provenance, we would expect the Abisha Scroll to be referred to if it were known at the time this book was composed. But it is not mentioned. For example, in chapter 23, the high priest Eleazar, grandfather of Abisha, hands Joshua a copy of the Torah and tells him that this is to be his guide to the Promised Land. Then, in chapter 38, we are told that the Levites made copies of the Torah. It is significant that no mention is made of any Torah scroll written by Abisha. Another chapter deals with the priority of the Samaritan version over the Jewish version, but no mention is made of the Abisha Scroll.[16]

The existence of scrolls among the Samaritans is first hinted at in the Samaritan chronicles (late 14th century) in a discussion of the heretical sectarian activities of one Sakta, who, with his followers, appeared to consider the scroll handle an object of veneration. According to Abu'l Fath, the Samaritan chronicler, Sakta and his followers were among the heretics and sectaries who sprang into being in the era following the rule of Baba Rabba, that is, sometime in the late third or fourth century C.E. Sakta's account leads us to suspect that a controversy was brewing among the Samaritans about the value of writing the sacred scriptures in codex form, suggesting that the scroll had been the common form for sacred scriptures up to that time. But there is no mention, or even hint, of the existence of the Abisha Scroll in support of the argument that scrolls were superior to codices. This, of course, is an argument from silence and does not prove that the Abisha Scroll did not exist earlier.

The first mention of the Abisha Scroll does indicate a somewhat earlier date. The reference is in the margin of a copy of an early Samaritan chronicle known as *Tolidah* (the Genealogy), composed or written in 1149. In the autograph manuscript itself, there is no reference to the Abisha Scroll. But in a copy of this chronicle made in 1346, a marginal gloss notes that the Abisha Scroll is housed in the old Stone Synagogue at Elon Moreh (on the lower slopes of Mount Gerizim). The Samaritans started their ceremonial festival processions for Passover and the other pilgrim festivals from this synagogue and walked up the hill carrying a Pentateuch scroll. (Nowadays they start from a synagogue near the top of the mountain.)

This marginal note also tells of a tragedy that befell the Abisha Scroll. On a particular festival (perhaps the second day of Sukkot/Pentecost), there was an earthquake while the priest was holding the scroll on the mountain. The priest was apparently affected by the quake and was stricken by an illness. An emendation to the text of the *Tolidah* says that "God sent a fiery snake which reared up beneath his legs [that is, the legs of the priest holding the scroll] and tore out a piece of his flesh." The scroll case fell open, and the scroll was picked up by the wind and torn. It seems that only the end of the Book of Numbers and the Book of Deuteronomy were saved. The statement as to what was saved is carefully worded but is nevertheless ambiguous, so we cannot be sure what was saved and what was lost. A supergloss—an additional note—says that the end of the book was lost.[17]

Remember that in the latter half of the 14th century, Abu'l Fath wrote that the Abisha Scroll had been missing but was rediscovered. This would seem to indicate that the Abisha Scroll had been carefully restored after the earthquake and was once again being used for the sacred offices, although it may not have been put at risk again on the climb up the mountain.

Since Abu'l Fath's day, there have been numerous references to the Abisha Scroll. They indicate that the scroll was seldom unrolled and that it was in poor condition. From a letter dated 1715, we learn that the scroll was kept in the house of the high priest and taken out only for great festivals. The letter also describes the scroll as torn. A certain Salih ibn Ibrahim, writing in 1849, notes that part of Deuteronomy 21:15 was duplicated and that he was given permission to erase the error with a knife. He adds that he was also given permission to repair the scroll. Incidentally, although Father Castro in his edition of the scroll does not comment on the erasure referred to in Salih ibn Ibrahim's letter, we can see traces of this erasure in Castro's published text, so we can be certain that the photographs published in Castro's edition[18] are in fact of the Abisha Scroll.

The first detailed description of the scroll is by John Mills, the secretary of the Anglo-Biblical Institute, who went to stay with the Samaritans for three months in 1861 so that he could bring back a report about them for members of the institute. Mills' description gives the impression that, despite patches and tears, the Abisha Scroll was more or less intact. From subsequent descriptions, we know that Mills was wrong. The scroll is not merely torn and patched but is a crazy quilt from a series of sources. For example, if you look at Castro's plate 12 (see photo, page 234), you can see that the column is formed of two parts, the top of which was once the lower part of a column; the way the writing is spread in the center of the column (i.e., the bottom of the top part) is characteristic of the bottom of columns of text. Samaritan scholar Moses Gaster, who saw the scroll early in this century, noted that in some places the scroll was illegible; in other places, letters had been rewritten; and "the scroll consists mainly of a mass of patches held together by a backing. Altogether it is in such a dilapidated condition that only the utmost care in handling it will preserve it."[19]

Another observer indicated that the condition of the scroll was so bad and the patching so extreme that it even interfered with the *tashqil*.[20] Scribes have tried at various times to restore what they knew to be the *tashqil* but have interfered with it as little as possible. Although it is difficult to read and there are some discrepancies between what we see today and what Abu'l Fath described, we cannot claim that there has been deliberate forgery.[21]

Castro detected six different hands in the oldest parts of the scroll, including scribal restorations. In itself, this does not indicate that the scroll as it presently exists was written over a long period of time. Samaritan scribes sometimes worked in shifts so that several scribes worked on the same text. However, that is not the case here. The hands are widely different, reflecting a chronological range of 800 years. The most recent hands are on patches at the tops and bottoms of columns where the scroll had been badly worn. The oldest, Castro's hand A, appears only at the end of Numbers and Deuteronomy. This was apparently the part that was saved after the earthquake.[22]

Our knowledge of Samaritan paleography (the study of the shape and position of letters as they change over time) is now so advanced that we can confidently date at least some parts of the scroll. From Castro's photographs, we can see very clearly that hand A, in which the cryptogram was written, is a Nablus hand of the first half of the 12th century C.E. (and therefore cannot be the hand of the great-grandson of Aaron, the priest of the Exodus).[23]

That does not mean that other hands in the scroll may not be even earlier. For the scroll is not a unit but a series of fragments and pieces put together

PATCHWORK REPAIRS. Numerous repairs and restorations of the dilapidated Abisha Scroll over the centuries have resulted in a crazy quilt of patches. The column seen here consists of two parts. An unknown restorer took the bottom portion of a column containing the appropriate text from another scroll and patched it onto the upper half of this column. The wide spacing of the letters near the bottom of the patch (near the center of the picture) is typical of the bottom of a column. *Photo: Plate 12,* Sefer Abisa, *by F. Castro*

to make a complete Torah scroll. It could be that the restorer (who reinserted the section rescued from the earthquake into a whole scroll) cannibalized even older material to reconstruct the scroll. Unfortunately Castro did not publish the photographs of the first part of the scroll (from Genesis to the middle of Numbers) because most of it was recent, although he recognized that there were older pieces among the recent additions. Some of these might have pre-dated the initial reconstruction and could have been reused during subsequent refurbishment. We have no way of knowing this, so we can describe only the end of the scroll. Moreover, even in the part we can examine, we can see traces of two other cryptograms in column 66 and columns 72-73, which strengthens the argument that different scrolls have been cannibalized to recreate this one.

Both the argument from silence (the absence of references to the Abisha Scroll before the 14th century) and the argument from paleography refute the claim that the Abisha Scroll actually comes from the hand of Aaron's great-grandson. But there is additional evidence in the language of the cryptogram itself. The words *on them be the favor of the Lord* indicate that the cryptogram was written after the advent of Islam, because that particular phrasing was borrowed by the

Samaritans from Islam.[24] Thus it could not have been written earlier than the seventh century.

We can, therefore, dismiss out of hand the claim that Abisha, the great-grandson of Aaron, inscribed the *tashqil*. But we are left with a mystery as to just who and what are described in the cryptogram. Perhaps there was another Abisha with the same name and forebears who lived 2,000 years later. Castro takes this position and argues for an unknown Abisha in the 11th century, suggesting that all that has happened is that 1,000 years was dropped out of the dating in the cryptogram of the scroll. This sometimes happens in Samaritan dating systems and does not prove an intent to deceive. But we know of no such Abisha in the 11th century, and the careful wording of the remainder of the cryptogram argues against the accidental dropping of a number.

Another scholar argues that the 13th year refers to a hiatus in the high priesthood in the 13th century C.E., when the priesthood of Shechem (modern Nablus) was assumed by Ithamar ben Amram of Damascus, the 13th year referring to the 13th year after this event.[25] Another scholar argues that the Abisha Scroll is connected with the Stone Synagogue from which it was carried on the day of the earthquake.[26] The Stone Synagogue was the pride and joy of the Samaritans, for it was built by High Priest Aqbun in the third or fourth century C.E. and was a substitute for the temple, which was destroyed by John Hyrcanus in 128 B.C.E. Although the temple was confiscated by Zeno in the fifth century (after the revolt of 484), it was returned to the Samaritans by the early Fatimid caliphs in the 11th century and rebuilt by the Samaritan patron, Ab Gillujah of Tyre. The site remained in Samaritan hands until it was lost to the Muslims in the 14th century.

Another possibility is that the 13th year refers to a return to the Promised Land from Damascus in the middle of the 12th century, a date that more or less coincides with the paleographic evidence. In 1137, some 500 Samaritan men, women and children, perhaps half the Samaritan population of Shechem, were abducted by one Bazwadj, the general of the Damascene army. They were ransomed by a very wealthy Samaritan, Ab Gillujah of Acre, and returned home. The homecoming of a substantial part of the population may well have been likened to entry to the Promised Land and a sign of God's redemption and grace.[27] According to the Samaritan chronicles, this same Ab Gillujah rebuilt the Stone Synagogue and equipped it with trumpets for announcing the festive days and summoning the faithful, as had been the case in the old Samaritan temple. We must assume that the restored Stone Synagogue was provided with a scroll or scrolls for worship.

We know that in this period a literary revival took place and numerous scrolls were written for newly refurbished Samaritan synagogues.[28] The chronicles tell us, too, that Ab Gillujah financed other construction works, including an aqueduct for the community in Awerta. The era of prosperity after the return from captivity might have given the impression that the days of Divine

Displeasure were over and the Days of Divine Favor were at hand, as suggested in the famous cryptogram. If we assume that 13 years after the return from Damascus was the period when the synagogue was rebuilt and furnished with a scroll, we arrive at a date of around 1150 for the new scroll for the Stone Synagogue. If my judgment is correct, this jibes with the paleographic evidence as the date of the Abisha Scroll.

Unfortunately, we know of no Abisha in the 12th century. It may be, of course, that there was one who is not mentioned in any other source.[29] Perhaps the scribe, whoever he was, adopted the name of a famous antecedent in order to remain anonymous because he was working in an environment that could turn hostile again. The cryptogram might have been phrased as a reminder that the people had been restored to their homes 13 years earlier and that, for the first time since the Byzantine era, they were again in possession of their great Stone Synagogue and temple substitute on the slopes of Mount Gerizim and that fortune appeared to be smiling upon the community after very hard times indeed.[30]

Whatever the truth may be, the Abisha Scroll is indeed old—at least parts of it are—and it ranks as one of the oldest Torah scrolls in the world.

PART III

Language(s) and the Bible

Introduction

Our investigation into biblical composition and transmission naturally raises questions about language as well. The Bible was composed as separate documents in Hebrew, Aramaic and Greek; yet most readers know it as a single book in a single language. How does this transformation affect meaning? In what languages were the oral traditions and written documents that underlie the final text?

The Hebrew Scriptures span a millennium; does the language reflect a thousand years of evolution, the way English does, for example, from Beowulf to the Beach Boys? Should this range be reflected in English translations by rendering the earlier books in archaic, perhaps Shakespearean, diction and later ones in a more modern idiom? The New Testament has come down to us in Greek; is this the language Jesus and his followers spoke? Knowing the date of a Hebrew composition can help establish the likely meaning of words and allusions. Knowing that a different language underlies a text can help explain unusual constructions or diction.

Language is central to understanding the Bible. Wordplay and etymologies are everywhere. Adam calls his new mate *'ishah* (woman) because she is taken from *'ish* (man) (Genesis 2:23). The Valley of Eshkol was so named because the 12 Israelite spies picked a cluster—*'eshkol*—of grapes there (Numbers 13:24). The entire story of Jacob's early life echoes with the root *'qb* (trip, supplant). He was named *Ya'aqob* (Jacob/Heel-grabber) because at birth he grabbed the *'aqeb* (heel) of his brother Esau (Genesis, 25:26), who, after being tricked out of his seniority, exclaims, "He is rightly called *Ya'aqob* for he has twice tripped me up/supplanted me" (*ya'aqebeni*, Genesis 27:36).

But many basic linguistic questions are still unanswered. If Hebrew changed over time, if sources have been combined to create the current text, if concepts like justice, morality, soul, afterlife, even God, evolved, what is the meaning of these words in the text before us? Words that meant one thing to the original audience may mean something else—or nothing—to us. The covering of the Tabernacle in the wilderness (Exodus 26:14), *'orot teḥašim* in Hebrew, is variously translated as badger skins (King James Version), porpoise hides

(New English Bible), dolphin skins (New Jewish Publication Society), dugong hides (Revised English Bible) and fine leather (New Revised Standard Version). Or take the word *nešer* in Leviticus 11:13 and Exodus 19:4. Listed as a forbidden bird in the dietary laws of Leviticus, *nešer* appears in several modern translations as vulture. But in the beautiful image of Exodus, God carries his people on "the wings of eagles." Did *nešer* indicate two different birds to the original author and audience?

And who, exactly, deserves to be called original author and original audience? The prophet and the people who heard him? The compilers who preserved the narratives and the posterity they envisioned? Or the final redactors and their readers? Were the original utterances extemporaneous oracles or polished poetry, nomadic folklore or urbane literature, in colloquial speech or literary diction? Did the prophet and his audience understand them as part of an unfinished revelation that began with Genesis and the creation of the world?

Let us look more closely at Amos, for example, who describes himself as a herdsman and a dresser of sycamore trees and who was called to prophecy more or less against his will (1:1, 7:14). The same word, *noqed*, translated herdsman, is applied in 2 Kings 3:4 to King Mesha of Moab. Does this imply that Amos was not an unlettered farmer but a manager of royal estates or a cultic official of some sort, perhaps keeper of the sacrificial livestock? If so, his condemnation of luxury could be the product of intimate knowledge and not, as is usually explained, the shock of a rustic discovering the big city.

Amos' prophecies are arranged by similarity in content and structure. If he was an educated poet, he may have composed, polished and delivered them this way. The refrain, "Thus says the Lord:/ For three transgressions of [a particular people],/ And for four,/ I will not turn away its punishment" (KJV), might indicate that chapters 1 and 2 were originally conceived as one long poem. If Amos was an untutored farmer, it is more likely that later editors combined separate oracles because of their similarities.

Who saw fit to record these speeches—Amos himself, a private secretary, an impressed hearer, a royal stenographer? And who were the final editors—disciples of the prophet, the redactors of the Bible?

Similar questions have arisen about the image of Jesus. Palestinian Jewish society was multifaceted in the first century C.E. Most Jews spoke Aramaic in their day-to-day affairs. But Hebrew was the language of the Temple and ritual, and, as the Mishnah and Dead Sea Scrolls prove, of scholarship and literature as well. The official language of the Roman Empire, to which Palestine belonged, was Greek. Many Romans, however, presumably spoke Latin. Nazareth was a small Jewish village with about 400 inhabitants, but it was just three miles from Sepphoris, the capital of the Galilee, a Greco-Roman city with a population of 30,000—Jews, Romans, Greeks and Arabs. Thus, the romantic view of Jesus as a simple rural preacher is probably untenable. As a skilled carpenter, he may have worked in the wealthy homes of Sepphoris and associated with people of all social classes and could get by in two or three languages. If this is correct, implications abound concerning his teaching and the early records of it. What was the nature and extent of Jesus' education? Did he preach in Aramaic or Greek? Were verbatim sayings and parables preserved? If so, in which language or languages?

In the Gospels, which obviously incorporate earlier traditions, Jesus speaks Aramaic in a few scenes. He raises the dead girl with the words *Talitha cum* (Arise, my child; Mark 5:41), heals the deaf with the word *Ephphatha* (Be opened; Mark 7:34) and says on the cross *Eli, Eli, lema sabachthani* (My God, my God, why have you forsaken me?; Matthew 27:46; Mark 15:34). However, Joseph A. Fitzmyer believes that, because Jesus dealt with Hellenized clients, tax collectors, soldiers and Roman bureaucrats who spoke Greek, he almost certainly spoke Greek in addition to Aramaic. But Fitzmyer does not think Jesus taught in Greek or that the Gospels preserve the actual Greek words Jesus used. Then did Jesus teach in Aramaic or Hebrew? Were any of his sayings preserved verbatim?

Jesus lived and died a Jew, of course, and early Christianity everywhere exhibits Jewish characteristics—a fact that is often overlooked. George Howard maintains that ancient Greek manuscripts in which the tetragrammaton, the four-letter Hebrew designation for the Israelite God, is written in Hebrew, prove that Jewish Christians continued to follow established Jewish customs. When gentile Christians later substituted Greek translations, they changed the meaning of the text; for example, "Prepare the way of YHWH" in Hebrew became "Prepare the way of the Lord" (Mark 1:3), which implies something quite different.

A parallel situation exists with Latin loan words. We take no notice of such familiar words as *legion, mile* and *colony*—which are also borrowed from Latin—but they may have been new enough to call attention to themselves in a first century Greek or Aramaic composition. If they were used for special effect, as we might use voguish French words, translators would be hard pressed to convey this in English.

Distortions like these are endemic to translation, which can vary from literal to paraphrase. Literal translation goes beyond the word-for-word technique that gives us Hebraic expressions like "Song of Songs" and "living soul." It also extends to syntax, for in the opinion of Jerome, the author of the Latin Vulgate, in Holy Scripture "even the word order is sacred." This belief influenced biblical translators for 1,500 years, meshing later with the Renaissance reverence for classical sources and the Protestant commitment to the preeminence of the biblical text.

William Tyndale, a precursor of and a major influence on the translators of the King James Version, wrote that "the properties of the Hebrew tongue agreeth a thousand times more with the English than with the Latin," and therefore "in a thousand places thou needest not but to translate it into English word for word." And in his essay in *The Literary Guide to the Bible*,[1] Gerald Hammond argues that the strange syntax of the King James Version often mirrors the Hebrew; for example, Genesis 1:4, "And God saw the light, that it was good." To the extent, then, that English has a "biblical" style, it is in the sounds and rhythms of the King James Version.

Even when the need was felt in the late 19th century to update the King James Version, the watchword was moderation. Words that had fallen out of use—but not, for example, *thee* and *thou*—were replaced, as were words with changed meanings that caused confusion. However, the King James Version could still be seen in the Revised Version (1885), American Standard Version (1901), Revised Standard Version (1952) and New American Standard Bible (1971). The preface to the Revised Standard Version proudly proclaims that it "is not a new translation in the language of today....It is a revision which seeks to preserve all that is best in the English Bible as it has been known and used throughout the years." The less rigid New Revised Standard Version (1990), a reworking of the 1952 edition, is intended to be "as literal as possible, as free as necessary."

The thought-for-thought approach to translation requires the translator to extract meaning from the original and recast it in whatever words and syntax seem best. As we can readily see by comparing parallel passages in Philip W. Comfort's *The Complete Guide to Bible Versions*,[2] phrases may replace single words; sentences may be combined and rearranged; transitional words may be added to show logical connections. Thus, John 1:1 in the literal New American Standard Bible is one sentence, without subordination:

> In the beginning was the Word, and the Word was with God, and the Word was God.

In the New English Bible, on the other hand, the passage has an introductory subordinator, two extra clauses and two sentences:

> When all things began, the Word already was. The Word dwelt with God, and what God was, the Word was.

Some translators try to achieve what Eugene Nida calls "dynamic equivalence"—producing the same effect as the original text. Assuming that John was written in the normal, everyday language of his time (rather than in a literary style) the Good News Bible—Today's English Version translates our sample verse:

> Before the world was created, the Word already existed; he was with God, and he was the same as God.

Finally, the paraphrase approach frequently incorporates interpretations into the text. Thus, in *The Living Bible*, this verse reads:

> Before anything else existed, there was Christ, with God. He has always been alive and is himself God.

As this passage illustrates, paraphrase precludes all interpretations except the editor's—an obvious loss in poetic and prophetic passages, and a danger even in simple narrative passages.

Of course, labeling parts of the Bible poetic seems to contradict the previous assumption that biblical language is the normal, everyday idiom. In fact, New Testament Greek ranges from something like careless speech in Revelation to polished prose in Hebrews, a distinction seldom apparent in translations. Making such comparisons about Hebrew is riskier because surviving documents do not preserve much of the language of personal letters, business records or colloquial speech. The Siloam Inscription celebrating the completion of King Hezekiah's water tunnel (mentioned in 2 Kings 20:20 and 2 Chronicles 32:3-4,30) is presumably literary. And even military dispatches, like the Lachish Ostraca, may not be written in colloquial language because learning to read and write may have meant learning special written diction. Thus, scholars can only speculate about when particular words or constructions are used for literary effect and when they were the only words or constructions available.

It used to be said, for example, that ancient Hebrew had a small vocabulary. Some modern translators, therefore, believed they could improve the accuracy and literary quality in English by rendering a single Hebrew word in a variety of English words. Rather than the quaint or archaic "Adam knew Eve" of the King James Version for Genesis 4:1, for example, they preferred "lay with" or "had intercourse with" because these are more idiomatic in modern English. It seems proper to ask, however, if the Hebrew original was idiomatic—or literary.

When Martin Buber and Franz Rosenzweig explained the philosophy of their German translation of the Hebrew Bible, which appeared between 1925 and 1961, they contended that the recurrence of key words in Hebrew was an artistic device that created cohesion and depth of meaning in seemingly artless prose. Robert Alter pursued this idea to great advantage in *The Art of Biblical Narrative*.[3] Alter argued that repetition is an artistic device and does not reflect an impoverished lexicon.

This would affect how the verse we have been examining is translated. The Hebrew root used in this verse, *yada'*, also means "know" or "experience." If *yada'* were the only Hebrew word for sexual intercourse, and it happened to be a homonym with the word for *know*, then "Adam *knew* Eve" would convey the wrong tone in English. Common, everyday Hebrew would have been rendered in a strange English locution. But because there were other Hebrew words for sexual union—*šakab* and *šagal*—the use of *yada'* in Genesis 4:1 must have been deliberate, an echo of the same root word for the Tree of Knowledge and the serpent's words that "God knows you will be like gods, *knowing* good and evil." In this case, "Adam *knew* Eve" correctly captures the Hebrew, but idiomatic modern phrases do not.

When we consider the size of the Bible, this becomes a formidable problem with no easy solution. Ironically, Marc Brettler praises the translators of the New Jewish Publication Society version for their attempts to find one-to-one correspondences between Hebrew and English words. But the editor of this version, Harry M. Orlinsky, maintains in *Notes on the New Translation of the Torah*[4] that "it is incorrect, if not misleading to reproduce [a Hebrew] term by a single English term throughout."

The concern for accurate translation derives, of course, from the religious significance of the Bible. Translators have been burned at the stake. People have killed and been killed over the difference between *congregation* and *church*, *elder* and *priest*. Biblical translations, almost by definition, embody religious interpretations. Should the Hebrew of Psalm 2:12 be rendered "Kiss the Son" as it is in the King James Version, "Kiss the king" as it is in the New English Bible, or "Pay homage in good faith" as it is in the New Jewish Publication Society version? The answer depends as much on religious as linguistic considerations.

Among Protestant Bibles, the King James Version, first published in 1611, long ago became the Authorized Version. Despite many revisions, the KJV still appeals to traditionalists. Somewhat more conservative are the J. B. Phillips Version (1947-1963), Good News Bible—Today's English Version (1966-1978), New American Standard Bible (1971), and New International Version (1978). On the liberal side is the New English Bible (1961-1970), although the revision of this version, the Revised English Bible (1989), is closer to the mainstream. *The Living Bible* is evangelical.

The Catholic counterpart to the King James Version in age and stature is the Rheims-Douay Version (1582, 1609-1610), revised by Bishop Challoner in 1750. The New American Bible (1970) is a translation from the Hebrew and Greek rather than the Vulgate. The widely praised Jerusalem Bible (1966) incorporates current research in Hebrew and Greek; a revised New Jerusalem Bible appeared in 1986.

The Jewish Publication Society has published two translations—The Holy Scriptures (1917), a revision of the Revised Version of 1885; and Tanakh: The Holy Scriptures (3 vols., 1962-1982), a scholarly translation into contemporary English also called the New JPS version. A traditional rabbinic translation published by Mesorah Publications is called the Artscroll Tanakh.

Languages of Composition

Various books of the Bible were composed in Hebrew, Aramaic and Greek. It seems certain, however, that certain sections are not preserved in the original language. The Aramaic letters in the third chapter of Ezra are presumably verbatim copies of documents in the Persian royal archives. But the narrative leading up to the quoted letters is in Hebrew; the narrative following them is in Aramaic. In which language was the history composed? What accounts for the change of language?

Establishing the original language for parts of the New Testament is even more difficult. The Gospels have come down to us in Greek. But at least some—perhaps most, or all—of the underlying oral tradition must have been in Aramaic, the vernacular of Palestinian Jews. Moreover, regardless of the spoken language, literate members of society expected literature to be in Hebrew or Greek. Where does the New Testament fit?

CHAPTER 20

The Name of God in the New Testament

George Howard

George Howard argues that translating the Hebrew divine name YHWH as kyrios *or* theos *"blurred the original distinction between the Lord God and the Lord Christ." For example, "YHWH said to my Lord" became in Greek, "The Lord said to my Lord" (Matthew 22:44), and "Prepare the way of YHWH" became "Prepare the way of the Lord" (Mark 1:3).–Ed.*

In many early copies of the New Testament, sacred words (*nomina sacra*) are abbreviated. The earliest abbreviations stand for God, Lord, Christ and Jesus. Abbreviations of these words were formed by writing the first and last letters and placing a line over them. Thus, using English to illustrate, God would be written G̅D̅ and Lord L̅D̅. Attempts to differentiate and dignify the sacred name of God go back to Jews in pre-Christian times.

From the Dead Sea Scrolls we know that Jewish scribes often set off the divine name Yahweh (Yahweh is known as the tetragrammaton because it consists of four Hebrew consonant letters, *yod, he, vav, he,* often written in English YHWH) by writing the tetragrammaton in old paleo-Hebrew script, even when the scroll was otherwise written in square Aramaic script. An example is the Habakkuk Commentary found in Cave 1 of the Dead Sea caves. In the portion reproduced in the photograph on page 250, the tetragrammaton appears twice in paleo-Hebrew script: line 7 word 3 and line 14 word 7 (reading from right to left). The rest of the text is in square Aramaic script—the same script that is the basis for Hebrew today. The tetragrammaton is used in the Habakkuk Commentary only in biblical quotations. References to God in the commentary portion are made with the generic word *El* (God). This is also true in other Qumran documents (i.e., the Dead Sea Scrolls).

The Qumran covenanters also used other devices for abbreviating the name of God. Sometimes they would write four or five dots in place of the tetragrammaton. In the Community Rule, for example, the writer quotes Isaiah 40:3 as follows: "Prepare in the wilderness the way of . . . ." We know from the Masoretic text that the four dots stand for the tetragrammaton YHWH. This passage is quoted again in a document discovered in Qumran Cave 4 (4QTanḥumim) with four dots representing the divine name. Sometimes, when the tetragrammaton had been written by mistake, dots were placed above the letters, apparently as a way of canceling the word without actually erasing it.

From early on, Jews adopted the practice of not pronouncing the divine name when scripture was read aloud, even in prayer. The word *adonai* (Lord) was (and is to this day) read by Jews instead of the tetragrammaton even when YHWH appears on the page. Such practices as writing the divine name in archaic script, substituting dots for it or avoiding it altogether suggest that to Jews the sacred name of God was a word that required special written and oral treatment.

Passages from the Old Testament in which the divine name YHWH appears in the original Hebrew are often quoted in Christian scriptures. In these quotations, however, the divine name is usually translated into the Greek word *kyrios* (Lord), or occasionally *theos* (God). Both of these are generic words for God and are not limited to the Hebrew God whose name is Yahweh and who is represented in the Hebrew Bible by the tetragrammaton. Most Old Testament quotations in the New Testament come from the Septuagint, a Greek translation of the Old Testament made by Jews in pre-Christian times. In the Septuagint (or at least the later, extant Christian copies of it), the tetragrammaton is rendered as *kyrios*; the same practice is followed in the New Testament.

In 1944, William G. Waddell discovered the remains of an Egyptian papyrus scroll that contained part of the Septuagint (Papyrus Fuad 266) dating to the first or second century B.C.E. In no case, however, was YHWH translated as *kyrios*. Instead the tetragrammaton itself—*in square Aramaic letters*—was written into the Greek text. This parallels the use of the paleo-Hebrew script for the divine name in documents otherwise written in square Aramaic script by the Qumran covenanters.

An even closer parallel to Papyrus Fuad 266 can be found in second-century C.E. Jewish translations of the Old Testament into Greek by Aquila, Symmachus, and Theodotion. In 1897, Francis C. Burkitt published some fragments of Aquila's Greek Old Testament, which had been found in the debris of a *genizah* (a storeroom for worn out manuscripts) of the old synagogue in Cairo. These fragments, which are the underwriting of palimpsest (parchments that were erased and written over) fragments, clearly show the Hebrew tetragrammaton in paleo-Hebrew script written into an otherwise Greek text. A number of other similar examples have also come to light.

At the end of the 19th century, Giovanni Cardinal Mercati discovered a palimpsest in the Ambrosian Library of Milan containing parts of the Psalter to Origen's Hexapla (missing the Hebrew column). The Hexapla also contains the translations of Aquila, Symmachus and Theodotion. In all of the extant columns, although the texts are otherwise written in Greek, the tetragrammaton is written in square Aramaic script.

Fragments of Psalm 22 from Origen's Hexapla, which were found in the Cairo *genizah*, were published in 1900 by C. Taylor. These fragments show the tetragrammaton written into the Greek columns of Aquila, Symmachus and the Septuagint in the strange form of *PIPI*, a clumsy attempt to represent with Greek letters what the tetragrammaton looked like in Hebrew. The Greek letter *pi* (π) somewhat resembles the Hebrew letter *he* (ה).

The Fuad papyrus scroll, dating to the first or second century B.C.E., is the earliest example we have examined. Here, for the first time, is evidence that in pre-Christian times the divine name was *not always* translated with the Greek word *kyrios* in the Septuagint; sometimes the Hebrew word YHWH was preserved. Did the Jews always write the tetragrammaton in Hebrew into the text of their Greek Bibles? Could this have been a continuous tradition from the earliest Septuagint through the second century translations of Aquila, Symmachus and Theodotion? Or is the Fuad manuscript a maverick, the only one in which this was done?

In 1952, fragments of a scroll of the Minor Prophets in Greek were found in a cave at Naḥal Ḥever in the Judean Desert. Père Dominique Barthélemy announced the discovery of the scroll in 1953 and ten years later published a transcription of it. In all probability, the document dates to the beginning of the first Christian century. In these fragments, too, the tetragrammaton is written in Hebrew—in old-style script—in an otherwise Greek text.

At Qumran Cave 4, in a fragment of a Greek translation of Leviticus the divine name is also preserved in the pre-Christian Septuagint. In this scroll,

TETRAGRAMMATON. A fragment of the Minor Prophets Scroll found in the Naḥal Ḥever caves. The text is in Greek except for the tetra-grammaton (far left, lines 1 and 6, count-ing from the bottom), which is in paleo-Hebrew script. *Photo: Israel Antiquities Authority/Bruce and Kenneth Zuckerman/ West Semitic Research Project*

dated by Patrick W. Skehan to the first century B.C.E., the tetragrammaton is rendered in a Greek transliteration with the letters *IAO*.

Thus, in three separate pre-Christian copies of the Greek Septuagint Bible, the tetragrammaton is not translated *kyrios* even once. In fact, the tetragrammaton is not translated at all. We can now say with near certainty that it was a Jewish practice before, during and after the New Testament period to write the divine name in paleo-Hebrew or square Aramaic script or in transliteration into the Greek text of scripture. This is in striking contrast to Christian copies of the Septuagint and quotations from it in the New Testament, where the tetragrammaton is consistently translated as *kyrios* or *theos*.

Christian copies of the Septuagint reflect a practice radically different from the Jewish practice of designating the divine name. Or do they? We have already mentioned that Christians translated the tetragrammaton either as *kyrios* or *theos* but abbreviated these surrogates by writing only the first and last letters and placing a line over them to attract attention. What was the purpose of these Christian abbreviations?

In 1907, Ludwig Traube suggested that the *nomina sacra* were of Hellenistic Jewish origin. The first of these, he suggested, was *theos*, which was abbreviated without vowels so as to follow the Hebrew custom of writing consonants only. Soon *theos* was followed by *kyrios*, which became an alternate surrogate, and the first and last letters became an alternate contraction. According to Traube, these contractions gave rise to the belief that the important thing was that sacred words be written in abbreviated form. This resulted in a number of words being written in a similar way (for example, spirit, father and heaven). In 1959, A. H. R. E. Paap took up the issue again and argued that the system of contracted *nomina sacra* originated in Jewish-Christian Alexandria about 100 C.E.

It seems to me, however, that a stronger case can be made that the system of contractions is of gentile Christian origin. The divine name YHWH was and is the most sacred word in the Hebrew language. So it is hardly likely that any Jews would have removed it from their Bibles. Furthermore, we know now from discoveries in Egypt and the Judean desert that Jews wrote the tetragrammaton in Hebrew even in their Greek texts. In all likelihood, Jewish Christians felt the same way about the divine name and continued to preserve it in Hebrew in their Bibles. In a famous rabbinic passage (Talmud Shabbat 13.5), the rabbis discuss the problem of destroying heretical texts (probably including Jewish-Christian books). The problem arose because heretical texts contain the divine name, and wholesale destruction would include destruction of the divine name. This reinforces the theory that Jewish Christians did not translate the divine name into Greek.

Gentile Christians, unlike Jewish Christians, had no traditional attachment to the Hebrew tetragrammaton and no doubt often failed even to recognize it. Gentile scribes who had never before seen Hebrew writing (especially in archaic form) could hardly be expected to preserve the divine name. Perhaps this was one reason for the use of surrogates, like *kyrios* and *theos*. The contracted form of the surrogates indicated the sacred nature of the name in a way that was convenient for gentile scribes to write. At the same time the abbreviated surrogates may have appeased Jewish Christians who felt it necessary to differentiate the divine name from the rest of the text. After the system of

COLUMN 10 OF THE HABAKKUK COMMENTARY found in Cave 1 at Qumran contains two quotations from Habakkuk (2:13 and 2:14). Note especially line 7 word 3 (counting from the top and reading from right to left) and line 14 word 7, where a single word appears in a different script. The word is the ineffable name of God, Yahweh, known as the tetragrammaton because it contains four letters, *yod, he, vov, he.*

The tetragrammaton is written in the archaic Hebrew script although the remainder of the scroll is written in the newer, square Hebrew script, which is the basis for modern Hebrew writing. In the Habakkuk Commentary the tetragrammaton is used *only* in biblical quotations; elsewhere, references to God are written as the generic word *El* (God). *Photo: John C. Trever*

contractions had been in use for some time, the original purpose may have been forgotten, and many other words, which had no connection with the tetragrammaton, were also abbreviated.

Assuming that this theory is generally correct, I offer the following scenario of the history of the tetragrammaton in the Greek Bible as a whole, including both testaments. In the Old Testament, Jewish scribes always preserved the tetragrammaton in the Septuagint both before and after the New Testament period. In all probability, Jewish Christians also wrote the tetragrammaton in Hebrew. Toward the end of the first Christian century, when the church had become predominantly gentile, the motive for retaining the Hebrew name for God was lost and the words *kyrios* and *theos* were substituted in Christian copies of the Old Testament Septuagint. Both *kyrios* and *theos* were written in abbreviated form in a conscious effort to preserve the sacred nature of the divine name. Soon the significance of the contractions was lost and many other contracted words were added.

A similar pattern probably evolved with respect to the New Testament. Whenever the Hebrew form of the divine name appeared in the Septuagint, which the New Testament church used and quoted, the New Testament writers no doubt included the tetragrammaton in their quotations. But when the Hebrew form for the divine name was eliminated in favor of Greek substitutes in the Septuagint, it was also eliminated from New Testament quotations of the Septuagint.

Thus, toward the end of the first Christian century, the use of surrogates (*kyrios* and *theos*) and their contractions must have crowded out the Hebrew tetragrammaton in both testaments. Before long the divine name was lost to the gentile church except as it was reflected in the contracted surrogates or remembered by scholars. Soon even the contracted substitutes lost their original significance and were joined by a host of other abbreviated *nomina sacra* with no connection to the divine name at all.

Is there any way for us, at this late date, to calculate the effect of this change in the Bible on the second-century church? It is impossible to be certain, but the effect was probably significant. A number of passages that had been perfectly clear in the original must have become ambiguous. For example, the second-century church read "the Lord said to my Lord" (Matthew 22:44; Mark 12:36; Luke 20:42), a reading as ambiguous as it is imprecise. The first-century church probably read "YHWH said to my Lord."

To Christians in the second-century church, "Prepare the way of the Lord" (Mark 1:3) must have meant one thing because it immediately followed the words "the beginning of the gospel of Jesus Christ." But in the first century, it must have meant something else because they read "prepare the way of YHWH."

In the second century, 1 Corinthians 1:31 read "the one who boasts, let him boast in the Lord," which was probably considered a reference to Christ, who is mentioned in verse 30. But in the first century, it probably referred to God, mentioned in verse 29; they read "the one who boasts let him boast in YHWH."

These examples are sufficient to suggest that removing the tetragrammaton from the New Testament and replacing it with the surrogates *kyrios* and *theos* blurred the original distinction between the Lord God and the Lord Christ and, in many passages, made it impossible to tell which one was meant. This argument is supported by the fact that in a number of places where Old Testament quotations are cited, there is confusion in the discussions surrounding the quotation about whether to read God or Christ. Once the tetragrammaton was removed and replaced by the surrogate "Lord," scribes could not be sure if Lord meant God or Christ. As time went on, the two figures were brought into even closer unity until it was sometimes impossible to distinguish between them. Thus the removal of the tetragrammaton may have contributed significantly to the Christological and Trinitarian debates that plagued the church during the early Christian centuries.

Whatever the case, the removal of the tetragrammaton probably created a different theological climate from the one that existed during the New Testament period of the first century. The Jewish God, who had always been carefully distinguished from all others by the use of his Hebrew name, lost some of his distinctiveness with the passing of the tetragrammaton. How much he lost may be known only when we find a first-century New Testament in which the Hebrew name YHWH still appears.[1]

CHAPTER 21

Did Jesus Speak Greek?

Joseph A. Fitzmyer

What language did Jesus speak? In what language did he preach? Joseph A. Fitzmyer rejects the idea that a Hebrew or Aramaic original underlies the Greek New Testament text we now have. He accepts the mainstream view that the Gospels are Greek compositions that drew on earlier traditions. Is it possible then that some of these sources were in Greek and that they preserved the actual words of Jesus? To the question "Did Jesus Speak Greek?" Fitzmyer answers "Yes!" Jesus, he says, was a skilled craftsman in a cosmopolitan community, not an illiterate peasant in the hinterland. So, did Jesus teach in Greek? And are the words in the Gospels the actual Greek words Jesus used? These questions are explored in the following article.–Ed.

N o doubt Jesus spoke Aramaic. At that time, many local dialects of Aramaic had emerged, and Jesus, like other Palestinian Jews, would have spoken a local form of Middle Aramaic[1] called Palestinian Aramaic. Palestinian Aramaic, along with Nabatean Aramaic (spoken in the area around Petra in modern Jordan), Palmyrene Aramaic (spoken in central Syria), Hatra Aramaic (spoken in the eastern part of Syria and Iraq) and early Syriac (spoken in northern Syria and southern Turkey) were the five dialects that made up Middle Aramaic.

Until the discovery of the Dead Sea Scrolls (beginning in 1947), Palestinian Aramaic was attested in a few paltry inscriptions on tombstones and ossuaries (bone boxes). But among the Dead Sea Scrolls were more than a score of fragmentary texts written in Palestinian Aramaic. For the first time, we were in possession of a corpus of literary texts from which we could learn something about the form of Aramaic spoken by Palestinian Jews in the centuries prior to Jesus and contemporaneous with him.[2]

Although Aramaic was the dominant language, it was not the only language spoken in Palestine at that time. The Dead Sea Scrolls reveal that three languages were spoken in Palestine in the first and second centuries C.E.[3] In addition to Aramaic, some Jews spoke Hebrew or Greek—sometimes both.[4] Different levels of Jewish society, different kinds of religious training and other factors may have determined who spoke which languages.

Hebrew was used in the sectarian literature of the Essenes, the Jews who settled at Qumran adjacent to the caves where the Dead Sea Scrolls were found. They apparently wanted to reestablish the use of Hebrew, which had come to be known as the "sacred language" because it was the language of the Torah. During the Babylonian captivity (sixth century B.C.E.), when many Jews were exiled from their homeland, they had adopted the dominant *lingua franca*, Aramaic, a sister language of Hebrew. After their return, some of the returnees probably reverted to Hebrew, but the use of Hebrew does not seem to have been widespread.[5]

Groups like the Essenes, however, apparently tried to resurrect the "sacred language." Of course, Hebrew was still used in the Temple and in the emerging synagogues; the Law and the Prophets (the Torah and the Nevi'im) were read in Hebrew. But the majority of people apparently no longer understood Hebrew, as we know from the custom that gradually developed of reading Aramaic translations of scriptural readings after the readings in Hebrew. The Aramaic translations were delivered orally by people called *meturgemanim* (translators). In time, the Aramaic translations were written down. They are called Targumim (singular, Targum). Three examples of early Targumim were discovered among the Dead Sea Scrolls.[6]

Greek, of course, was in widespread use in the Roman Empire at this time. Even the Romans spoke Greek,[7] as inscriptions in Rome and elsewhere attest. It is hardly surprising, therefore, that Greek was also in common use among the Jews of Palestine.[8]

Hellenization of Palestine had begun even before the fourth-century B.C.E. conquest by Alexander the Great.[9] But after Alexander's conquest, Hellenistic culture spread quickly, especially under the Seleucid monarch Antiochus IV Epiphanes (second century B.C.E.) and later under certain Jewish Hasmonean and Herodian kings.

The earliest Greek text found in Palestine is the bilingual Edomite-Greek ostracon dated to the sixth year of Ptolemy II Philadelphus (277 B.C.E.).[10] The Greek names of three musical instruments are recorded in Aramaicized form in Daniel 3:5, probably imported along with the instruments themselves. But the number of times Greek words have turned up in Aramaic documents of the first or second century C.E. can almost be counted on the fingers of one hand.[11] Oddly enough, in the rabbinic writings of the third and fourth centuries C.E., we find widespread use of Greek words in Aramaic or Hebrew texts; by that time, Greek had made heavy inroads into the Semitic languages of Palestine.[12]

A host of early Jewish *littérateurs*, however, chiefly historians and poets, wrote in Greek.[13] The most important Palestinian Jews in this group were Flavius

Josephus (37/38-100 C.E.) and Justus of Tiberias. The latter was Josephus' bitter opponent during the First Jewish Revolt against Rome (66-70 C.E.). Justus had received a thorough Hellenistic education, and after the revolt he wrote "History of the Jewish War against Vespasian."[14] Josephus composed his own *Jewish War* to counteract the version of Justus.

Josephus comments on his knowledge of Greek at the end of *Antiquities of the Jews*:

> My compatriots admit that in our Jewish learning I far excel them. But I labored hard to steep myself in Greek prose [and poetic learning], after having gained a knowledge of Greek grammar; but the constant use of my native tongue hindered my achieving precision in pronunciation. For our people do not welcome those who have mastered the speech of many nations or adorn their style with smoothness of diction, because they consider that such skill is not only common to ordinary freedmen, but that even slaves acquire it, if they so choose. Rather, they give credit for wisdom to those who acquire an exact knowledge of the Law and can interpret Holy Scriptures. Consequently, though many have laboriously undertaken this study, scarcely two or three have succeeded (in it) and reaped the fruit of their labors.[15]

Josephus thus gives the impression that few Palestinian Jews of his day could speak Greek well. This does not necessarily mean, however, that they could not carry on ordinary conversations in, perhaps, broken Greek.

Josephus mentions that he acted as interpreter for the Roman general Titus when he addressed the Jewish populace toward the end of the war.[16] Josephus also tells us that he composed his *Jewish War* "in his native tongue,"[17] which must mean Aramaic, although no copies of the text have survived in this language. Subsequently, he translated the work into Greek[18] to provide people throughout the Roman Empire with a record of the Jewish revolt. This was not easy for him, and he used "some assistants for the sake of the Greek."[19] In his own words,[20] he still considered Greek a "foreign and unfamiliar" language.

Other evidence of the use of Greek in Palestine can be found in inscriptions. The large number of these indicate that Greek was used for public announcements.[21] Inscriptions on ossuaries—in Greek and Hebrew (or Aramaic), or in Greek alone—from the vicinity of Jerusalem[22] attest to the widespread use of Greek among first-century Palestinian Jews at all levels of society.[23]

The Romans destroyed Jerusalem and burned the Temple in 70 C.E. Despite their defeat, the Jews again revolted against Rome in 132 C.E.—the Second Jewish Revolt, also called the Bar-Kokhba Revolt after the military leader of the rebellion. By 135 C.E., the Jews were again defeated and Jewish nationhood was not reestablished for another 2,000 years. From the period between the two revolts, numerous papyri written in Greek have come to light—letters, marriage contracts, legal documents, literary texts and some in Greek shorthand (not yet deciphered).[24]

Among these texts are some letters written by the leader of the Second Jewish Revolt, Bar-Kokhba himself, to his lieutenants, surprisingly enough, in Greek.[25] One letter is remarkable because it bears the name Soumaios, which the editor, Baruch Lifshitz, thinks is a way of writing the name Šim'ôn in Greek. Together with the remainder of the name, *ben Kōsibāh*, this indicates that Bar-Kokhba's real name was Simon ben Kosiba. In this letter, he orders his lieutenants to send wooden beams and citrons for the celebration of Sukkot, and he admits that this letter "has been written in Greek because a [de]sire has not be[en] found to w[ri]te in Hebrew."[26] Thus, at a time when nationalist fever must have been running high among the Jews, the leader of the revolt—or someone close to him—frankly preferred to write in Greek. He did not find the *horma* (impulse, desire) to write *hebraisti*.

In Acts 6:1, early Jewish Christians of Jerusalem are referred to as *Hebraioi* and *Hellēnistai*, "Hebrews" and "Hellenists." Who are these Hellenists? Up to this point, the only Hellenists mentioned are converts from Jerusalem, who must all have been Jewish Christians. The word *Hellēnistai* also appears in Acts 9:29, where it clearly refers to Jews. Some commentators have tried to explain *Hellēnistai*, as "those who lived like Greeks"; I believe a better explanation is that the term refers to those who spoke Greek or, more precisely, those who habitually spoke only Greek.

Hellēnistai may have spoken little, if any, Hebrew or Aramaic. This is suggested by a reference in Philippians 3:5, where Paul stoutly refers to himself as "a Hebrew of Hebrews." Paul also spoke Greek. Thus *Hellēnistai*, as Charles Moule has suggested, probably designates Jerusalem Jews or Jewish Christians who habitually spoke Greek (and for that reason were more affected by Hellenistic culture), whereas *Hebraioi* designates Greek-speaking Jews and Jewish Christians who also spoke a Semitic language, probably Aramaic, which they normally used.[27]

Did Jesus speak Greek? The answer is almost certainly yes. A more difficult question, however, is whether or not he taught in Greek. Are any of the sayings of Jesus that are preserved only in Greek in the original language?

Most New Testament scholars agree that Jesus normally used Aramaic for both conversation and teaching.[28] Did he also speak Greek? The evidence already recounted of the use of Greek in first-century Palestine provides the background for a positive answer to this question. But there are also specific indications in the Gospels themselves.

All four Gospels describe Jesus conversing with Pontius Pilate, the Roman prefect of Judea, during his trial (Mark 15:2-5; Matthew 27:11-14; Luke 23:3; John 18:33-38). Even if we allow for obvious literary embellishment in these accounts, there can be little doubt that Jesus and Pilate engaged in some kind of conversation (compare the independent testimony in 1 Timothy 6:13, which refers to Jesus' "testimony" before Pilate). In what language did Jesus and Pilate converse? There is no mention of an interpreter. Pilate, a Roman, would probably not have been able to speak either Aramaic or Hebrew; so, the obvious answer is that Jesus spoke Greek at his trial before Pilate.

Another instance might be when Jesus encountered the Roman centurion (Matthew 8:5-13; Luke 7:2-10; John 4:46-53). Luke calls him *hekatontarchos*, which might indicate that he was a Roman centurion, or at least an officer in charge of a troop of Roman mercenaries in the service of Herod Antipas (perhaps that is why he is called *basiliskos* [royal official] in John 4:46). In any event, Luke 7:9 implies that he is a gentile. In what language did Jesus speak to the first gentile convert? Most likely in Greek.

In Mark 7:25-30, Jesus, having journeyed to the pagan area of Tyre and Sidon, converses with a Syro-Phoenician woman. The indigenous population of that area undoubtedly spoke a Semitic language, either Phoenician or Aramaic (sister languages), but the author of the Marcan account goes out of his way to identify the woman as *Hellēnis* (a Greek, Mark 7:26). This suggests that Jesus spoke to her in Greek.

Moreover, if there is any historical truth to the incident in John 12:20-22 where Greeks (*Hellēnes*) come to see Jesus, he must have conversed with them in Greek. The same is suggested in John 7:35, where Jesus says that he plans to "go off" to him who sent him, and the Jews speculate that he might mean he intends to go to "the Diaspora among the Greeks and teach the Greeks." The evangelist presumably thought that Jesus would teach the Greeks in Greek.

Hints like these in the stories about Jesus' ministry suggest that, at least on occasion, he did speak Greek. Moreover, the specific instances when Jesus apparently spoke Greek are consistent with his Galilean background. In Matthew 4:15, the area is referred to as "Galilee of the gentiles."[29] Having grown up and lived in the area, Jesus would have needed to know some Greek. Nazareth was only a one-hour walk from Sepphoris[30] and was near other cities of the Decapolis. Tiberias, on the Sea of Galilee, was built by Herod Antipas; the people there, too, were far more bilingual than the people in Jerusalem.[31]

Jesus would no doubt have shared this double linguistic heritage. Reared in an area where many inhabitants were Greek-speaking gentiles, Jesus, the "carpenter" (*tektōn*, Mark 6:3), like Joseph, his foster-father (Matthew 13:55), would have had to communicate with the gentiles in Greek. Jesus was not an illiterate peasant and did not come from the lowest stratum of Palestinian society; he was a skilled craftsman who had a house in Capernaum (Mark 2:15). He would naturally have conducted business with gentiles in Nazareth and neighboring Sepphoris in Greek. His parables reveal that he was familiar with Palestinian trade and government. His followers, especially the fishermen Simon, Andrew, James and John, would also have had to conduct their fish-mongering with gentile customers in Greek.[32] So Jesus almost certainly spoke some Greek.

The more difficult question is whether or not Jesus taught in Greek. This question is especially important because, if the answer is yes, this means, in the words of Aubrey W. Argyle, "We may have direct access to the original utterances of our Lord and not only to a translation of them."[33] Although Jesus probably spoke at least some Greek, it is unlikely that any of his teachings have come down to us directly in that language.

Those who argue otherwise often point out that no extant Christian documents are in Aramaic. Papias, a second-century bishop of Hierapolis in Asia Minor, said that Matthew had put together the *logia* (sayings) of Jesus "in the Hebrew dialect" (= Aramaic),[34] but no one has ever seen them. More important, all four Gospels were composed in eastern Mediterranean areas outside of Palestine. That is why they are in Greek; they are the immediate products of a non-Palestinian Christian tradition, which has many indications of Palestinian, Semitic (especially Aramaic) roots.

Another point sometimes made by those who contend that Jesus taught in Greek is that a number of Jesus' disciples had Greek names—Andrew, Philip and even Simon (a Grecized form of Hebrew *Šim'ôn*). Levi/Matthew, a toll collector, would have had to deal with people in Greek (Luke 5:27). Similarly, technical Greek names have crept into the Hebrew or Aramaic used by the upper classes—for example, the Jewish judicial and legislative council is called sanhedrin, from Greek *synedrion*. In addition, they argue, Greek terms used in the Gospels were retained because they were uttered in Greek. One example is *epiousios*, the bread for which Christians pray in the Our Father, which is usually rendered "daily" for want of a better word, but which even Origen recognized as a neologism.[35] A second example is *ho huios tou anthropou*, which is usually rendered "Son of Man" but which is a Greek barbarism. All of these examples suggest the influence of Greek language and culture on Palestinian Jewish life but do not prove that Andrew, Philip or Levi normally spoke to Jesus in Greek. As for the word *epiousios*, no one knows how to analyze it or translate it.

Part of the problem with arguing that Jesus' words in the Greek Gospels are in the original language is that the Gospels themselves are not in word-for-word agreement. How can we determine which form is original? Did Jesus recite the Our Father prayer with five petitions, as it is preserved in Luke 11:2-4, or with seven petitions, as it is preserved in Matthew 6:9-13? One could naively maintain that he recited it both ways. That is a possible solution, but is it convincing? The same would have to be said about the different versions of eucharistic institution (Mark 14:22-24; Matthew 26:26-28; Luke 22:17-20). In all three Synoptic Gospels, Jesus says the bread is his body, but not in the same words. In Matthew, he says, "Take, eat; this is my body", in Mark, "Take, this is my body"; in Luke, simply, "This is my body." In Matthew and Mark, Jesus tells his disciples at the Last Supper to drink of the wine, which is his blood, but his precise words vary. Even if the words of Jesus are preserved in the original language, our next problem would be to determine which Greek form of his words is the original.

Some scholars have attempted to analyze some of the Greek words to show that this was indeed the original language. For example, the word *hypokritēs* (hypocrite) is a compound Greek word (= Greek preposition *hypo*, "under," + the root *krin-*, "judge"), a form that does not exist in Semitic languages. *Hypokritēs* literally means one who answers, but in classical and Hellenistic Greek it came to mean not only interpreter or expounder, but also orator, and even actor on a stage,[36] one who spoke from behind a dramatic mask. From the reference to play-actor, the word came to mean dissembler or pretender. But the Greek word *hypokritēs* has no counterpart in either Hebrew or Aramaic.[37] This does not mean, however, that Jesus' original words were in Greek. Actually, the word *hypokritēs* appears in the Greek translation of the Hebrew Scriptures known as the Septuagint (Job 34:30, 36:13), where the Hebrew word *ḥānēph*, which means a godless or impious person, is translated *hypokritēs*; so the word must already have had some currency among Jewish speakers. Among Greek-speaking Jews of the Diaspora, *hypokrisis* (hypocrisy) was one word for lying and deceit.[38]

Moreover, the word *hypokritēs* never appears in the Gospel of John. In Luke it is used to describe disciples and other people, the crowds (Luke 6:17, 12:56). It also appears frequently in the other two Synoptic Gospels as a term for Pharisees (Matthew 7:5 = Luke 6:42; Mark 7:6 = Matthew 15:7; Luke 13:15; Matthew 6:2,5,16, 22:18, 23:13,14,15). Mark and Matthew have undoubtedly put on the lips of Jesus an opprobrious Greek word that they and their contemporaries had already begun to use when referring to their Jewish opponents. We cannot conclude from such evidence that Jesus himself used the Greek term *hypokritēs* to refer to the Pharisees or anyone else.

In a trenchant linguistic analysis, G. H. R. Horsley has shown convincingly that the Greek of the Gospels is not "Jewish Greek,"[39] and yet it is Semitized enough to reflect a Palestinian matrix.[40] But there is no evidence that the Greek preserves didactic sayings of Jesus addressed to the crowds or to his followers. As Barnabas Lindars has remarked, "Careful analysis of the sayings shows again and again that the hypothesis of an Aramaic original leads to the most convincing and illuminating results."[41]

Just as some scholars have attempted to show that some of Jesus' teachings were originally in Greek, others have tried to show—equally unconvincingly—that his words were derived from a Hebrew *Vorlage* (source).[42] That Jesus at times used Hebrew is suggested in the Lucan version of his visit to the synagogue in Nazareth (Luke 4:16-19), where he is portrayed as opening a scroll of Isaiah, finding a certain passage (Isaiah 61:1-2) and reading it. If that detail is historical and not part of Luke's programmatic scene, then Jesus would have read Isaiah in Hebrew.[43] There is no mention of an Aramaic Targum in this passage. So Jesus may have been a trilingual Palestinian Jew, capable of reading at least some Hebrew and of speaking some Greek. But Aramaic was his dominant language.

It is important to keep in mind the three stages of the gospel tradition. Stage one includes what Jesus of Nazareth said and did from approximately 1 to 33 C.E.; stage two includes what the disciples and apostles taught and preached about Jesus between 33 and 66 C.E. Stage three includes what the evangelists sifted from Jesus' teaching and then redacted, each in his own literary and rhetorical style and for his own evangelical purposes. This last stage occurred sometime between about 66 and 95 C.E. The canonical Gospels reflect stage three of the gospel tradition much more than stage one. Unless we keep this in mind, we are in danger of lapsing into fundamentalism, i.e., of equating the Greek of stage three with the Aramaic of stage one.

In short, what has come down to us about Jesus' words and deeds is part of a Christian tradition in Greek. But that tradition was not originally conceived or formulated in Greek. None of the Gospels purports to be a stenographic report or cinematographic reproduction of the ministry of Jesus of Nazareth. The only thing we are told Jesus himself wrote, he wrote on the ground (John 8:6-8)—and the evangelist did not record it.

So the answer to the question of whether or not Jesus spoke Greek is yes, sometimes, although we have no real record of it. Did Jesus teach and preach in Greek? Probably not, but if he did, there is no way to sort out what he taught in Greek from what we have inherited in the Greek version of the Gospels.

A F T E R W O R D

Dr. Charles Abraham of San Diego disagrees with Fitzmyer's conclusion. He believes that Jesus did, in fact, preach in Greek.

Matthew 16:18 says "You are Peter and on this rock I will build my community."[1] The Greek text reads "σὺ εἶ Πέτρος, καὶ ἐπὶ ταύτῃ τῃ ´ πέτρᾳ οἰκοδομήσω μου τήν ἐκκλησίαν."

Assuming this is an accurate report of a historical event, Fitzmyer's conclusion is hardly incontrovertible. Either (1) Jesus not only spoke and taught in Greek, but also knew the language well enough to coin spontaneously a highly sophisticated literary pun (based on Peter [Petros in Greek] and rock [*petra* in Greek]), or (2) the primacy of Rome itself and Saint Peter's dogmatic tradition must be reevaluated. The Petros/petra pun works only in Greek, not in Hebrew and not in Aramaic, the suggested linguistic *Vorlage* of the Gospel.

Even the German Protestant theologian, Franz Delitzsch, as thoroughly educated as he was in Semitics, Talmud and medieval Jewish literature, could not convey the pun in his Hebrew translation of the New Testament. He contents himself with the Hebrew lexical item sl' (rock), conveying the idiomatic sense but destroying the literary wordplay of this most doctrinal passage of Western Christendom.

Did Jesus teach and preach in Greek? The inherited Greek tradition of the Gospels would have us think so. **BAR** *19:1 (1993), p. 68*

Fitzmyer replies:

The text of Matthew 16:18, which Dr. Abraham mentions as an indication that Jesus taught in Greek because of the play on Peter's name ("You are Peter and upon this rock I will build my church"), might seem important and hence ought to have been included in my article. There are several aspects of that verse, however, that seem to have escaped Dr. Abraham's attention.

First, Dr. Abraham is correct that a pun is involved in the use of Petros (in English, "Peter," and French, "Pierre") and *petra* (in English, "rock," but in French, "pierre"), despite the difference in gender (masculine Petros and feminine *petra*).

Second, for Dr. Abraham to claim in 1992 that "the Petros/petra pun works only in Greek, not in Hebrew and not in Aramaic" is amazing. He cites the "German Protestant theologian, Franz Delitzsch," who, in his translation of the New Testament into Hebrew published in 1877, could only use Hebrew sl' (rock) to convey the sense of the Greek *petra*, thus destroying "the literary wordplay." Dr. Abraham is, of course, correct that the play on words can not be expressed in Hebrew. But many things have come to light since the time of Delitzsch; Dr. Abraham seems to be unaware of the Aramaic discoveries of this century that bear upon the interpretation of Matthew 16:18. For it is now apparent that the pun was perfectly possible in Aramaic.

Third, in the New Testament, Peter is sometimes called Kēphas, which is explicitly explained as Petros in John 1:42 (see also Galatians 1:18, 2:9; 1 Corinthians 1:12 et al.). Kēphas is a grecized form of Aramaic Kēphā'. Kepha' is now clearly attested. It appears as a patronymic in a list of witnesses to a document, *šhd,'qb br kp'*, "witness: 'Aqab, son of Kepha'."[2] Moreover, the common noun *kēphā'* (rock, crag) appears several times in Qumran Aramaic texts. I cite only one example from the Targum of Job from Qumran Cave 11: *[b]kp' yskwn wyqnn*, "[on] the crag it (the black eagle, cf. Hebrew Job 39:28) dwells and makes its nest" (11QtgJob 33:9). See further 11QtgJob 32:1 (= Hebrew Job 39:1). *Kēphā'* also occurs several times in the Cave 4 texts of Enoch: 4QEn^e4 iii 19 (= 1 Enoch 89:29); 4QEn^c 4:3 (= 1 Enoch 89:32); 4QEn^a 1 ii 8 (= 1 Enoch 4).[3] In most of these instances *kēphā'* means "crag," part of a mountain.

This evidence reveals that the Greek pun reflects a realistic Aramaic substratum. I retrovert Jesus' saying into contemporary Aramaic: *'attāh Kēphā' (hū') we'al kēphā' dēn, 'ebnêh qehālî*, "You are Peter, and on this rock I will build my church," or in French, "Tu es Pierre, et sur cette pierre je bâtirai mon église."

Fourth, though the Greek name Petros appears also in John 1:42 and elsewhere in the New Testament, one wonders why the Matthean Jesus did not say, *sy ei Petros kai epi toutō tō petrō oikodomēsō mou tēn ekklēsian*, using the masculine form of the common noun *petros* (rock, stone) attested in the language since the time of Homer. Because of the change in gender to the feminine *petra*, a German scholar, August Dell, concluded in 1916 that the saying was not Jesus' words (*kein Jesuswort*) but the creation of Greek-speaking Christians. Part of the problem encountered here is that the name Petros does not occur in the Greek language prior to the New Testament. After that it occurs frequently, undoubtedly in imitation of the apostle's name, given to Simon by Jesus.[4]

Because the foregoing evidence reveals that the pun was possible in Aramaic as well as in Greek and because of the problem of the Greek name Petros, I considered that Matthew 16:18 was not pertinent to the discussion of whether or not Jesus spoke Greek. I still consider it irrelevant, despite the widespread belief reflected in Dr. Abraham's letter. Will such Aramaic parlance continue to fall upon deaf ears? **BAR** *19:1 (1993), p. 68*

In a recent related article,[5] Pieter van der Horst provides additional evidence for the widespread use of Greek among Jews in the Hellenistic world. Dean W. Chapman disputes van der Horst's interpretation of the evidence.

I agree with Pieter van der Horst that funerary inscriptions deserve more attention from scholars than they have usually received. I question, however, whether these inscriptions support van der Horst's claim that "for a great part of the Jewish population the daily language was Greek, *even in Palestine*" (emphasis mine).

The 1,600 Jewish epitaphs he cites include examples from all over the Mediterranean world over an 800-year period. The question for New Testament scholars, however, is not whether Jews in Rome spoke Greek (which would hardly be surprising!), or even whether or not the rabbis, after the Roman destruction of Jerusalem, preferred Greek to Aramaic, but to what extent Greek penetrated the (supposedly Aramaic-speaking) area of the Holy Land before 70 C.E. This drastically reduces the body of data.

One must also consider if funerary inscriptions provide an effective population sample. They are certainly heavily skewed in the direction of the wealthy. The other 90 percent of the population (which would include virtually the entire "Jesus movement") were simply laid in the ground with no (enduring) inscriptions. I would anticipate a positive correlation between wealth, on the one hand, and the esteem in which the language of the (Roman) oppressor was held in an occupied country, on the other. Such a correlation would weaken the significance of funerary inscriptions for drawing conclusions about "a majority of the Jews in Palestine."

Greek was introduced by foreign oppressors into a strongly xenophobic and rigid culture. This may be the reason Josephus writes that "our people do not welcome those who have mastered the speech of many nations...though many have laboriously undertaken this study [of Greek], scarcely two or three have succeeded..." (quoted by Fitzmyer). Indeed, the Talmud states that the Gamaliel family had to get permission even to study Greek, their justification being that it was necessary in their work with the Roman government (Babylonian Talmud Sotah 49b). The Pharisees were loathe to acquire Greek, and I am inclined to believe that opposition was even stronger among rural peasants. (Compare, for instance, the resistance to English among the French-speaking natives of Quebec, even though many of them do business frequently with English-speaking Canadians and residents of the U.S.)

Thus, the use of Greek in epitaphs does not require that the majority of Jews in Palestine in the time of Jesus spoke Greek regularly or even that they were familiar with it; and there are good reasons to believe otherwise.

What is missing from the discussion is a sociological model that would clarify two major issues: (1) the nature, means and extent of penetration of a foreign language in a conquered peasant society; and (2) the effect of losing the primal city (Jerusalem) on acceptance of the conqueror's language.
BAR *19:1 (1993), p. 70*

Pieter van der Horst explains:

Mr. Chapman has made some perceptive critical remarks about my article, for which I am grateful. I will comment briefly. He says that it is hardly surprising that Jews in Rome spoke Greek. Well, the situation is not so simple. Compare Syrian epitaphs with Jewish epitaphs from Rome. The vast majority of Syrian epitaphs in Rome are in Latin, not Aramaic or Greek. This shows that the Jews, because they were relatively isolated, did not adopt the majority language but maintained their own language, which was Greek.

If we restrict ourselves to data from the Holy Land in the period before 70 C.E., we find, for instance, that of the approximately 250 ossuaries and other inscriptions from Jerusalem, some 40 percent are in Greek, and most of the epitaphs from the Goliath family in Jericho are in Greek.

Moreover, not only the wealthy knew Greek, as Professor Fitzmyer convincingly demonstrated in his article. Jesus, who certainly did not belong to the wealthy upper class, knew and occasionally used Greek, which was no longer regarded as the language of the oppressor, which was Latin. I never said, however, that a majority of the Jews in Palestine spoke Greek (as Mr. Chapman quotes); what I said was that "a majority of the Jews in Palestine and the western Diaspora spoke Greek," by which I meant that a majority of all Jews taken together spoke Greek. When I said that "for a great part of the Jewish population the daily language was Greek, even in Palestine" I did not mean a majority; a great part can be a quarter or a third.

It is not correct that the Gamaliel family had to have permission to study Greek. The passage in the Babylonian Talmud says that they had to get permission to learn Greek wisdom (that is, literature and philosophy), and it is explicitly stated that "the Greek language and Greek wisdom are distinct" (Sotah 49b)! So there was no objection to Jews learning the Greek language.

Finally, I agree with Mr. Chapman that a sociological model would clarify the issues under consideration. I hope that someone knowledgeable in sociolinguistics will accept this challenge. **BAR** *19:1 (1993), p. 70*

Theory of Translation

Most people think translating from one language to another is a simple, straightforward process—word (a) in the first language equals word (A) in the second, (b) equals (B), (c) equals (C), and (abc) in the first language equals (ABC) in the second. This approach probably works well enough for ordering food or asking directions, but not much more. This kind of translating will not result in a meaningful version of a theological thought.

Robert Frost once defined poetry as the part of a poem that is lost in translation. In the following essays, a linguistic scholar explores the problems and limitations of the translator's art.

CHAPTER 22

Concern for the Text versus Concern for the Reader

Harvey Minkoff

How should one translate "I am the bread of life" for readers who snack on bread and eat something else as their dietary staple? How can a translation capture the intimate relationship between language and culture?

Making the Bible available to everyone is now called accessibility. And the complex issue of what can—or should—be done to make a translation accessible is explored in the following article. Scholars distinguish between "text-oriented" and "reader-oriented" translations. The former tend to be literal renderings of the original, even if the results sound alien to the new-language audience; the latter make the reader feel more at home, although they may compromise the cultural integrity of the original. What then should be done? To a large extent, the answer depends on whether the translator believes the message of the Bible is universally meaningful to people as they are or that people must modify their lives to enter the biblical community embodied in a particular language, time and place. Comparing the New English Bible to the New Jewish Publication Society version illustrates the differences in practice.—Ed.

The purpose of translating seems simple enough—to transfer meaning from one language to another. For public notices, traffic signs and other everyday needs, this is not difficult. But for literature—even pseudoliterature like political speeches—meaning lies in the interplay between what the author intends to say, what the text actually says, style and cultural setting, and how the audience interprets the text.

Let's say the president of the United States announces to the world that "it's third down and 20 on arms control" or "Khomeini isn't Marcus Welby." How can these be translated so they have the same meaning to an audience in France or China, where people know little or nothing about football or American television?

When translating this presidential language from English to French or Chinese, should we try to transfer the *text* or the *audience reaction* from one language to another? In other words, where does the meaning lie—in the *words* or in the *audience reaction* to the words?

Take biblical passages like "I am the bread of life" (John 6:35) or "Your sins shall be white as snow" (Isaiah 1:18). What does the former mean in a society where rice, rather than bread, is the dietary staple, or the latter to people who have never seen snow?

If we conclude that meaning lies in the text, then we will want a "text-oriented," or "overt," translation, even if it is alien to the audience. A text-oriented translation tends to be literal and word for word. On the other hand, if meaning inheres in audience reaction to the text, we may prefer a "reader-oriented," or "covert," translation, even if it compromises the cultural integrity of the original.[1] Reader-oriented translations tend to be more interpretative than literal.

Our Western tradition of literal translations of biblical texts goes back at least as far as the Septuagint, the widely influential translation of the Bible from Hebrew into Greek produced by the Jews of Alexandria in the third century B.C.E. Because the Septuagint translators believed that every word in the Bible came from God, they tried to retain the Hebrew flavor of the original. They made no attempt to capture in Greek the full sense of the original Hebrew. Indeed, this was obviously impossible when even the word order was considered divine and not to be changed except on rare occasions.

Thus, word order is on the Talmud's list of a dozen places where the Septuagint introduced "changes." For example, the opening phrase of Genesis consists of the three Hebrew words *bere'šit bara' 'elohim*, which literally means "in-the-beginning created God." The word order is adverb-verb-noun, which is the norm in Hebrew; the Greek word order in the Septuagint is noun-verb-adverb, "God created in the beginning." According to talmudic commentaries, this deviation was acceptable because it obviated the possibility that an unwary reader might mistake "in-the-beginning" for the name of God's creator.[2]

The Septuagint translation was especially important to early Christian writers. New Testament quotations of Jewish Scriptures generally reflect the Septuagint version where it differs from the Hebrew. So it is easy to understand how the underlying concept of literal translation in the Septuagint became entrenched and established a tradition of translation that still exists.

This translation tradition has given us English expressions that mirror biblical Hebrew in vocabulary as well as syntax. For example, the Hebrew word *nefeš* ranges semantically—depending on the context—from "soul" to "being" to "person." But literal translators of the Bible—who believed they were respecting the Hebrew base of the text—translated *nefeš* consistently as "soul." Thus, we have "The man became a living *soul*" instead of *being* (Genesis 2:7), and "Jacob went down to Egypt with 70 *souls*" instead of *persons* (Genesis 46:27). This in turn led to an expansion of the semantic range of the word *soul* in English. As a result, we have such nonbiblical coinages as "poor soul" and "not a soul was there."

Another example of this phenomenon occurs in syntax. The model of the Hebrew superlative in "song of songs" and "king of kings"—which should more properly be translated "great song" and "great king"—has produced English phrases such as "in my heart of hearts" and "horror of horrors."[3]

At the end of the fourth century, Jerome produced the official Latin version of the Bible for the church—called the Vulgate because it was the *editio vulgata* (standard edition) and was written in the language of the *vulgus* (common people). But Jerome had already done a lot of translating before he worked on the Bible, and the idea that meaning can be divorced from the words themselves is often attributed to him. In fact, Jerome's work was often attacked for this reason.

Jerome's most famous defense of his method of translation is the letter *Ad Pammachium*, usually subtitled *de optimo genere interpretandi* (concerning the best way to translate). In the letter, he dismisses the accusation that he does not translate word for word with the argument that he never distorts the sense of the original. He then declares that he translates *non verbum e verbo, sed sensum de sensu* (not word for word, but sense for sense).

This phrase has been widely quoted, but the qualification that follows has often been overlooked—and, for our purposes, it is a very important qualification indeed—*ubi et verborum ordo mysterium est* (except for Holy Scripture where even the word order is sacred).[4]

Because of his commitment to the text of scripture, Jerome created "translation stock," or mechanical equivalents; he matched specific Hebrew words with Latin equivalents instead of choosing the best translation in each context from a range of synonyms and alternatives. For example, he rendered Hebrew *bara'* as *creavit* (created) even when the result was meaningless, as in Genesis 2:3, where Jerome translated the Hebrew phrase *bara' la'asot* as *creavit ut faceret* (created to do) instead of "proposed to do," or "set himself to do" (as in the New English Bible). So in Jerome's translation the verse reads "God rested from the work that he *created* to do"—which is all but meaningless.[5]

It is clear from Jerome's defense and his practice that his goal in *biblical* translation, as distinct from other types of translation, was to follow the word order unless this thoroughly distorted the sense of the text. This tradition can be traced from one translation to another in English as well as in other European languages.

Occasionally, even before the modern era, other approaches were tried. Take, for example, the Bay Psalm Book, published in 1640, only ten years after the settlement of the Massachusetts Bay Colony. This translation is usually ridiculed for harsh and unmusical verse and is patronizingly called the sincere work of brave but overworked pioneers.[6] Here is the beginning of Psalm 23 from the Bay Psalm Book:

> The Lord to mee a shepheard is,
>   want therefore shall not I.
> Hee in the folds of tender grasse,
>   doth cause mee downe to lie:
> To waters calme mee gently leads
>   restore my soule doth hee:
> Hee doth in paths of righteousnes
>   for his names sake leade mee.

It is indeed difficult to defend this as poetry, but it does foreshadow a new theory of translation—that the audience is paramount. As the translators of the Bay Psalm Book pointed out in the preface:

> The Psalms are penned in such verses as are suitable to the poetry of the Hebrew language...and if in our English tongue *we are to sing them*, then as all our English songs (according to the course of our English poetry) do run in metre, so ought David's Psalms be translated into metre....[And] as the Lord hath hid from us the Hebrew tunes, lest we should think ourselves bound to imitate them...every nation without scruple might follow as the graver sort of tunes of their own country songs....[7] [emphasis added]

In other words, the original Hebrew psalms were meant to be sung in public worship; the purpose of the new English versions was therefore similar. Moreover, the Puritan ministers wanted psalms that farmers in their fields and women at their spinning wheels could sing. They wanted verses that lent themselves to easy memorization and catchy tunes. Although the rhythm of these translations has been justifiably compared to a hammer pounding on an anvil, the poems probably accomplished their purpose. They were sung! And for all we know, they may have replicated the effect of the Hebrew psalms on the original audience.

Of course, discovering the original intention of the text is not always possible. But even assuming that we can, it is questionable that the same "intent" *can* be conveyed in a different language. Two languages seldom, if ever, arise from similar cultures and histories. Where there are differences, the translator is likely to find himself in the predicament described by Michael Bullock:

> No amount of sympathy on the translator's part will enable him to visualize how...the German novelist X would have written his stylistically highly original novel if he had been an English novelist writing in English....The fact is, he would not have written it.[8]

A translator must weigh each element and decide what can be changed or omitted and what must be retained at all costs. As John Beekman, a theorist for the Wycliffe Bible Translators, pointed out, sometimes a biblical author "chose words whose form and function are equally important. At other times...form was included only because it served as a natural vehicle carrying the functional meaning."[9] A translator must distinguish between the two because sometimes an image just contributes to the meaning, and sometimes the image is the meaning. Something that makes perfect sense in one culture may be wrong, obscure or even meaningless in another. This, of course, is at the heart of the current debate over "de-sexing" the Bible. Determining whether God is a Father or a Parent, whether Jesus is a Son or a Child, is not a simple matter.

And the problem does not stop there. What should a translator do with a text that assumes familiarity with people, events and other texts that are common knowledge in the original culture but alien to the audience of the translation? And what can he do with a text that alludes to its own language?

In Genesis 30:24, for example, Rachel calls her first son Joseph (Hebrew *yoseph*) because, competing with her husband's three other wives, she prays, "May God add (*yoseph*) another." Perhaps a translator could note the pun in a footnote, intrusive though it might be.

It would be more difficult, however, to handle the connection between the name Isaac (Hebrew *yiṣḥak*, "he laughs") and the many occurrences of laughter in Genesis 18 and 21 from the same root (*Ṣ-Ḥ-K*). In the text, "Sarah laughed" (*tiṣḥak*) upon hearing the angel's prediction that at the advanced age of 90 she would bear a child (Genesis 18:12); and again in Genesis 21:6, immediately after the child's naming, Sarah says: "All who hear will laugh" (*yiṣeḥak*).[10] Preserving these connections in translation is almost impossible.

And how can a translator hope to capture in English what is obvious in Hebrew—that *'Adam* was so named because he was taken from *'adamah*, which is *'adom* like *dam*? It simply does not *mean* the same thing to say he was called *Man* (*'adam*) because he was taken from *earth* (*'adamah*), which is *red* (*'adom*) like *blood* (*dam*).

Also, the Hebrew text of Genesis 2-4 moves seamlessly between "the man" (*ha-'adam*) and *'Adam* (the name) suggesting that the story is not about two people named Adam and Eve but about "Everyman" and "Life-Mother." There it is, plain as day in the Hebrew. But how do you translate this into English?

These problems only skim the surface, yet Eugene Nida, president of the American Bible Society and a linguist who knows as much about translating as anyone, denies "the impossibility of translation." Says Nida, "Anyone who is involved in the realities...is impressed that effective interlingual communication is always possible, despite seemingly enormous differences in linguistic structures and cultural features." An effective translation can be made through what he calls "dynamic equivalence," that is, producing the same effect as the original in the translation.[11]

In modern times, Christians have been more open to this kind of translation than Jews. As Nida and William L. Wonderly have noted in "Linguistics and Christian Missions":

> In contrast with Judaism and Hinduism, which were not primarily interested in extension by missionary effort...Christianity was from the beginning concerned with an effective communication of its message to all men everywhere, such as could be accomplished only through the native idioms. [T]his concern early led to an interest in translation.[12]

For this reason, it seems to me, Christian Bible translators often try to clothe "universal truths" in native dress, whereas Jewish translators require that readers accept the text on its own terms. For extreme examples, we can compare the zealously fundamentalist *Living Bible*, a Christianization of Jewish Scriptures,[13] with the *Living Torah*, the translators of which state in the introduction that their interpretations consistently "reflect the final decision in Jewish law."

At a less charged level, the contrast is evident in the way translators handle imagery. In Latin America, the Christian experience has been reworked for various Indian cultures. Thus parables about foxes (Matthew 8:20) have become parables about coyotes in Mazahua, Mexico; locusts (Mark 1:6) are changed to flying ants in Ayutla Mixteco, Mexico; pulque (Matthew 9:17) replaces wine in Mezquital Otomi, Mexico; people stick out their chins (Mark 15:29) in place of shaking their heads in Huitoto, Peru; and calling from the door (Acts 12:17) replaces knocking in Chol, Mexico.[14] Even in English, Adam and Eve's fig-leaf clothes (Genesis 3:7) have been changed to aprons (King James Version), breeches (Genevan Bible) and loincloths (New English Bible).

Contrasting theories of translation may be found even in two of the best recent translations, the New Jewish Publication Society (NJPS) translation and the New English Bible (NEB), a British Protestant project. The editor-in-chief of the NJPS translation, Harry M. Orlinsky, has stated that "the first and exclusive obligation of a translator is to the text," and thus, for example, "thou" in addressing God was eliminated, because "the Hebrew Bible itself never made any distinction between God or man or animal" in the pronouns.[15] In contrast, although the NEB translators were aware of the arguments against using "thou," Geoffrey Hunt tells us that the NEB committee wanted this version to be "as intelligible to contemporary readers as the original was to its first readers," and "the public in general for whom NEB was intended were not considered ready for the general use of 'you' in address to God."[16]

I do not mean to imply that the NJPS version is unintelligible or that the NEB version does not respect the text. But even in a simple matter like this, which has no obvious theological overtones, we can see the consequences of different orientations.

Let us conclude by comparing the two translations of Genesis 35:1-5, a passage chosen almost at random (see box on following page). The differences are

Two Translations Compared (Genesis 35:1-5)

"God said to Jacob, 'Arise, go up to Bethel and remain there; and build an altar there to the God who appeared to you when you were fleeing from your brother Esau.' So Jacob said to his household and to all who were with him, 'Rid yourselves of the alien gods in your midst, purify yourselves, and change your clothes. Come, let us go up to Bethel, and I will build an altar there to the God who answered me when I was in distress and who has been with me wherever I have gone.' They gave to Jacob all the alien gods that they had, and the rings that were in their ears, and Jacob buried them under the terebinth that was near Shechem. As they set out, a terror from God fell on the cities round about, so that they did not pursue the son of Jacob."
NJPS

"God said to Jacob, 'Go up to Bethel and settle there; build an altar there to the God who appeared to you when you were running away from your brother Esau.' So Jacob said to his household and to all who were with him, 'Rid yourselves of the foreign gods which you have among you, purify yourselves, and see your clothes are mended. We are going to Bethel, so that I can set up an altar there to the God who answered me in the day of my distress, and who has been with me all the way that I have come.' So they handed over to Jacob all the foreign gods in their possession and the rings from their ears, and he buried them under the terebinth-tree near Shechem. Then they set out, and the cities round about were panic-stricken, and the inhabitants dared not pursue the son of Jacob."
NEB

without religious import, but they highlight the contrast between overriding loyalty to the text in one case and concern for the audience in the other. Where the NJPS translation reads "change your clothes," NEB reads "see your clothes are mended." The striking difference in this case is the result of different interpretations of a Hebrew word and does not reflect loyalty to the text as opposed to concern for audience understanding.

But this is not true in other cases. NJPS reads "terror from God," which is taken directly from the Hebrew and makes no concession to a modern audience. The same word in NEB reads "panic-stricken." Likewise, NJPS uses the word "fleeing," which is more old-fashioned than the NEB "running away." A Western reader may not know that "terebinth" in the NJPS version refers to a tree, but "terebinth-tree" in the NEB version has a built-in explanation. (On the other hand, "in the day of my distress" in the NEB is more literal than "when I was in distress" in NJPS.)

The NJPS "Arise, go up" and "Come, let us go up" are less idiomatic than the NEB "Go up" and "We are going." The NJPS translation reflects, even if it does not precisely preserve, the Hebrew "inception," or auxiliary verb, construction. The NEB, on the other hand, is more concerned with preserving the effect of idiomatic language on the English reader.

Similarly, NJPS tries to preserve the pervasive Hebrew particle *wa-*, usually translated "and"; thus they include "*and* build an altar" as well as "*and* I will build an altar." In contrast, NEB simply reads "build an altar" and "so that I can set up an altar."

In NJPS a Hebrew relative clause is translated "that were in their ears"; in NEB the clause is reduced to a prepositional phrase, "from their ears." In NJPS the antecedent of "they did not pursue" seems to be "cities," just as it is in the Hebrew; in NEB an explanatory subject, "the inhabitants," has been added.[17]

In the end, the NEB translators—who, in Mark 6:37, say Jesus' disciples spent 20 pounds instead of 200 denarii—are apt to resolve difficulties by emending, rearranging or otherwise tampering with the received Hebrew text—even to the extent of dividing the Song of Songs into different parts attributed to different speakers—in an attempt to make the text accessible to modern readers.

Of course, concern for the reader has a venerable tradition. Alexander Pope rendered the *Iliad* in rhymed couplets in iambic pentameter (five feet per line) even though the classical Greek is in long, multiline sentences in unrhymed dactylic hexameters (six feet per line). Pope used rhymed couplets because that was the usual poetic form in Augustan England. Moreover, in an English translation, dactylic hexameters would have created a strange effect that would not have been experienced by the original Greek audience.

But once we accept accessibility as a goal, it is hard to know where to stop. In various English translations of classical Roman authors, the technical, culture-specific term *patres et plebes* (the two groups in the Roman senate) has been translated as "Lords and Commons"; *praetor* (a Roman magistrate) as "Lord Chief Justice"; and *comitium* (the place of assembly in Rome) as "Parliament"—all of which conjure up images of Englishmen in London.[18]

Returning to two biblical phrases we mentioned earlier—"Your sins shall be white as snow" and "I am the bread of life"—John Beekman has convincingly defended translating these for certain cultural groups as "Your sins shall be white as cotton" and "I am the tortilla of life." As Beekman explains:

> Many groups in Mexico consider bread to be second best and inferior to tortillas, or look upon it as dessert or party food. This function does not correspond to the idea Jesus had in mind....To use a literal equivalent for bread in spite of its incompatible functional meaning, introduces a wrong equivalence.[19]

According to this line of reasoning, we might translate "an evil spirit from the Lord came upon Saul" (1 Samuel 16:14) as "Saul was depressed" or "Saul went into a royal depression."

If we continue to pursue accessibility as a goal, where we end up is anybody's guess. Perhaps one day we will have a special Bible translation for government bureaucrats modeled on George Orwell's well known "translation" of

Ecclesiastes 9:11 into bureaucratese. In the King James Version the passage reads as follows:

> I turned and saw under the sun, that the race is not to the swift, nor the battle to the strong, neither yet bread to the wise, nor yet riches to men of understanding, nor yet favor to men of skill; but time and chance happeneth to them all.

Here is Orwell's parody in bureaucratic language:

> Objective consideration of contemporary phenomena compels the conclusion that success or failure in competitive activities exhibits no tendency to be commensurate with innate capacity, but that a considerable element of the unpredictable must invariably be taken into account.[20]

CHAPTER 23

Coarse Language in the Bible
It's Culture Shocking!

Harvey Minkoff

Another aspect of the translator's challenge is taken up in the article that follows. Readers are certainly surprised—sometimes shocked—when they come across what they consider gutter or bathroom language in Holy Scripture. But the contrast between text and reader orientation illustrates why the Bible may contain words or subjects that shock modern readers and may skirt other subjects that we discuss openly. What is considered taboo or offensive, and therefore requires euphemism, varies from culture to culture. Because the Bible was written not only in foreign languages, but also in foreign lands and at different times, "what requires a euphemism in the original language may not warrant one in translation, and what the original author had no qualms about saying explicitly may require circumlocution in the culture of the translation."

We must also keep in mind that the authors or redactors of the Bible often tailored their work to accomplish specific goals. Some may have used strong language to shock or embarrass readers. Translators today, however, must weigh the reaction of congregations that hear such language as part of the liturgy. Because canonization changed the function of the Bible, translators today write for a different audience and purpose.—Ed.

In my recent article on the problems of Bible translation,[1] I distinguished two styles—reader-centered (covert) translation and text-centered (overt) translation. The first style tries to convey to the reader the *impression* of an original text in the language of the translation. The second style retains linguistic and cultural elements of the original, which may leave the reader in the new language feeling like a stranger looking in from the outside. A reader's letter to the editor picks up on this distinction and raises some interesting issues. Here is the letter:

"Overt" and "covert," as Harvey Minkoff uses them, are well chosen terms when applied to changes made by Oxford University Press in the Oxford Study Edition of the New English Bible with Apocrypha.

The predecessor of the Oxford Study Edition, the NEB with Apocrypha printed by Oxford and Cambridge University Presses in 1970, lists Judges 1:14 as: "As she sat on the ass, she broke wind, and Caleb said, 'What do you mean by that?' " In the newer Study Edition, the "same" NEB (printed in New York by Oxford University Press) has: "As she sat on the ass, she made a noise, and Caleb said, 'What did you mean by that?' "

When I spoke with Oxford in New York, an editor explained to me that, while the "break wind" translation continues in the English printed NEB, the "covert" translation (Minkoff's word) is used in the American edition. "That sounds like scholarship knuckling under to political pressure," I responded. Some American Christian groups objected to the wording, he explained—to his credit, a bit sheepishly. The editor went on to explain that there is a good deal of language in the OT that is "coarse" and for which audiences are not ready. When I asked whether other changes had been made as a result of political pressure, he assured me there had been none.

Bible Review could do us all a service and get Minkoff and Oxford to discuss this particular passage, as well as to air other areas where we delicate American mortals are being protected from the coarse language of scripture, and where we might expect such protection in the future.

Bruce Reeves
Diablo Valley College
Pleasant Hill, California

Because I wanted to show the pervasive significance of the distinction between reader-centered (covert) translations and text-centered (overt) translations, I concentrated in my article on normal vocabulary, word order and repetition. But, of course, where the culture and language themselves are central to the text, as with taboos and euphemisms, the problems of translation are increased by an added set of conflicting demands and considerations. And this is the essence of the problem raised by Professor Reeves.

Let us look first at the passage Reeves cites. The books of Joshua and Judges recount the Israelite conquest of Canaan. A short episode repeated in both books concerns the conquest of the city of Debir, the old name of which was Kiriath-Sepher, a site about eight miles southwest of Hebron now identified as Tell Rabud.[2] In the British edition of the New English Bible (NEB), this episode (Joshua 15:15-19 = Judges 1:12-15) reads as follows:

> From there they marched against the inhabitants of Debir, formerly called Kiriath-Sepher. Caleb said, "Whoever attacks Kiriath-Sepher and captures it, to him I will give my daughter Achsah in marriage." Othniel, son of Caleb's younger brother Kenaz, captured it, and Caleb gave him his daughter Achsah. When she came to him, he incited her to ask her father for a piece of land. As she sat on the ass, she broke wind, and Caleb said, "What did you mean by that?" She replied, "I want to ask a favor of you. You have put me in this dry Negeb; you must give me pools of water as well." So Caleb gave her the upper pool and the lower pool.[3]

What happened—at least according to the British edition of the NEB—is that Othniel, the hero of Kiriath-Sepher, was unhappy with the dowry (waterless land in the Negev desert) that came with his bride, Achsah. So Othniel complained to his new wife. She, in turn, complained—in a particularly gross way, according to the British edition of the NEB—to her father, Caleb, who then gave her some additional land with springs.

In his letter to the editor, Reeves notes that in the Oxford Study Edition of the NEB, which was written for an American audience, the critical verse is changed from "As she sat on the ass, she broke wind" to "As she sat on the ass, she made a noise." Reeves wonders where else "we delicate American mortals are being protected from the coarse language of scripture."

The ironic references to "delicate Americans" and "coarse language of scripture" address two important, but complicated, problems—first, difficulties specific to this passage and, second, the role of euphemisms in general.

The meaning of this passage is uncertain in several places, as we can readily see by comparing the latter half of the NEB translation to the same passage in the New Jewish Publication Society (NJPS) translation:

> His younger kinsman, Othniel the Kenizzite, captured it; and Caleb gave him his daughter Achsah in marriage. When she came [to him], she induced him to ask her father for some property. She dismounted from her donkey, and Caleb asked her, "What is the matter?" She replied, "Give me a present, for you have given me away as Negeb-land; give me springs of water." And Caleb gave her Upper and Lower Gulloth.

Let us look at some of the questions raised by these two renderings. Is Othniel the son of Caleb's younger brother, Kenaz, or is he a Kenizzite and Caleb's younger kinsman? Did Othniel incite Achsah, or did Achsah induce Othniel to make the request? Was Achsah given land in the Negeb, or was she given away like Negeb-land, that is, without a dowry? Did Caleb give her pools, or did he give her a place named Gulloth, which by coincidence happens to mean "pools"? Finally, did Achsah break wind to express her dissatisfaction, or did she get down from her donkey?

The Hebrew word at the crux of the problem is *tiṣnaḥ* (תצנח). The word *tiṣnaḥ* is rendered "descend" in most translations, including the NJPS. Thus, Judges 1:14 and Joshua 15:18 in the King James Version (KJV) read "she lighted from off her ass," and the Jerusalem Bible (JB) reads "she jumped down from her donkey."

The verbal root of *tiṣnaḥ* is ṢNḤ (*ti*- is a prefix indicating third person singular feminine). This is the only word based on this root in the Hebrew Bible. But *tiṣnaḥ* does appear in one other passage, Judges 4:21. This is the story of how Jael kills the sleeping Sisera with a tent spike. The KJV reads "[she] smote the nail into his temples, and fastened it [*tiṣnaḥ*] into the ground"; the NJPS reads "[she] drove the pin through his temple till it went down [*tiṣnaḥ*] to the ground." They differ as to whether the implied subject of *tiṣnaḥ* is Jael or the spike (a feminine noun in Hebrew), but in both translations the verb conveys the idea of descent.[4]

In contrast, the NEB reads: "[she] drove the peg into his skull as he lay sound asleep. His brains oozed out [*tiṣnaḥ*] on the ground." Here, *tiṣnaḥ* is rendered as "oozed," and the subject "brains" is added, presumably because it is required by the context.

Because the root ṢNḤ is rare and obscure, the traditional translation is, in fact, a scholarly hypothesis. In the 1894 translation of Wilhelm Gesenius' *Hebrew and Chaldee Lexicon to the Old Testament Scriptures*, the definition is "to descend, to let oneself down, e.g., from an ass."[5] But in a later work, *A Hebrew and English Lexicon of the Old Testament* by Francis Brown, Samuel R. Driver and Charles A. Briggs, which is also based on Gesenius' monumental German work, the authors add that the "meaning [is] inferred fr[om] context."[6] And Georg Fohrer's *Hebrew and Aramaic Dictionary of the Old Testament*, citing Joshua 15:18 and Judges 1:14, says the word means "clap the hands ?, bend down ?"[7]

The version in the NEB that relates this root to breaking wind is, in large part, the result of scholarship by Godfrey Driver, an eminent Semiticist and Arabic specialist who was chairman of the NEB Old Testament Translation Panel. Driver's argument is as follows:

> [T]he LXX [the Septuagint, a third-century B.C.E. Greek translation of the Hebrew Bible] says [in this passage] "and she murmured and cried out" and the Vulg[ate, a fourth-century C.E. Latin translation] says "and she sighed," both renderings implying that she expressed her displeasure by making some sort of noise....What *ṣnḥ* really means is "belched" or "broke wind."[8]

Driver then gives examples from Akkadian, Arabic and Greek to show that "breaking wind was an extremely common expression in the ancient world for indicating disgust or contempt."

But this explanation has not been generally accepted by Bible scholars and translators. Arthur Gibson notes that the translators of the Septuagint rendered the two identical occurrences of *tiṣnaḥ* in Judges 1:14 and Joshua 15:18 with three different Greek words implying, significantly, an oral sound—and in Judges 4:21 with a fourth meaning, "it descended." He concludes that "they were confused, or guessing" and therefore cannot be invoked as support for Driver's argument.[9]

Roger A. Bullard, one of the translators of Today's English Version of the Bible, characterizes the NEB rendering of *tiṣnaḥ* in Judges 1:14 as "teased out of Arabic."[10] And F. F. Bruce complains that in the NEB "conjecture has been resorted to much more freely than in most of the older English versions— or even in others of more recent date."[11]

I asked Donald Kraus, senior editor of the Bible Department of Oxford University Press in New York, why the translation "she broke wind" in the British edition of the NEB was changed to "she made a noise" in the Oxford

Study Edition. He suggested that the change may have been motivated by scholarly objections to the British translation, combined with the feeling that an American audience might not be comfortable with the British version.[12] His preference, Kraus said, is that translations should be as accurate as possible. But he acknowledged that in the case of the Bible, which is used for public readings and in liturgical contexts, other considerations come into play.

And this brings us to the larger issue of euphemisms in the Bible and in Bible translations. A euphemism is the substitution of a word that may be taboo, offensive or disagreeable with a more acceptable word. There are some euphemisms in the original text of the Bible.

For example, in the Hebrew text sometimes the word "bless" (*barak*) is used instead of "curse" to avoid the phrase "cursing God"—which would, of course, be blasphemous. This happens in the famous story of Naboth's vineyard. King Ahab of Israel has everything a king could want—except the vineyard of his neighbor, Naboth. Jezebel, Ahab's Phoenician wife, hatches a plan whereby Naboth will be killed and Ahab can seize Naboth's vineyard. (The plan is carried out, and the prophet Elijah confronts the king with the famous line, "Hast thou killed and also taken possession?") Jezebel's plan involves two scoundrels who falsely accuse Naboth of cursing God. For this crime, the unjustly accused Naboth is stoned to death. But in the two relevant passages, the Hebrew text says that the scoundrels charged Naboth with "blessing" God, not "cursing" him (1 Kings 21:10,13). Obviously, the author recoiled from blasphemous words like "cursing God." Almost all English translations, however, translate "bless" (*barak*, ברך) as "curse," "revile" or "blaspheme" God:

> **NEB:** ...charge him with cursing God and the king.
>
> **NJPS:** You have reviled God and the king.
>
> **JB:** You have cursed God and the king.
>
> **KJV:** Thou didst blaspheme God and the king.

Elsewhere in the Bible, to avoid expressing a disagreeable thought, death is rendered in various metaphors: "sleep an endless sleep" (Jeremiah 51:39), "go the way of all the earth" (1 Kings 2:2), "be gathered to his people" (Genesis 49:33). And bodily functions are frequently veiled: "Adam knew Eve his wife" (Genesis 4:1), "the manner of women" (Genesis 18:11), "that which comes out of you" (Deuteronomy 23:13 [verse 14 in the Hebrew]).

Because what is taboo, offensive or disagreeable varies from culture to culture, translating euphemisms presents special problems. Euphemisms required in the original language may not be necessary in the translation, and some things the original author had no qualms about saying explicitly may require circumlocution in the culture of the translation. As I have already noted, English translators of 1 Kings 21:10 do not show the same fear of blasphemy as the Hebrew authors did. And some modern translators boldly proclaim their liberation in matters of sex and personal hygiene. A good example of this is

in Deuteronomy 23:12-13 (in Hebrew, verses 13-14). The Hebrew word is
şe'ateka (צֵאָתְךָ):

> **NEB:** You shall have a sign outside the camp showing where you can
> withdraw. With your equipment you will have a trowel, and when you
> squat outside, you shall scrape a hole with it and then turn and cover
> your excrement.

> **NJPS:** Further, there shall be an area for you outside the camp, where
> you may relieve yourself. With your gear you shall have a spike,
> and when you have squatted you shall dig a hole with it and cover up
> your excrement.

> **JB:** You must have a latrine outside the camp, and go out to this; and you
> must have a mattock among your equipment, and with this mattock,
> when you go outside to ease yourself, you must dig a hole and cover
> your excrement.

> **KJV:** Thou shalt have a place also without the camp, whither thou shalt
> go forth abroad: And thou shalt have a paddle upon thy weapon; and it
> shall be, when thou wilt ease thyself abroad, thou shalt dig therewith, and
> shalt turn back and cover that which cometh from thee.

John Beekman and John Callow note that in many cultures adultery is
referred to euphemistically rather than directly: in Chinantee, Otomi, Trique,
Mixtec and Chol of Mexico, the required locution is "talk to another
woman/man"; among the Colorado of Ecuador, it is "walk with others"; and
the Tagabili of the Philippines speak of "stepping on his/her partner."[13]

Some of the things the authors of the Bible were willing to say modern
English translators find embarrassing. Peter Mullen, a vicar in the diocese of
York, suggests that sin, the devil and the hereafter make moderns uncomfortable, so some translators try to avoid these subjects. For example, in the
Sermon on the Mount, the beatitudes are customarily translated "Blessed are
the poor in spirit, for theirs is the kingdom of heaven," etc. (Matthew 5:3-11);
but in the Jerusalem Bible, "happy" is substituted for "blessed." Mullen calls
this "a failure of nerve":

> Reward in heaven is being played down here, one suspects, in deference
> to modern man's famous doubts about the reality of the world to come.
> But these beatitudes speak of a more enduring benediction than any-
> thing conveyed by the word "happy"....They are so bland, these translators.
> Everything must be inoffensive, bland.[14]

Mullen also suspects "a typical piece of the NEB's daintiness" in the use
of "good-for-nothing" in 1 Samuel 25:25 where the KJV reads "man of Belial."
As Mullen explains, "The characterization of evil has indeed suffered
the debilitating effect of the friendly euphemism if the Devil's son is only
good-for-nothing."[15]

Mullen is on shakier ground here because the Hebrew *beliya'al* (בְּלִיַּעַל)
may originally have meant "worthless" and become a name for the devil

only after the time of the Hebrew Bible.[16] But the charge of daintiness merits consideration.

The function of taboo or offensive expressions, in contrast to euphemisms, is mostly to shock. When taboo or offensive words are used by someone who is known to avoid such language, they can carry great force.

In the Hebrew Bible, the root *ŠKB* (שכב), lie (with), is regularly used for sexual intercourse. But on four occasions, the more direct verb *ŠGL* (שגל) is used. Scholars agree that *ŠGL* was a word for sexual intercourse, but it may or may not have been considered vulgar (therefore, we cannot supply an exact English translation). In each of the four instances, *ŠGL* is used in a threat or condemnation, and always with the clear intention of shocking the audience. In Deuteronomy 28:28-30: "The Lord will strike you with madness, blindness and dismay....You will be betrothed to a woman, but a stranger will *ŠGL* her." In Isaiah 13:16: "Their infants will be smashed on the ground, their houses ransacked, and their wives *ŠGL*[ed]." In Jeremiah 3:1-2: "You have played the harlot with many lovers....Where haven't you been *ŠGL*[ed]?" In Zechariah 14:2: "The city shall be captured, the houses ransacked, and the women *ŠGL*[ed]."

Obviously, the authors deliberately chose strong language–if not vulgarisms–to horrify, upset and rattle their readers. Everything they love, readers are told, will be abused, debased or destroyed.

What have English translators done with these lines? Taking the first example (Deuteronomy 28:30) as a representative case, the English translators miss the tone entirely except in the NEB. The Hebrew word *ŠGL* is gritty and down-to-earth. When people heard these threats and condemnations, they gasped at the language and shuddered at the image. "Enjoy her" and "have her" simply do not deliver the required emotional punch. And even "ravish" does not fit in Jeremiah 3:2, where the woman is being accused of seeking lovers to *ŠGL*. Yet even here "ravished" is used in the NEB as well.

Modern English translators, unfortunately, do not usually distinguish between the voice of the biblical narrator and the voices of the characters in the stories. In translation, everyone speaks the same homogenized language. In the original Hebrew, the characters in the stories sometimes speak a more colloquial, "spoken" language, the quality of which is often lost in translation. Thus, for example, Godfrey Driver of the NEB wanted Exodus 2:9 to read "Hey, you! The child–get it suckled for me" instead of "Here is the child. Suckle him for me."[17] And David Daiches proposed "Hey! Listen to this dream I've had" (Genesis 37:6) for the KJV "Hear, I pray you, this dream which I have dreamed."[18]

On occasion, the characters in the stories even use language some might consider too coarse for the Bible. Take the story of how David got his wife, Abigail (1 Samuel 25). Abigail, a beautiful, intelligent woman, is married to a wealthy man named Nabal. Nabal's shepherds tend their flocks near David's band of outlaws, who treat them kindly and even protect them. When David's young men later seek hospitality from Nabal, they are turned away. For this, the Lord strikes down Nabal, and Abigail becomes David's wife. But this account gets ahead of the story. When it is reported to David that his young men had been unceremoniously turned away by Nabal, he becomes furious. David and his band set out to massacre Nabal and the men of his family. David swears (1 Samuel 25:22): "May God curse me if I leave alive *maśtin beqir*" (משתין בקיר). The Hebrew words are not vulgar, but this is a coarse way to refer to men. The phrase is used by an angry David about to murder Nabal and the men of his family. The King James Version translation reads "any that pisseth against the wall."

The Oxford English Dictionary says that "piss" was borrowed from French as a euphemism and was not considered impolite at the time of the KJV. The situation is now different, of course, and this accounts for our surprise at Job 18:11 in the NEB: "The terrors of death suddenly beset him and make him piss over his feet."

The NJPS translation of the relevant phrase, "a single male," in the story about David and Nabal indicates in a footnote: "Lit[erally,] 'one who pees against a wall.'" Only the NEB, with "a single mother's son," even attempts to capture the original tone in a parallel English idiom.

A similar problem arises in 2 Kings 18:27 where the emissary of the Assyrians besieging Jerusalem calls on the Israelite soldiers on the city walls to surrender. All hope is lost, he tells them. Their allies have fallen, their gods have abandoned them, and they will soon be reduced to eating their own ____ and drinking their own ____.

The Hebrew words in those two slots are quite explicit soldier-talk: חריהם and שיניהם. A footnote to this passage in the Jerusalem Bible calls attention to the "graphic description of the straits to which a beleaguered city is reduced." Yet the JB translation, like other modern English versions, sanitizes the horror by having the angry Assyrian soldier threaten to make his enemies "eat their own dung and drink their own urine."

But what should a modern translator do? This is, after all, the Bible. And that is the crux of the problem. The original authors did not intend to write "the Bible." Nevertheless, what they wrote *became* the Bible. As Richard Elliott Friedman explains:

> One confronts questions of conception. What did the author of any given portion of the book perceive his work to be? Did he see himself as a historian, a narrator, an artist; in the service of history, God, the king, the people of Israel? One must then apply the same questions to the redactors [editors]....Are the conceptions of author and author, or author and redactor, at odds?[19]

To these, we must add the conceptions of audience, translator and history.

Whatever the biblical authors and editors may have intended, they didn't conceive of the Bible as we do. Whether they were prophets calling on a specific population to repent or historians illustrating God's hand in Israel's destiny, they did not picture themselves writing pericopes for sermons and noble sentiments for liturgical use. In other words, their purpose was not to produce a Bible for public reading in houses of worship. Once the Bible became "sacred" (as distinct from inspired), however, it did enter the liturgy. And then coarse language became a problem.

When the Jews returned from the Babylonian Exile, many of them spoke Aramaic, which was the official language of the Babylonian and Persian empires; many did not even understand Hebrew (as witness, for example, Nehemiah 13:23-27). Therefore, when Ezra read aloud to the people from the Torah in Hebrew, his assistants were "translating and giving the sense, so they [the people] understood the reading" (Nehemiah 8:8).[20] The practice of translating public readings of the Bible lasted for hundreds of years.

By the second century C.E., the Mishnah[21] (see Megillah 4.10) codified the following rules for public readings:

> The incident of Reuben [in which he sleeps with his father's concubine, Genesis 35:22] is read in the synagogue but not translated....The stories of David [how he desired Bathsheba and killed her husband, 2 Samuel 11:2-17] and Amnon [who raped his half-sister Tamar, 2 Samuel 13:1-14] are read but not translated.[22]

And a later talmudic commentary adds (Megillah 25b):

> The rabbis taught: Wherever an indelicate expression is written in the text, we substitute a more polite one in reading. For *yišgalenah* [ישגלנה from *ŠGL*, Deuteronomy 28:30, as I have already illustrated earlier in this article] read *yiškabenah* [ישכבנה from *ŠKB*, "lie down with"]...For *ḥorehem...šinehem* [חריהם...שיניהם, "excrement...urine," 2 Kings 18:27] read *ṣo'atam...meme raglehem* [צואתם...מימי רגליהם, "deposit...feet-water"].[23]

Why did the rabbis feel they had to be more polite than the biblical authors themselves? A 17th-century commentator, Rabbi Samuel Eliezer Edels, explains that a distinction had to be made between private study and public worship. Because the written text was not amended, anyone who took the trouble to study Hebrew could read the original, but the dignity of communal worship required the substitution of less explicit language during public readings. And comments by other Hebrew scholars raise the intriguing possibility that, even if the Hebrew word was not coarse, cognates in colloquial Aramaic or Arabic of later Jewish communities might be vulgar. In this case, the unlearned, catching a familiar word or two in the Hebrew, would be misled or shocked.[24]

Concern for the sensibilities of the unlearned and unsophisticated remains high on the list of translators' priorities. It crops up time and again. For example, in an article in *Notes on Translation*, a forum for the Summer Institute of Linguistics and the Wycliffe Bible Translators, Katharine Barnwell warns translators to "remember that the meaning of a translation is not what the translator wants or aims to communicate, but what the hearer actually understands."

She argues that a translation of the Bible "must be such that it is acceptable to the church."[25] In the same publication, John Banker argues that "the translator needs to study receptor language figures of speech to find out how they can be used to produce naturalness and proper style in the translation." But he admits that "first, the translator must determine whether a particular stylistic feature is appropriate to scripture in general," and that "if the church leaders are against using the feature...it would seem wise in most cases to forgo the use of [it]."[26]

Bruce Hollenbach urges translators to respect the religious feelings of the target community. Noting that many denominations look to the Bible, he writes, "We want everyone who might possibly be willing and able to read these translated Scriptures to do so and be exposed more richly to the Word of God by doing so." It follows, therefore, Hollenbach says, that "we should be careful to exclude from our translation any doctrinal bias that could unnecessarily offend people."[27]

Hollenbach's major concern is doctrine, but his point applies equally well to offensive language. Significantly, just when reformers were updating the language of biblical translations and liturgy, David Crystal and Derek Davy, two pioneers in the study of linguistic style, warned against introducing "a variety of English which is too colloquial or informal," which might blur "the distinctive purpose of religious language."[28]

A translator must decide if the intended audience is made up of scholars or the general public, if the text will be used for silent reading or liturgy, and if it will be used at home or in a house of worship. Ideally, a translation should be appropriate for any audience. But in practice, this has proved to be impossible. And, as I was constantly aware while writing this article, the only thing a translator can know for sure is that whatever he decides, someone will be offended.

Word Studies

Language, of course, is more than words. But words are certainly at the heart of language. Unless we know what the words mean, we cannot hope to capture the poetry or reproduce the emotional impact of words in a translation.

The Bible spans more than a thousand years of linguistic history. During that time, new words entered biblical languages, old ones fell out of use and many others changed meaning. Scholars have suggested that New Testament authors did not always know the meaning of the Hebrew Scriptures they were quoting. Do we?

CHAPTER 24

Words That Occur in the Bible Only Once

Frederick E. Greenspahn

Frederick E. Greenspahn discusses the difficulties of translating hapax legomena, *words that occur only once, in the Hebrew Bible. Because we learn what words mean by comparing them in different contexts, the meanings of these 1500 or so words cannot be deduced in the usual way. More* hapax legomena *appear in poetic books than prose. In Job, for example, the erudite passages attributed to God are filled with one-time words. Whenever possible, scholars compare the biblical context with the appearance of the word in nonbiblical contexts; they also look for cognates in related languages and propose emendations. In the two studies of important, but enigmatic, words that follow, these scholarly techniques are evaluated.–Ed.*

For more than a thousand years, students of the Hebrew Bible have been intrigued by words that occur only once in the text. In medieval Jewish manuscripts, these unique words were marked with the Hebrew letter *lamed*, an abbreviation for the Aramaic word *layt*, which means "there is no other." The Masoretes, medieval scholars who attempted to preserve and fix the authentic Hebrew text, compiled lists of these words, presumably for the benefit of scribes who might otherwise have thought that, because they were unique, these words had been copied wrong. Medieval Jewish interpreters of the Bible described words for which they could find no parallels as "one of a kind" or words with no "friend," "brother," or even "father and mother."

Modern scholars too have been impressed with these words in the Bible. They call them *hapax legomena* (singular, *hapax legomenon*, which means "once said" in Greek).[1] The term was first used by pre-Christian Greeks to identify rare words in classical Greek literature.

The most reliable way to determine the meaning of a Hebrew word, or any word for that matter, is from the context, in other words, how the word is used in different settings. Different contexts, however, are precisely what *hapax legomena* do not have because they occur only once, in a single context from which the meaning can be inferred.

Useful insights about the meaning of rare Hebrew words can sometimes be derived from ancient translations, which, because they were produced at a time closer to the biblical writings, reflect knowledge not available to us. Unfortunately, this approach is often problematic. We have no way of knowing if an ancient translator used a Hebrew text different from ours or simply guessed at the meaning of words he did not know.

Through the ages, scholars have tried several approaches to the problem of translating words with only one context. One approach has been to correlate rare words with other, more common words. Because similar-sounding letters, such as *b* and *p* or *d* and *t*, are sometimes interchangeable in Hebrew, medieval scholars sometimes equated words with one of these letters with words having the other member of the pair.

For example, Lamentations 3:16 reads that God has *k-p-sh* me in ashes. *K-p-sh* is a *hapax legomenon*; we don't know for sure what it means. One conjecture is that it means God has "covered" me with ashes. This is the King James translation. Several scholars, however, have compared the root *k-p-sh* with the more familiar root *k-b-sh*, which means "subdue." These scholars suggest that *k-p-sh* may be an otherwise unattested variant of *k-b-sh*. On this basis, the New Jewish Publication Society translation, for example, tells us God has "ground [i.e., subdued] me into the ashes."

Claiming that rare words are often the result of scribal errors, modern scholars sometimes correct these "mistakes," sometimes on the basis of manuscript evidence, sometimes even on a hypothetical basis. In one well known instance, scholars have puzzled for centuries over the meaning of the root *n-l-h* in Isaiah 33:1, where the prophet warns that treachery awaits the evildoer when he *n-l-h* his treachery. Thus *n-l-h* is a *hapax legomenon* with no known meaning. The meaning "finished" seems clearly required by the context, so scholars have suggested that *n-l-h* is a scribal error for *k-l-h*, which in fact does mean "finish." In ancient Hebrew script, the signs for *k* (כ) and *n* (נ) are similar and could easily have been confused by a scribe.

Cognates in related languages sometimes provide additional contexts for unique words. In the Middle Ages, cognates usually had to be found in rabbinic or even Arabic texts. Today, archaeologists have a wide array of resources from which to choose, including ancient Semitic languages, such as Akkadian, Ugaritic and Eblaite, which have now been deciphered. Cognates are not, however, always reliable. For example, the German word *sterben* means "die"; the English cognate is "starve." The meanings are obviously not identical.

Describing the importance of Ugaritic texts discovered about half a century ago, one scholar has written: "The meaning of words occurring only once in the Hebrew Bible...but fairly frequently in Ugaritic can now be determined with reasonable certainty."[2] Most recent discoveries have not been as helpful in unlocking the meaning of *hapax legomena* as this quotation suggests, however. Few ancient Hebrew inscriptions of any length have been discovered to which we can compare biblical *hapax legomena*. Even dramatic finds like the Dead Sea Scrolls have not been very helpful in this respect. The modern decipherment of Akkadian, the language of the Assyrians and Babylonians in the second and first pre-Christian millennia, has provided information crucial for understanding only a handful of *hapax legomena* verbs in the Bible. Ugaritic sources have been crucial to unlocking the meaning of only two *hapax legomena* verbs.

This is not to say that information from these languages is unimportant; indeed, it has enhanced our understanding of the cultural environment of the ancient Near East in which the Bible was written and given us insight into the meaning of many biblical words. But these languages have been of limited use for translating *hapax legomena* simply because most *hapax legomena* were understood long before these ancient languages were discovered and deciphered.

One might expect that it would be more difficult to understand and translate words that occur in only one context than words that appear numerous times, but this is not always true. Often the information available from a single context is more than sufficient. The verb *n-b-ḥ*, for example, occurs only in Isaiah 56:10: "They are all dumb dogs that cannot *n-b-ḥ*." The word clearly means "bark," an inference supported by the fact that the word has precisely the same meaning in several other Semitic languages.

Other biblical *hapax legomena* were used by the ancient rabbis rather familiarly, suggesting that the meanings were clear at that time. Indeed, where cognates are useful, the most productive source has been early rabbinic literature (in both Hebrew and Aramaic), which has been known since antiquity. When one adds Arabic, which has been familiar to biblical scholars since at least the Middle Ages, it is easy to see why students of the Bible have had relatively little difficulty with *hapax legomena*. Despite the longstanding fascination with words that occur only once, most of them are not particularly obscure or difficult. In fact, ancient, medieval and modern scholars alike agree about the meaning of many of them—not what one would expect for words no one really understands.

How many *hapax legomena* are there? Scholars have produced several lists, but no two are exactly alike. There are several reasons for this. First, they had to decide what to do with words that occur only once but are related to other, more frequent words. Can the English word *sing* truly be considered a *hapax legomenon* if it occurs alongside the word *song*? To avoid confusion, scholars generally distinguish between absolute *hapax legomena*, words that are not related to any other words, and non-absolute *hapax legomena*, which are.

More difficult problems in identifying *hapax legomena* are posed by passages that are repeated in the Bible. Chronicles, for example, contains much of the same material found in Kings; Psalm 18 is essentially the same as 2 Samuel 22. And the description of building the tabernacle in Exodus 35-39 is almost exactly the same as the description in Exodus 25-31, where God commands that the tabernacle be constructed. Words that occur in two identical passages and nowhere else, such as the words commonly translated "ledge" in Exodus 27:5 and 38:4, "ivory" in 1 Kings 10:22 and 2 Chronicles 9:21, and "ankle" in 2 Samuel 22:37 and Psalm 18:37, are regarded by some as *hapax legomena* because they occur in only one context, whereas others say they occur twice. Disagreements have also arisen about words that occur several times in a single biblical passage; the word for "sack" appears 14 times in Genesis 43-44 but nowhere else; "sweep" occurs twice in Isaiah 14:23 but nowhere else.

Once these technical problems have been resolved, it is possible to draw up a list of biblical *hapax legomena*. The Hebrew Bible contains about 300 absolute *hapax legomena* and more than 1,200 non-absolute *hapax legomena*, depending on how you define the term.

The lists of *hapax legomena* also show that these words are not spread evenly throughout the Bible but are concentrated in certain books. The Song of Songs,[3] for example, has a larger proportion of them than any other book of the Bible; Chronicles, a historical book, has the smallest. Poetic books consistently have more *hapax legomena* than prose books, which is not surprising because poetic language is usually different from common speech. One can carry this analysis further.

The book of Job has the second largest proportion of *hapax legomena*; even within Job, however, rare words are distributed in identifiable patterns. God uses *hapax legomena* four times as often as Job; Job's speeches contain more *hapax legomena* than the speeches of his three friends. It seems both reasonable and appropriate that God's vocabulary be more erudite than man's.

Another matter for discussion is *why* some words occur only once. Medieval scholars assumed that a single occurrence was accidental. But we know these words must have been understood, or biblical authors would not have used them. The fact that they are rare to us may simply mean that only a fraction of ancient Israelite literature has survived.

In fact, the reason words occur infrequently may have nothing to do with Hebrew or with the Bible. In all texts, indeed in all bodies of linguistic material, whether written or oral, a certain number of words occur only once. The 1500 or so absolute *hapax legomena* in the Hebrew Bible represent roughly one-quarter of the total vocabulary. Compared to other literatures, this is a relatively small proportion. For example, 55 percent of the words in Shakespeare's *Julius Caesar* and 47 percent in the Gospel of Mark are *hapax legomena*. Because the Hebrew Bible is a much longer work, previously used words are likely to be repeated, just as new, hitherto unused words are likely to be added. In any event, the Bible does not contain an unduly large number of rare words.

Although the Bible comprises only a small part of ancient Israelite literature (in the Bible itself other books are mentioned, as in Joshua 10:13), a certain proportion of the vocabulary in any work—usually between one-third and two-thirds—will, by statistical necessity, be rare. (About 60 percent of the words in this article occur only once!) *Hapax legomena* are simply a fact of linguistic life.

Statisticians have shown that rare words in a particular book are probably rare in the language as a whole. But this does not necessarily mean they are difficult. English words like *aspirin* and *zebra* occur much less frequently than *book* or *table*, but we understand them perfectly well. The words *brother*, *see* and *half* occur only once in this article but are not likely to cause problems for most readers. Some words are rare by nature. In other words, one cannot assume that a rarely used word has been miscopied. In fact, biblical scholars often work on the principle that if one must choose between two possible readings, the more difficult reading should be chosen because scribes are more likely to have "corrected" a rare word they thought was wrong than to have "created" a new word by miscopying a common word.

This is not to say that we understand every word in the Bible (obviously, the opposite is the case); but rare words are not necessarily difficult. Indeed, the meaning of common words can sometimes be more problematic. The noun *ahavah*, derived from a common root meaning "to love," occurs about 40 times in the Hebrew Bible; but some scholars have suggested it should be translated "leather" in Song of Songs 3:10 to fit with other concrete words in that verse. Accordingly, this occurrence of a common word has been turned into a *hapax legomenon*. Of course, we cannot prove whether or not such an interpretation is correct. (In the recent translations I examined, "leather" appears only in the New English Bible.)

For all the attention *hapax legomena* have attracted, their one-time occurrence would seem less important than scholars over the past thousand years have thought.

CHAPTER 25

Red Sea or Reed Sea?
What Yam Sûp Really Means

Bernard F. Batto

Did the Red Sea part for the Israelites during the Exodus? The Hebrew words yam sûp *are frequently rendered "Red Sea," but the geographical difficulties of this identification have caused scholars to place the miracle at a Sea of Reeds. Bernard F. Batto offers an innovative solution to the meaning of* yam sûp *based on the cosmic and mythic connotations of the story. According to Batto, the Israelites emerged from the chaos of slavery by crossing the "Sea at the End of World."–Ed.*

If there is one thing sophisticated students of the Bible *know*, it is that *yam sûp*, which has traditionally been translated Red Sea, really means Reed Sea and that the Israelites crossed the Reed Sea on their way out of Egypt.

Well, it doesn't and it wasn't and they're wrong!

Yam sûp (pronounced "yahm soof") appears many times in the Bible. In a number of places, it clearly refers to the body of water we know as the Red Sea (including the two northern fingers, the Gulf of Suez and the Gulf of Eilat or the Gulf of Aqaba).

Note that I do not say that *yam sûp* literally *means* Red Sea. The literal meaning of *yam sûp* is part of the problem. *Yam* indeed means sea; that much is clear and agreed. But the word for red is *adam* (pronounced "a-dahm"), not *sûp*. So Red Sea should be *yam adam*, not *yam sûp*. From the context, however, we know that in a number of biblical references, *yam sûp* does refer to the body of water we know as the Red Sea.

Look, for example, at 1 Kings 9:26, where we are told that "King Solomon built a fleet of ships at Ezion-Geber near Elath [or Eilat] on the shore of the *yam sûp* in the land of Edom." From the other geographical references, it is absolutely clear that *yam sûp* here refers to the northeastern finger of the Red Sea, known today as the Gulf of Eilat or the Gulf of Aqaba.

Or consider Jeremiah 49:21. Jeremiah prophesies that the dying babies of Edom will cry, and "the sound of screaming shall be heard at the *yam sûp.*" A glance at a map indicates that the *yam* (sea) referred to is again the northeastern finger of what we call the Red Sea and that *yam sûp* refers to the body of water we call the Red Sea. (For other examples, see Numbers 21:4 and, with less certainty, Numbers 14:25; Deuteronomy 1:40 and 2:1; and Judges 11:16.)

One especially important reference, to which we shall return later in this article because it describes the Israelite journey out of Egypt, is Numbers 33. This passage contains the list of ancient camping stations of the Exodus, all the way from Rameses and Succoth in Egypt to Kadesh and the land of Edom. In verse 8, we are told that the Israelites "passed through the sea (*yam*) into the wilderness." Which "sea," we are not told. Then the Israelites traveled for three days and camped at Marah. Then they left Marah and went to Elim. Then they left Elim and camped by the *yam sûp.* It is obvious that they had reached the northwestern finger of the Red Sea, which we call the Gulf of Suez. Here *yam sûp* again refers to the body of water we call the Red Sea, a five-day journey, at least, from the sea the Israelites miraculously passed through.

On the basis of these geographical referents, it is easy to understand how the traditional translation of *yam sûp* came to be Red Sea. In the earliest known translation of the Bible—from Hebrew to Greek—*yam sûp* is consistently translated as Erythra Thalassa, which means Red Sea. This Greek Bible, known as the Septuagint, was translated in about 300 B.C.E. In Saint Jerome's Latin translation known as the Vulgate (from about 400 C.E.), *yam sûp* is translated Mare Rubrum—Red Sea. From the Vulgate translation, Red Sea became firmly entrenched in Western tradition, appearing again, for example, in the King James Version.

The Red Sea/Reed Sea problem arises because *yam sûp* is also used in the Bible as the name of the body of water that parted to allowed the Israelites to pass through and then came together to drown the Egyptians. The most important of these biblical passages is in Exodus 15, which scholars consider to be one of the oldest, if not the oldest, and most archaic poems in the entire Bible. Known as the Song of the Sea,[1] Exodus 15 is a celebration of the miracle of the sea by which the Israelites were saved from Pharaoh's pursuing horsemen:

> I will sing to the Lord, for he has triumphed gloriously;
> Horse and driver he has hurled into the sea (*yam*).
>   ....
> Pharaoh's chariots and his army he has cast into the sea (*yam*);
> And the pick of his officers are sunk in the *yam sûp.*
>
> Exodus 15:1,4

In later biblical books, the sea that parted for the Israelites is consistently referred to as *yam sûp.* In Joshua 2:10, for example, Rahab, the harlot who let the Israelite spies into Jericho, tells them, "We have heard how the Lord

dried up the water of the *yam sûp* before you when you came out of Egypt."
When the Lord parted the Jordan River to allow the Israelites to cross,
Joshua told his people that this was just what "the Lord your God did
to the *yam sûp* which he dried up for us until we passed over" (Joshua 4:23).
(See also Joshua 24:6; Deuteronomy 11:4; Psalms 106:7,9,22; 136:13-15;
and Nehemiah 9:9.)

Traditionally, *yam sûp* has been translated Red Sea in these passages, too.
But something seems wrong with this translation. It doesn't seem to fit the geography, quite apart from the fact that the Gulf of Suez is more than 20 miles wide.
Moreover, there is absolutely no philological reason to think that *sûp* means
"red" or anything like it.

Thus was born the translation Reed Sea. Translating *yam sûp* as Reed Sea
arguably solves all these problems. The Reed Sea allegedly fits the geography,
is a body of water that could dry up under the force of a heavy wind, and *sûp*
is arguably based on an Egyptian etymology meaning "reed."

We don't know who first suggested the translation Reed Sea. The
11th-century medieval French Jewish commentator known as Rashi accepted
a connection between *yam sûp* and a marsh overgrown with reeds.[2] Ibn Ezra,
a Spanish Jewish commentator of the 12th century, commenting on the meaning of *yam sûp* in Exodus 13:18, notes that, "Some say that it is so called
because reeds grow round about it." Martin Luther may have been acquainted
with such opinions; he translated *yam sûp* as *Schilfmeer* (meaning Reed Sea).

Among modern scholars, Heinrich Brugsch in 1858 was apparently the
first to develop a comprehensive, coherent theory of the Reed Sea, including
the alleged connection between biblical *yam sûp* and *p3-ṯwf(y)* (pronounced
approximately "pi thoof") of the Egyptian texts.[3]

These Egyptian texts are the principal pillar of the Reed Sea hypothesis.
According to this argument, these texts establish that *yam sûp* literally means
"Sea of Papyrus" or "Sea of Reeds." Etymologically, we are told, Hebrew *sûp* is
a loan-word from Egyptian *ṯwf*, which means "papyrus" (reeds). This etymology is supposed to be proved in biblical passages where *sûp* refers to vegetation growing along the banks of the Nile. For example, in Exodus 2:3,5, the
baby Moses is hidden from Pharaoh who has threatened to kill all newborn
Hebrew males; he is hidden among the *suph* (reeds) by the bank of the Nile
(see also Isaiah 19:6).

One Egyptian text, known as Papyrus Anastasi III, supposedly even speaks
of a "Papyrus Marsh" or "Papyrus Lake" not far from the city of Rameses
(= Tanis?), the very place from which the biblical narrative says the Israelites
began their journey out of Egypt (Exodus 12:37).

The Reed Sea hypothesis has now become so widely accepted that one can
scarcely pick up a handbook or treatise on the Bible, regardless of the author's
theological affiliation or scholarly bent,[4] that does not espouse the theory that
yam sûp means Reed Sea when referring to the body of water the Israelites

passed through on their way out of Egypt. The ubiquity of the hypothesis is even reflected in modern critical translations of the Bible. Although English versions normally adhere to the traditional rendering of Red Sea, almost every respected translation of the Book of Exodus now includes at least an annotation that *yam sûp* actually means Reed Sea when it refers to the body of water the Israelites passed through and in which the Egyptians drowned.[5]

The Reed Sea solution is not as simple as it seems, however. Right off the bat, we have the problem of how to translate those passages where *yam sûp* has nothing to do with the Exodus (such as 1 Kings 9:26, cited above) and where the body of water referred to is clearly the Red Sea. Here, we have no choice but to translate *yam sûp* as the Red Sea. And that is regularly done when *yam sûp* obviously refers to the Red Sea or when the referent is not obvious to the translator. Translations are not consistent from Bible to Bible, but we regularly find *yam sûp* translated two ways—in the same Bible translation! Check your own Bible translation, for example, at Exodus 15:4 and 1 Kings 9:26.

Another problem with translating *yam sûp* as Sea of Reeds is the supposed etymological connection between *sûp* and reeds. There are no reeds in the Red Sea (or in the Gulf of Suez). The ancients would surely not apply *yam sûp* to what we call the Red Sea if *yam sûp* were intended to refer to reeds. In short, a translation such as Sea of Papyrus Reeds is inappropriate when applied to the Red Sea because papyrus does not grow in those salty waters!

Finally, the connection between *yam sûp* and Egyptian *p3-twf* does not stand up under scrutiny. There can be no doubt that the Egyptian word for papyrus, *twf*, passed into Hebrew as a loan-word, *sûp*, with a slight modification in pronunciation as required by Hebrew phonology. Hebrew *sûp* means papyrus in Exodus 2:3,5 and Isaiah 19:6. Nevertheless, Egyptian *p3-twf* has nothing to do with the biblical *yam sûp*.

Let us look more closely at the evidence. The hieroglyphic signs in question (𓆎𓈖𓏲𓏏) are written in Latin letters as *p3-twf*. The definite article is *p3*, and *twf* means "papyrus." The phrase appears a number of times in Egyptian texts. It refers, however, to a papyrus marsh *area* or *district*, not to a lake or body of water.[6] In some texts, *p3-twf* is used to designate a district or area where papyrus grows and where animals are pastured and agricultural enterprises undertaken.

In hieroglyphic writing, an unpronounced sign called a determinative is often included in the spelling to indicate the class of noun. Thus the determinative for god is added to the phonetic signs for gods, so we know which names refer to gods. The determinative for plant always accompanies *p3-twf*. Occasionally it is written with the determinative for town, but never is it written with the determinative for lake or water. Moreover, the term *p3-twf* does not indicate a specific area. Several places in the eastern delta of the Nile are referred to as *p3-twf*.[7]

The text most often cited in support of the connection between *p3-twf* and *yam sûp* is, as I noted earlier, Papyrus Anastasi III, which describes the residence of Pharaoh Rameses II (often identified as the pharaoh of the Exodus): "The papyrus marshes *p3-ṭwf* come to it [the pharaoh's residence] with papyrus reeds, and the Waters-of-Horus with rushes."[8] This text hardly indicates a single lake or body of water called the Reed Sea.

Indeed, the identification of *p3-ṭwf* as a body of water owes more to the desire to find confirmation for the hypothetical Reed Sea of the Bible than to the internal evidence of the Egyptian texts. Egyptian *p3-ṭwf* would hardly ever have been understood as referring to a body of water apart from the biblical term *yam sûp*. In Roland de Vaux's recent classic, *The Early History of Israel*,[9] he translates *p3-ṭwf* as "the land of the papyrus."

I believe there is another, wholly satisfactory way out of this dilemma. *Yam sûp* for the ancients had a symbolic as well as historical meaning. Indeed, the symbolic meaning preceded the historical meaning. Symbolically, *yam sûp* means Sea of the End, the sea at the end of the world. Historically, it came to mean the Red Sea and what lay beyond.

The word *sûp* should be connected not with Egyptian *p3-ṭwf* but with the Semitic root *sûp*, meaning "to come to an end" or "to cease to exist." The Hebrew word *sôp* simply means "end." *Yam sûp* is the equivalent of *yam sôp*. This association has been suggested by Norman Snaith, who correctly argues that *yam sûp* thus refers to "that distant scarcely known sea away to the south, of which no man knew the boundary. It was the sea at the end of the land."[10]

What we call the Red Sea came to be known as the *yam sûp* because it was regarded by the ancients as the sea at the end of the world. Interestingly enough, the Greeks applied the name Red Sea (*Erythra Thalassa*) not only to our Red Sea but also to the Indian Ocean[11] and, later, when they discovered it, even to the Persian Gulf.[12] The phrase Red Sea could even be vaguely used to designate remote, faraway places.[13] Likewise in Jewish intertestamental literature, the designation Red Sea included the Persian Gulf and everything to the south. Thus, both the fragmentary Aramaic text from the Dead Sea Scrolls known as the Genesis Apocryphon (21.17-18) and *Antiquities of the Jews* (1.1.3) by Josephus, the famous first-century C.E. Jewish historian, state that the Tigris and Euphrates empty into the Red Sea. The Book of Jubilees (third or second century B.C.E.) says that Eden and the lands of India and Elam (Persia) all border on the Red Sea (8.21, 9.2). It is thus clear that the ancients thought of the Red Sea as a continuous body of water that extended from the Red Sea through the Indian Ocean to the Persian Gulf and that included all connecting oceans to the south. Presumably the earlier Israelites also included in the designation *yam sûp* all the connecting oceans to the south.

The designation *yam sûp* thus had both a geographical and a symbolic meaning. The Sea of the End means not just the sea at the physical end of the world but also the place where noncreation or nonexistence begins.

In the ancient Near East, the idea of the sea carried with it many mythological connotations. A common theme in cosmogonic myths from Mesopotamia
to Egypt was the creation of the cosmos through some kind of primeval battle against the forces of chaos. Chaos, variously named Leviathan, Rahab and
the dragon, was most commonly known simply as Sea (Akkadian Tiamat,
Canaanite Yamm). Creation meant that which was most solidly formed, the dry
land, out of the chaos of the sea. At the center of the cosmos stood the cosmic
mountain, the home of the creator deity. At the opposite pole lay the realm of
chaos, uncreated and unformed, the most graphic symbol of which was the
sea. To the ancients, this feared and apparently limitless abyss really was the
end of the world. This was what the Hebrews called *yam sûp*.

Mythic cosmic elements are surely embedded in the term *yam sûp* as it is
used in the Bible. Indeed these elements unlock new meaning in the biblical
text. Moreover, the "fit" is so good that it corroborates the theory. Consider,
for example, the Song of the Sea (Exodus 15), one of the most ancient passages
in the entire Bible. This justly famous poem in archaic Hebrew celebrates the
deliverance of the Israelites:

> Then Moses and the Israelites sang this song to the LORD.
> They said:
> I will sing to the LORD, for He has triumphed gloriously;
> Horse and driver He has hurled into the sea.
> The LORD is my strength and might;
> He is become my salvation.
> This is my God and I will enshrine Him;
> The God of my father, and I will exalt Him.
> The LORD, the Warrior—
> LORD is His name!
> *Pharaoh's chariots and his army*
> *He has cast into the sea;*
> *And the pick of his officers*
> *Are sunk in the* yam sûp.
> The deeps covered them;
> They went down into the depths like a stone.
> Your right hand, O LORD glorious in power,
> Your right hand, O LORD, shatters the foe!
> In Your great triumph You break Your opponents;
> You send forth Your fury, it consumes them like straw.
> The floods stood straight like a wall;
> The deeps froze in the heart of the sea.
> The foe said,
> "I will pursue, I will overtake,
> I will divide the spoil;
> My desire shall have its fill of them.

I will bare my sword—
My hand shall subdue them."
You made Your wind blow, the sea covered them;
They sank like lead in the majestic waters.
Who is like you, O LORD, among the gods;
Who is like You, majestic in holiness,
Awesome in splendor, working wonders!
You put out Your right hand,
The underworld swallowed them.
In Your love You lead the people You redeemed;
In Your strength You guide them to Your holy abode.
The peoples hear, they tremble;
Agony grips the dwellers in Philistia.
Now are the clans of Edom dismayed;
The tribes of Moab—trembling grips them;
All the dwellers in Canaan are aghast.
Terror and dread descend upon them;
Through the might of Your arm they are still as stone—
Till Your people cross over, O LORD,
Till Your people cross whom You have created.[14]
You will bring them and plant them in Your own mountain,
The place You made to dwell in, O LORD,
The sanctuary, O LORD, which Your hands established.
The LORD will reign for ever and ever!

Modern source critics have identified four different textual strands in the Pentateuch. These four strands are labeled J (for Yahwist in its Germanic form), E (for Elohist), P (for Priestly writer) and D (for Deuteronomist). The Song of the Sea, however, is independent of any of the textual strands that have been interwoven to form the biblical text as we know it. Moreover, the Song of the Sea is also recognized to be older even than J, the earliest textual strand.

The Song of the Sea follows the basic pattern of ancient mythological cycles, such as Enuma Elish, the Mesopotamian epic about the god Marduk, and the Ugaritic cycle concerning the god Baal. In these mythological texts, the creator god overcomes his watery foe of chaos, brings order out of this chaos and creates a people in the process. The creator god then retires to his mountain sanctuary to rule over his newly ordered cosmos.[15]

As has often been observed, the biblical description in Exodus 15 is heavily dependent on mythological language. The defeat of the historical pharaoh plays only a minor role in the poem. The struggle against the pharaoh is portrayed as part of a larger battle between the deity and the powers of chaos; the pharaoh is identified with the chaotic powers and is destroyed with them. For this reason, the pharaoh is submerged in the sea and defeated along with the sea.

In this biblical poem, the *yam* in verse 4a is the equivalent of the sea dragon in ancient Near Eastern mythologies. In the second half of verse 4, *yam* is paired with *yam sûp*, which here means literally Sea of End/Annihilation. The *yam sûp* was the sea at the end of the earth, which in the ancient mind was fraught with connotations of primeval chaos.[16]

These mythical associations explain the presence of *yam sûp* in the Song of the Sea. Traditional mythical language is used to express the belief that the emergence of Israel as a people during the Exodus was a creative act by Yahweh equal to the creation of the cosmos. The Egyptians, the evil force that threatens the existence of this new creation, are appropriately cast into the sea where they perish. A more powerful symbol for nonexistence can scarcely be found than submergence in the Sea of End/Annihilation.

Philological confirmation of the connotations emanating from the word *sûp* may be found in a passage from Jonah. The word *sûp* is used there in a prayer of thanksgiving Jonah delivers from the belly of the whale just after he has been rescued from watery chaos:

> I called out in my distress to Yahweh
>   and he answered me;
> From the belly of Sheol I cried
>   and you heard my voice.
> You had cast me into the deep,
>   in the midst of Sea
>   and River surrounded me.
> All your breakers and your billows
>   passed over me.
> Then I said, "I am driven
>   away from your presence.
> How can I continue to look
>   to your holy temple?"
> The waters engulfed me up to the neck;
>   the Abyss surrounded me;
>   *sûp* was bound to my head.
> To the foundations of the mountains I descended;[17]
>   the underworld and its bars closed after me forever.
> But you brought my life up from the Pit,
>   O Yahweh, my God.
> When my soul went faint within me,
>   I remembered Yahweh;
> And my prayer came unto you,
>   into your holy temple.
> Those who worship vain idols
>   forsake their true loyalty.

> But I with acclamations of thanksgiving
>> will sacrifice to you.
> What I have vowed I will pay;
>> deliverance is from Yahweh.

Sûp is usually translated in this passage as "seaweed," "weeds," or the like. Seaweed doesn't grow, however, in the depths of the sea. And there is surely no philological basis for a translation like "seaweed." What *sûp* really means is the End/Annihilation. *Sûp* here is parallel to the abyss that surrounded the prophet and the waters that engulfed him up to his neck. In the same way, the End/Annihilation was bound to his head. All the images in the psalm concern the realm of primeval chaos: Sheol, the Pit, and the underworld as the abode of Death; the Sea Dragon under the twin names of Sea and River; the primeval Abyss (*tehom*) and associated terms, "the deep," "breakers," "billows," "waters"; the foundations of the mountains in the underworld. Clearly, context requires that *sûp* have something to do with the cosmic battle against chaos.

In Jonah, as in the Song of the Sea in Exodus 15, God rules from his holy temple or mountain, a continuation of the primordial battle against the nihilistic forces of chaos. God's holy mountain, where his temple is located, is the center of the cosmos, or orderly creation. To the ancient mind, the farther away from the center of the cosmos one goes, the farther one moves into the realm of chaos or noncreation. The spatial image is both vertical and horizontal. Vertically, the heavens are the source of existence and creation; the underworld and the abyss are the places of death and nonexistence. Horizontally, the land around the mountain of one's god is known and understood and therefore thought of as the most "created." The sea, which lies beyond the limits of the land, is unsolid, unformed—in other words, "uncreated." Thus, the sea and the abyss are simultaneously symbolic and real to the ancient mind.

In the same way, *yam sûp* had both a symbolic meaning and a real meaning. When it refers to the body of water that engulfed the Egyptians after the Israelites passed through, it has a symbolic meaning. Elsewhere, it refers to a particular body of water, the Red Sea, which for the ancients was really the Sea at the End of the World. But *yam sûp* never refers to the Reed Sea.

Yam sûp came to refer to the Red Sea because the Israelites, like other ancient peoples, did not distinguish the Red Sea from the oceans farther south. To their way of thinking, the Red Sea—the *yam sûp*—was the sea at the end of the earth. It was a real place, but it also extended to the end of the world and thus carried enormous symbolic and mythic weight.

It is interesting to note how the sea figures in each of the textual strands that make up the narrative account in Exodus 13:17 through Exodus 14:30. Although there are minor disagreements among scholars about how to divide the text, critics generally agree on the division among the three strands represented in this passage. These three strands are J and E (which were combined into JE by a so-called redactor or editor at an early stage) and P. I have set forth the division among the three strands in an endnote.[18]

In the J narrative the sea is not identified; it is called simply *ha-yam* (the sea, Exodus 14:21b).[19] The seabed is bared by a strong east wind that blows all night. Towards morning, God somehow panics the Egyptians, who flee headlong into the dry seabed. When the waters flow back to their normal place, the Egyptians are drowned, and the Israelites are free to continue on their way. Of the three textual strands, J is accepted as the oldest (probably tenth or ninth century B.C.E.), and in this version the sea clearly has symbolic connotations. The Egyptians are drowned in primeval chaos.

The textual strand known as E is scarcely represented in the sea narrative. There are no clear references to any miracle at the sea in this strand. The only possible reference to the sea is in 14:25a, which talks about chariot wheels clogging. This allusion to God's clogging the chariot wheels so that the Egyptians could not drive may fit in with the setting of a dry seabed, but it is equally appropriate for a flight story. We do not know what the original E account contained. Not much of it has been left by the redactor.

The P narrative tells the familiar story. Trapped between the sea and the pursuing Egyptians, the Israelites cry to Yahweh for help. Yahweh commands Moses to stretch out his staff over the sea, and the sea is split in two. The Israelites march dry-shod through the middle of the sea between walls of water to the right and to the left with the Egyptians in pursuit. After the Israelites have crossed, Moses again raises his staff and the waters return; the trapped Egyptian army perishes in the midst of the sea. Here too, the place of the miracle is designated simply as the sea. Accordingly, some scholars have argued that P, like J, did not connect the miracle with *yam sûp*. It is more likely, however, that P did identify the sea of the miracle with *yam sûp*.

As I have shown elsewhere,[20] P is responsible for editing the Exodus narrative and the wilderness journey to conform to the camping stations listed in Numbers 33. But there is one very important exception. In Numbers 33, the station at the sea of the crossing (verse 8) is distinct from *yam sûp* (verses 10-11), where the Israelites arrive some three camping stations later. In the Exodus narrative, however, P deliberately suppressed the latter station at *yam sûp* and changed the setting of the miraculous crossing from an unnamed sea to *yam sûp*. You can easily observe this for yourself. Compare the stations listed in Exodus 13:20, 14:2, 15:22-23 and 15:27-16:1 with the parallel list in Numbers 33:5-11. By telescoping the stations at the sea and at *yam sûp* into one, P surely wanted the reader to understand the defeat of Pharaoh as happening in *yam sûp*.

On the one hand, P clearly intended to historicize his account by providing concrete chronological and geographical referents. It must be assumed, then, that P intended *yam sûp* as a specific, identifiable body of water. On the other hand, P also wished to play upon the cosmic and mythic elements connoted by the *yam sûp*. In P's retelling of the Exodus, the *yam sûp* is split, and the

Israelites—freed from the slavery of Pharaoh—emerge as God's new creation (even as Marduk cleaved Tiamat in twain and out of her carcass created the cosmos).

The splitting of the sea is clearly reminiscent of the West Semitic myth of the creator god overcoming his watery foe of chaos. Various commentators have noted that P's account of creation (Genesis 1) alludes in various places to the common Semitic creation myth, including the reference to the "darkness upon the face of the abyss" (Hebrew *tehom*, which is a cognate of the Akkadian Tiamat). P describes the universal flood as an irruption of the abyss into creation (Genesis 7:11, 8:2).

In P's flood story, the creator once again has to defeat the nihilistic power of evil (the waters) encroaching upon the kingdom of God. In P's version of the Exodus story, the Israelite deliverance from Egypt is another instance of the creator's continuing battle against contemporary manifestations of chaos represented by the sea. By splitting the sea so "that the people of Israel might go through the midst of the sea on dry land" (Exodus 14:16), God once more demonstrated his creative power over chaos. Just as he did in the creation and the flood accounts, the creator caused dry land to appear in the midst of the abyss, in effect making the realm of chaos recede before a superior, positive power. The people of God, of course, walked in the realm of creation (dry land), while the Egyptians were submerged into the realm of noncreation (sea).

P was not the only biblical author to portray Egypt as the embodiment of chaos. In Isaiah 30:7, Egypt, again in the role of opponent of Yahweh, is called "Rahab the quelled." Rahab is one of the names of the primeval sea dragon. Also, in Ezekiel 29:3, Pharaoh, together with all Egypt, is depicted as "the great sea dragon" (*tannim*), an epithet of Leviathan (see Isaiah 27:1, 51:9-11). Thus, by portraying the Exodus from Egypt as an extension of the creative will of God, P placed himself solidly within Israel's theological traditions.

The cosmological and mythological concepts embodied in the biblical account of the miracle of the sea are foreign to us post-Enlightenment readers, but they were an important source for creative theologizing by biblical writers, both in Exodus and elsewhere. The Exodus narrative should not be read as a historical account of what actually transpired. Biblical writers were less interested in reporting historical data than in symbolizing for their contemporaries the salvational significance of their traditions. The significance of those original symbols has been lost in our modern scientific and technological world. Nevertheless, if we are to understand the Exodus as the ancient Israelites did, we must also learn to understand the meaning of their symbols.

AFTERWORD

In response to a question from Robert Billig of New York City, Batto explains how the translation Red Sea came about:

The Septuagint translators did not translate the Hebrew word *sûp* as "red." Rather, they correctly understood *yam sûp* to refer to the body of water they called the Red Sea (Erythra Thalassa) and translated accordingly. There are several theories as to why the Greeks called it the Red Sea in the first place. The name is usually attributed to the reddish color of either the surrounding cliffs or the coral reefs within the sea itself. Other authorities note that strong winds often blow clouds of desert sand that settle on the water in great reddish streaks. Still others call attention to the presence of certain algae that can give the waters a reddish hue. In any case, one should compare analogous geographic names, such as the Red River, the Black Sea, the Black Forest, the Blue Nile, etc. The Red Sea, or Arabian Sea, like many other places, has borne a variety of names over the centuries. Interestingly, one of the ancient Egyptian names for it was the Great Green Water, a name that also applied to other seas, such as the Mediterranean.[1] ***BAR** 10:6 (1984), p. 12*

Rev. Norman Friedmeyer of Hebron, Nebraska, believes Batto is wrong about the condition of the Red Sea in antiquity:

Batto says that *yam sûp* could not refer to a Sea of Reeds because "there are absolutely no reeds in the Red Sea (or in the Gulf of Suez)." He says the ancients would surely not have referred to reeds if there were none.

That may be correct, but it doesn't seem fair to state categorically what conditions once were, based on what they are today. Things have a way of changing over the millennia. For example, many mountainous areas give evidence of having been under water at one time. And again, the country of Lebanon was at one time forested with cedar trees, stately and valuable enough to be exported for the construction of palaces and temples. Pictures of Lebanon today do not hint at that kind and density of vegetation. ***BAR** 10:6 (1984), p. 14*

Batto replies:

Rev. Friedmeyer has confused two very distinct situations. It is true that the hills of Lebanon (and Palestine) have been denuded of forests within historical time, as is amply documented in records stretching from the third millennium B.C.E. to modern times. Long before David and Solomon began acquiring the prized cedar of Lebanon for their magnificent building projects, royal expeditions from both Mesopotamia and Egypt had already exploited those mountains for their lumber. And the trees that escaped the successive war machines of Roman, Crusader and Muslim armies were devoured by Turkish locomotives in our own century.

The presence of marine fossils and sedimentary deposits in mountainous regions is quite a different case. These ordinarily derive from geological activities that antedate the historical period by millions of years. There is absolutely no evidence of major climatic or geological changes in the Sinai Peninsula or the Red Sea within the historical period.

Thus, one may safely assume that papyrus did not grow in the Red Sea in biblical times. Papyrus grows in fresh water. The Red Sea has a higher saline content than the ocean itself, because a narrow southern channel restricts ocean currents that might otherwise dilute the saline concentration caused by rapid evaporation from the high winds and extreme temperatures in that region. *BAR* 10:6 (1984), p. 14

Dwight Sullivan of Bisbee, Arizona, takes issue with Batto's summary rejection of the supernatural:

Bernard Batto states: "The Exodus narrative should not be read as a historical account of what actually transpired in those days," and "The significance of those original symbols, so meaningful when first written, has been lost in our modern scientific and technological world."

This presents something perplexing to me. I admire the archaeologists' quest for the truth and their attempts to seek "what actually transpired in those days." But it is unsettling to realize that one of the assumptions in the method to establish fact, a method based on principles of scientific research, is that the supernatural is ruled out as a possible explanation. The very basis of proof for establishing "what really happened" has this unproven assumption in it. Isn't this a blind spot in the archaeologist's world view, possibly limiting his or her openness? If there were supernatural phenomena, then how would the archaeologist by his criteria of reality and proof be able to detect it? In other words, if there were a miracle with Moses crossing the Red Sea, then how could the archaeologist ever interpret the event other than as symbolic, mythical or traditional? *BAR* 10:6 (1984), p. 10

George L. Faull of Fort Wayne, Indiana, raises a similar objection:

How can any ancient historian tell of a miracle without "post-Enlightenment scholars" making the story part of a myth of the neighboring pagans? Such foolishness does not deserve the name of scholarship.

Does Mr. Batto think there is any connection between the Parable of the Lost Sheep and Little Bo Peep who lost her sheep? Could there be a connection between the Genesis story of Eve being tempted to eat the forbidden fruit and Little Miss Muffet? Is it possible the serpent in the JEPD account has become a spider in the M.G. (Mother Goose) account? Then again, is it possible that

Paul referred to the story of the three little pigs when he spoke of men building on wood, hay and stubble? Perhaps if we saw "the significance of these original symbols, so meaningful when first given," we would better understand in this "modern scientific and technological age" what the scriptures mean. *BAR* 10:6 (1984), p. 10

But Edward Rosenberry of Newark, Delaware, finds some valuable insights in Batto's argument:

Bernard Batto makes a strong case. Whether or not his hypothetical derivation of *suph* (*soph*, end) is correct, the view that some contexts call for a symbolic rather than a geographical reading is highly persuasive. The prayer of Jonah cited in confirmation certainly derives more force from a sea felt to be associated with ultimate annihilation than from one improbably and irrelevantly clogged with weeds.

The association of *suph* with Sheol and Abyss in the Jonah passage, and especially with the speaker's anguished sense of being cast out of the presence of God, suggests a collateral confirmation overlooked by Mr. Batto—namely that Jonah's secret destination in taking flight from the Lord was Tarshish. Though the name of Tarshish is freighted with symbolic values in its approximately 20 occurrences in the Old Testament—a kind of Shangri La of the maritime world—it has never been shown to have had any physical existence. Even if one accepts its occasional conjectural identification with Tartessos, near the Strait of Gibraltar, Tarshish remains essentially symbolic, a place of fabulous promise in a terminally remote location.

The conjunction of Jonah's mythical goal with his expressed sense of the sea as a moral or metaphysical wilderness lends considerable credibility to the idea of *yam suph* as a place that exists at least as much in the mind as on the map. *BAR* 10:6 (1984), p. 12

Modern Translations

Facing problems in every verse and contro-
versy at every turn, a Bible translator faces
a daunting prospect. The following reviews
of some recent translations illustrate just
how daunting.

CHAPTER 26

The New King James Version

William Griffin

In 1975, Thomas Nelson Publishers undertook a revision of the King James Version, apparently to counterbalance the more radical modern translations. Staff members were required to affirm their belief that "the Scriptures were the uniquely inspired Word of God, free from error...." William Griffin finds that the resulting New King James Version is both easy to read and true to the "rhythms, meaning and beauty" of the 1611 original. He likes the addition of quotation marks, the modernized punctuation and the simplified syntax. He is not as happy with the retention of italics to indicate words omitted in idiomatic Hebrew–for example, the verb to be–because to the modern reader, italics imply emphasis, not omission, and therefore convey the wrong meaning.–Ed.

The venerable King James Version of the Bible has not been revised since 1769. This year (1982), Thomas Nelson Publishers managed to bring the King James Version into the 20th century without sacrificing the beloved cadences and familiar archaic language.

The King James Version of the Bible, originally published in 1611, eventually became the official Bible of Protestants and was praised by Catholics and non-Christians as well. The KJV was accurate for its time; it was intelligible; and when read aloud, it was lyrical and majestic.

The KJV translation has aged slowly and gracefully. Between 1611 and 1769, the original underwent four major revisions (and hundreds of minor revisions). An anonymous editor at Cambridge University updated it in 1629. Cambridge scholars produced two more versions—one by John Bois in 1638 and one by Thomas Paris in 1762. The current edition is Benjamin Blainey's revision of 1769, which was produced at Oxford University. Religious authorities in Great Britain designated the 1769 version "official," and although hundreds of other Bibles have since been produced, the King James Version has remained dominant through the centuries.

In 1975, the plethora of Bibles being generated by modern publishing houses prompted Thomas Nelson Publishers to undertake a revision of the King James Version. A team of more than 130 Bible scholars was assembled. All of them were Christian, and all were required to sign statements declaring their belief that "the Scriptures were the uniquely inspired Word of God, free from error in the original autographs." The Old Testament was under the general editorship first of William White, then of James Price, both of Dropsie University in Philadelphia. The New Testament was under the general editorship of Arthur Farstad of Dallas Theological Seminary.

Each scholar submitted his translation of a book of the Bible to the executive editor of his testament, who, in turn, submitted it to Rev. William H. McDowell, professor of philosophy and religion at Florida Southern College. McDowell checked the book for grammatical accuracy, literary style and effective communication and passed it on to the oversight committees, which perused the translations afresh.

Meetings were held. Differences were debated. If a consensus could not be reached, the majority vote carried. The goal was to achieve equivalence with the King James Version, and the changes are very much of the common-sense variety.

• The clutter of punctuation is reduced; there are fewer colons and semicolons.
• Archaic verbs and pronouns have been modernized; *showeth* has become *show*; *thee* and *thou* now read *you*.
• Pronouns referring to God, which were not capitalized in the original King James Version, have been capitalized.
• Modern 20th-century words have replaced 17th-century words when the original meaning has changed; *naughtiness* in James 1:21 now reads *wickedness*.
• Very long sentences have been broken up.
• Quotation marks have been added to indicate more easily who is speaking and precisely what is being said.
• Some 17th-century nouns that have acquired theological significance, like *atonement* and *righteousness*, have been retained.
• Footnotes have been added to indicate variant readings.

In the 19th and 20th centuries, a significant number of ancient manuscripts of the Bible (some among the Dead Sea Scrolls) have been discovered. After studying these manuscripts, some recent revisers decided to remove certain words and phrases from the scriptures. The Nelson scholars, however, decided not to incorporate any changes in the text based on these manuscripts; instead, the publisher decided that "in those few places where the majority of the manuscripts did not support a word or phrase, that fact could best be indicated in a footnote....It was the editors' conviction that the use of footnotes would encourage further inquiry by readers."

"It was like keeping three balls in the air at the same time," said Farstad, who was a member of the executive committees of both testaments. "It was like juggling biblical Hebrew and Greek, the English of the King James Version and contemporary English."

After seven years of exhaustive biblical research and linguistic study, Nelson's Bible was published. It is both easy to read and preserves the rhythms, meaning and beauty of the original 1611 version.

One distracting aspect of the original King James Version has, unfortunately, been retained; words for which there is no Hebrew equivalent are set in italics—for example, the verb *to be*, which is often omitted in Hebrew (although it is understood in context). This unnecessary italicization tends to emphasize these words, which was not the intention of the original authors and is confusing to the modern reader.

Portions of this article are reprinted with permission from Publishers Weekly *(August 20, 1982).*

CHAPTER 27

The Torah, The Prophets *and* The Writings:
A New Jewish Translation

Marc Brettler

Marc Brettler offers a short course in translation theory in his review of the New Jewish Publication Society version. He notes that because this edition ("the first Bible translation executed by a panel of Jewish scholars since the Septuagint") relies on the Masoretic text rather than combining ancient witnesses, the resultant translation is not an eclectic text, "which might never have existed," like the New English Bible. He also prefers the New Jewish Publication Society translation to the New English Bible because the compilers attempted to find one-to-one correspondences between Hebrew and English words.–Ed.

The publication of the third section of the Hebrew Bible, *The Writings*, marks the completion of the New Jewish Publication Society Bible translation, abbreviated NJPS. This is the first Bible translation by a panel of Jewish scholars since the Septuagint, the Greek translation of the Bible was completed in Alexandria, Egypt, two millennia ago.

Like the Septuagint, the new translation was done at different times by various scholars: *The Torah* (the five books of Moses) was published first in 1963; *The Five Megilloth and Jonah*[1] in 1969; *The Prophets* in 1978; and *The Writings* in 1982.

Because each volume represents the point of view of one committee or individual, it is impossible to speak of "the" NJPS translation as one work. *The Torah* bears the stamp largely of Harry M. Orlinsky, who prepared the original draft of the translation for the committee (Orlinsky himself, E. A. Speiser and H. L. Ginsberg). *The Prophets* reflects the influence of Ginsberg. *The Writings* was completed by an entirely different committee, including *BAR* Advisory Board members Jonas Greenfield and Nahum Sarna. The third member of the committee for *The Writings* was Moshe Greenberg.

Unlike the earlier volumes, *The Writings* does not bear the stamp of any one individual.

Any translation of an ancient work is a major undertaking. The translator must attempt to enter the mind of the original author and sense the environment in which he or she worked. The translator must master ancient languages and styles. Finally, he or she must transfer his or her understanding of an ancient culture into a modern language, which is necessarily culturally foreign to the original.

Translating the Hebrew Bible has unique problems. First, it is not clear which text should be used as the basis for translation. The first complete, vocalized Hebrew Bible texts date from the early 11th century C.E. This is between 13 and 22 centuries later than the original Hebrew text. The complete vocalized Hebrew Bibles from the 11th century and later, which are relatively uniform, are called Masoretic texts after the Masoretes, Jewish scribes and scholars who flourished in the second part of the first millennium. Masoretes preserved the reading traditions of the consonantal Hebrew text current in their own communities by inserting vowel points, accent marks and cantillation notes to indicate proper liturgical reading.

The tradition preserved in the Masoretic text, abbreviated MT by scholars, is not, however, the only extant textual tradition of the Bible. The Dead Sea Scrolls, which date from the late third century B.C.E. to the first century C.E., preserve many passages that differ from the MT. The early translations of the Bible into Greek, Latin, Aramaic and Syriac, completed in the late centuries B.C.E. and the early centuries C.E., also differ from the MT sometimes. Some early rabbinic Midrashim (expositions of the biblical text) cite Hebrew texts that also differ from the MT.

Although the MT is the earliest complete vocalized Hebrew text of the Bible incorporating the efforts of Jewish scholars to preserve the correct reading tradition of their sacred text, it does contain some inaccuracies. Better readings have been found in the Dead Sea Scrolls or in ancient translations. This presents the Bible translator with a fundamental problem. For every single verse, he must decide which text—the Masoretic text, the Dead Sea Scroll text or the text of an ancient translation—he should use as the basis for his translation and interpretation.

The New Jewish Publication Society translation is based on the MT, which is the Jewish *textus receptus*. The implications of this decision can best be appreciated by comparing the NJPS to, for example, the New English Bible (NEB), which was completed under the guidance of the late British Semitist, Sir Godfrey Driver. Psalm 116:8, for example, reads in the NJPS, "You (God) have delivered me from death, my eyes from tears, my feet from stumbling." This is a straightforward rendition of the Hebrew MT. The NEB translation, however, reads: "He has rescued me from death, and my feet from stumbling." This translation is based partly on the Greek Septuagint. Where the MT reads "You," the Septuagint reads "He." In this respect, the NEB follows the Septuagint. The NEB also relies on the Peshitta, a Syriac (Aramaic) translation, in which the phrase "my eyes from tears" is omitted. No one knows for sure if these variants in the ancient translations originated with the translators from Hebrew to Greek or Syriac, or if one or another translation was based on an older Hebrew manuscript. Furthermore, even if we could prove that the Hebrew text used by the ancient translators was different from the MT, should we assume that text is superior to the MT? Such issues are difficult, if not impossible, to resolve, and no standard procedure—either steadfast adherence to the MT or consistent use of divergent ancient translations or the Dead Sea Scrolls—is sound. Every variant presents the translator with new problems.

In many cases, scholars have determined that the MT cannot be original; another ancient version may preserve a correct text, or a sound alternate reading may be reconstructed by conjectural emendation. Nevertheless, the NJPS translators decided to translate one Hebrew text, the MT, rather than combining ancient texts to create an eclectic original text (Ur-text), which might never have existed. In the NJPS, there are no conflate texts like the NEB translation of Psalm 116, which is based one-third on the Hebrew text, one-third on the Greek translation and one-third on the Syriac translation.

Despite their decision to adhere to the MT, however, there are several places where NJPS translators did not do so; this is particularly apparent in *The Prophets*, where changes to the MT are indicated by notes, such as "emendation yields...," or "so 1QIs[a] [the large Isaiah scroll found near the Dead Sea]," or "these words are supplied in some of the ancient versions." Thus, the reader is told that the ancient version presents a "better" reading than the MT, and he or she may decide if the editors' opinion is correct. For example, Ezekiel 3:12, an important text in the liturgy, is translated, "Blessed is the presence of the LORD in His place." The careful reader, however, will note that this phrase is contextually odd and syntactically difficult. Thus, a note indicates, "Emendation yields: 'as the Presence of the LORD rose from where it stood.'" "This emendation is plausible because it explains all of the difficulties in the verse and involves only one change in the MT text—the word *brwk* (blessed) is changed to *brwm* (as...rose), based on the assumption that an ancient *m* (ﬦ) could have been accidentally changed to the graphically similar *k* (ﬧ).

Although this change is very likely, the editors have nevertheless refrained from inserting it into the text. Instead, they have rendered us a double favor—they have given us a translation of the text as it exists in the MT and have indicated the more likely text in a note.

Another difficulty in translating the Hebrew Bible, perhaps the most serious problem of all, is understanding the meaning of the original text. The New Testament was written in Koiné Greek, which is known from many contemporaneous inscriptions, but there are few contemporaneous Hebrew inscriptions outside the Bible. Thus, the main sources for determining the meaning of a word in the Hebrew Bible are occurrences elsewhere in the Bible and occurrences in related Semitic languages such as Akkadian, Ugaritic or Arabic. Methodological difficulties abound, because defining a biblical word by its use in the Bible may result in circular reasoning, and defining a word by its use in a related language may give the Hebrew word a meaning it never had. Imagine trying to interpret the sentence "Read this book" if the only way to reconstruct the meaning of *read* was to compare it to the etymologically related German word *raten* (to advise)!

The Bible is also difficult to translate because many passages are recognized as literary masterpieces. A translator must thus attempt to recreate the beauty of the original. Early volumes of the NJPS were praised for clarity of expression and literary beauty. This is certainly true also in *The Writings*, where the editors have been particularly careful to use particular English words for each Hebrew word whenever possible. This one-to-one correspondence allows much of the structure of the original text, which is often based on subtle repetitions of words or roots, to shine through. For example, in Psalm 121, the psalmist expresses his belief in God's perpetual watchfulness, and therefore helpfulness, through a six-fold repetition of the root *šmr* (keep, guard), through the repetition of *yanum* (slumber) in consecutive verses and by repetition of God's name (YHWH) in the proclamation ending the psalm. Any attempt to convey the power, and thus the full meaning, of the original must reflect this structure.

All of these repetitions are reflected in NJPS. But in NEB, although the root *šmr* is translated "guard" or "guardian," *yanum* is translated "sleep" in verse 3 and "slumber" in verse 4. Thus, the reader of this translation would not realize that verse 4 picks up on the idea of verse 3, emphasizing and expanding it. The Revised Standard Version (RSV) translates each of these terms consistently but uses the weak "keep/keeper" to render *šmr*. Certainly, "guardian," as in "the LORD is your guardian," which is used in NJPS and many other translations, more accurately captures the strength of the Hebrew *šmr* than "The LORD is your keeper." Finally, the Jerusalem Bible does not capture the power of the final proclamation because the repetition of YHWH is rendered "He." (Perhaps the Jerusalem Bible deviates from the traditional Hebrew text; if so, this is not noted and is methodologically unsound in this instance.) Thus, NJPS comes closest to capturing the power and eloquence of the original psalm, both by a consistent rendering of the patterns of the Hebrew and by careful selection of appropriate translation equivalents.

In the NJPS translation, this one-to-one correspondence between English and Hebrew terms extends beyond individual psalms or chapters, sometimes to entire books and sometimes to the entire Hebrew Bible. But occasional mistakes are inevitable. In Proverbs 7:27, the wiles of dangerous "alien women" are described. In their zeal to be picturesque, the NJPS translators tell us that "Her house is a highway to Sheol." The Hebrew word rendered "highway" is *derek*. But *derek* is translated as "way" two verses earlier. Thus, the editors have inadvertently broken the literary connection between verses 25 and 27. Similarly, for no obvious reason, *kəsil*, always translated "dullard" in Proverbs, is rendered "the foolish" in Psalm 49:10. Such inconsistencies are more common between the volumes edited by different committees. *Ma'al baḥerem* is

---

Psalm 121—Four Translations

I turn my eyes to the mountains;
  from where will my help come?
My help comes from the LORD,
  maker of heaven and earth.
He will not let your foot give way;
  your guardian will not slumber.
See, the guardian of Israel
  neither slumbers nor sleeps!
The LORD is your guardian,
  the LORD is your protection
at your right hand.
By day the sun will not strike you,
  nor the moon by night.
The LORD will guard you from
  all harm;
  He will guard your life.
The LORD will guard your going
  and coming
  now and forever.

      **New Jewish
      Publication Society
      Version (NJPS)**

If I lift up my eyes to the hills,
  where shall I find help?
Help comes only from the LORD,
  maker of heaven and earth.
How could he let your foot stumble?
  How could he, your guardian, sleep?
The guardian of Israel
  never slumbers, never sleeps.
The LORD is your guardian,
  your defence at your right hand;
The sun will not strike you by day
  nor the moon by night.
The LORD will guard you against
  all evil;
  he will guard you, body and soul.
The LORD will guard your going and
  your coming,
  now and for evermore.

      **New English Bible
      (NEB)**

I lift my eyes to the mountains;
  where is help to come from?
Help comes to me from Yahweh,
  who made heaven and earth.
No letting our footsteps slip!
  This guard of yours, he does not doze!
The guardian of Israel
  does not doze or sleep.
Yahweh guards you, shades you.
  With Yahweh at your right hand
Sun cannot strike you down by day,
  nor moon at night.
Yahweh guards you from harm,
  he guards your lives,
He guards your leaving, coming back,
  now and for always.

      Jerusalem Bible (JB)

I lift up my eyes to the hills.
  From whence does my help come?
My help comes from the LORD,
  who made heaven and earth.
He will not let your foot be moved,
  he who keeps you will not slumber.
Behold, he who keeps Israel
  will neither slumber nor sleep.
The LORD is your keeper;
  the LORD is your shade
  on your right hand.
The sun shall not smite you by day,
  nor the moon by night.
The LORD will keep you from all evil;
  he will keep your life.
The LORD will keep
  your going out and your coming in
  from this time forth and for evermore.

      **Revised Standard
      Version (RSV)**

translated "proscription" in Joshua 22:20 and "committed a trespass against the proscribed thing" in 1 Chronicles 2:7. These inconsistencies may eventually be corrected.

We have mentioned the difficulty of determining the correct meaning of ancient Hebrew words. The NJPS editors make judicious use of comparative Semitics for this purpose. After carefully weighing the many innovative suggestions for new meanings of Hebrew words and roots based on ancient and modern Semitic languages, the editors often opted to retain the traditional meanings. This contrasts sharply with the NEB, which makes free use of cognate languages, even when it is unlikely that a Hebrew word has the same meaning as an equivalent Semitic word or when an innovative suggestion is contextually impossible.

I will give only one example to illustrate how the NJPS uses comparative linguistics to elucidate a biblical text. The difficult word *mimsak* appears twice in the Bible, in Isaiah 65:11 and in Proverbs 23:30. Neither context is specific enough to define the word. The derivation is traditionally understood as the root *msk* (to mix); *mimsak* then means "mixed/spiced/well-blended wine." In NJPS, however, the word is translated "the cups." This likely rendering is based in part on a Ugaritic tablet, which includes a list of vessels. *Mmsk* is listed immediately after *spl* (a bowl), suggesting that they might be related items. In Isaiah 65:11, the *mimsak* is being "filled"; thus a vessel, such as a cup, seems a more appropriate translation than a mixed drink. In Proverbs 23:30, excessive drinkers are depicted as "investigating" or "probing" a *mimsak*. Here too, a vessel whose bottom is being searched as the contents are drained is appropriate. Thus the NJPS translates Proverbs 23:30: "Those whom wine keeps till the small hours. Those who gather to drain the cups." This translation, which does not appear in other major English translations, probably comes closest to the original Hebrew.

Many new translations in the NJPS are based on (re)discoveries of what Hebrew words mean through internal Hebrew linguistics rather than new relationships between Hebrew words and Semitic relatives. This is unique to the NJPS and was fostered by constant consultation of medieval Jewish commentaries. Medieval commentators, working without concordances, had unrivaled mastery of the text and often saw interrelationships between Hebrew words in different places in the Bible that have eluded modern scholars. In Job 18:12, Job's "friend" Bildad describes the evildoer. RSV translates the difficult Hebrew into nearly unintelligible English: "His strength (*'on*) is hunger-bitten, and calamity is ready for his standing (*ṣelaʿ*)." NEB translates, "For all his vigor (*'on*), he is paralyzed with fear; strong as he is, disaster awaits him (*ṣelaʿ*)." This is certainly a clear image, but it has little relation to the extant Hebrew text as traditionally understood using classical Hebrew grammar. NJPS translates, "His progeny (*'on*) hunger, disaster awaits his wife (*ṣelaʿ*)." This translation is based largely on the Aramaic Targum, an early Jewish translation of the Bible with a long and complex history, and on the commentaries of Rashi, the noted 11th-century Jewish French exegete. The Targum and Rashi must have sensitized the translators to texts such as Psalm 78:51 and 105:36, where 'on is parallel to "firstborn" and thus may connote "progeny," and to Genesis 2, where a ṣela', literally a "rib," is used in the description of the creation of the first woman. This is one of many cases in the NJPS where the translators have sifted through a vast body of Jewish exegesis to rediscover translations often different from, and superior to, the standard translations.

The preceding comments have suggested how difficult, and often subjective, translating the Bible can be. A final virtue of the NJPS is the frequent acknowledgment of these difficulties. Instead of indicating that a text is obscure or difficult, many modern translators guess at meaning without indicating that the translation is a guess. In the NJPS, "Meaning of Hebrew uncertain" appears frequently. Such notes may enclose one or two words, a chapter, such as Psalm 68 ("The coherence of this psalm and the meaning of many of its passages are uncertain"), or the entire poetic section of Job. These notes remind the reader of the many difficulties of translating the Hebrew Bible and should caution him or her against drawing far-reaching historical or theological conclusions from certain difficult texts.

The best way to convey the qualities of the NJPS translation is to compare a passage from this translation to three commonly used translations (see p. 313). I have chosen Psalm 121 for comparison because it is both beautiful and well known. Readers who know Hebrew are encouraged to compare the translations to the original, to see how the NJPS most closely approaches the Hebrew meaning. A careful comparison reveals substantial differences among the translations and suggests that the NJPS is the most precise and elegant rendering of the Hebrew text.

Literary style, philological precision and humility about our ability to understand the Bible make the NJPS translation invaluable for both casual Bible readers and serious Bible students. I hope the contradictions and inaccuracies in the three separate volumes of *The Torah*, *The Prophets* and *The Writings* will be resolved, and that the Jewish Publication Society will soon publish a one-volume English edition for lay readers and a Hebrew-English edition for students of the Hebrew Bible.[2]

A F T E R W O R D

Adam Mikaya of Washington, D.C., notes a number of places where the New Jewish Publication Society translation does not use one-to-one correspondences between Hebrew and English words:

The Hebrew word *ulam* is a part of Solomon's temple. In 1 Kings 6:3, it is translated "portico"; in 1 Chronicles 28:11 and 2 Chronicles 3:4, it is translated "porch."

The *debir* was the Holy of Holies in Solomon's temple. *Debir* is translated "shrine" in 1 Kings 6; it is translated "inner sanctuary" in 2 Chronicles 3:16 and 5:7. (To make matters more confusing, *kodesh* is translated "sanctuary" in 2 Chronicles 5:11.)

In 1 Kings 6:27, *bayit* is translated "chamber"; elsewhere in the same chapter, it is translated "house."

In 1 Kings 6:36, *hatzar* is translated "enclosure." In 1 Kings 7:12, the same word referring to the very same place is translated "court," as in courtyard....

Finally, in Genesis 15:18, God makes a "covenant" (*brit*) with Abraham; in Genesis 21:27, Abraham and Abimelech make a "pact" (*brit*); and in 1 Kings 5:26 (5:12 in other English translations), Solomon and Hiram make a "treaty" (*brit*)–three English words for the same Hebrew word. This is not the end, however; in Deuteronomy 7:2, the Israelites are told to grant the Canaanites and others no "terms" (*brit*, again), so this is a fourth English word for the same Hebrew word. **BAR** *9:2 (1983), p. 24*

Brettler responds:

Mr. Mikaya's sharp eyes have caught some of the many inconsistencies that often detract from the high quality of the NJPS translation. Certain inconsistencies within the translation are desirable, however, and should not be "corrected." I will use Mr. Mikaya's examples to illustrate where the translators have improperly or properly rendered the same Hebrew word with two or more English equivalents.

The difference in translation of the same word in parallel passages in Kings and Chronicles is irksome. I can only point out that the two books, which belong to different segments of the Jewish canon, were translated by two different committees. The *Writings* committee occasionally "corrects" inaccurate or inelegant renderings by the earlier *Prophets* committee. This explains many of the inconsistencies cited by Mr. Mikaya....

On the other hand, differences in translation for the same Hebrew word are often unavoidable and are sometimes even desirable, because similar words in different languages cover different semantic ranges. Thus, the Hebrew word *brit* is used in the Bible for agreements between kings, agreements between commoners and agreements between individuals and God. No one English word can cover all of these uses without sounding awkward. Thus, the variety of translations for *brit* in NJPS is not only excusable, but also desirable. Between God and a person, a *brit* is a covenant; between rulers, it is a treaty; between two people, it is a pact. **BAR** *9:2 (1983), p. 24*

P. J. Rosenbloom of Bloomington, Minnesota, believes the NJPS translation is not the first modern translation by a Jewish committee working from the Hebrew:

In fact, in 1908 the Jewish Publication Society had decided, together with the Central Conference of American Rabbis, to "cooperate in bringing out the new translation." Instead of trying to harmonize the translations of individual contributors, the work was to be done by a board of editors. This board as finally constituted had seven members—Dr. Solomon Schechter, Dr. Cyrus Adler, Dr. Joseph Jacobs, Dr. Kaufman Kohler, Dr. David Philipson, Dr. Samuel Schulman and Professor Max Margolis. There was equal representation of the Jewish Theological Seminary of America, the Hebrew Union College of Cincinnati and Dropsie College for Hebrew and Cognate Learning in Philadelphia. For one year, Professor Isaac Friedlander was a member of the board instead of Schechter.

In addition to these distinguished men, a subcommittee reviewed all other known translations in various countries since the Septuagint. These translations, made by individual experts in their respective fields, were taken into account. Due weight was given to the Septuagint and other ancient versions. Non-Jewish authorities were consulted as well.

The new translation may be—and undoubtedly is—in many ways superior to the translation completed in 1915 and finally published in 1917. But the 1917 publication is also one in which we can take a great deal of pride. **BAR** *9:2 (1983), p. 24*

Brettler replies:

The 1917 Jewish Publication Society translation was a landmark work incorporating many keen insights of the late Professor Max Margolis, who was noted for scholarship relating to the biblical text and the versions. Despite its claims, however, this translation was not an *independent* translation by a committee working from the Hebrew text. Harry Orlinsky comments in his *Notes on the New Translation of the Torah*,[1] "For, in truth, that version [the 1917 JPS] was essentially but a modest revision of the Revised Version of 1885, a revision that was only a small percentage of the whole." Thus, my contention is accurate that NJPS is the first modern translation by a Jewish committee made directly from the Hebrew text. **BAR** *9:2 (1983), p. 26*

In the Beginning,[2] *an innovative translation of Genesis by Everett Fox, elicited these comments from Brettler:*

This new translation and concise commentary are unique among English Bible translations. Fox's orientation derives from an extensive study of the Buber-Rosenzweig translation, which was begun by these two Jewish thinkers in 1925 and completed by Buber in 1962 (Rosenzweig died in 1929). The underlying assumption of the Buber-Rosenzweig translation was that the Bible was originally oral literature and was intended to be read aloud. This assumption led to three corollaries: (1) the text should be printed in lines that reflect oral recitation; (2) the ancients were acutely aware of the connections between names and similar sounding words in the surrounding narrative, and this must be reflected in the translation; (3) *Leitwörter*, leading words, that recur throughout a book or unit, should be translated with the same word to retain the ties between the various contexts.

Fox's unique translation is based on these principles. *In the Beginning* is, in Fox's words, a translation "in the Buber-Rosenzweig tradition."

Setting verses into poetic lines or cola (singular, colon) increases the impact on the reader or listener. For example, God's command that Abraham sacrifice Isaac in Genesis 22:1-2 is generally printed in prose; thus, the action proceeds too quickly for the emotional impact of the momentous command to be appreciated. Fox renders these lines:

> Now after these events it was
> that God tested Avraham
> and said to him:
> "Avraham!"
> He said,
> "Here I am."
> He said:
> "Pray take your son
> your only-one,
> whom you love,
> Yitzhak
> and go-you-forth..."

In verse two, Fox captures the likely tension in Abraham's mind when God initially withholds the name of the sacrificial victim. Rashi, the 11th-century Jewish French Bible exegete, cites a Midrash that captures this feeling: "Your son." He (Abraham) said, "I have two sons." "Your only-one." He (Abraham) said, "Each one is his mother's only son." (God) said, "Whom you love." He (Abraham) replied, "I love them both." Then he (God) said, "Yitzhak (Isaac)."

The buildup to the name Isaac is lost in many translations; the New English Bible, for example, renders, "Take your son Isaac, your only son, whom you love...."

Fox's rendition of the entire Hebrew text in one form, not distinguishing between poetry and prose, is appropriate because the traditional Hebrew text rarely distinguishes between poetry and prose, and, in fact, there was probably no classification of literature into these two mutually exclusive categories in ancient Israel.

The connection between names and narrative is reflected in Abigail's comment to David about her churlish husband, Nabal (1 Samuel 25:25): "For he is exactly like his name; his name is Nabal (churl) and churlishness is his style." Fox brings out such connections by translating names like Jacob as "Yaakov/Heel-Holder" (Genesis 25:26) and then translating 27:36 as "Is that why his name is called Yaakov/Heel Sneak? For he has now sneaked against me twice." In this rendition, the connections between Hebrew *akev* (heel), which Yaakov (Jacob) grasped at birth (Genesis 25:26), and Jacob's nature—or shall I say fate—as a sneak (*vayaakveni*) (Genesis 27:37) are made as explicit in English as they are in Hebrew. In other translations, such folk etymologies are usually relegated to notes, and the immediacy of the connections is often lost.

Repetition of words within units or between units is an important characteristic of biblical narrative. For example, the words *lek leka* (go you forth) frame God's commands to Abraham; they are used in Genesis 12:1, where God tells Abraham to leave for Canaan, and in Genesis 22:2, where God tells him to offer up Isaac. This phrase is found nowhere else in Genesis, and the repetition is an intentional narrative device to frame God's trials of Abraham. Fox's translation is the only one that encourages the reader to notice this framing device.

Significant word repetitions within one unit can be illustrated from Genesis 11:1-9, the story of the Tower of Babel, where Fox faithfully reflects these recurrences. In their excitement to build a tower, "lest we be scattered over the face of all the earth!" the builders say "come now" twice (11:3-4), and God counters with the words "come now" (11:7) when he forces the project to a halt. In another instance, the people express their fear of being scattered upon the face of the earth (11:4), and four verses later God punishes them with what they feared, "So YHWH scattered them." By reflecting the Hebrew text precisely, Fox picks up messages expressed through structure and literary repetitions....

Any project of this kind is bound to have some awkward or inconsistent renderings. I do not understand how Noah's ark (8:4) "came to rest...on the seventh day of the New-Moon" (translate month) or how (4:12) "soil...give[s] strength" (translate produce). Furthermore, the underlying contention of Buber, Rosenzweig and Fox that the whole Bible is oral and was originally spoken is not entirely convincing. Still, this translation and short commentary are a pleasure to read, whether alone, with the Hebrew text, or in conjunction with longer commentaries or other translations. It is the best translation available for reading aloud and for appreciating the structure of the Hebrew text.
BR *1:2 (1985), p. 8*

Authors

HARVEY MINKOFF, editor, is professor of linguistics at Hunter College in New York City and the author of nine books, including *Visions and Revisions* (Prentice-Hall, 1990) and *Exploring America: Perspectives on Critical Issues* (Harcourt Brace, forthcoming). Minkoff works in many languages, including French, Spanish, Hebrew, Latin, Yiddish and Aramaic.

DAVID E. AUNE, professor of theology at Loyola University in Chicago, is the author or editor of many books, including *The New Testament in Its Literary Environment* (Westminster Press, 1987) and *Hellenistic Culture and the New Testament* (Anchor Bible Reference Library, forthcoming).

BERNARD F. BATTO is associate professor of Old Testament at DePauw University in Indiana and Old Testament book review editor of *Catholic Biblical Quarterly*. Batto excavated Tell Halif (Lahav) and is the author of *Slaying the Dragon: Mythmaking in the Biblical Tradition* (Westminster/John Knox Press, 1992) and many other books and articles.

JOSEPH BLENKINSOPP is John A. O'Brien Professor of Biblical Studies at Notre Dame University. He coordinated excavations at the Greek Orthodox site at Capernaum on the Sea of Galilee in the 1980s and is the author of many articles and books, including "The Prophetic Literature" in *Harper Bible Commentary* (Harper & Row, 1988) and *Ezekiel: A Commentary* (John Knox Press, 1989).

MARCUS J. BORG is Hundere Distinguished Professor of Religion and Culture at Oregon State University, past chair of the Historical Jesus Section of the Society of Biblical Literature and a Fellow of the Jesus Seminar. Borg is the author of several books, including *Meeting Jesus Again for the First Time* (HarperSanFrancisco, 1994) and *Jesus in Contemporary Scholarship* (Trinity Press International, forthcoming).

JAMES BRASHLER has been dean of the Ecumenical Institute at Saint Mary's Seminary in Baltimore, Maryland, since 1984. Brashler is known for his work on the cultural context of earliest Christianity and Second Temple Jerusalem and was a member of the team that translated the Nag Hammadi Codices. His translation of the Coptic Apocalypse of Peter will appear in the critical edition of Nag Hammadi Codex VII, edited by Birger Pearson (Brill, forthcoming).

MARC BRETTLER is associate professor of Near East and Judaic studies at Brandeis University. He specializes in biblical historiography, medieval Jewish biblical interpretation and literary study of the Bible. Brettler contributed some 20 articles to the *Anchor Bible Dictionary* and *Harper's Bible Dictionary*. Most recently, he co-edited *Minhah le-Nahum: Biblical and Other Studies Presented to Nahum M. Sarna in Honour of his 70th Birthday*, Journal for the Study of the Old Testament Supplement 154 (Sheffield, 1993).

FRANK MOORE CROSS was the Hancock Professor of Hebrew and Other Oriental Languages at Harvard University from 1958 to 1992, when he retired. One of the leading Bible scholars in the world, Cross was a member of the original team of scholars that deciphered the Dead Sea Scrolls. A past president of both the Society of Biblical Literature and American Schools of Oriental Research, Cross has written many books and articles, including *The Ancient Library at Qumran and Modern Biblical Studies* (rev. ed., Baker Book House, 1980).

ALAN D. CROWN is head of the department of Semitic studies at Sydney University and a leading authority on the Samaritan Pentateuch. His publications include *A Bibliography of the Samaritans* (Scarecrow, 1984) and *Biblical Studies Today* (Chevalier, 1975).

JOSEPH A. FITZMYER is professor emeritus of biblical studies at the Catholic University of America in Washington, D.C. He is the author of *Responses to 101 Questions on the Dead Sea Scrolls* (Paulist Press, 1992), *The Gospel According to Luke*, Anchor Bible 28, 28A (Doubleday, 1983) and *A Christological Catechism: New Testament Answers* (rev. ed., Paulist Press, 1991). Fitzmyer was a member of the original team of scholars who studied, translated and published the Dead Sea Scrolls.

DAVID NOEL FREEDMAN is Arthur F. Thurnau Professor of Biblical Studies at the University of Michigan and general editor of the Anchor Bible series. His many publications include *The Unity of the Hebrew Bible* (University of Michigan Press, 1991), *Pottery, Poetry, and Prophecy* (Eisenbrauns, 1981) and (with F.I. Andersen) *Hosea*, Anchor Bible 24 (Doubleday, 1980).

FREDERICK E. GREENSPAHN is professor of Judaic and religious studies at the Iliff School of Theology, University of Denver, author of *Hapax Legomena in*

Biblical Hebrew (Scholars Press, 1984) and editor of *Scripture in the Jewish and Christian Traditions: Authority, Interpretation, Relevance* (Abingdon Press, 1982).

LEONARD J. GREENSPOON is professor of religion at Clemson University. A scholar of biblical translations, Greenspoon is author of *Max Leopold Margolis: A Scholar's Scholar*, Biblical Scholars in North America 15 (Scholars Press, 1987) and many articles.

WILLIAM GRIFFIN is former religious editor for *Publishers Weekly* and a writer, editor, book reviewer and literary agent who lives in New Orleans, Louisiana.

DARRELL HANNAH has a Masters of Divinity from Southern Baptist Theological Seminary in Louisville, Kentucky, and a Masters of Theology in New Testament textual criticism from Regent College in Vancouver, British Columbia. Hannah is now a Ph.D. candidate in the Department of Theology at Cambridge University Divinity School.

ROY W. HOOVER is Weyerhaeuser Professor of Biblical Literature and professor of religion at Whitman College in Walla Walla, Washington. Hoover is co-editor (with Robert W. Funk) of *The Five Gospels: The Search for the Authentic Words of Jesus* (Polebridge Press, 1993) and *The Gospel of Luke*, Scholar's Bible Series (Polebridge Press, forthcoming).

GEORGE HOWARD is head of the department of religion at the University of Georgia and former president of the Society for Biblical Literature, Southeastern Region. Howard is author of *Paul: Crisis in Galatia. A Study in Early Christian Theology* (Cambridge University Press, 1990 [1979]) and translator of *The Teaching of Addai* (Scholars Press, 1981).

HELMUT KOESTER is John H. Morison Professor of New Testament and Winn Professor of Ecclesiastical History at the Harvard Divinity School. Among his many books are *Ancient Christian Gospels: Their History and Development* (SCM/Trinity International Press, 1992), the two-volume *Introduction to the New Testament* (de Gruyter, 1980; Fortress Press, 1982) and *Trajectories through Early Christianity* (Fortress Press, 1971).

P. KYLE McCARTER, JR., is William Foxwell Albright Professor of Biblical and Ancient Near Eastern Studies and acting chairman of the department of classics at Johns Hopkins University in Baltimore. A few of his recent publications are "The Mysterious Copper Scroll: Clues to a Hidden Treasure?" (*Bible Review* 8:4 [1992]) and "Canaan, Canaanites," "Canaan, Conquest of" and "High Place(s)" in *Oxford Companion to the Bible* (Oxford University Press, 1991).

STEPHEN J. PATTERSON has been assistant professor of New Testament studies at Eden Theological Seminary in Saint Louis since 1988. He is co-author (with John Kloppenborg, Marvin Meyer and Michael Steinhauser) of *The Q-Thomas Reader* (Polebridge Press, 1990) and author of *The Gospel of Thomas and Jesus* (Polebridge Press, 1993). He is also a contributing editor to *Bible Review.*

HERSHEL SHANKS is editor of *Biblical Archaeology Review* and *Bible Review* and president of the Biblical Archaeology Society. Shanks is the editor and author of many books, including *Understanding the Dead Sea Scrolls* (Random House, 1992) and *The Search for Jesus: Modern Scholarship Looks at the Gospels* (Biblical Archaelogy Society, 1994).

WILLIAM R. STEGNER is professor of New Testament at Garrett-Evangelical Theological Seminary in Evanston, Illinois. Stegner's particular interest is the Jewish background of the New Testament. His books include *Narrative Theology in Early Jewish Christianity* (Westminster/John Knox Press, 1989) and *An Introduction to the Parables* (University Press of America, 1977).

EMANUEL TOV is J. L. Magnes Professor of Bible at the Hebrew University in Jerusalem. He is one of the editors of the Hebrew University Bible Project and editor-in-chief of the Dead Sea Scrolls publication project. Among his many books are *Textual Criticism of the Hebrew Bible* (Fortress Press/Van Gorcum, 1992), *The Text-Critical Use of the Septuagint in Biblical Research*, Jerusalem Biblical Studies 3 (Simor Press, 1981) and *The Greek Minor Prophets Scroll from Naḥal Ḥever*, Discoveries in the Judaean Desert 8 (Clarendon Press, 1990).

Endnotes

A General Introduction
(pages xi-xii)

1. David Rosenberg, ed., *Congregation* (Orlando, FL: Harcourt Brace Jovanovich, 1987).

2. Frank Kermode, *The Genesis of Secrecy* (Cambridge, MA: Harvard University Press, 1979).

PART I
Overview
(pages 2-7)

1. Nahum Sarna, *Exploring Exodus* (New York: Schocken Books, 1986).

2. Joseph Blenkinsopp, "The Documentary Hypothesis in Trouble," *BR* 1:4 (1985). Reprinted on pp. 10-21 in this volume.

3. Hans-Georg Gadamer, *Truth and Method* (New York: Crossroad, 1982).

4. Charles A. Briggs, *General Introduction to the Study of Holy Scripture* (Grand Rapids: Baker Book House, 1970).

5. Richard Elliott Friedman, *The Creation of Sacred Literature* (Berkeley: University of California Press, 1981).

6. John Barton, *Reading the Old Testament* (Louisville: Westminster/John Knox Press, 1984).

7. Robert Alter and Frank Kermode, eds., *The Literary Guide to the Bible* (Cambridge, MA: Harvard University Press, 1987).

8. Brevard S. Childs, *Introduction to the Old Testament as Scripture* (Philadelphia: Fortress Press, 1979).

9. Childs, *The New Testament as Canon: An Introduction* (Philadelphia: Fortress Press, 1985).

10. Alter, *The Art of Biblical Narrative* (New York: Basic Books, 1981).

11. David Noel Freedman, *The Unity of the Hebrew Bible* (Ann Arbor: University of Michigan Press, 1991).

12. Isaac M. Kikawada and Arthur Quinn, *Before Abraham Was: The Unity of Genesis 1-11* (Nashville: Abingdon Press, 1985).

13. Helen Elsom, "The New Testament and Greco-Roman Writing" in Alter and Kermode, *Literary Guide*, pp. 561-578.

1. Blenkinsopp
(pages 10-21)

"The Documentary Hypothesis in Trouble" first appeared in **BR** Winter 1985.

1. Richard Simon, *Histoire critique du Vieux Testament* (Rotterdam: R. Leers, 1678; repr. of 1685 ed., Geneva: Slatkine Reprints, 1971).

2. Johann Gottfried Eichhorn, *Introduction to the Old Testament* (Leipzig: Weidmann, 1803).

3. Julius Wellhausen, *Prolegomena to the History of Israel* (Berlin: Georg Reimer, 1883; repr., Atlanta: Scholars Press, 1994).

4. Otto Eissfeldt, *The Old Testament: An Introduction*, trans. Ackroyd, 3d ed. (New York: Harper & Row, 1965).

Related Articles in *BR* and *BAR*
Harold Bloom, *The Book of J*, reviewed by Baruch Halpern, *BR* 7:1 (1991).

Richard Elliott Friedman, "Is Everybody a Bible Expert? Not the Authors of *The Book of J*," *BR* 7:2 (1991).

Hershel Shanks, "An Interview with David Noel Freedman, Part I: How the Hebrew Bible and the Christian Old Testament Differ," *BR* 9:6 (1993).

Shanks, "An Interview with David Noel Freedman, Part II: The Undiscovered Symmetry of the Bible," *BR* 10:1 (1994).

John Van Seters, *Prologue to History: The Yahwist as Historian in Genesis*, reviewed by Richard Elliott Friedman, *BR* 9:6 (1993).

James VanderKam, *In the Beginning: Creation and the Priestly History*, a review, *BR* 8:5 (1992).

2. McCarter
(pages 23-31)

"A New Challenge to the Documentary Hypothesis" first appeared in **BR** April 1988.

1. Isaac M. Kikawada and Arthur Quinn, *Before Abraham Was: The Unity of Genesis 1-11* (Nashville: Abingdon Press, 1985).

2. See Tikva Frymer-Kensky, "What the Babylonian Flood Stories Can and Cannot Teach Us about the Genesis Flood," *BAR* 4:4 (1978).

3. See Emanuel Tov, "The Saga of David and Goliath: How a Biblical Editor Combined Two Versions," *BR* 2:4 (1986). This article is reprinted on pp. 51-61 in this volume.

Related Articles in BR and BAR
Yohanan Aharoni, *Arad Inscriptions: Judean Desert Studies*, reviewed by P. Kyle McCarter, Jr., *BAR* 8:3 (1982).

Robert B. Coote and David Robert Ord, *In the Beginning: Creation and the Priestly History*, reviewed by James VanderKam, *BR* 8:5 (1992).

P. Kyle McCarter, Jr., "A Major New Introduction to the Bible," *BR* 2:2 (1986).

Robert W. Suder, *Hebrew Inscriptions: A Classified Bibliography*, reviewed by P. Kyle McCarter, Jr., *BAR* 11:5 (1985).

3. Freedman
(pages 34-46)

"The Nine Commandments: The Secret Progress of Israel's Sins" first appeared in **BR** December 1989.

1. This article is from Freedman's book, *The Unity of the Hebrew Bible* (Ann Arbor: University of Michigan Press, 1991), and was rewritten for *BR*.

2. It is no accident that Samuel, Kings and Chronicles are the three longest books (by word count) in the Hebrew Bible (between 24,000

and 26,000 words each) and therefore the most likely to be divided. The division may have occurred when the Greek translations of these books were made because the translations are longer than the originals. We can speculate that the books had reached the practical limit in terms of scroll length and that anything longer had to be literally divided.

3. The author is well known as the general editor of the Anchor Bible series, probably the leading Bible commentary in modern times.—Ed.

4. There are several ways of counting the Decalogue. Different religious bodies have assigned numbers to them in different ways. The numbering here reflects what might be called the consensus position to which most scholars adhere.

5. In Deuteronomy 5:12 the word is "observe."

6. The full text reads as follows: "You shall not desire [or covet] your neighbor's house. You shall not desire your neighbor's wife, his man or maidservant, his ox or his ass, or anything at all that belongs to your neighbor" (Exodus 20:17). The version in Deuteronomy 5:21 (5:18 in Hebrew) differs slightly from the version in Exodus. In Exodus the neighbor's house comes before the neighbor's wife; in Deuteronomy the order is reversed. In Exodus the word for desire or covet (*taḥmod*) is repeated; in Deuteronomy *taḥmod* is used the first time, but a synonym, *titawweh*, is used for desire or covet the second time.

Related Articles in BR and BAR
David Noel Freedman, letter: Freedman Replies to Pettinato on Ebla Checking, *BAR* 7:2 (1981).

Freedman, *Pottery, Poetry, and Prophecy: Studies in Early Hebrew Poetry*, reviewed by James L. Kugel, *BAR* 7:2 (1981).

Freedman, "What the Ass and the Ox Know—But the Scholars Don't," *BR* 1:1 (1985).

Freedman, "But Did King David Invent Musical Instruments?" *BR* 1:2 (1985).

Freedman, letter: Did Gesenius (and Others) Anticipate Freedman? *BR* 1:3 (1985).

Freedman, "Who Asks (or Tells) God to Repent?" *BR* 1:4 (1985).

Freedman, "Is It Possible to Understand the Book of Job?" *BR* 4:2 (1988).

David Noel Freedman and Leona G. Running, *William Foxwell Albright*, reviewed by Hershel Shanks, *BAR* 2:2 (1976).

David Noel Freedman and K.A. Mathews, *The Paleo-Hebrew Leviticus Scroll (11QpaleoLev)*, reviewed by Hershel Shanks, *BAR* 11:5 (1985).

Hershel Shanks, Interview with David Noel Freedman, *BAR* 6:3 (1980).

Shanks, "An Interview with David Noel Freedman, Part I: How the Hebrew Bible and the Christian Old Testament Differ," *BR* 9:6 (1993).

Shanks, "An Interview with David Noel Freedman, Part II: The Undiscovered Symmetry of the Bible," *BR* 10:1 (1994).

Hershel Shanks and Benjamin Mazar, eds., *Recent Archaeology in the Land of Israel*, reviewed by David Noel Freedman, *BAR* 10:2 (1984).

Moshe Weinfeld, "What Makes the Ten Commandments Different?" *BR* 7:2 (1991).

4. Tov
(pages 51-61)

"The David and Goliath Saga" first appeared in **BR** *Winter 1986.*

1. These and other cases are examined in *Empirical Models for Biblical Criticism*, ed. Jeffrey H. Tigay (Philadelphia: University of Pennsylvania Press, 1985). The present article is adapted from a chapter by Professor Tov in that volume.

2. Manuscripts of the LXX vary somewhat. I will be referring to the oldest Greek manuscripts. Later LXX manuscripts, such as the one used in Origen's Hexapla, were "corrected" toward the MT.

3. In this case, as with other inconsistencies, it is possible to explain them away by interpreting one description or the other as an exaggeration.

Related Articles in BR and BAR

Trude Dothan and Moshe Dothan, *People of the Sea: The Search for the Philistines*, and Neal Bierling, *Giving Goliath His Due: New Archaeological Light on the Philistines*, reviewed by Jane C. Waldbaum, *BAR* 19:3 (1993).

Emanuel Tov, letter: Who Killed Goliath? *BR* 3:3 (1987).

Tov, "Computers and the Bible," *BR* 4:1 (1988).

"When Did the Philistines Arrive in Canaan? Multiple Clues Help Unravel the Mystery," *BAR* 17:2 (1991).

6. Stegner
(pages 66-71)

"The Baptism of Jesus: A Story Modeled on the Binding of Isaac" first appeared in **BR** *Fall 1985.*

1. In Matthew and Luke, the account of Jesus' baptism directly follows the account of his birth and infancy and is, in effect, introduced by the birth and infancy narratives. Mark does not include a birth and infancy section; the story of Jesus' baptism in Mark, therefore, plays a different role.

2. George Foot Moore, *Judaism in the First Centuries of the Christian Era: The Age of the Tannaim*, 2d ed. (New York: Schocken Books, 1971), vol. 1, p. 539.

3. There is considerable scholarly debate about the dates of the Targums. Although they may have been edited and "published" considerably later than the New Testament (some say as late as the seventh or eighth century C.E.), various passages are obviously much earlier. This is true of the material relating to the binding of Isaac. We have a number of clues suggesting that the targumic versions of the story of the binding of Isaac were well known in New Testament times. For example, the works of Philo and Josephus and other first-century documents all describe Isaac's voluntary submission to sacrifice. Even more significant is that the targumic material locates the binding of Isaac on the Temple Mount in Jerusalem. In the targumic accounts, when Isaac looks up from the altar he has a vision of God's glory, known in rabbinic literature as the Shekhinah, who dwelt in the Temple. In this way, the Targums use the binding of Isaac to prove the legitimacy of Jerusalem and the Temple as the sole place of sacrifice. This makes good sense only before 70 C.E., when the Romans destroyed the Temple, and suggests that those details were incorporated into the story before the destruction.

4. The three Targums to Genesis 22:10.

5. Targum Pseudo-Jonathan to Genesis 22:14. The other two Targums, namely Neofiti and the Fragmentary Targum, use "the glory of the Shekhinah of the Lord." There is little difference between these two expressions.

6. The three Targums to Genesis 22:10.

7. Here I am especially indebted to the analysis of Fritzleo Lentzen-Deis, *Die Taufe Jesu nach den Synoptikern: Literarkritische und gattungsgeschichtliche Untersuchungen*, Frankfurter

theologische Studien 4 (Frankfurt am Main: Joseph Knecht, 1970), pp. 97-248.

8. The Revised Standard Version says the "heavens opened"; a more accurate translation is that the heavens "split."

9. In the parallel synoptic accounts, where Mark uses "Spirit," Luke uses "Holy Spirit" (Luke 3:22) and Matthew uses "Spirit of God" (Matthew 3:16).

10. Efraim E. Urbach, *The Sages: Their Concepts and Beliefs*, trans. Israel Abrahams (Jerusalem: Magnes Press, 1975), p. 43. Also see the discussion by Alan Unterman, "Shekhinah" in *Encyclopaedia Judaica*, vol. 14, cols. 1349-1354.

11. Arthur Marmorstein, "The Holy Spirit in Rabbinic Legend" in *Studies in Jewish Theology: The Arthur Marmorstein Memorial Volume*, ed. J. Rabinowitz and M.S. Lew (Freeport, NY: Books for Libraries Press, 1972), vol. 2, p. 131.

12. Some commentators suggest that the phrase "Thou art my beloved Son" is a quotation from Psalm 2:7 applied to Jesus by the heavenly voice. But the Psalm says, referring to Israel's king, "You are my son," not "my beloved son." The absence of "beloved" is a serious objection to this view.

13. G. Schrenk in Gerhard Kittel and Gerhard Friedrich, eds., *Theological Dictionary of the New Testament*, trans. and ed. Geoffrey W. Bromiley, 10 vols. (Grand Rapids: Eerdmans, 1964-1976), vol. 2, p. 740ff.

14. Some commentators argue that the Gospel phrase "with thee I am well pleased" is a quotation from Isaiah 42:1. Again, however, the verb in Isaiah is different: "Behold my servant...in whom my soul *delights*."

15. See 1 Corinthians 5:7: "For Christ, our paschal lamb, has been sacrificed." In John 1:29 Jesus is referred to as the "Lamb of God."

16. Unlike theories that attribute different parts of the message of the heavenly voice to different parts of the Old Testament, this theory has the advantage of simplicity. Both parts of the statement are derived from the same story, the binding of Isaac.

17. Some Bibles, such as the popular Revised Standard Version, refer to the Song of Songs as the Song of Solomon, the traditional title based on the customary attribution to Solomon. See Jack M. Sasson, "Unlocking the Poetry of Love in the Song of Songs," *BR* 1:1 (1985).

18. "Song of Songs," ed. Maurice Simon, in

Midrash Rabbah, ed. H. Freedman and Simon (London: Soncino Press, 1939), p. 86.

19. Geza Vermés, *Scripture and Tradition in Judaism* (Leiden: Brill, 1973), p. 195.

20. For our purposes, it does not matter whether the tearing of the curtain is a sign of God's judgment on the Temple or a sign that access to God is now open and visible as a result of the cross.

21. This is a device known as *gazera shava*, which is an "analogy of expressions; that is, an analogy based on identical or similar words occurring in two different passages of Scripture" (Moses Mielziner, *Introduction to the Talmud*, 4th ed. [New York: Bloch, 1969], p. 143). According to exegetical practice, if one of the passages in which the word occurs is obscure, its meaning is to be ascertained from the other passage.

Related Articles in *BR* and *BAR*

Dale C. Allison, Jr., "The Baptism of Jesus and a New Dead Sea Scroll," *BAR* 18:2 (1992).

Lippman Bodoff, "God Tests Abraham, Abraham Tests God," *BR* 9:5 (1993).

Robin M. Jensen, "The Binding or Sacrifice of Isaac: How Jews and Christians See Differently," *BR* 9:5 (1993).

Victor H. Matthews and Don C. Benjamin, *Old Testament Parallels: Laws and Stories from the Ancient Near East*, a review, *BAR* 18:2 (1992).

Jo Milgrom, *The Binding of Isaac: The Akedah– A Primary Symbol in Jewish Thought and Art*, reviewed by Jack Riemer, *BR* 5:6 (1989).

Jack Riemer, "The Binding of Isaac– Rembrandt's Contrasting Portraits," *BR* 5:6 (1989).

David Ulansey, "The Heavens Torn Open: Mark's Powerful Metaphor Explained," *BR* 7:4 (1991).

7. Borg
(pages 74-84)

"What Did Jesus Really Say?" first appeared in **BR** *October 1989.*

1. Robert W. Funk, Roy Hoover and the Jesus Seminar, *The Five Gospels: The Search for the Authentic Words of Jesus* (New York: Macmillan, 1993). The fifth gospel in the study is the apocryphal Gospel of Thomas.

2. See Marcus J. Borg, "A Renaissance in Jesus

Studies," *Theology Today* 45 (1988), pp. 280-292.

3. Cullen Murphy, "Who Do Men Say That I Am?" *The Atlantic* (December 1986), pp. 37-58; John P. Meier, "Jesus Among the Historians," *The New York Times Book Review* (December 21, 1986), pp. 1, 16-19.

4. Headlines about the Jesus Seminar often highlight whatever is most likely to cause offense—"Scholars Say Jesus Was Often Misquoted," "Scholars Question Roots of Scripture," "Scholars Seek to Discredit Christ," "Why Do These Scholars Call Themselves Christian?"

5. "Mainstream" biblical scholarship is the kind of biblical scholarship practiced in most university departments of religious studies and seminaries of mainstream denominations, and thus in the training of their clergy (I refer generally to Lutherans, Methodists, Presbyterians, Episcopalians, Congregationalists, Disciples of Christ, some Baptists and, increasingly since World War II, Roman Catholics). "Fundamentalist" and much "conservative-evangelical" biblical scholarship is based on a different framework for understanding the Gospels, explicitly or implicitly affirming that the historical truthfulness of the Gospels is "guaranteed" by God.

6. These differences can be discerned easily by anybody who spends even a short time examining "synoptic" texts of Matthew, Mark and Luke printed in parallel columns. The most widely used edition is Burton H. Throckmorton, ed., *Gospel Parallels*, 5th ed. (Nashville: Thomas Nelson, 1992).

7. For an accessible summary description of the criteria, see W. Barnes Tatum, *In Quest of Jesus: A Guidebook* (Atlanta: John Knox Press, 1982), pp. 76-77. For a more sustained discussion, see Norman Perrin, *Rediscovering the Teaching of Jesus* (New York: Harper & Row, 1967), pp. 15-49; Perrin seems to me to give too much priority to the criterion of dissimilarity.

8. Although the majority of mainstream scholars accept the two-source theory, a movement centered around Prof. William R. Farmer of Southern Methodist University has been pressing vigorously for reexamination of this position. See, for example, Farmer's *Jesus and the Gospel: Tradition, Scripture, and Canon* (Philadelphia: Fortress Press, 1982).

9. In the judgment of some scholars, the Gospel of Thomas contains material as old as any material in the canonical Gospels. For a representative treatment, see Stevan L. Davies, *The Gospel of Thomas and Christian Wisdom* (New York: Seabury Press, 1983). For the story of the discovery and significance of the Nag Hammadi documents, see esp. John Dart, *The Jesus of Heresy and History: The Discovery and Meaning of the Nag Hammadi Gnostic Library* (San Francisco: Harper & Row, 1988). See also James Brashler, "Nag Hammadi Codices Shed New Light on Early Christian History," *BAR* 10:1 (1984), p. 54. Reprinted in this volume on pp. 173-181.

10. According to the kosher laws of the Hebrew Bible, food is divided into categories of "clean" and "unclean." Only the former may be eaten. See Leviticus 11 and Deuteronomy 14.

11. There is near unanimity among mainstream scholars about Jesus' use of parables and proverbs/aphorisms. For a representative treatment, see the work of John Dominic Crossan, esp. *In Parables* (New York: Harper & Row, 1973), and *In Fragments: The Aphorisms of Jesus* (San Francisco: Harper & Row, 1983). For a more recent treatment, see Bernard B. Scott, *Hear Then the Parable* (Philadelphia: Fortress Press, 1989).

12. For a fuller discussion of the positive and negative forms of the criterion of dissimilarity and a sustained critique of the latter, see Borg, *Conflict, Holiness and Politics in the Teachings of Jesus* (Lewiston, NY: Edwin Mellen Press, 1984), pp. 20-24, 283-285.

13. See, for example, Samuel G.F. Brandon, *Jesus and the Zealots: A Study of the Political Factor in Early Christianity* (Manchester: Manchester University Press/New York: Scribners, 1967).

14. The perception of corrosiveness arises, at least partly, from confusion about the relationship between historical judgments and theological convictions. To use an example from this essay, whether or not Jesus said (or thought) he was both Lord and Christ should not be confused with whether or not he was (or is) Lord and Christ. For the early Christians, as for Christians today, he was certainly both, even though he may not have spoken of himself in those terms. To use an illustration from our national history, George Washington is quite properly referred to as the "Father of Our Country," even though he did not think of himself that way. In other words, the truth of the New Testament perception of Jesus as both Lord and Christ is not dependent upon whether or not Jesus used exalted titles himself.

15. It is important to note that one cannot settle historical questions by "belief." The fact that I believe something to be true has no bearing on whether or not it is true. Whether or not I believe that Lincoln wrote the Gettysburg Address on the back of an envelope has nothing to do with whether or not he did. Thus belief cannot be used to make historical judgments, not even to tip the scales when the evidence is evenly balanced. See what Van A. Harvey calls "the morality of historical judgment" in *The Historian and the Believer: The Morality of Historical Knowledge and Christian Belief* (New York: Macmillan, 1966).

16. For my own picture of the historical Jesus and his significance, see Borg, *Jesus: A New Vision. Spirit, Culture, and the Life of Discipleship* (San Francisco: Harper & Row, 1987). This book was reviewed by Adela Yarbro Collins, *BR* 5:5 (1989); excerpts from this review are reprinted on pp. 87-88 in this volume.

Related Articles in *BR* and *BAR*

Marcus J. Borg, "Jews and Gentiles," *BR* 6:1 (1990).

Borg, "On Red, Pink, Gray and Black," *BR* 6:2 (1990).

Borg, "Different Ways of Looking at the Bible," *BR* 8:4 (1992).

Michael Grant, *Jesus: An Historian's View of the Gospels*, reviewed by George W. Buchanan, *BAR* 5:6 (1979).

Barbara Thiering, *Jesus and the Riddle of the Dead Sea Scrolls: Unlocking the Secrets of His Life Story*, reviewed by Hershel Shanks, *BAR* 18:5 (1992).

Ian Wilson, "Are These the Words of Jesus?" *BR* 7:3 (1991).

Borg, Afterword
(pages 85-88)

1. Robert W. Funk, Roy Hoover and the Jesus Seminar, *The Five Gospels: The Search for the Authentic Words of Jesus* (New York: Macmillan, 1993).

2. Robert W. Funk, Bernard B. Scott and James R. Butts, eds., *The Parables of Jesus: Red Letter Edition* (Sonoma, CA: Polebridge Press, 1988).

3. Robert W. Funk and Mahlon H. Smith, *The Gospel of Mark: Red Letter Edition* (Sonoma, CA: Polebridge Press, 1991).

4. Marcus J. Borg, *Jesus: A New Vision. Spirit, Culture, and the Life of Discipleship* (San Francisco: Harper & Row, 1987).

5. H. Richard Niebuhr, *Christ and Culture* (New York: Harper, 1956).

8. Koester and Patterson
(pages 89-104)

"Does the Gospel of Thomas Contain Authentic Sayings of Jesus?" first appeared in **BR** April 1990.

1. Edgar Hennecke and Wilhelm Schneemelcher, *New Testament Apocrypha*, 2 vols. (Philadelphia: Westminster Press, 1963), vol. 1, p. 60.

2. For a summary of the discovery of the manuscripts and their subsequent marketing, see James M. Robinson and Richard Smith, eds., *The Nag Hammadi Library in English*, 3d rev. ed. (San Francisco: Harper & Row, 1988), pp. 22-26.

3. The work of translating these manuscripts and preparing them for publication has fallen to the Coptic Gnostic Library Project of the Institute for Antiquity and Christianity, in Claremont, California. Facsimiles of all writings, prepared by the institute, were published by Brill (Leiden) from 1972 to 1978. English translations of all writings can be found in Robinson and Smith, *Nag Hammadi Library*. Critical editions with introduction and notes are in the process of publication in the Nag Hammadi Studies series.

4. Pahor Labib, *Coptic Gnostic Papyri in the Coptic Museum of Old Cairo*, vol. 1 (Cairo: Government Press [Antiquities Department], 1956). Within a year, the East German scholar Johannes Leipoldt had published a German translation of the Gospel of Thomas: "Ein neues Evangelium: Das Koptische Thomasevangelium übersetzt und besprochen," *Theologische Literaturzeitung* (TL) 83 (1958), cols. 481-496, republished in *Koptisch-gnostische Schriften aus den Papyrus-Codices von Nag Hammadi*, ed. Johannes Leipoldt and Hans-Martin Schenke, Theologische Forschung 20 (Hamburg-Bergstedt: Reich and Evangelischer Verlag, 1959). The Coptic text was published a year later with French, German and English translations: *The Gospel According to Thomas: Coptic Text Established and Translated*, ed. Antoine Guillaumont et al. (Leiden: Brill, 1959; recent ed., San Francisco: Harper & Row, 1984). A flurry of scholarly activity soon followed.

5. They were published in a series of notices by the Egypt Exploration Fund, London, edited and translated by Bernard P. Grenfell and Arthur S. Hunt: *LOGIA IESOU: Sayings of Our Lord* (1897); *New Sayings of Jesus and Fragment of a Lost Gospel from Oxyrhynchus* (1904); *The Oxyrhynchus Papyri*, part 4 (1904), pp. 22-28. The literature about these fragments is listed in Hennecke and Schneemelcher, *New Testament Apocrypha*, vol. 1, pp. 99, 105, 110-111.

6. Oxyrhynchus Papyrus 1 preserves the Greek original of the Gospel of Thomas, Sayings 28-33; Oxyrhynchus Papyrus 654, the first seven sayings; and Oxyrhynchus Papyrus 655, Sayings 37-40.

7. A new edition of these Greek texts, by Harold W. Attridge, is now available in *Nag Hammadi Codex II, 2-7*, ed. Bentley Layton, Nag Hammadi Studies 20 (Leiden/New York: Brill, 1989).

8. Robert M. Grant, "Notes on the Gospel of Thomas," *Vigiliae Christianae (VC)* 13 (1959), pp. 170-180; this article was followed by a book co-authored with David Noel Freedman, *The Secret Sayings of Jesus* (Garden City, NY: Doubleday, 1960).

9. Ernst Haenchen, "Literatur zum Thomasevangelium," *Theologische Rundschau* 27 (1961/1962), pp. 147-178, 306-338, a critical survey of the first publications on the Gospel of Thomas; and *Die Botschaft des Thomas-Evangeliums* (Berlin: Alfred Töpelmann, 1961), his translation and commentary.

10. Gilles Quispel, "The Gospel of Thomas and the New Testament," *VC* 11 (1957), pp. 189-207. Quispel defended and elaborated his hypothesis in a number of articles published in subsequent years.

11. Oscar Cullmann, "Das Thomasevangelium und die Frage nach dem Alter der in ihm enthaltenen Tradition," *TL* 85 (1960), pp. 321-334.

12. Hugh Montefiore, "A Comparison of the Parables of the Gospel According to Thomas and the Synoptic Gospels," *New Testament Studies* 7 (1960-1961), pp. 220-248; republished in *Thomas and the Evangelists*, ed. Montefiore and Henry E.W. Turner, Studies in Biblical Theology 35 (Napierville, IL: A.R. Allenson/London: SCM, 1962).

13. The Syriac translation of John 14:22 refers to a disciple named Judas Thomas, that is, Judas the twin; in the standard Greek text it says "Judas (not Iscariot)." In the New Testament Epistle of Jude (= Judas), we are told that Jude is "the brother of James" (who is the brother of Jesus). In the Gospel of Thomas, there is a connection between James the righteous one (Jesus' brother), who is designated as the leader of the church (Gospel of Thomas, Saying 12), and (Judas) Thomas, the apostle who knows the secret wisdom (Gospel of Thomas, Saying 13), but no family relationship between Jesus, James and Thomas is established.

14. Except where noted, all citations from the Gospel of Thomas follow the translation of Thomas O. Lambdin in Layton, *Nag Hammadi Codex II, 2-7*, vol. 1.

15. The most perceptive recent book that helps to explain the world of the parable is by James Breech, *The Silence of Jesus: The Authentic Voice of the Historical Man* (Philadelphia: Fortress Press, 1982).

16. See Helmut Koester, "Three Thomas Parables" in *The New Testament and Gnosis: Essays in Honor of Robert McL. Wilson*, ed. A.H.B. Logan and A.J.M. Wedderburn (Edinburgh: T & T Clark, 1983), pp. 195-203.

17. The most comprehensive treatment of this question can be found in Kurt Rudolph, *Gnosis: The Nature and History of an Ancient Religion* (Edinburgh: T & T Clark, 1983), see esp. pp. 275-294.

18. John S. Kloppenborg, *The Formation of Q: Trajectories in Ancient Wisdom Collections* (Philadelphia: Fortress Press, 1987). Kloppenborg confirms earlier studies of the development of Q, such as Dieter Luhrmann, *Die Redaktion der Loqienquelle* (Neukirchen: Neukirchener Verlag, 1969).

19. In the Gospel of Thomas, these sayings correspond to Q = Luke 11:27-28,33,34-36,39,52 and 12:2,3,10,13-15,16-21,22,33-34,39,49,51-53,56; also Luke 17:20-21,22,34, which probably belonged to the same section of Q.

20. See Marcus J. Borg, "What Did Jesus Really Say?" *BR* 5:5 (1989). Reprinted on pp. 74-84 of this volume.

21. Joachim Jeremias, *Unbekannte Jesusworte*, 2d ed. (Guetersloh: Guetersloher Verlagshaus, 1983 [1963]).

22. Johannes Bauer, "Echte Jesusworte" in *Evangelien aus dem Nilsand*, ed. W.C. van Unnik (Frankfurt: Verlag Heinrich Scheffer, 1960), pp. 126-127.

Related Articles in *BR* and *BAR*

Ron Cameron, ed., *The Other Gospels: Non-*

Canonical Gospel Texts, reviewed by Charles W. Hedrick, *BAR* 10:1 (1984).

John S. Kloppenborg, Marvin W. Meyer, Stephen J. Patterson and Michael G. Steinhauser, *The Q-Thomas Reader*, reviewed by Joseph A. Fitzmyer, *BR* 7:1 (1991).

Helmut Koester, "Using Quintilian to Interpret Mark," *BAR* 6:3 (1980).

Koester, *Introduction to the New Testament*, vol. 1, *History, Culture and Religion of the Hellenistic Age*; vol. 2, *History and Literature of Early Christianity*, reviewed by Harold W. Attridge, *BAR* 9:5 (1983).

Koester, "Parallels between Thomas and Q," *BR* 6:2 (1990).

Koester, "The Gospel of Thomas and the Jews," *BR* 6:4 (1990).

Robert J. Miller, "The Gospels That Didn't Make the Cut," *BR* 9:4 (1993).

Stephen J. Patterson, "Q–The Lost Gospel," *BR* 9:5 (1993).

Hershel Shanks, "How to Break a Scholarly Monopoly–The Case of the Gospel of Thomas," *BAR* 16:6 (1990).

Koester and Patterson, Afterword
(pages 105-107)

1. Rudolf Bultmann, *History of the Synoptic Tradition*, trans. John Marsh, rev. ed. (New York: Harper & Row, 1968).

2. Joachim Jeremias, *The Parables of Jesus*, trans. S.H. Hooke, 3d rev. ed. (London: SCM, 1972).

9. Brettler
(pages 108-112)

"How the Books of the Hebrew Bible Were Chosen" first appeared in **BR** August 1989.

Related Articles in BR and BAR
James L. Crenshaw, "Ecclesiastes–Odd Book In," *BR* 6:5 (1990).

Harvey Minkoff, "How Many Books?" *BAR* 18:4 (1992).

Brettler, Afterword
(page 113)

1. Edward J. Young, *An Introduction to the Old Testament* (Grand Rapids: Eerdmans, 1958; rev. ed., London: Tyndale, 1964).

2. Gleason Archer, *A Survey of Old Testament Introduction* (Chicago: Moody Press, 1964).

10. Hoover
(pages 114-120)

"How the Books of the New Testament Were Chosen" first appeared in **BR** April 1993.

1. *First Clement*, which is concerned with quelling church disputes and teaching the divine origins of church order and apostolic succession, is not part of the New Testament, although it was widely cited and often regarded as authoritative in the second century.

2. See George Howard, "Canon–Choosing the Books of the New Testament," *BR* 5:5 (1989).

3. See Helmut Koester and Stephen J. Patterson, "The Gospel of Thomas: Does It Contain Authentic Sayings of Jesus?" *BR* 6:2 (1990). Reprinted on pp. 89-104 in this volume.

4. Some scholars date the Muratorian Canon to the fourth century, about the same time as Eusebius' list of canonical books.

5. The opening lines have not been preserved. The extant Latin text begins in midsentence and refers to Luke as the third gospel. Many scholars infer from this that the missing opening lines referred to Matthew and Mark.

6. Compiled from references in Irenaeus' writings. See Bruce M. Metzger, *The Canon of the New Testament: Its Origin, Development, and Significance* (New York: Oxford University Press, 1987), pp. 153-156.

7. Eusebius *Historia Ecclesiastica* [*Ecclesiastical History*] 6.25, 3-14.

8. Irenaeus *Adversus Haereses* [*Against Heresies*] 3.11.8.

9. Eusebius *Vita Constantini* [*Life of Constantine*] 4.2. Cited by William R. Farmer, *Jesus and the Gospel: Tradition, Scripture, and Canon* (Philadelphia: Fortress Press, 1982), p. 186.

Related Articles in BR and BAR
Philip W. Comfort, *Early Manuscripts and Modern Translations of the New Testament*, reviewed by Bruce M. Metzger, *BR* 8:4 (1992).

Geoffrey Mark Hahneman, *The Muratorian Fragment and the Development of the Canon*, reviewed by Robert J. Miller, *BR* 10:1 (1994).

Bruce M. Metzger, *The Canon of the New Testament: Its Origin, Development, and Significance*, reviewed by George Howard, *BR* 5:2 (1989).

Robert J. Miller, "The Gospels That Didn't Make the Cut," *BR* 9:4 (1993).

Hoover, Afterword
(pages 121-125)

1. Ron Cameron, ed., *The Other Gospels: Non-Canonical Gospel Texts* (Philadelphia: Westminster Press, 1982).

11. Shanks
(pages 126-138)

"Don't Let Pseudepigrapha Scare You" first appeared in **BR** *Summer 1987.*

1. James H. Charlesworth, ed., *The Old Testament Pseudepigrapha*, 2 vols. (Garden City, NY: Doubleday 1983-1985).

2. See James M. Robinson and Richard Smith, eds., *The Nag Hammadi Library in English*, 3d rev. ed. (San Francisco: Harper & Row, 1988).

3. Some manuscripts of Enoch had been brought to Europe in 1773, but they were not translated into English until 1821 and into German in 1833.

4. In a survey of New Testament scholarship from 1926 to 1956, Professor Robert Grant observed that the only real advances were made by critical scholars and historians rather than scholars who were looking only for the message: "The permanent achievements [of this period 1926-1956] were made by those whose goal was understanding rather than proclamation. They did not sell their birthright as critics and historians for what has been called a 'pot of message'" (Robert Grant, "American New Testament Study, 1926-56," *Journal of Biblical Literature* 87 [1968], p. 50).

5. A selection of the major Pseudepigrapha was published in 1984, edited by H.F.D. Sparks, *The Apocryphal Old Testament* (New York: Oxford University Press/Oxford: Clarendon Press).

6. James H. Charlesworth, *The Old Testament Pseudepigrapha and the New Testament: Prolegomena for the Study of Christian Origins*, Society for New Testament Studies Monograph Ser. 54 (Cambridge, UK: Cambridge University Press, 1985).

7. This is not an exact quotation. Professor Charlesworth clarified the language for purposes of this article.

We should not forget that in the first century the Romans recognized the Great Sanhedrin (*Sanhedrin Gedolah*) as the ruling Jewish body in Jerusalem. But as Charlesworth points out, "An establishment must be distinguished from a normative theological system."

It is true that "without any doubt, the cult in Jerusalem was dominant." But this went "hand in glove with a rejection of the priestly ruling class—considered by some religious Jews to be illegitimate—and the deep and ancient traditions that the present Temple is but an imperfect model of the future earthly, heavenly, or eschatological (perhaps messianic) Temple...The cult not only proved to be a unifying force in Judaism, it also tended to spawn differences, as the struggles for control, as well as the corruption within the priesthood, produced opposition."

8. Alan F. Segal, *Rebecca's Children: Judaism and Christianity in the Roman World* (Cambridge, MA: Harvard University Press, 1986).

9. All the verbs in Jude are in the aorist tense, signifying events that were seen holistically as past. The cumulative effect is to denote the end of a whole process.

10. The Ethiopian Falashas canonized Enoch.

Related Articles in *BR* and *BAR*

Robert H. Eisenman, "The Testament of Kohath," *BAR* 17:6 (1991).

Michael E. Stone, ed., *Jewish Writings of the Second Temple Period: Apocrypha, Pseudepigrapha, Qumran Sectarian Writings, Philo, Josephus*, reviewed by Stuart S. Miller, *BR* 6:1 (1988).

Shanks, Afterword
(pages 139-140)

1. James H. Charlesworth, ed., *The Old Testament Pseudepigrapha*, 2 vols. (Garden City, NY: Doubleday, 1983-1985).

2. Robert H. Charles, ed., *The Apocrypha and Pseudepigrapha of the Old Testament in English*, 2 vols. (Oxford: Clarendon Press, 1913).

PART II
Introduction
(pages 142-146)

1. Hershel Shanks, ed., *Understanding the Dead Sea Scrolls* (New York: Random House, 1992).

2. James A. Sanders, "Understanding the Development of the Biblical Text" in *The Dead Sea Scrolls: After Forty Years*, ed. Hershel Shanks (Washington, DC: Biblical Archaeology Society, 1991), pp. 56-73.

3. Elaine Pagels, *The Gnostic Gospels* (New York: Random House, 1979).

4. Leonard H. Brockington, *The Hebrew Text of the Old Testament: The Readings Adopted by the Translators of the New English Bible* (Oxford: Oxford University Press, 1973).

5. Randolph V.G. Tasker, ed., *The Greek New Testament* (London: Oxford University Press, 1964).

6. Philip W. Comfort, *Early Manuscripts and Modern Translations of the New Testament* (Wheaton, IL: Tyndale House Publishers, 1990).

12. Cross
(pages 148-161)

"The Text behind the Text of the Hebrew Bible" first appeared in **BR** Summer 1985.

1. The English edition was published by Yadin shortly before his death: Yigael Yadin, *The Temple Scroll*, 3 vols. (Jerusalem: Israel Exploration Society, 1983); a popular version was also published, *The Temple Scroll* (New York: Random House, 1985). See also "The Temple Scroll–The Longest and Most Recently Discovered Dead Sea Scroll," *BAR* 10:5 (1981).

2. See Paul W. Lapp, "Bedouin Find Papyri Three Centuries Older than the Dead Sea Scrolls," *BAR* 4:1 (1978); and Frank Moore Cross, "The Historical Importance of the Samaria Papyri," ibid.

3. Josephus *Contra Apionem* 1.42.

4. It must be recognized that Josephus was writing a polemical work addressed to a Greek-speaking audience, and he does, on occasion, overstate or exaggerate.

5. The Hexapla was a work of six or more columns in which the first column contained the Hebrew text of the Bible; the second column, a transliteration of the Hebrew text into Greek script; the third, the recension of Aquila; the fourth, the recension of Symmachus; the fifth, Origen's revised text of the Septuagint; and the sixth column, the recension of Theodotion.

6. For a contemporary evaluation of the medieval variants in manuscripts of the Hebrew Bible and rabbinical literature, see Moshe H. Goshen-Gottstein, "Hebrew Biblical Manuscripts: Their History and Their Place in the HUBP Edition," *Biblica* 48 (1967), pp. 243-290; and Cross, "The History of the Biblical Text in the Light of Discoveries in the Judean Desert,"

Harvard Theological Review 57 (1964), pp. 281-299, esp. 287-292. Both papers are republished in Cross and Shemaryahu Talmon, eds., *Qumran and the History of the Biblical Text* (Cambridge, MA: Harvard University Press, 1975), pp. 42-89 (Goshen-Gottstein), pp. 177-195 (Cross).

7. The history of textual scholarship of this era–the emergence of the "one-recension" theory, the "archetype" theory and the confusion of the two in subsequent scholarly discussions– is given definitive treatment by Goshen-Gottstein in the article listed above (note 6).

8. In fact, the Nash Papyrus had already given a glimpse of an earlier stage of the Pentateuchal text before the fixing of the rabbinic recension, but its witness was largely ignored. See William F. Albright, "A Biblical Fragment from the Maccabaean Age: The Nash Papyrus," *Journal of Biblical Literature* 56 (1937), pp. 145-176.

9. A review of the biblical text from Qumran and publication data on those that have been edited may be found in Patrick W. Skehan, "Qumran Littérature" in *Supplément au Dictionnaire de la Bible*, vol. 9, cols. 805-828; cf. Cross, *The Ancient Library of Qumran*, rev. ed. (Grand Rapids: Baker Book House, 1980), pp. xi-xxi (preface to German edition, supplementing 1961 English edition).

10. The Book of the Minor Prophets included (in traditional order) Hosea, Joel, Amos, Obadiah, Jonah, Micah, Nahum, Habakkuk, Zephaniah, Haggai, Zechariah and Malachi. The Murabba'at Minor Prophets Scroll extends from the middle of Joel to the beginning of Zechariah.

11. The term *Masoretic* refers to the schools of Masoretes, Jewish biblical scholars of the late Middle Ages who handled and standardized traditions of punctuation (including vocalization), accentuation, divisions, etc., of the consonantal (unpointed) text of the medieval Hebrew Bible.

12. See Pierre Benoit, Jozef T. Milik and Roland de Vaux, *Les grottes de Murabba'at*, Discoveries in the Judean Desert 2 (Oxford: Clarendon Press, 1961), pp. 75-85 (plates 19-24), 181-205 (plates 56-73).

13. See Cross, "The Contribution of the Qumran Discoveries to the Study of the Biblical Text," *Israel Exploration Journal* (*IEJ*) 16 (1966), pp. 81-95, and esp. 282 n. 21.

14. The paleo-Hebrew script survives to the present day in manuscripts of the Samaritan

Pentateuch. The Jewish character of the Hellenistic and Roman periods, the ancestor of the modern Hebrew book-hand, is a derivative of the Aramaic script of the Persian chancelleries.

15. 2 Maccabees 2:14 contains an interesting reference to the massive destruction of books in the Antiochan conflict and their replacement by Judah.

16. The first evidence of the proto-rabbinic text in Samuel is found in the recension of the Theodotionic School, the so-called Kaige recension. This systematic Greek recension from the end of the first century B.C.E. is inspired by principles similar to those that emerged in the era of Hillel and, no doubt, may be assigned to scholars of the same party that published the rabbinic recension. The Hebrew text used as the basis of this revision is Pharisaic-rabbinic, to be sure, not identical with the fully-fixed Pharisaic Bible. The revision of the Kaige recension by Aquila brought the Greek text fully in line with the rabbinic recension.

17. See Cross, "The History of the Biblical Text in the Light of Discoveries in the Judean Desert" *IEJ* 16 (1966), p. 291. Dominique Barthélemy notes Josephus' reference to increased contacts between the Palestinian Jewish community and the Babylonian Jewish community during the reign of Herod (*Antiquities of the Jews* 17:24-27); see his *Études d'histoire du texte de l'Ancien Testament* (Fribourg: Editions Universitaires, 1978), p. 241f.

18. This textual tradition has also been called "proto-Masoretic," a designation that perhaps should be reserved for early exemplars of the rabbinic recension.

19. Sukkah 20a. Hillel's "establishment of the Torah" has, of course, been understood heretofore to apply to his role in the interpretation of oral and written law, or even figuratively to his exemplary "living the Torah." Cf. Efraim E. Urbach, *The Sages: Their Concepts and Beliefs*, trans. Israel Abrahams (Jerusalem: Magnes Press, 1975), pp. 588, 955 n. 91.

20. Josephus' canon of 22 books no doubt was the same as the traditional Hebrew canon that has been transmitted to us. For the reckoning, see note 24.

21. Josephus *Contra Apionem* 1.37-41.

22. The "Council of Jamnia" is a common and somewhat misleading designation of a particular session of the rabbinic academy (or court) at Yabneh, during which it was asserted that Ecclesiastes and Song of Songs "defile the hands," i.e., are holy scripture. The session in question was held about 90 C.E., although even this date is far from certain. The academy was founded by Yohanan ben Zakkai, a disciple of Hillel. It was presided over by Gamaliel II, a descendant of Hillel, during much of the era between the two Jewish revolts against Rome. The academy, in effect, resurrected the institution of the Sanhedrin, which exercised religious authority over the Jewish community before the Roman destruction of Jerusalem in 70 C.E.

23. See S. Leiman, *The Canonization of the Hebrew Scripture: The Talmudic and Midrashic Evidence*, Transactions of the Connecticut Academy of Arts and Sciences (Hamden, CT: Archon Books, 1976), esp. pp. 72-120.

24. Josephus is not alone in his testimony. We are now able to reconstruct an old canonical list, the common source of the so-called Bryennios List and the canon of Epiphanius, which must be dated to the end of the first century or the beginning of the second century of the Common Era. It is a list of biblical works "according to the Hebrews" and includes the same 22 books listed in Josephus and echoed in the independent canonical lists of Origen and Jerome. The 24-book canon mentioned in Fourth Ezra (c. 100 C.E.) and in the rabbinic sources is doubtless identical in content but reckons Ruth and Lamentations separately. The pairing of Ruth with Judges and Lamentations with Jeremiah is quite old, to judge from its survival in the Septuagint and the testimony of Origen to the Hebrew ordering.

25. In the case of Ecclesiastes, it is not without interest that the book has proven to be much earlier than scholars generally thought. A copy of the work from about 200 B.C.E. is known from Qumran, and a composition date as early as the Persian period can not be excluded.

13. Cross
(pages 162-169)

"Original Biblical Text Reconstructed from Fragments" first appeared in **BR** *Fall 1985.*

1. The name of Naḥash has often been taken as meaning "snake," not an inappropriate appellation. In fact, it is a shortened term (nickname) of Naḥash-tob, meaning "good luck"—*mazal tov* in modern Hebrew.

2. See Frank Moore Cross, *Canaanite Myth and Hebrew Epic: Essays in the History of the Religion*

of Israel (Cambridge, MA: Harvard University Press, 1973), p. 266 and references.

3. For a detailed discussion (and photograph) of the fragment of Samuel, see Cross, "The Ammonite Oppression of the Tribes of Gad and Reuben: Missing Verses from 1 Samuel 11 Found in 4QSamuelª" in *History, Historiography, and Interpretation*, ed. H. Tadmor and M. Weinfeld (Jerusalem: Magnes Press, 1983), pp. 148-158.

4. See Alexander Rofé's comments in *Israel Exploration Journal* 32 (1982), pp. 129-133. I anticipated such views in the paper cited in note 3.

5. See Cross, "Notes on the Ammonite Inscription from Tell Siran," *Bulletin of the American Schools of Oriental Research* 212 (1973), esp. p. 15, where the title on the Tell Siran bottle and the Amman citadel inscription are discussed.

6. See Cross, "The Dead Sea Scrolls and the People Who Wrote Them," *BAR* 3:1 (1977).

7. The term apocalyptic in the strict sense means "pertaining to an apocalypse," a salient genre of the literature of the religious movement described here. Apocalypse means "revelation" in Greek and came to mean a seer's revelation of last things (eschatological events), e.g., the apocalypse of John, commonly called the Revelation of John. We shall use the term apocalyptic in a wider sense to designate a religious movement marked by an eschatological viewpoint found *inter alia* in the apocalypses.

8. The treatment of Jewish mysticism has undergone a similar transformation in contemporary scholarship; it is now regarded as a major component of Jewish history, owing largely to the research of Gershom Scholem and his students.

9. I extend special thanks to Hershel Shanks for his editorial labors in combining material from two unpublished papers and one recently published paper to put together a first draft of this article and "The Text behind the Text of the Hebrew Bible," printed in this volume on pp. 148-161.

Related Articles in *BR* and *BAR*

Frank Moore Cross, "The Historical Importance of the Samaria Papyri," *BAR* 4:1 (1978).

Cross, "Phoenecians in Brazil?" *BAR* 5:1 (1979).

Hershel Shanks, "Frank Moore Cross—An Interview, Part I: Israelite Origins," *BR* 8:4 (1992).

Shanks, "Frank Moore Cross—An Interview,

Part II: The Development of Israelite Religion," *BR* 8:5 (1992).

Shanks, "Frank Moore Cross—An Interview, Part III: How the Alphabet Democratized Civilization," *BR* 8:6 (1992).

Cross, Afterword
(pages 170-172)

1. James A. Sanders, "Understanding the Development of the Biblical Text" in *The Dead Sea Scrolls: After Forty Years*, ed. Hershel Shanks (Washington, DC: Biblical Archaeology Society, 1991), p. 62.

2. Andrew Greeley and Jacob Neusner, *The Bible and Us: A Priest and a Rabbi Read Scripture Together* (New York: Warner Books, 1990).

3. The allusion here is to the second volume of Rabbi Abraham Joshua Heschel's *The Prophets* (New York: Harper & Row, 1971).

4. Jacob Neusner, William S. Green and Ernest S. Frerichs, eds., *Judaisms and Their Messiahs at the Turn of the Christian Era* (Cambridge, UK/New York: Cambridge University Press, 1987).

5. Jacob Neusner, "Story-Telling and the Incarnation of God in Formative Judaism" in *The Incarnate Imagination: Essays in Theology, the Arts and Social Sciences in Honor of Andrew Greeley, A Festschrift*, ed. Ingrid H. Shafer (Bowling Green, OH: Bowling Green State University Popular Press, 1988).

14. Brashler
(pages 173-181)

"Nag Hammadi Codices Shed Light on Early Christianity" first appeared in **BAR** *January/ February 1984.*

1. Elaine Pagels, *The Gnostic Gospels* (New York: Random House, 1979).

2. *Coptic* refers to the language and culture of Christians in Egypt from approximately the second century C.E. to the present. Coptic, the final stage in the development of the ancient Egyptian language, is written in the Greek alphabet and incorporates many Greek words. The use of Coptic as a popular language gradually died out after the Muslim conquest of Egypt in the seventh century, but before that it was the language of a rich but little known literary and liturgical corpus, of which the Nag Hammadi manuscripts are some of the best known examples.

Gnostic (pronounced "nostik") refers to the beliefs and practices of a variety of religious groups that relied on secret knowledge revealed to a select few. (Gnosis is the Greek word for this nonempirical insight.) Gnostic teachers frequently combined spiritual wisdom from several sources and traditions, including Christian, Jewish, Greco-Roman, Egyptian and Iranian, into syncretistic systems reserved for their own devotees. In these systems, physical and historical ways of understanding reality and human experience were rejected in favor of spiritual and mystical modes of understanding.

Some scholars reserve the term Gnostic for the developed systems of heretical Christian teachers of the second century C.E., such as Basilides and Valentinus. Others use the term *gnosis* (note the lower case *g*) as a general term. It is important to remember that Gnostic does not always mean "heretical." The definition of orthodoxy was an ongoing process that had not been completed when Gnostic ideas and practices flourished.

3. *Codex* (plural, codices) is the Latin word for book. In English it has come to refer to handmade books, of which the Nag Hammadi Codices are among the oldest surviving examples.

4. In the scholarly literature devoted to the study of the Nag Hammadi Codices, a system of Roman numerals for each codex followed by an Arabic number in italics for the tractate within that codex is generally accepted. Most scholars add page and line numbers of the original Coptic manuscript after the codex and tractate reference; sometimes the tractate reference is omitted. Thus II.*1*:11,18-22 is a reference to lines 18-22 on page 11 in the first tractate of Nag Hammadi Codex II. This tractate is known as the Apocryphon of John.

5. Pagels' use of the term *gospels* in the title and the text is only partially justified by Gnostic writings such as the Gospel of Thomas, the Gospel of Philip, the Gospel of the Egyptians (once mistakenly referred to as the Gospel to the Egyptians) and the Gospel of Truth. She refers more to other Gnostic writings and even the writings of the church fathers than she does to the Gnostic gospels. The publishers may have had something to do with the provocative use of the term Gnostic gospels in the title of the book.

6. Elaine Pagels, *The Johannine Gospel in Gnostic Exegesis: Heracleon's Commentary on John,*

Society of Biblical Literature Monograph Ser. 17 (Nashville: Abingdon Press, 1973).

7. Elaine Pagels, *The Gnostic Paul: Gnostic Exegesis of the Pauline Letters* (Philadelphia: Fortress Press, 1975; recent ed., Philadelphia: Trinity Press International, 1992).

Related Articles in BR and BAR

Ron Cameron, ed., *The Other Gospels: Non-Canonical Gospel Texts,* reviewed by Charles W. Hedrick, *BAR* 10:1 (1984).

John Dart, *The Jesus of Heresy and History: The Discovery and Meaning of the Nag Hammadi Gnostic Library,* reviewed by James Brashler, *BR* 6:1 (1990).

James M. Robinson, ed., *The Nag Hammadi Library in English,* reviewed by James M. Brashler, *BR* 6:1 (1990).

Brashler, Afterword
(pages 182-183)

1. Published in *BR* 6:1 (1990), p. 10: James M. Robinson and Richard Smith, eds., *The Nag Hammadi Library in English,* 3d rev. ed. (San Francisco: Harper & Row, 1988); John Dart, *The Jesus of Heresy and History: The Discovery and Meaning of the Nag Hammadi Gnostic Library* (San Francisco: Harper & Row, 1988).

2. Bentley Layton, *The Gnostic Treatise on Resurrection from Nag Hammadi,* Harvard Dissertations in Religion 12 (Missoula, MT: Scholars Press, 1979); *The Gnostic Scriptures* (Garden City, NY: Doubleday, 1987).

3. Layton, *Gnostic Treatise,* p. 5.

4. Walter C. Till, *Koptische Grammatik,* 4th ed., Lehrbucher für das Studium der orientalischen und afrikanischen Sprachen 1 (Leipzig: Verlag Enzyklopadie, 1970; originally published, Leipzig: Harrassowitz, 1955).

5. Walter E. Crum, *Coptic Dictionary* (Oxford/NY: Oxford University Press, 1990; originally published, Oxford: Clarendon Press, 1939).

15. Greenspoon
(pages 184-195)

"Truth and Legend about the Septuagint" first appeared in **BR** August 1989.

1. The English translation used in this article is from R.J.H. Shutt, "Letter of Aristeas (A New Translation and Introduction)," which can be found in James H. Charlesworth, ed., *The Old*

Testament Pseudepigrapha, vol. 2 (Garden City, NY: Doubleday, 1985). The well known collection of ancient documents edited by Robert H. Charles (*The Apocrypha and Pseudepigrapha of the Old Testament in English*, 2 vols. [Oxford: Clarendon Press, 1913]) also contains an English translation of the Letter of Aristeas prepared by H.T. Andrews. Shutt's renderings are more up to date, but Andrews' introduction and notes are fuller.

Moses Hadas provides an authoritative translation along with almost 100 pages of introductory discussion in his study of the letter, *Aristeas to Philocrates* (New York: Harper, 1951). Hadas is a reliable guide to almost everything written about this document up to that time.

For a discussion of issues since then, interested readers can consult with confidence two works: Sidney Jellicoe, *The Septuagint and Modern Study* (Oxford: Oxford University Press, 1968), and *Studies in the Septuagint: Origins, Recensions, and Interpretations* (New York: Ktav, 1974), edited by Jellicoe. In his brief introduction and notes, Shutt provides even more recent coverage in a few areas.

2. See Jellicoe, *The Septuagint and Modern Study*, p. 30.

3. Scholars who support royal patronage, for these or other reasons, include Dominique Barthélemy, "Pourquoi la Torah a-t-elle été traduite en grec?" in *On Language, Culture and Religion: In Honor of Eugene A. Nida*, ed. Matthew Black and William A. Smalley (The Hague: Mouton, 1974), republished in Barthélemy, *Études d'histoire du texte de l'Ancien Testament* (Fribourg: Editions Universitaires, 1978); and Elias J. Bickerman, "The Septuagint as a Translation," *Proceedings of the American Academy for Jewish Research* 28 (1959), pp. 1-39.

4. They include Henry Barclay Swete, *An Introduction to the Old Testament in Greek*, rev. Richard R. Ottley (Cambridge, UK: Cambridge University Press, 1914); Jellicoe; John W. Wevers, "Proto-Septuagint Studies" in *The Seed of Wisdom: Essays in Honour of T. J. Meek*, ed. William S. McCullough (Toronto: University of Toronto Press, 1964); and, most vigorously, Sebastian Brock, "The Phenomenon of Biblical Translation in Antiquity," *Alta* 2:8 (1969), pp. 96-102, and "The Phenomenon of the Septuagint," *Oudtestamentische Studiën* 7 (1972), pp. 11-36.

5. Philo *De Vita Mosis*.

6. The same conclusion was reached by a few scholars of previous generations. More recent research has strengthened this view. Readers are encouraged to look in particular at the work of Wevers, who has been engaged for some years in reconstructing the earliest Septuagint text for the books of the Pentateuch. These texts and accompanying studies are being published as part of the Göttingen Septuagint Project.

7. Wevers, *Text History of the Greek Numbers* (Göttingen: Vandenhoeck & Ruprecht, 1982), p. 94.

8. For some details, see Hadas, *Aristeas to Philocrates*.

9. See J.A.L. Lee, *A Lexical Study of the Septuagint Version of the Pentateuch* (Chico, CA: Scholars Press, 1983). None of this evidence allows for exact dating of the Septuagint. A date as early as the reign of Ptolemy II is possible, however. But the environment Lee established is also decidedly Egyptian—and this goes against numerous statements in the Letter of Aristeas that elders from Jerusalem were responsible for preparing the translation. Perhaps the crucial point for the author of the letter was that the Hebrew text used by the translators (whatever their origin) had Eleazar's wholehearted approval.

10. A number of scholars have made this point, none more effectively than Harry M. Orlinsky in "The Septuagint as Holy Writ and the Philosophy of the Translators," *Hebrew Union College Annual* 46 (1975), pp. 89-114.

11. Robert G. Bratcher in *The Word of God: A Guide to English Versions of the Bible*, ed. Lloyd R. Bailey (Atlanta: John Knox Press, 1982), p. 165.

12. This suggestion is not original with me. I do, however, find it convincing.

Related Articles in BR and BAR

Marc Brettler, letter: The Earliest Bible Translation, *BR* 5:6 (1989).

Leonard J. Greenspoon, "Major Septuagint Manuscripts—Vaticanus, Sinaiticus, Alexandrinus," *BR* 5:4 (1989).

"How the Septuagint Differs," *BAR* 2:2 (1976).

16. Brettler
(pages 198-204)

"Old Testament Manuscripts: From Qumran to Leningrad" first appeared in BR *August 1990.*

1. Darrell Hannah, "New Testament Manuscripts: Uncials, Minuscules, Palimpsests and

All That Stuff," *BR* 6:1 (1990). This article is reprinted on pp. 205-211 in this volume.

2. All scrolls from Qumran are numbered. For biblical texts, the first number is the cave in which they were found (1-11); this is followed by Q, for Qumran, then the biblical book in abbreviated form and a superscript letter, which differentiates between different manuscripts of the same work from the same cave. Thus 1QIsa[a] is the first manuscript ([a]) of Isaiah (Isa) from Cave 1 at Qumran (1Q).

3. See Leonard J. Greenspoon, "Mission to Alexandria: Truth and Legend About the Creation of the Septuagint, the First Bible Translation," *BR* 5:4 (1989). Reprinted on pp. 184-195 in this volume.

4. Pesher texts are commentaries on events referred to in prophetic literature and Psalms as actualized prophecy, that is, events taking place during the author's lifetime. Pesher texts provide important background information for the study of the Gospels.

5. An important *genizah* was rediscovered at the end of the last century in the Old Jewish Synagogue in Fostat, or Old Cairo. The documents found there have proved invaluable for the study of medieval Jewry and traditional Jewish texts. According to one estimate, the Cairo *genizah* yielded fragments of several thousand biblical manuscripts.

6. For a history of the Aleppo Codex, see Harvey Minkoff, "The Aleppo Codex: Ancient Bible from the Ashes," *BR* 7:4 (1991). This article is reprinted on pp. 212-222 of this volume.

Related Articles in *BR* and *BAR*

Magen Broshi, *The Damascus Document Reconsidered*, reviewed by Hershel Shanks, *BAR* 18:4 (1992).

"Facsimile Leningrad Codex Is Planned," *BR* 7:1 (1991).

"Genizah Collection at Cambridge University Preserves 2,000 Years of History," *BAR* 8:5 (1982).

Leonard J. Greenspoon, "Major Septuagint Manuscripts—Vaticanus, Sinaiticus, Alexandrinus," *BR* 5:4 (1989).

Michael L. Klein, *Genizah Manuscripts of Palestinian Targum to the Pentateuch*, a review, *BAR* 13:3 (1987).

Hershel Shanks, "An Interview with David Noel Freedman, Part I: How the Hebrew Bible and the Christian Old Testament Differ," *BR* 9:6 (1993).

Shanks, "An Interview with David Noel Freedman, Part II: The Undiscovered Symmetry of the Bible," *BR* 10:1 (1994).

Roger S. Wieck, "Visual Glories—The Hebrew Bible in Medieval Manuscripts," *BR* 5:2 (1989).

17. Hannah
(pages 205-211)

"New Testament Manuscripts: Uncials, Minuscules, Palimpsests, etc." first appeared in **BR** *February 1990.*

1. Paleography (literally "old writing") is the study of the manuscript itself rather than the text. When attempting to date manuscripts, paleographers are especially concerned with the script, i.e., the style of letters used. We have so many papyri from Egypt that a definite progression in the style of script from one period to the next can be seen.

2. Y.K. Kim, "Palaeographical Dating of ℘46 to the Later First Century," *Biblica* 69:2 (1988), pp. 248-257.

3. Bruce M. Metzger, *The Text of the New Testament: Its Transmission, Corruption, and Restoration*, 2d ed. (Oxford: Oxford University Press, 1968), pp. 40-41.

4. Kurt Aland and Barbara Aland, *The Text of the New Testament*, trans. Erroll F. Rhodes (Grand Rapids: Eerdmans, 1987), pp. 101-102; Metzger, *New Testament*, p. 6.

5. Cf. Metzger, *New Testament*, p. 9.

6. The most up-to-date numbering of each class of manuscripts is found in Aland and Aland, *Text of the New Testament*, p. 74.

7. Metzger, *New Testament*, p. 4.

8. Metzger, *New Testament*, p. 63.

Related Articles in *BR* and *BAR*

David Daniell, ed., *Tyndale's New Testament*, reviewed by Harvey Minkoff, *BR* 6:3 (1990).

Hamchand Gossai, "The Old Testament among Christian Theologians," *BR* 6:1 (1990).

Lisbon Bible 1482, reviewed by Joseph Gutmann, *BR* 7:1 (1991).

18. Minkoff
(pages 212-222)

"The Aleppo Codex: Ancient Bible from the Ashes" first appeared in **BR** *August 1991.*

1. See the deposition given by Rabbi Tawwil in 1958, after his immigration to Israel, and the 1976 interview of Mordecai Fahham in Amnon Shamosh, *Ha-Keter: The Story of the Aleppo Codex* (Jerusalem: Machon Ben Zvi, 1986), pp. 39-41, 161-162 (in Hebrew).

2. Hebrew words generally have two components, a root and a grammatical portion. The root, usually three consonants (X-X-X), establishes the semantic field: *l-m-d* "studying," *g-z-l* "stealing," *d-r-š* "searching." The grammatical portion is a pattern of vowels and certain consonants that fits into the root; for example, XaXXan "one who does," XaXaX "third-person-masculine, simple past tense." Thus, *lamdan* "scholar," *gazlan* "thief," *daršan* "preacher," *lamad* "he studied," *gazal* "he stole," *daraš* "he searched." Other patterns give *melamed* "teacher," *talmid* "student," *derašah* "exegesis," *midrash* "commentary." Analyzing words in an advertisement, Geoffrey Sampson (*Writing Systems: A Linguistic Introduction* [Stanford, CA: Stanford University Press, 1985], pp. 89-92) finds that only 30 percent have more than one possible reading, even in isolation; in context none is ambiguous.

3. Writing in France during the 11th century, Rabbi Solomon ben Isaac (Rashi) says in his commentary to this passage in the Talmud that the reader "moves his hand according to the melody. I have seen this among readers who come from the land of Israel." For illustration of the modern Italian style, as well as convincing arguments that the "melody" is actually a chant, see Avigdor Herzog, "Masoretic Accents" in *Encyclopaedia Judaica*, vol. 11, cols. 1098-1111.

4. Even after a thousand years, the Masoretic undertaking is the subject of considerable controversy and polemic, both Jewish/Christian and Catholic/Protestant. For various evaluations of the Masorah, see Aron Dotan, "Masorah" in *Encyclopaedia Judaica*, vol. 16, cols. 1401-1482; Moshe H. Goshen-Gottstein, "Hebrew Biblical Manuscripts: Their History and Their Place in the HUBP Edition," *Biblica* 48 (1967), pp. 243-289, and "The Aleppo Codex and the Rise of the Massoretic Bible Text," *Biblical Archaeologist* 42:3 (1979), pp. 145-163; Judah D. Eisenstein, "Massoret" in *Ozar Yisrael*, 10 vols. (New York: Pardes, 1951), vol. 6, pp. 255-256 (in Hebrew); Shemaryahu Talmon, "The Old Testament Text" in *The Cambridge History of the Bible*, vol. 1, ed. P.R. Ackroyd and C.F. Evans (Cambridge, UK: Cambridge University Press, 1963-1970), pp.

159-198; Bleddyn J. Roberts, "The Old Testament: Manuscripts, Text and Versions" in *Cambridge History*, vol. 2, ed. G.W.H. Lampe, pp. 1-26; John Reumann, "The Transmission of the Biblical Text" in *The Interpreter's One-Volume Commentary on the Bible*, ed. Charles M. Layman (Nashville: Abingdon Press, 1982 [1971]), pp. 1225-1236; Otto Eissfeldt, *The Old Testament: An Introduction*, trans. Ackroyd, 3d ed. (New York: Harper & Row, 1965), pp. 678-693; Meyer Waxman, *A History of Jewish Literature*, 2d ed. (South Brunswick, NJ: Thomas Yoseloff, 1960), vol. 1, pp. 153-166.

5. See Dotan, "Masorah," col. 1405; and Eisenstein, "Soferim" in *Ozar Yisrael*.

6. Soferim 1.10, 12.8-12. See also Abraham Cohen, ed., *The Minor Tractates of the Talmud* (London: Soncino Press, 1971), vol. 1, p. 215 n. 44.

7. The Hebrew word *dikduk* has come to mean grammar. In Ben Asher's day, it probably still had a denotation closer to the root *DWK* (examine, detail).

8. English preface to the facsimile edition of *Keter Aram Zova*, ed. Mordecai Breuer (Jerusalem: Magnes Press, 1976).

9. Quoted in Yitzhak Ben-Zvi, "Ben Asher's 'Keter Torah'—A Brand Plucked from the Fire," *Sinai* 43 (1958), p. 9 (in Hebrew).

10. Details for the following historical survey were culled from many sources. The general history of Aleppo owes much to Abraham Marcus, *The Middle East on the Eve of Modernity: Aleppo in the Eighteenth Century* (New York: Columbia University Press, 1989). For the description of Jewish life, see also Raphael Patai, *The Vanished Worlds of Jewry* (New York: Macmillan, 1980), pp. 138-141; Elkan Nathan Adler, "Aleppo" in *Universal Jewish Encyclopedia*, vol. 1, pp. 167-168; Eliyahu Ashtor, "Aleppo" in *Encyclopaedia Judaica*, vol. 2, cols. 562-564; Azriel Eisenberg, *Jewish Historical Treasures* (New York: Bloch, 1968), pp. 78-79; Norman A. Stillman, *The Jews of Arab Lands: A History and Source Book* (Philadelphia: Jewish Publication Society, 1979), pp. 105-107, 318-321.

11. Marcus, *The Middle East*, pp. 27-36.

12. See Marcus, *The Middle East*, chap. 2, "The People: Groups, Classes, and Social Contrasts," and chap. 9, "The Urban Experience: Neighborhood Life and Personal Identity"; and Adler, "Aleppo," p. 168.

13. Marc Brettler, "Old Testament Manuscripts:

From Qumran to Leningrad," _BR_ 6:4 (1990). Reprinted on pp. 198-204 of this volume.

14. See, for example, Ben-Zvi, "The Codex of Ben Asher," _Textus_ 1 (1960), pp. 1-16; D.S. Loewinger, "The Aleppo Codex and the Ben Asher Tradition," ibid., pp. 59-111; Lazar Lipschutz, "Mishael Ben Uzziel's Treatise on the Differences Between Ben Asher and Ben Naphtali," part 1 (text), _Textus_ 2 (1962), pp. 1-58, part 2 (analysis), _Textus_ 4 (1964), pp. 1-29; Israel Yeivin, _The Aleppo Codex: A Study of Its Vocalization and Accentuation_ (Jerusalem: Magnes Press, 1968), and "The New Edition of the _Biblia Hebraica_: Its Text and Massorah," _Textus_ 7 (1969), pp. 114-123; Breuer, "Review of Yeivin's _Aleppo Codex_," _Leshonenu_ 35 (1970-1971), pp. 85-98, 175-191, and _The Aleppo Codex and the Accepted Text of the Bible_ (Jerusalem: Mossad Harav Kook, 1976); Dotan, "The Aleppo Codex and _Dikdukei ha-Te'amim_," _Leshonenu_ 2 (1972), pp. 167-185; Goshen-Gottstein, "The Aleppo Codex and the Rise of the Massoretic Bible Text"; Jordan S. Penkower, "Maimonides and the Aleppo Codex," _Textus_ 9 (1981), pp. 39-128.

15. Goshen-Gottstein, "The Textual Criticism of the Old Testament: Rise, Decline, Rebirth," _Journal of Biblical Literature_ 102:3 (1983), p. 396.

Related Articles in BR and BAR
Alan Millard, "Were Words Separated in Ancient Hebrew Writing?" _BR_ 8:3 (1992).

19. Crown
(pages 223-236)

"Is the Abisha Scroll 3,000 Years Old?" first appeared in **BR** _October 1991._

1. Abisha is the Samaritan form; in Hebrew Bibles and English translations, the name is Abishua.

2. Jerome refers to this meaning in Homily 42: "A Samaritan (_Samarites_) that is a guardian," in Jerome, _Homilies on Psalms_, trans. Marie Ewald, Fathers of the Church, vol. 48 (Washington, DC: Catholic University of America Press, 1964), Psalm 127.

3. August F. Von Gall, _Der hebräische Pentateuch der Samaritaner_ (Giessen: Alfred Töpelmann, 1914-1918; repr. 1966).

4. The Jews in antiquity maintained that the Samaritans were the offspring of intermarriage with the imported foreign population.

5. Edward Robertson, "Concerning the Abisha Scroll," _Bulletin of the John Rylands Library (BJRL)_ 19:2 (1935), pp. 412-437.

6. See Moses Gaster, Manuscript 863, fol. 138, in the John Rylands Library; also in Alan D. Crown, "A Critical Reevaluation of the Samaritan Sepher Yehoshua" (Ph.D. diss., Sydney University, 1967).

7. John Mills, _Nablus and the Modern Samaritans_ (London, 1864), pp. 308-315.

8. Described in Georg Rosen, "Alte Handschriften des samaritanischen Pentateuch," _Zeitschrift der deutschen morgenländischen Gessellschaft_ 18 (1864), pp. 582-589.

9. A photograph is reproduced in John Whiting, "The Last Blood Sacrifice, a Samaritan Rite in Palestine," _National Geographic_ (January 1920).

10. See R.E. Moody, "Samaritan Material at Boston University: The Boston Collection and the Abisha Scroll," _Boston University Graduate Journal_ 5:10 (1957), pp. 158-160; James D. Purvis, "Studies on the Samaritan Materials in the W.E. Barton Collection in the Boston University Library" in _Proceedings of the Fifth World Congress of Jewish Studies, 1965_ (Jerusalem: World Union of Jewish Studies, 1972), vol. 1, pp. 134-143; Paul Kahle, "The Abisha Scroll of the Samaritans" in _Studia Orientalia Ioanni Pederson, Septuagenario_ (Helsinki: E. Munksgaard, 1953), pp. 188-192.

11. Robertson, "Concerning the Abisha Scroll," p. 27 n 2.

12. Father Federico Perez Castro, _Sefer Abisa, Textos y Estudios del Seminario Filologico Cardenal Disneros_ (Madrid: CSIC, 1959).

13. See Paul Stenhouse, _The Kitab al-Tarikh of Abu'l Fath_ (Sydney: Mandelbaum Publications, 1982).

14. Yitzhak Ben-Zvi, "Sepher Abisha," _Eretz-Israel_ 5 (1958), pp. 240-252 (in Hebrew).

15. I refer here to the older Arabic version (the oldest extant manuscript is dated to the 14th century, but this version may be a century earlier); the Hebrew version is a very late translation from the Arabic (the date of the translation is unknown, but all our manuscripts belong to the late 19th and early 20th centuries, and the translation cannot be much earlier than these manuscripts). For published editions, see T.W.J. Juynboll, _Chronicon Samaritanum Arabice conscriptum, cui Titulus est Liber Josuae_ (Leiden,

1848); a translation is published in Oliver T. Crane, *The Samaritan Chronicle or the Book of Joshua, the Son of Nun* (New York: John Alden, 1890). Quotations from the Arabic version appear in the 15th-century Jewish history *Sepher Yuchasin* by Abraham Zacuto.

16. Robertson (in a review of Father Castro's *Sefer Abisa* in *Vetus Testamentum* 12:2 [1962], pp. 228-235) claims to have found such a reference, but it is not in the J.C. Scaliger manuscript published by Juynboll (see note 15). He may have been looking at a later version of the Book of Joshua.

17. Kahle ("The Abisha Scroll of the Samaritans" and *The Cairo Geniza* [Oxford: Blackwell, 1959]) and John Bowman (*Transcript of the Original Text of the Samaritan Chronicle Tolidah* [Leeds, UK: Leeds University Oriental Society, 1954]) have argued the opposite, namely that the end part of the scroll is the only original part and that all the rest was lost and replaced. The actual text reads: "This Abisha b. Pinhas has written the book of the Torah and it is found until the present day in the town of Shechem in the house of the high priests and its history is very surprising and is reported by those handing down daily events. The resting place of this holy book was in the Stone Synagogue situated in Elon Moreh and the community used to come round to see it on the Monday called Yom Awerta. And it happened on this day that the priest who had the duty to carry it had a nocturnal pollution early in the day. He washed himself in the morning secretly, carried [the scroll] from the synagogue up to Gilgal in Ephraim where they used to glorify it and were standing in file at Gilgal. And at the time when the scroll was opened there happened a great earthquake with thunder and lightnings and a mighty storm pulled out the scroll from the weak case in which it was housed, it was lifted up and whirled away into the air by the storm while the community saw it, trembling and crying. They strengthened their hearts and seized the end of the book which is preserved in the house of the priest in Shechem until this day...." A supergloss has been added that reads as follows: "A little was torn from it and that is from Numbers 35.2-Deuteronomy 34.10."

18. Castro, *Sefer Abisa*.

19. Gaster, *The Samaritans: Their History, Doctrines and Literature*, Schweich Lectures for 1923 (London: Oxford University Press, 1925; repr. 1976, 1980).

20. Robertson, review of *Sefer Abisa*.

21. The standard edition of the *tashqil* cryptogram is probably the one published by Castro in *Sefer Abisa*, p. xl. He indicates the text to be "I am Abisha, the son of Phineas, the son of Eleazar, the son of Aaron, the High Priest, upon them be the favor of the Lord and His glory. I wrote this sacred book at the entry to the Tent of Assembly on Mount Gerizim, Bethel, in the thirteenth year of the rule of the Israelites in the land of Canaan and all its surrounding borders. Thanks to God. Amen."

In a letter to Moses Gaster (appendix 4 in Gaster's *The Samaritans*), the Samaritan high priest Jacob ben Aaron set out the *tashqil* but omitted the words "and all its surrounding borders" and changed the word "rule" to "settlement." The word "all" in the phrase "all its surrounding borders" is omitted by several readers. The differences between Castro's and Gaster's versions are highlighted in all transcriptions. (See the long discussion of the form of the *tashqil* in Ben-Zvi, *Sefer Hašomronim* [Tel Aviv, 1935], pp. 233-250.) It is clear that the disputed words can only be guessed at.

22. Robertson, in his review of *Sefer Abisa* (see notes 12, 16), however, argues that hand A is later than the hand of cols. 21-43 and 88-92.

23. Given the difference in size of the scripts between a codex and a scroll and the freedom that the scribe of the codex had to use ligatures, the script of the main part of the Abisha Scroll may even be in the same hand as the Cambridge Add. MS 1846, which dates from close to 1149 C.E. See Crown, "Samaritan Majuscule Palaeography," *BJRL* 60:2 and 61:1 (1978), pp. 1-55, esp. 30, and plates 1A, 1B.

24. Likewise, the disputed word "dominion" (read either as *malikhut* or *mamlechet*) represents part of the formulary used by the Samaritans for expressing dates after the Hegira.

25. Von Gall, *Der hebräische Pentateuch.*

26. Ben-Zvi, "Sepher Abisha," pp. 240-252.

27. See Benjamin Z. Kedar, "The Frankish Period" in *The Samaritans*, ed. Crown (Tübingen: J.C.B. Mohr, 1989), pp. 82-94, for a discussion of these events.

28. Kedar, "The Frankish Period," pp. 89-90.

29. If there was, he wrote nothing else known to us. See Crown, "Index of Scribes, Witnesses, Owners and Others Mentioned in Samaritan Manuscripts," *BJRL* 68:2 (1986), pp. 317-372.

30. This hypothesis would also account for the silence of the author of the *Tolidah* concerning

the Abisha Scroll. The scroll would have been known to him, but he would have known its origin and would not have wanted to attribute it to Abisha in his chronicle.

Related Articles in *BR* and *BAR*

Alan D. Crown, "The Importance of the Samaritan Pentateuch," *BR* 8:1 (1992).

Reinhard Pummer, "The Samaritans—A Jewish Offshoot or a Pagan Cult?" *BR* 7:5 (1991).

Pummer, letter: Pummer's View at Odds with the Bible, *BR* 8:1 (1992).

PART III
Introduction
(pages 238-243)

1. Gerald Hammond, *The Literary Guide to the Bible* (Cambridge, MA: Harvard University Press, 1987).

2. Philip W. Comfort, *The Complete Guide to Bible Versions* (Wheaton, IL: Tyndale House Publishers, 1991).

3. Robert Alter, *The Art of Biblical Narrative* (New York: Basic Books, 1981).

4. Harry M. Orlinsky, *Notes on the New Translation of the Torah* (Philadelphia: Jewish Publication Society, 1969).

20. Howard
(pages 246-252)

"The Name of God in the New Testament" first appeared in **BAR** March 1978.

1. For further details, see George Howard, "The Tetragram and the New Testament," *Journal of Biblical Literature* 96 (1977), pp. 63-83.

Related Articles in *BR* and *BAR*

Gabriel Barkay, "The Divine Name Found in Jerusalem," *BAR* 9:2 (1983).

Willis Barnstone, *The Other Bible*, reviewed by George Howard, *BR* 4:1 (1988).

David Estrada and William White, Jr., *The First New Testament*, reviewed by George Howard, *BAR* 6:1 (1980).

George Howard, letter: Difficulty with Rabbinic Script, *BR* 3:2 (1987).

Howard, letter: Remains Unconvinced, *BR* 3:2 (1987).

Bruce M. Metzger, *Manuscripts of the Greek*

Bible: An Introduction to Palaeography, reviewed by George Howard, *BAR* 10:1 (1984).

Choon-Leong Seow, "The Ineffable Name of Israel's God," *BR* 7:6 (1991).

21. Fitzmyer
(pages 253-260)

"Did Jesus Speak Greek?" first appeared in **BAR** September/October 1992.

1. See Joseph A. Fitzmyer, "The Phases of the Aramaic Language" in *A Wandering Aramean: Collected Aramaic Essays*, Society of Biblical Literature Monograph Ser. 25 (Missoula, MT: Scholars Press, 1979), pp. 57-84.

2. See Fitzmyer and Daniel I. Harrington, *A Manual of Palestinian Aramaic Texts (Second Century B.C.-Second Century A.D.)*, Biblica et orientalia 34 (Rome: Biblical Institute Press, 1978).

3. See Fitzmyer, "The Languages of Palestine in the First Century A.D." in *Wandering Aramean*, pp. 29-56. Cf. Jonas C. Greenfield, "The Languages of Palestine, 200 B.C.E.-200 C.E." in *Jewish Languages: Theme and Variations: Proceedings of Regional Conferences of the Association for Jewish Studies Held at the University of Michigan and New York University in March-April 1975*, ed. H.H. Paper (Cambridge, MA: Association for Jewish Studies, 1978), pp. 143-154; Jehoshua M. Grintz, "Hebrew as the Spoken and Written Language in the Last Days of the Second Temple," *Journal of Biblical Literature (JBL)* 79 (1960), pp. 32-47; Robert H. Gundry, "The Language Milieu of First-Century Palestine: Its Bearing on the Authenticity of the Gospel Tradition," *JBL* 83 (1964), pp. 404-408; Shmuel Safrai, "Spoken Languages in the Time of Jesus," *Jerusalem Perspective* 4 (1991), pp. 3-8, 13.

4. Since Palestine was under Roman domination after the conquest of Pompey in 63 B.C.E., Latin was also used at times, as we know from inscriptions written in that language. Latin, however, seems to have been confined more or less to official use by Romans and for Romans or other visitors from the Roman empire. See Fitzmyer, *Wandering Aramean*, pp. 30-32.

On triglossia, see Jozef T. Milik, *Ten Years of Discovery in the Wilderness of Judaea*, Studies in Biblical Theology 26 (London: SCM, 1959), pp. 130-133. Whether or not Hebrew in a form approaching Mishnaic Hebrew "was the normal language of the Judaean population in the

Roman period," as Milik claims, may be questioned. Cf. Pinchas Lapide, "Insights from Qumran into the Languages of Jesus," *Revue de Qumrân* (1972-1975), pp. 483-501.

5. Grintz (see note 3) argues that it was, but neither his arguments nor his evidence is rigorous enough to establish his point. Cf. John A. Emerton, "The Problem of Vernacular Hebrew in the First Century A.D. and the Language of Jesus," *Journal of Theological Studies* 24 (1973), pp. 1-23.

6. The Targum of Job from Qumran Cave 11 (J.P.M. van der Ploeg and A.S. van der Woude, *Le targum de Job de la grotte xi de Qumrân* [Leiden: Brill, 1971]); and the Targumim of Leviticus and Job from Qumran Cave 4 (Milik, *Qumrân Grotte 4.II: I. Archéologie; II, Tefillin, mezuzot et targums (4Q128-4Q157)*, Discoveries in the Judaean Desert 6 [Oxford: Clarendon Press, 1977], pp. 86-90).

7. See J. Kaimio, *The Romans and the Greek Language*, Commentationes humanarum litterarum 64 (Helsinki: Societas Scientiarum Fennica, 1979).

8. See Pieter W. van der Horst, "Jewish Funerary Inscriptions—Most Are in Greek," *BAR* 18:5 (1992).

9. See Martin Hengel, *Judaism and Hellenism: Studies in Their Encounter in Palestine during the Early Hellenistic Period*, 2 vols. (Philadelphia: Fortress Press, 1974). For a later period, see Baruch Lifshitz, "L'Hellénisation des Juifs de Palestine: A propos des inscriptions de Besara (Beth Shearim)," *Revue biblique* 72 (1965), pp. 520-538; "Du nouveau sur l'hellénisation des Juifs en Palestine," *Euphrosyne*, new ser. 4 (1970), pp. 113-133.

10. Discovered at Khirbet el-Kom in 1971. See Lawrence T. Geraty, "The Khirbet el-Kom Bilingual Ostracon," *Bulletin of the American Schools of Oriental Research* 220 (1975), pp. 55-61.

11. Four examples can be found in Fitzmyer, *Wandering Aramean*, p. 41. Some others could now be added to that list. Cf. Aubrey W. Argyle, "Greek among the Jews of Palestine in New Testament Times," *New Testament Studies (NTS)* 20 (1973-1974), pp. 87-89.

12. See Saul Lieberman, *Hellenism in Jewish Palestine: Studies in the Literary Transmission, Beliefs and Manners of Palestine in the I Century B.C.E.-IV Century C.E.*, Texts and Studies of JTSA 18 (New York: Jewish Theological Seminary, 1950; 2d ed., 1962); "How Much Greek in Jewish Palestine?" in *Biblical and Other Studies*, ed. Alexander Altmann (Cambridge, MA: Harvard University Press, 1963), pp. 121-141; *Greek in Jewish Palestine: Studies in the Life and Manners of Jewish Palestine in the II-IV Centuries C.E.*, 2d ed. (New York: Feldheim, 1965).

13. A list can be found in Carsten Colpe, "Jüdisch-hellenistische Literatur," *Der Kleine Pauly: Lexikon der Antike 2* (Stuttgart: Drückenmiller, 1967), pp. 1507-1512. Cf. Carl R. Holladay, *Fragments from Hellenistic Jewish Authors*, vol. 1, *Historians*, Society of Biblical Literature Texts and Translations (SBLTT) 20, Pseudepigrapha Ser. (PS) 10 (Chico, CA: Scholars Press, 1983), and vol. 2, *Poets*, SBLTT 30, PS 12 (Atlanta: Scholars Press, 1989). Not all these Jewish authors, however, lived in Palestine.

14. See Holladay, *Fragments*, vol. 1, pp. 371-376.

15. Josephus *Antiquities of the Jews* 20.12.1, sec. 263-265.

16. Josephus *The Jewish War* 5.9.2, sec. 361.

17. Josephus *Jewish War* 1.1.2, sec. 6.

18. Josephus *Jewish War* 1.1.1, sec. 3.

19. Josephus *Against Apion* 1.9, sec. 50.

20. Josephus *Antiquities* 1.1.1, sec. 7.

21. See Fitzmyer, *Wandering Aramean*, p. 35.

22. Some of these are found in Fitzmyer and Harrington, *Manual of Palestinian Aramaic Texts*; others in Jean-Baptiste Frey, *Corpus Inscriptionum Iudaicarum*, 2 vols. (Vatican City: Pontificio Istituto di Archeologia Cristiana, 1950-1952), vol. 2, sec. 882-883, 887-891, 964-970, 972, 983-986, 991-1000. Cf. *Supplementum Epigraphicum Graecum*, vol. 6, sec. 849; vol. 8, sec. 179-186, 197, 201, 208-209, 221, 224; vol. 17, sec. 784; vol. 19, sec. 922; vol. 20, sec. 483-492; L.H. Kant, "Jewish Inscriptions in Greek and Latin," *Aufstieg und Niedergang der römischen Welt* II. 20/2 (1987), pp. 671-713.

23. See H.J. Leon, *The Jews of Ancient Rome* (Philadelphia: Jewish Publication Society, 1960), p. 75. Cf. Henri Leclercq, "Note sur le grec néotestamentaire et la position du grec en Palestine au premier siecle," *Les études classiques* 42 (1974), pp. 243-255; Gerard Mussies, "Greek as the Vehicle of Early Christianity," *NTS* 29 (1983), pp. 356-369, and "Greek in Palestine and the Diaspora" in *The Jewish People in the*

First Century: Historical Geography, Political History, Social, Cultural and Religious Life and Institutions, ed. Safrai and M. Stern, Compendia rerum iudaicarum ad Novum Testamentum 1-2 (Assen: Van Gorcum/ Philadelphia: Fortress Press, 1976), pp. 1040-1064.

Eric M. Meyers and James F. Strange (*Archaeology, the Rabbis and Early Christianity* [Nashville: Abingdon Press, 1981], pp. 62-91) go so far as to say, "It appears that sometime during the first century B.C.E. Aramaic and Greek changed places as Greek spread into the countryside and as knowledge of Aramaic declined among the educated and among urban dwellers....Aramaic never died, though it suffered a strong eclipse in favor of Greek." This eclipse was not characteristic, however, of the first century C.E.

24. See Pierre Benoit et al., *Les grottes de Murabba'at*, Discoveries in the Judaean Desert 2 (Oxford: Clarendon Press, 1961), sec. 89-107, 108-112, 114-116, 164. Cf. A.R.C. Leaney, "Greek Manuscripts from the Judaean Desert" in *Studies in New Testament Language and Text: Essays in Honour of George D. Kilpatrick on the Occasion of His Sixty-fifth Birthday*, ed. J.K. Elliott, Novum Testamentum Supplement (NovTSup) 44 (Leiden: Brill, 1976), pp. 283-300.

25. See Lifshitz, "Papyrus grecs du desert du Juda," *Aegyptus* 42 (1962), pp. 240-256 (+ 2 plates); Yigael Yadin, "New Discoveries in the Judaean Desert," *Biblical Archaeologist* 24 (1961), pp. 34-50; "More on the Letters of Bar Kochba," ibid., pp. 86-95. See also Naphtali Lewis, *The Documents from the Bar Kokhba Period in the Cave of Letters: Greek Papyri*, Judean Desert Studies (Jerusalem: Israel Exploration Society, 1989).

26. See Fitzmyer, *Wandering Aramean*, p. 36.

27. Charles F.D. Moule, "Once More, Who Were the Hellenists?" *Expository Times* (*ExpTim*) 70 (1958-1959), pp. 100-102. Cf. J.N. Sevenster, *Do You Know Greek? How Much Greek Could the First Jewish Christians Have Known?* NovTSup 19 (Leiden: Brill, 1968), p. 37.

28. See W. Sanday, "The Language Spoken in Palestine at the Time of Our Lord," *Expositor* 1:7 (1878), pp. 81-99, and "Did Christ Speak Greek?—A Rejoinder," ibid., pp. 368-388; A. Meyer, *Jesu Muttersprache: Das galiläische Aramäisch in seiner Bedeutung für die Erklärung der Reden Jesu* (Leipzig: Mohr [Siebeck], 1896); Gustaf Dalman, *The Words of Jesus Considered in the Light of Post-biblical Jewish Writings and*

the Aramaic Language (Edinburgh: T & T Clark, 1902), and *Jesus-Jeshua: Studies in the Gospels* (London: SPCK, 1929; repr., New York: Ktav, 1971), p. 1037; Friedrich Schulthess, *Das Problem der Sprache Jesu* (Zurich: Schulthess, 1917); Charles C. Torrey, *Our Translated Gospels: Some of the Evidence* (New York: Harper, 1936); Andre Dupont-Sommer, *Les Araméens* (Paris: Maisonneuve, 1949), p. 99; Matthew Black, "The Recovery of the Language of Jesus," *NTS* 3 (1956-1957), pp. 305-313, and *An Aramaic Approach to the Gospels and Acts*, 3d ed. (Oxford: Clarendon Press, 1967); A. Diez Macho, *La lengua hablada por Jesucristo*, 2d ed., Maldonado 1 (Madrid: Fe católica, 1976); Paul Kahle, "Das zur Zeit Jesu gesprochene Aramäisch: Erwiderung," *Zeitschrift für die neutestamentliche Wissenschaft* 51 (1960), p. 55; Edward Y. Kutscher, "Das zur Zeit Jesu gesprochene Aramäisch," ibid., pp. 46-54; H. Ott, "Um die Muttersprache Jesu: Forschungen seit Gustaf Dalman," *Novum Testamentum* (*NovT*) 9 (1967), pp. 1-25; J. Barr, "Which Language Did Jesus Speak?—Some Remarks of a Semitist," *Bulletin of the John Rylands Library* 53 (1970-1971), pp. 9-29; Barnabas Lindars, "The Language in Which Jesus Taught," *Theology* 86 (1983), pp. 363-365.

29. In Isaiah 8:23, however, the phrase (*gelîl haggôyim*) is used as a description of "the land west of the Jordan," northern Galilee, inhabited by pagans even in the time of the eighth-century prophet. Whether that is a stringent argument for that area in first-century Palestine is not apparent. J.M. Ross, who maintains that Greek was widely used in lower Galilee, doubts that it was true of northern Galilee (*Irish Biblical Studies* 12 [1990], p. 42).

30. See Richard A. Batey, "Sepphoris—An Urban Portrait of Jesus," *BAR* 18:3 (1992).

31. See Sean Freyne, *Galilee from Alexander the Great to Hadrian 323 B.C.E. to 135 C.E.: A Study of Second Temple Judaism* (Notre Dame, IN: University of Notre Dame/Wilmington, DE: Glazier, 1980), pp. 101-154.

32. See J.A.L. Lee, "Some Features of the Speech of Jesus in Mark's Gospel," *NovT* 27 (1985), pp. 1-36. The abundance of parataxis in this early Gospel is often cited as evidence of the influence of Aramaic.

33. Argyle, "Did Jesus Speak Greek?" *ExpTim* 67 (1955-1956), p. 93.

34. Papias, quoted in Eusebius *Ecclesiastical History* 3.39.16.

35. See Fitzmyer, *The Gospel According to Luke*, Anchor Bible 28, 28A (Garden City, NY: Doubleday, 1981-1985), pp. 904-906.

36. Pindar *Fragments* 140b; Aristophanes *Wasps* 1279; Plato *Republic* 2.373b.

37. Argyle, "'Hypocrites' and the Aramaic Theory," *ExpTim* 75 (1963-1964), pp. 113-114.

38. Testament of Benjamin 6:4-5; Psalms of Solomon 4:6; 2 Maccabees 6:25.

39. G.H.R. Horsley, "The Fiction of 'Jewish Greek'" in *New Documents Illustrating Early Christianity*, 5 vols. (North Ryde, N.S.W., Australia: Macquarie University, 1981-1989), vol. 5, pp. 5-40. But that fiction is often repeated; e.g., Ben Zion Wacholder, *Eupolemus: A Study of Judaeo-Greek Literature* (Cincinnati: Hebrew Union College, 1974), p. 256: "In the Gospels Jesus speaks Judaeo-Greek."

40. See Klaus Beyer, *Semitische Syntax im Neuen Testament: Band I, Satzlehre Teil 1*, 2d ed., Studien zur Umwelt des Neuen Testaments (Göttingen: Vandenhoeck & Ruprecht, 1968); A. Ceresa-Gastaldao, "Lingua greca e categorie semitiche del testo evangelico," *Storia e preistoria dei Vangeli* (Genoa: Università di Genova, Facoltà di lettere, 1988), pp. 121-141; Elliott C. Maloney, *Semitic Interference in Marcan Syntax*, Society of Biblical Literature Diss. Ser. 51 (Chico, CA: Scholars Press, 1981).

41. Lindars, "The Language in Which Jesus Taught," *Theology* 86 (1983), p. 364.

42. See Harris Birkeland, *The Language of Jesus*, Avhandlinger utgitt av Det Norske Videnskaps-Akademi i Oslo II. Hist.-Filos. Klasse 1954/1 (Oslo: Jacob Dybwad, 1954). Cf. Jean Carmignac, *The Birth of the Synoptic Gospels* (Chicago: Franciscan Herald, 1987); Claude Tresmontant, *The Hebrew Christ: Language in the Age of the Gospels* (Chicago: Franciscan Herald, 1989). These claims have been adequately refuted by Pierre Grelot, *L'Origine des evangiles: Controverse avec J. Carmignac* (Paris: Cerf, 1986).

43. The text is composite, being a quotation of Isaiah 61:1a,b,d, 58:6d, 61:2a. It omits "to heal the broken-hearted" (61:1c) and "the day of vengeance of our God" (61:2b). As such, it is scarcely derived directly from the Hebrew or the Septuagint.

Related Articles in BR and BAR

Elias J. Bickerman, *The Jews in the Greek Age*, reviewed by Louis H. Feldman, *BR* 5:1 (1989).

Joseph A. Fitzmyer, letter: Did Jesus Live with the Essenes in the Wilderness? *BAR* 11:1 (1985).

Howard Clark Kee, *What Can We Know about Jesus*, a review, *BR* 7:3 (1991).

John Riches, *The World of Jesus: First Century Judaism in Crisis*, a review, *BR* 7:3 (1991).

J. Robert Teringo, *The Land and People Jesus Knew: A Comprehensive Handbook on Life in First-century Palestine*, reviewed by James F. Strange, *BAR* 12:4 (1986).

Pieter van der Horst, "Jewish Funerary Inscriptions—Most Are in Greek," *BAR* 18:5 (1992).

Fitzmyer, Afterword
(pages 261-264)

1. New Jerusalem Bible, Reader's Edition, p. 1166.

2. E.G. Kraeling, *The Brooklyn Museum Aramaic Papyri Elephantine* (New Haven, CT: Yale University Press, 1953), p.226; Walter Baumgartner, *Hebräisches und Aramäisches Lexikon zum Alten Testament* (Leiden: Brill, 1974), p. 468.

3. See Jozef T. Milik, *The Books of Enoch: Aramaic Fragments of Qumran Cave 4* (Oxford: Clarendon Press, 1976), pp. 146-147, 204-205, 243-244.

4. For further details on all these points, one may consult Joseph A. Fitzmyer, "Aramaic Kepha' and Peter's Name in the New Testament" in *Text and Interpretation: Studies in the New Testament Presented to Matthew Black*, ed. Ernest Best and Robert M. Wilson (Cambridge, UK: Cambridge University Press, 1979), pp. 121-132, repr. in Fitzmyer, *To Advance the Gospel: New Testament Studies* (New York: Crossroad, 1981), pp. 112-124.

5. Pieter W. van der Horst, "Jewish Funerary Inscriptions—Most Are in Greek," *BAR* 18:5 (1992).

22. Minkoff
(pages 266-274)

"Concern for the Text versus Concern for the Reader" first appeared in **BR** *August 1988.*

1. Marilyn Gaddis Rose, "Translation Types and Conventions" in *Translation Spectrum*, ed. Rose (Albany: State University of New York Press, 1981), p. 32: "In overt translation the receiving reader or listener knows that the text is a translation and recognizes that it is bound to the source culture....Covert translations, on the

other hand, are almost accidentally in a language other than the original, for they are not bound to a specific culture."

2. Soferim 1.8. Modern editions of the Septuagint do not contain this reading. See also Eliyahu Kitov, *Sefer Hatoda'ah* (Jerusalem: Machon Lehoza'at Sefarim, 1958), vol. 1, pp. 195-196, English trans., *The Book of Our Heritage* (Jerusalem: 'A' Publishers, 1968), vol. 1, pp. 320-322; "Masseketh Soferim," ed. Israel W. Slotki, in *The Minor Tractates of the Talmud*, ed. Abraham Cohen (London: Soncino Press, 1971), vol. 1, pp. 213-214. The possibility of misunderstanding the Hebrew in this way was never considered, probably because as a learned language it required study and supervision. In contrast, Greek was the everyday language of Alexandria and might be read casually or carelessly.

3. Lists of common words and phrases taken from the Bible used to be commonplace in histories of the English language. See, for example, Otto Jespersen, *Growth and Structure of the English Language* (1905), sec. 250-253 (Garden City, NY: Doubleday, 9th ed., 1955), pp. 252-255.

4. Epistle 57, see *Jerome: Lettres*, ed. Jerome Labourt (Paris, 1953), vol. 3, p. 59.

5. See Harvey Minkoff, "Some Stylistic Consequences of Aelfric's Theory of Translation," *Studies in Philology* 73:1 (1976), pp. 29-41. E.F. Sutcliffe ("Jerome" in *The Cambridge History of the Bible*, vol. 2, ed. G.W.H. Lampe [Cambridge, UK: Cambridge University Press, 1963-1970], p. 96) translates *verborum ordo* as "the precise character of the words." But Jerome's point remains the same—translating the Bible is different from translating anything else.

6. In contrast, Zoltán Haraszti (*The Enigma of the Bay Psalm Book* [Chicago: University of Chicago Press, 1956], p. vi) believes that "the work is no literary treasure trove; yet much of the ridicule heaped upon it seems undeserved."

7. I have modernized the spelling. Susan Bassnett-McGuire (*Translation Studies* [London: Methuen, 1981], p. 47) notes that since the "political function" of early English translations was "to make the complete text of the Bible accessible, this led to a definite stance on priorities by the translator."

8. Michael Bullock, "Enquête" in *Quality in Translation*, ed. E. Cary and R.W. Jumpelt (New York: Macmillan, 1963), p. 149.

9. John Beekman, "Lexical Equivalence Involving Consideration of Form and Function" in *Notes of Translation*, ed. Beekman (Santa Ana: Summer Institute of Linguistics, 1965), p. 91.

10. In addition, this same root is the bridge to the story of how Ishmael, son of Abraham's maid-concubine Hagar, is soon afterward driven from his home for "mocking" (*meṣaḥek*, 21:9). And it appears again when King Abimelech realizes that Rebecca is Isaac's wife, not his sister, when he sees them "sporting" (*meṣaḥek*, Genesis 26:8).

11. Eugene Nida, "Science of Translation," *Language* 45:3 (1969), p. 483 n. 1. See also his "Linguistics and Ethnology in Translation Problems," *Word* 1 (1945), pp. 194-208, repr. in *Language in Culture and Society*, ed. Dell Hymes (New York: Harper & Row, 1964).

12. Nida and William Wonderly, "Linguistics and Christian Missions" in *Language Structure and Translation: Essays by Eugene A. Nida*, ed. Anwar S. Dil (Stanford, CA: Stanford University Press, 1975), p. 193.

13. See, for example, Eldon Jay Epp's negative review, "Should 'The Book' Be Panned?" *BR* 2:2 (1986), pp. 36-41, which labels *The Living Bible* "inaccurate, inconsistent, biased and otherwise seriously flawed"; and Barry Hoberman, "Translating the Bible," *The Atlantic* (February 1985), which calls *The Living Bible* "an inaccurate and tendentious paraphrase...that has been repudiated by virtually all responsible biblical scholars" (p. 47).

14. See Beekman, "Lexical Equivalence," pp. 93-111.

15. Harry M. Orlinsky, *Notes on the New Translation of the Torah* (Philadelphia: Jewish Publication Society, 1969), pp. 39-40.

16. Geoffrey Hunt, *About the New English Bible* (Cambridge, UK: Oxford and Cambridge University Presses, 1970), pp. 22, 52.

17. See also Sidney Greenbaum, "Three English Versions of Psalm 23," *Journal of English Linguistics* 17 (1984), pp. 1-23, which, in a comparison of 13 features, finds the King James Version "clearly more faithful" to the Hebrew than the NEB (p. 19).

18. See Bassnett-McGuire, *Translation Studies*, pp. 57-58.

19. Beekman, "Lexical Equivalence," pp. 88-89.

20. George Orwell, "Politics and the English Language" in *Shooting an Elephant and Other*

Essays (New York: Harcourt, Brace & World, 1945).

Related Articles in *BR* and *BAR*

Harvey Minkoff, "Semite, Semitic, Semitic Languages," *BR* 5:3 (1989).

Minkoff, "How Bible Translations Differ," *BAR* 18:2 (1992).

Kenneth V. Mull and Carolyn Sandquist Mull, "How a Generic Term for Skin Diseases in the Hebrew Bible Became 'Leprosy' in English Translation," *BR* 8:2 (1992).

23. Minkoff
(pages 275-284)

"Coarse Language in the Bible: It's Culture Shocking!" first appeared in **BR** *April 1989.*

1. Harvey Minkoff, "Problems of Translations—Concern for the Text versus Concern for the Reader," *BR* 4:4 (1988). Reprinted on pp. 266-274 in this volume.

2. See "Where Is Biblical Debir?" *BAR* 1:1 (1975).

3. There are some minor differences between the two passages. In this article, I use the text of Judges.

4. In medieval liturgical Hebrew ṢNḤ meant "descend"; modern Israeli Hebrew has added the sense "parachute." See Avraham Even-Shoshan, *Ha-milon Ha-ḥadaś* (Jerusalem: Kiryat Sefer, 1979), vol. 5, p. 2245. But these meanings are based on the traditional interpretation of the biblical verses and are therefore not independent evidence.

5. Wilhelm Gesenius, *Hebrew and Chaldee Lexicon to the Old Testament Scriptures*, trans. S.P. Tregelles (London: Samuel Bagster, 1894).

6. Francis Brown, Samuel R. Driver and Charles A. Briggs, *A Hebrew and English Lexicon of the Old Testament* (New York: Oxford University Press, 1951 [1906]), p. 856. This edition was overseen by Godfrey Driver, Samuel R. Driver's son.

7. Georg Fohrer, *Hebrew and Aramaic Dictionary of the Old Testament*, trans. W. Johnson (Berlin: de Gruyter, 1973).

8. Godfrey R. Driver, "Problems of Interpretation in the Heptateuch" in *Mélanges bibliques: Rédigés en l'honneur de André Robert*, Travaux de l'Institut Catholique de Paris 4 (Paris: L'Institut Catholique de Paris, 1957),

pp. 73-75. I am grateful to Suzanne Siegel of the Hunter College library for helping me track down Driver's far-flung publications.

9. Arthur Gibson, "ṢNḤ in Judges 1:14: NEB and AV Translations," *Vetus Testamentum* 26 (1976), pp. 275-283. Solomon Mandelkern (*Qonqordanṣiah le-Tanakh [Concordance on the Bible]* [Leipzig: Veit, 1896; rev. ed., New York: Shulsinger, 1955], p. 999, s.v. ṢNḤ) attributes the Septuagint renderings in Judges 1:14 and Joshua 15:18 to a reading of *tiṣrah* rather than *tiṣnaḥ*; but the NEB translation assumes the traditional reading *tiṣnaḥ*. See Leonard H. Brockington, *The Hebrew Text of the Old Testament: The Readings Adopted by the Translators of the New English Bible* (Oxford: Oxford University Press, 1973), pp. 32, 35.

10. Roger A. Bullard, "The New English Bible" in *The Word of God: A Guide to English Versions of the Bible*, ed. Lloyd R. Bailey (Atlanta: John Knox Press, 1982), pp. 55-56. And he says of "oozed" in 4:21: "the translators have apparently given it a different meaning. (I don't know this; they may well be letting the hypothetical root-meaning of the Arabic root color this rendering as well.) In the first place, it is not clear how they have determined the subject of this verb, since it is not expressed....What the panel has done with this word is a mystery to me."

11. F.F. Bruce, *The English Bible: A History of Translations from the Earliest English Versions to the New English Bible* (Oxford/New York: Oxford University Press, 1970), p. 248.

12. I wish to thank Donald Kraus for his graciousness in searching Oxford's files and library to answer my questions.

13. John Beekman and John Callow, *Translating the Word of God* (Dallas: Summer Institute of Linguistics, 1986), p. 105.

14. Peter Mullen, "The Religious Speak-Easy" in *Fair of Speech: The Uses of Euphemism*, ed. D.J. Enright (Oxford/NY: Oxford University Press, 1985), pp. 164-165. In later editions the Jerusalem Bible replaced "happy" with "blessed."

15. Mullen, "The Religious Speak-Easy," p. 160. See also p. 164: "There is a great deal of this polite drawing-room chat in most new translations of the Bible, as if sin were not bad but only bad form."

16. Brown, S. Driver and Briggs (*A Hebrew and English Lexicon*, p. 116) give the etymology as a compound of *beli* (without) and *ya'al* (worth,

use, profit). See also Mandelkern, *Concordance*, p. 202; Theodor H. Gaster, "Belial" in *Encyclopaedia Judaica*, vol. 4, cols. 428-429.

17. G. Driver, "Colloquialisms in the Old Testament" in *Mélanges Marcel Cohen: Études de Linguistique, Ethnographie et Sciences Connexes*, ed. David Cohen (The Hague: Mouton, 1970), p. 232.

18. David Daiches, "Translating the Bible," *Commentary* (May 1970), p. 63.

19. Richard Elliott Friedman, "Sacred History/Sacred Literature" in *The Creation of Sacred Literature: Composition and Redaction of the Biblical Text*, ed. Friedman, Near Eastern Studies 22 (Berkeley/Los Angeles: University of California Press, 1981), p. 1.

20. Following the NJPS translation. See Genesis Rabbah 36.8: "R Yudan said,...'and they read in the book of the Law of God' refers to *miqra'* [the Hebrew text]; *meporaś* refers to *targum* [a translation]." Similar statements are found in Babylonian Talmud Megillah 3a and Nedarim 37b, and Jerusalem Talmud Megillah 28b. For "targum" as "translation" rather than "translation into Aramaic," see "Genesis Rabbah," ed. H. Freedman, in *Midrash Rabbah*, ed. Freedman and Maurice Simon (London: Soncino Press, 1939), vol. 1, pp. 293-294.

21. The Mishnah (from the Hebrew "to repeat") is a body of Jewish oral law, specifically, a collection of oral laws compiled by Rabbi Judah the Prince in the second century C.E.

22. See "Megillah," ed. Simon, in *The Babylonian Talmud*, ed. Isidore Epstein (London: Soncino Press, 1938), pp. 151-154.

23. Simon, "Megillah," pp. 151-154.

24. See Samuel Eliezar Edels ("Maharsha"), "Ḥiddushei Halakhot ve-Aggadot" in *Tractate Megillah* (New York: Pardes, 1944), appendix, p. 10, col. 1. See also Adin Steinsaltz' marginalia to Megillah 25b in his edition of *Talmud Bavli* (Jerusalem: Israel Institute for Talmudic Publications, 1983), p. 109. I am indebted to my father, Rabbi Michael Minkoff, for these references.

25. Katharine Barnwell, "Toward Acceptable Translations," *Notes on Translation* 95 (1983), pp. 19-26.

26. John Banker, "How Can We Improve Translations Stylistically?" *Notes on Translation* 94 (1983), pp. 16-21.

27. Bruce Hollenbach, "Translating without

Offense," *Notes on Translation* 119 (1987), pp. 50-54.

28. David Crystal and Derek Davy, *Investigating English Style* (Bloomington: Indiana University Press, 1969), pp. 149-150.

24. Greenspahn
(pages 286-290)

"Words That Occur in the Bible Only Once" first appeared in **BR** *February 1985.*

1. Frederick E. Greenspahn, *Hapax Legomena in Biblical Hebrew* (Chico, CA: Scholars Press, 1984).

2. Peter C. Craigie, "The Tablets from Ugarit and Their Importance for Biblical Studies," *BAR* 9:5 (1983).

3. See Jack M. Sasson, "Unlocking the Poetry of Love in the Song of Songs," *BR* 1:1 (1985).

Related Articles in *BR* and *BAR*

Michael Fishbane, *Biblical Interpretation in Ancient Israel*, reviewed by Frederick E. Greenspahn, *BR* 1:1 (1985).

Greenspahn, letter: How Many Words in the Hebrew Bible? *BR* 1:2 (1985).

25. Batto
(pages 291-301)

"Red Sea or Reed Sea?: What Yam Sûp Really Means" first appeared in **BAR** *July/August 1984.*

1. The Song of the Sea is referred to as the Song of Moses or the Song of Miriam by some scholars.

2. A.M. Silberman, ed., *Pentateuch with Rashi's Commentary Translated into English: Exodus* (London: Shapiro, Valentine & Co., 1930), p. 67.

3. Heinrich Karl Brugsch, *L'Exode et les monuments égyptiens* (Leipzig, 1875); see Henri Cazelles, "Les localisations de l'Exode et la critique littéraire," *Revue biblique* 62 (1955), p. 323. The identification of *p3-twf* with biblical *yam sûp* is also espoused by Ricardo Caminos (*Late Egyptian Miscellanies*, ed. and trans. Caminos [London: Oxford University Press, 1954], p. 79) and Pierre Montet (*Egypt and the Bible* [Philadelphia: Fortress Press, 1968], p. 64).

4. Representative examples include the following: Yohanan Aharoni and Michael Avi-Yonah, *The Macmillan Bible Atlas* (New York:

Macmillan, 1968), p. 40; Bernhard W. Anderson, *Understanding the Old Testament*, 3d ed. (Englewood Cliffs, NJ: Prentice-Hall, 1975), p. 68; John Bright, *A History of Israel*, 2d ed. (Philadelphia: Westminster Press, 1972), pp. 120-121; Cazelles, "Les localisations de l'Exode," pp. 321-364, esp. 340-343; Brevard S. Childs, *The Book of Exodus*, Old Testament Library (Philadelphia: Westminster Press, 1974), p. 223; Frank Moore Cross, *Canaanite Myth and Hebrew Epic: Essays in the History of the Religion of Israel* (Cambridge, MA: Harvard University Press, 1973), p. 128; Jack Finegan, *Let My People Go* (New York: Harper & Row, 1963), pp. 77-89; Siegfried Herrmann, *A History of Israel in Old Testament Times*, trans. John Bowden (Philadelphia: Fortress Press/London: SCM, 1975), pp. 62-64; J.E. Huesman, "Exodus from Egypt" in *New Catholic Encyclopedia*, vol. 5, pp. 741-748, esp. 745-746; Norbert Lohfink, *Das Siegeslied am Schilfmeer: Christliche Auseinandersetzungen mit dem Alten Testament* (Frankfurt: Joseph Knecht, 1965), pp. 102-128; John L. McKenzie, *Dictionary of the Bible* (Milwaukee: Bruce, 1965), p. 723; J.L. Mihelic, "Red Sea" in *Interpreter's Dictionary of the Bible*, 4 vols. (Nashville: Abingdon Press, 1962), vol. 4, pp. 19-21; Martin Noth, *Exodus*, Old Testament Library (Philadelphia: Westminster Press, 1962), pp. 107-111; John C. Rylaarsdam, "Exodus: Introduction and Exegesis" in *Interpreter's Bible*, vol. 1 (Nashville: Abingdon Press, 1952), pp. 930-931; G.E. Wright, *Biblical Archaeology*, rev. ed. (Philadelphia: Westminster Press, 1962), pp. 60-62, and "Exodus, Route of" in *Interpreter's Dictionary of the Bible*, vol. 2, pp. 197-199. The Reed Sea hypothesis is given as a possibility, without endorsement, by Moshe Brawer and Avi-Yonah, "Red Sea" in *Encyclopaedia Judaica*, vol. 14, cols. 14-16; Gaalyahu Cornfeld, ed., *Pictorial Biblical Encyclopedia* (New York: Macmillan, 1964), pp. 302-303; Bustanay Oded, "Exodus" in *Encyclopaedia Judaica*, vol. 6, cols. 1042-1050, esp. 1048-1050.

5. The Revised Standard Version and the New American Bible are examples of Bibles containing this annotation. The New English Bible gives Sea of Reeds as an alternative translation. The editors of the New International Version append a corrective note at each occurrence: "Hebrew *Yam Suph*; that is, 'Sea of Reeds.'" The New Jewish Publication Society and the Jerusalem Bible both translate *yam sûp* as the Sea of Reeds.

6. The eight certain references in Egyptian texts have been carefully collated and annotated by

Alan H. Gardiner, *Ancient Egyptian Onomastica* (New York: Oxford University Press, 1947), vol. 2, pp. 201-202.

7. Much of this evidence comes from the authority on hieroglyphics, Sir Alan Gardiner; he thus refutes his own conclusion that the connection between *p3-twf(y)* and biblical *yam sûp* is "beyond dispute"; see Gardiner, *Ancient Egyptian Onomastica*, vol. 2, pp. 201-202.

8. Translated by Caminos, *Late Egyptian Miscellanies*, p. 74.

9. Roland de Vaux, *The Early History of Israel* (Philadelphia: Westminster Press, 1978), p. 377.

10. "פוּס-םי: The Sea of Reeds: The Red Sea," *Vetus Testamentum* 15 (1965), pp. 395-398, esp. 397-398. See also J.A. Montgomery, "Hebraica (2) *yam sûp* (The Red Sea) = Ultimum Mare?" *Journal of the American Oriental Society* 58 (1938), pp. 131-132. It has been objected that *sôp* is an Aramaic word introduced into Hebrew at a late date; see M. Wagner, *Die lexikalischen und grammatikalischen Aramäischen in alttestamentlichen Hebräisch*, Beihefte zur Zeitschrift für die alttestamentliche Wissenschaft 96 (Berlin: Alfred Töpelmann, 1966), p. 87. However, the occurrence of verbal forms of this root in Amos 3:15; Psalm 73:19; Jeremiah 8:13; and Zephaniah 1:2-3 indicates that *sôp* need not be considered a late Aramaism in Hebrew; see G. Ahlström, "Joel and the Temple Cult in Jerusalem," Vetus Testamentum Supplement 21 (1971), pp. 2-3.

11. Herodotus 1, 180 and Pindar *Pythian Odes* 4, 448, in the fifth century B.C.E.

12. Xenophon *Cyropaedia* 8.6.10, fourth century B.C.E.

13. See Henry G. Liddell and Robert Scott, *A Greek-English Lexicon* (New York: Harper, 1876 [1856]), s.v. erythros II.

14. *Am zû qanîta* means "the people whom you have *created*," not "the people whom you have purchased" (Revised Standard Version) or "ransomed" (New Jewish Publication Society). Although *qanâ* normally does mean "to acquire," a second meaning of "to create" is now established from extrabiblical texts wherein one of the titles of the god El is "creator of heaven and earth"; see Cross and David Noel Freedman, "The Song of Miriam," *Journal of Near Eastern Studies* 14 (1955), p. 249. The reluctance of Paul Humbert ("Qana en hébreu biblique" in *Opuscules d'un hébraïsant* [Université de Neuchatel, 1958], pp. 166-174) to accept this meaning because of the parallel

to *'am zû ga'al ta* ("the people whom you have redeemed," verse 13) is unwarranted; *ga'al* (to redeem) is elsewhere paralleled by verbs of "creation" (Deuteronomy 32:6; Isaiah 43:1, 44:24, 54:4). The concept of God creating Israel as a people is present elsewhere in Malachi 2:10 and frequently in Second Isaiah; for the latter, see Carroll Stuhlmueller, *Creative Redemption in Deutero-Isaiah*, Analecta biblica 43 (Rome: Biblical Institute Press, 1970), pp. 193-229.

15. See Cross, *Canaanite Myth*, pp. 138-44; Patrick D. Miller, *The Divine Warrior in Early Israel* (Cambridge, MA: Harvard University Press, 1973), pp. 113-117; Stig I.L. Norin, *Er Spaltete das Meer: Die Auszugsüberlieferung in Psalmen und Kult des alten Israel*, Coniectanea biblica, Old Testament Ser. 9 (Lund: C.W.K. Gleerup, 1977), pp. 77-107.

16. One is reminded that, in the Israelite conception, the earth was an island of dry land surrounded on all sides by, and floating in, the primeval waters of chaos (Psalms 24:1-2, 104:5-7, 136:6). E. Levine (*The Aramaic Version of Jonah* [Jerusalem: Jerusalem Academic Press, 1975], pp. 75-77) relates that in later midrashic tradition, Jonah, while in the belly of the fish, was shown the path of the Israelites through the Red Sea (b. Sotah 45b; Midrash Jonah, h.l.; Yal. 551: Rashi, Comm. ad h.l.); this was possible, according to Ibn Ezra and Kimchi ad h.l., because "the Red Sea extends to, and mingles with the waters of Jaffa."

17. The punctuation of the Masoretic text followed here makes better sense than the common modern practice of editing the text according to strictly metrical considerations (*Biblia Hebraica* [Kittel], *Biblia Hebraica Stuttgartensia*, etc.).

18. To J, I assign the following verses: 13:21-22, 14:5b-6,9a,10b,11-14,19b,20,21b,24,25b,27b,30-31. To E, I assign the following: 13:17-19, 14-5a,7,19a,25a. To P, I assign the following: 13:20, 14:1-4,8,9b-10a,10c,15-18,21a,21c-23,26-27a,28-29.

19. The small "b" indicates the second half of the verse. Scholars divide biblical verses into colons or parts, designated "a" and "b," and sometimes a third colon, designated "c."

20. Bernard F. Batto, "The Reed Sea: *Requiescat in Pace*," *Journal of Biblical Literature* 102 (1983), pp. 27-35.

Related Articles in *BR* and *BAR*
Bernard Batto, "When God Sleeps," *BR* 3:4 (1987).

Eliezer D. Oren, "How Not to Create a History of the "Exodus"—A Critique of Goedicke's Theories," *BAR* 7:6 (1981).

"Scientists Part the Red Sea," *BAR* 18:5 (1992).

Hershel Shanks, "The Exodus and the Crossing of the Red Sea, According to Hans Goedicke," *BAR* 2:3 (1981).

Shanks, "In Defense of Hans Goedicke," *BAR* 8:3 (1982).

Frank J. Yurco, "Did Pharaoh Drown in the Red Sea?" *BAR* 18:3 (1992).

Batto, Afterword
(pages 302-304)

1. See further Maurice Copisarow, "The Ancient Egyptian, Greek and Hebrew Concept of the Red Sea," *Vetus Testamentum* 12 (1962), pp. 1-13.

26. Griffin
(pages 306-308)

"*The New King James Version*" first appeared in **BAR** November/December 1982.

Related Articles in *BR* and *BAR*
Jack P. Lewis, *The English Bible from KJV to NIV: A History and Evaluation*, reviewed by Bart D. Ehrman, *BR* 8:5 (1992).

The Washburn College Bible: King James Text, Modern Phrased Version, reviewed by Robert Sugar, *BAR* 7:3 (1981).

The Word of God—A Guide to English Versions of the Bible, reviewed by Lloyd R. Bailey, *BAR* 10:6 (1984).

27. Brettler
(pages 309-315)

"*The Torah, The Prophets and The Writings: A New Jewish Translation*" first appeared in **BAR** November/December 1982.

1. The five megilloth are the Song of Songs, Ruth, Lamentations, Ecclesiastes and Esther.

2. Since this article was written, a revised one-volume English edition has been published (*Tanakh: A New Translation of the Holy Scriptures According to the Traditional Hebrew Text* [Philadelphia: Jewish Publication Society, 1985]), but work on a Hebrew-English edition has been postponed indefinitely.—Ed.

Related Articles in *BR* and *BAR*
Marc Brettler, letter: NJPS Not Consistent, *BAR* 9:2 (1983).

Brettler, letter: Slighting the 1917 NJPS Bible, *BAR* 9:2 (1983).

Everett Fox, *Genesis and Exodus*, a review, *BR* 7:5 (1991).

John H. Gabel and Charles B. Wheeler, *The Bible as Literature: An Introduction*, reviewed by Marc Brettler, *BR* 5:4 (1989).

Baruch A. Levine, *Leviticus*, reviewed by Mordechai Coogan, *BR* 8:1 (1992).

Jacob Milgrom, *Numbers*, reviewed by Mordechai Coogan, *BR* 8:1 (1992).

Milgrom, *Leviticus 1-16: A New Translation with Introduction and Commentary*, reviewed by James VanderKam, *BR* 8:4 (1992).

Nahum Sarna, *Exodus*, reviewed by Mordechai Coogan, *BR* 8:1 (1992).

Sarna, *Genesis*, reviewed by Mordechai Coogan, *BR* 8:1 (1992).

Moshe Weinfeld, *Deuteronomy 1-11: A New Translation with Introduction and Commentary*, reviewed by James VanderKam, *BR* 8:4 (1992).

Brettler, Afterword
(pages 316-319)

1. Harry M. Orlinsky, *Notes on the New Translation of the Torah* (Philadelphia: Jewish Publication Society, 1969), p. 10.

2. Everett Fox, *In the Beginning: A New English Rendition of the Book of Genesis*, 2d ed. (New York: Schocken Books, 1983). The first edition of this translation appeared as a complete issue of *Response*, vol. 14 (summer 1972).

Subject Index

Scripture Index